Charles Gayarré

Aubert Dubayet

Or, The two Sister Republics

Charles Gayarré

Aubert Dubayet
Or, The two Sister Republics

ISBN/EAN: 9783337138776

Printed in Europe, USA, Canada, Australia, Japan

Cover: Foto ©ninafisch / pixelio.de

More available books at **www.hansebooks.com**

AUBERT DUBAYET

OR

THE TWO SISTER REPUBLICS

BY

CHARLES GAYARRÉ

AUTHOR OF "THE HISTORY OF LOUISIANA," "PHILIP II. OF SPAIN,"
"THE SCHOOL FOR POLITICS," "INFLUENCE OF THE
MECHANICAL ARTS," "FERNANDO DE LEMOS,'
ETC., ETC.

"It will be a curious spectacle to watch the progress of those twin sisters, the American and French Republics." — AUBERT DUBAYET

BOSTON
JAMES R. OSGOOD AND COMPANY
1882

PREFATORY REMARK.

IN this work the substance is history; the form only is romance. It can not, therefore, be properly called a novel. It is history, but with its nudities embellished under the glittering gossamer veil of fiction. History is marble, and remains forever cold, even under the most artistic hand, unless life is breathed into it by the imagination—that creative power granted by God to man. Then the marble becomes flesh and blood—then it feels, it thinks, it moves, and is immortal. This is what I have attempted.

THE AUTHOR.

INTRODUCTION.

In the composition which I venture to present to the public under the title of " Aubert Dubayet ; or, the Two Sister Republics," as a sequel to " Fernando de Lemos," there are three historical characters not so well and so extensively known as many of the others who figure in its pages. For this reason, I deem it expedient to give the short biographical sketches which follow :

AUBERT DUBAYET

was born in New Orleans, on the 17th of August, 1759. His father was adjutant-major in the small body of troops which France kept, at that epoch, in her colony of Louisiana, soon destined to be transferred to Spain. The subject of this notice entered in early life the French army, and under Rochambeau served in America during the war of independence between Great Britain and the United States. He was in France at the commencement of her revolution in 1789, and hastened to take an active part in public affairs. At that time he published a pamphlet against admitting the Jews to the rights of citizenship. But he afterward became one of the principal advocates for Liberal innovations, without running into excesses, and in 1791 was elected to the Legislative Assembly, in which he acted a conspicuous part, and whose presi dent he was for two weeks. In 1793, he resumed his military career, and was made Governor of Mayence (Mentz), on the Rhine, which, after an obstinate defense, he was compelled to surrender to the King of Prussia. Aubert Dubayet speedily rose to the grade of lieutenant-general, commanded as general-in-chief in La Vendée, and, being defeated at Clisson by the Royalists, or the *Chouans*, as they were called by the republicans, became the object of denunciations, against which he successfully defended himself. Employed again at Cherbourg, where he displayed great intelligence and activity, he was called by the Directory to the post of Minister of War, which he held only three months, being appointed Minister Plenipotentiary of the Republic at Constantinople, where he closed his active and romantic career on the 17th of December, 1797, when he was hardly more than thirty-eight years old.

ETIENNE BERNARD ALEXANDRE VIEL

was born in Louisiana, on the 31st of October, 1736, and died on the 16th of December, 1821, at the College of Juilly, in France, where he had been educated, and where, in his turn, after having become a Jesuit, he had devoted himself to the education of youth. He resided several years in that part of Louisiana called Attakapas, and formerly occupied by Indians who were men-eaters. He made himself much beloved by those to whose spiritual welfare he had attended. He is known in the erudite world by a very beautiful translation in Latin verse of Fenelon's Telemachus; also by some small poems in Latin which he presented to the public in 1816, under the

title of " Miscellanea Latino Gallica," and by an excellent French translation of the " Ars Poetica," and
of two of Horace's Odes.

JOSEPH LAKANAL

was a priest and a professor of *belles-lettres* before the
revolution of 1789. He broke, in 1791, the vows
which bound him to the Catholic, Apostolic, and
Roman Church. In 1792, he became a member of
the National Convention, in which, when the question was presented, he voted for the death of Louis
XVI., without appeal and without reprieve. In March,
1793, he was commissioned by the National Convention to demolish the Château de Chantilly, the famous
seat of the Condés, princes of the blood, and to convert to the use of the Republic all the gold, silver,
copper, lead, and iron which he could extract from
that magnificent edifice. He also took possession of
all the papers of that royal and heroic race. As a
member of the Committee on Public Education he
showed great zeal and intelligence, and, in consequence of it, was chosen, at a later period, to be a
member of the French Institute. On the 1st of June,
1793, he caused the National Convention to issue a
decree taking away from the cities, towns, and villages
of France all such names as reminded the people of
royalty, and giving them other appellations which he
indicated. On the 17th of April, 1794, he proposed
to erect a monument to those citizens who had perished in attacking the Tuileries on the 10th of
August, 1792, and in helping to slaughter the one
hundred Swiss Guards on duty in the palace. He

·was the author of the decree establishing primary and central schools all over France. On the 17th of October, 1795, he spoke with great vehemence against such of the people of Paris as had, two days before, risen against the Assembly; he advocated a severe repression of such attempts, and proposed the expulsion from that city of all those who were not residents in it before 1789. He also advised the formation of a guard to protect the Legislative Body. He entered the " Council of Five Hundred " on the 30th of October, 1795, and ceased to be a member on the 20th of May, 1797. He was one of the executive commissaries of the Government, when, having opposed the *coup d'état* of the 18th *Brumaire,* he was removed by Bonaparte soon after the latter became First Consul. He was, however, appointed censor or proctor in the Bonaparte Lyceum, and filled its functions until 1809. At the restoration of the Bourbons, the regicide fled from France and came to the United States. He established himself in Kentucky, on the banks of the Ohio, as generally reported, from which he was called to Louisiana, to be put at the head of the College of Orleans, which had long flourished under a wise and esteemed administration. The appointment of Lakanal was offensive to a large portion of the population, and that institution soon ceased to exist. After the revolution of 1830, he returned to France, where he died, leaving descendants in New Orleans.

CONTENTS.

CHAPTER XIV.

CHAPTER XV.

CHAPTER XVI.

CHAPTER XVII.

CHAPTER XVIII.

CHAPTER XIX.

CHAPTER XX.

CHAPTER XXI.

AUBERT DUBAYET;

OR,

THE TWO SISTER REPUBLICS.

CHAPTER I.

THE ABBÉ VIEL AND AUBERT DUBAYET—A TERRIBLE SECRET.

In the month of November, in the year 1779, on one of those exquisite autumnal days so peculiar to Louisiana, when merely to inhale the balmy atmosphere is a feast of the senses, two men were standing on the left bank of the Mississippi, in front of Toulouse street. The sun, verging toward the western horizon, was gilding with its last rays the roofs of New Orleans and the tops of the tall moss-covered trees, which looked like gray-bearded giants, on the opposite side of the river, in the rear of several plantations then existing where the town of Algiers has since grown up. A vessel was in sight, just turning round a projecting curve, and was fast coming up with all her sails swelling under the breath of a strong breeze, which impelled her onward like a thing of life. One of those men was a youth, about twenty-one years old; the other had reached fully double the age of his companion. The former, elegantly dressed after the fashion of the time, was Jean Baptiste Annibal Aubert Dubayet, a native of Louisiana, and a

son of Adjutant-Major Dubayet, who had long served
in the small body of troops which France had maintained in her colony of Louisiana before its cession
to Spain, and who had lately died, leaving a widow
and an only son—the one now before us. The young
man had just returned from Europe, where he had
received a complete classical education in a college of
Jesuits. His companion wore the costume of an ecclesiastic, and belonged to the celebrated religious
order founded by Loyola. He also was born in Louisiana. But he had in early life gone to France, and
had subsequently become a teacher in the institution
where Aubert Dubayet had recently graduated with
distinguished honors. Conceiving for his pupil a
strong attachment, he had returned with him to New
Orleans. He was called *L'abbé* Viel. The *abbé* was
an unsurpassed Latin and Greek scholar, and was so
wedded to ancient literature that he admired nothing of the modern, except the poem of Telemachus,
by Fénélon. Perhaps it was because the work of the
archbishop of Cambrai had been evidently inspired
by Homer and Virgil, and the subject had been taken
from the quarry of antiquity with all the approved
and traditional machinery of gods and goddesses.
The only fault he found with that production was its
being written in French and in prose. "Otherwise,"
he said, "it would have been a grand epic poem,
ranking next to the Iliad, the Odyssey, and the Eneid."
Wherefore he had translated it into Latin verse, really
worthy of the Augustan age. This learned Jesuit,
although a truly pious man, was, it must be confessed,
more familiar with the classics than with the Bible
and the writings of the fathers of the Church. He
had in particular a sort of devotional attachment to

Horace, who was his oracle and whom he quoted on every occasion. Hence, deploring that the great majority of his countrymen could not profit by the philosophical and literary principles of him whom he called " The sage of the Sabine farm," he had ventured to translate into French some of the epistles of that poet and his *Ars Poetica.* His Latin translation of Telemachus, published in a costly edition by the voluntary and spontaneous subscription of some of his pupils and admirers, had gained him considerable reputation, increased by his French translations of Horace, although he frequently regretted the impropriety of having travestied that author in a language so very inferior to the original, " and yet it is better," he would say, " thus to present to the ignorance of the modern world this great luminary of the ancient—pale, distorted, and obscured as its light may be by passing through the medium of an opaque and coarse glass, than not present it at all." The *abbé* considered as a profound ignoramus any one who did not have at his fingers' end the Latin language; and, as to the Greek, he deeply commiserated the unfortunate man who was not acquainted with its beauties. He always carried about him, safely stowed at the bottom of his literary carpet-bag, and with as much care as his breviary, some compositions of his own, in Latin, of course, which he had decorated with the title of *Miscellanea Latino Gallica*—" Latino-Gallic Miscellanies." These he would occasionally read by scraps to his most intimate friends and favorite pupils. It was only when in his eightieth year, that he could be prevailed upon to overcome his modesty and to lay before the public any original production of his own mind. To the entreaties of his admirers during

half a century he had constantly replied that there
are few things worth publishing after the master-
pieces of antiquity. " I, for one," he declared, "will
not be guilty of such presumption." But, in extreme
old age, a short time before he died in France at the
college of Juilly, where he had been educated and
where he ended his life, engaged to the last in dis-
charging the duties of a professor, he changed his
mind—the paternal fondness of the author for his
literary progeny having probably so increased with
years as to become irresistible.

Such was the individual who, on the day and at the
hour I have mentioned, stood with Aubert Dubayet
on the bank of the Mississippi, and watched with
keen interest the rapid approach of the vessel which
I have described, and which sported conspicuously
the white flag of France. It was a large merchant
ship from Bordeaux. Pointing to her with his index,
" News, news from France, from our beloved France!"
exclaimed the *abbé*, joyfully. " This *navis jactantibus
austris*, this tempest-beaten ship, will rejoice our
hearts. Let us go on board." By this time the ship
had dropped her anchor near the bank of the river,
but not so near as to permit communication with her
without the assistance of a boat. *L'abbé* Viel and
Aubert Dubayet, throwing themselves into one, were
soon on deck, and exchanging warm greetings with
the captain, whom they knew well and with whom
they had once crossed the Atlantic.

" Ha, ha!" exclaimed the learned Jesuit, patting
the broad chest of the rugged captain, " *illi robur, &
æs triplex circa pectus erat, qui fragilem truci com-
misit pelago ratem primus.*"

" Still spouting your confounded lingo, which I

don't understand," said the captain, smiling good-
humoredly. "I take it for granted that you are asking me in Latin for a bottle of claret. Let us go
down for it. Besides, I have for you in my cabin a
package of letters. Follow me; I lead the way."

"Agreed," said the incorrigible *abbé*, " *recepto dulce
mihi furere est amico*, which means, captain, that I
hope to drink your health many a time before you
are drowned in that villainous element on which you
live."

When they were below deck, " Pray, be seated on
this sofa, gentlemen," said the captain. " Steward,
bring glasses and our oldest claret." The order was
soon obeyed, and pledges of good wishes exchanged
over the ruby-looking liquid. " Now," continued the
captain, drawing a package from his desk and handing
it over to the *abbé*, " here are letters for you both. I
must on deck to give orders, whilst you commune
with your distant friends. Break the seals open without ceremony. Make yourselves at home and comfortable. The claret will remain before you and at
hand," and, bowing to his guests, he ran up the steep
steps by which they had come down, and his voice of
command was heard above, giving orders to his crew.

The two men were soon immersed in the reading
of their letters. " O, how happy I feel, father!" exclaimed Aubert Dubayet, addressing the ecclesiastic.
" Here is a letter from Augustin Calandrano, and one
from Joseph Lakanal, my chums at college and your
favorite pupils. Both are provided for. Augustin Calandrano, or rather Tintin Calandro, as we used to call
him by abbreviation, is chief musician of the princess
de Lamballe's chapel, with a good salary and an occupation suited to his taste and peculiar nature, and

Joseph Lakanal, who has entered the holy orders, to which he was inclined at school, has obtained, through the influence of the princess, at the solicitation of Tintin, the situation of professor of belles-lettres in the academy of the city of Toulouse.

"I rejoice at it with all my heart," replied *L' abbé* Viel. "*O fons Blandusiæ, non sine floribus, aras donaberis hædo, cui frons turgida cornibus primis*, which means that, to-morrow, when saying mass, I shall offer special thanks for these news. But night comes apace, my son; let us retire. I can no longer read even the superscription of this letter. Before we go, however, as our news are so cheering, let us make a libation to the gods. *Per Bacchum*, this wine is excellent. *Nunc est bibendum*, Horace would certainly have said on such an occasion. Fill up, boy; here is a bumper to the prosperity of the gentle Calandro and of the oak-ribbed Joseph Lakanal, for they are very unlike, although intimate friends. May they ever remain so!" Down went the glorious liquid, titillating the throat of the good-natured scholar-priest, who smacked his lips after the operation was over. The *abbé* was temperate, but he knew how to enjoy a generous cup of unadulterated wine. After the third glass he used to say on convivial occasions: "*Jam satis est*, enough; it is enough." At that moment the captain, returning from the deck above, joined them and called for another bottle.

"No, no," said the *abbé*. "*Non ego te, candide Bassareu, invitum quatiam, nec variis obsita frondibus sub divum rapiam*, which means, my sea-faring friend: I will not abuse thy gifts, O Bacchus, nor shall I, by taking off my wig in a fit of inebriation, uncover the nakedness of my bald head, which ought to remain hid." The *abbé*, as we see, had rather an original and eccentric way of translating his favorite author, when in a familiar mood, for the benefit of his unlearned friends.

At the corner of Bourbon and St. Philip streets stood the dwelling house of the Dubayet family. It had, at the time our story begins, only three inmates, widow Dubayet, Aubert Dubayet, her son, and the *abbé* Viel. In the week following the arrival of the French vessel, on a certain evening, widow Dubayet, a lofty-looking dame, dressed in mourning weeds and still retaining considerable traces of faded beauty, was reclining in a large arm-chair in front of a chimney where blazed a cheerful fire. She looked sad and in bad health, sighing occasionally, particularly when she looked at an oil portrait hung over the mantelpiece; it represented an officer in full regimentals, and wearing on his breast the decoration of the Cross of St. Louis. There was such a strong likeness between that portrait and young Dubayet, that it was easy to guess what had been the relationship existing between the two persons. It was a remarkably handsome face, with an expression of great decision of character stamped upon it. The lady had her eyes fixed on those features still living on the canvas before her and in her fond recollection, when her son entered in full ball costume. He approached his mother respectfully, and imprinted a kiss on her forehead. "His image!" muttered the widow to herself, as she gazed at him admiringly, and said:

"Where are you going, Aubert?"

"To an entertainment, mother, at the house of Olivier de Maison Rouge."

The widow grew deadly pale and carried her hand

to her heart, as if a sudden pang had shot through
it. "My son," she said with a tremulous voice, "I
thought I had requested you not to frequent that
house."

"I tried to obey you, mother," replied the youth.
"God knows what efforts I made. It happened, however, to be too late when you spoke. My own affections I might have controlled for your sake. But
when I discovered that I had secured the heart of
Emilie de Maison Rouge, I knew of no satisfactory
reason why I should crush it."

"Can you believe, Aubert, that there was none satisfactory to your mother when she addressed such a
request to you?"

"Your reasons, whatever they may be, you have
not been pleased to make known to me. For me,
therefore, they do not exist, and perhaps it is better
now that they should not be communicated, for I may
as well, mother, avail myself of this opportunity to
inform you that I am engaged to Emilie de Maison
Rouge."

"Engaged! affianced!" shrieked the widow, as she
rose from her seat and advanced toward her son with
a face which was the very picture of horror and despair. "You," she said, "you, Aubert Dubayet, marry
Emilie de Maison Rouge! Never, never!"

So shocked and astonished was Aubert at the condition in which he saw his mother that he could only
stammer out: "Mother, what is the matter? What
is the cause of this terrible excitement? What can
be said against the Maison Rouges? They are fully
our equals; they rank among our best families, and
the breath of scandal has never attacked them. I
have long been aware of your personal dislike to them

But on what is it founded? And should any such thing, or any unaccountable prejudice, be in the way of your son's happiness and honor? I say honor, for my honor is pledged. How could I break my engagement? Ask for my life, but not for more. I can not consent to disgrace my father's name."

"Boy," exclaimed the lady impetuously, " dare not interrogate me. I forbid that marriage in God's name, whatever may be the consequences. That is enough. It can not, it shall not ever take place."

"Madam," replied Aubert, respectfully, but firmly, "I am of age to-morrow, and although it will grieve me much to displease you, that marriage shall take place in due time, unless you give me the most satisfactory reasons why it should not"; and, bowing low to his mother, he walked out.

Widow Dubayet stood motionless for a while in the middle of the room, and appeared to have assumed the rigidity of a statue. But at last, coming to herself as it were, she dropped on her knees and prayed fervently. Then she rose, and rang a little bell which she took from a table near her arm-chair. A black servant answered the summons. "Is *L'abbé* Viel in his room?" she inquired.

"Yes, madam."

"Tell him that I beg the favor of his coming to me instantly."

The *abbé* soon made his appearance, and widow Dubayet, advancing toward him with hurried steps, said : " Excuse my disturbing you at this late hour, father, but I shall not detain you long. I am much agitated, as you see, and need repose and solitude for the present. All I want to say is, that I must see you in the confessional at church to-morrow, at seven in the morning. I am sworn to a fearful secret, but I must break my oath. On that point I wish to consult you, and now, good-night."

The good *abbé* saw that this was not the moment to ask for any explanation, and retired in great surprise, without addressing one word to the lady, and without trying to soothe her evident anguish. But as he walked back slowly to his room through a dimly-lighted passage, he kept muttering to himself : " What earthquake is this? What is in the wind? There is a storm brewing surely. How shall I prepare for it? The omens are not favorable. Is it *prægnans canis, aut ab agro rava decurrens lupæ Lanuvino, fœtaque vulpes?* But, dog or wolf, I must conjure down the evil fiend. *Ego cui timebo, providus auspex ; antequam stantes repetat paludes imbrium divina avis immenentûm, oscinem corvum precesuscitabo solis ab ortu.* That is to say, I will, before going to bed, read two odes of Horace, two chapters of St. John, and repeat twice my evening prayers, adding a special one to St. Peter and St. Paul."

The next day when Aubert came to breakfast at the regular hour, he was astonished at being told that his mother had gone out, and, when she left the house, had given strict orders that the morning meal should not be delayed on her account, because it was more than probable that she could not return in time for it. As to *L'abbé* Viel, he had also risen very early, had gone out with Madam Dubayet, and came back alone, looking as if he were insane, crossing himself, and jabbering Latin with such gesticulations as to frighten all the servants, who thought that he must have met the devil, or some other awful apparition. " Tell Aubert, if he should inquire for me," had the *abbé* said

to one of the sable menials, "that I wish to be left
undisturbed in my room until dinner-time, and that
he must excuse my not joining him at the breakfast
table to-day." This increased Aubert's surprise, and
a presentiment of evil came over him. He hardly
tasted the repast which had been spread before him,
and retired to a room of which he had made a library
—a sanctum for the *abbé* and himself. There they
used to have their familiar daily chats — the *abbé*,
of course, leading the conversation, which seldom
ended without his carrying his pupil back to his
former studies of classical lore when on the benches
of the school. Aubert was listlessly holding a book
in his hand, and trying in vain to fix his attention on what he was attempting to read, when his
mother entered. He was painfully struck with the
evidence of deep suffering which he observed in her
face. She looked almost livid. Aubert rose, took her
hand, which shook like an aspen leaf, kissed it rever-
ently, and led her to a seat. She remained silent,
striving, as it were, to nerve herself, while one or
two slight spasmodic contractions of the lips showed
some deep agony at work in the heart's core. After
a pause which appeared to Aubert to last an age,
she said: "My son, are you still irrevocably bent on
that marriage?"

"How can it be otherwise, dearest mother, unless,
as I told you yesterday, you give me the most satisfactory reason for not keeping my plighted faith—a
reason which I can communicate to Emilie de Maison
Rouge, and which may free me from my obligations
without disgrace, although it may break my heart?"

"O my son, my son!" exclaimed the lady. "What
have you done, and what are you compelling me to

do! But, since it must be, let it be. O God! O
God! How dreadful are the consequences of sin!"
She drew from her bosom a letter which she presented
to her son, saying: "This is a communication from
Madam de Maison Rouge to your father. It accidentally, and I now say providentially, came to my
hand—providentially, because it will prevent the perpetration of a crime. It destroyed my happiness,
Aubert, but I long ago forgave your father, and promised him on oath never to divulge the secret to any
human being. My son, Emilie de Maison Rouge is
your sister."

Aubert leaped from his seat, uttered a wild, piercing cry, and fell senseless on the floor.

One month after this event, Emilie de Maison Rouge,
reduced to despair by the inexplicable desertion of
Aubert, who could not divulge to her the secret communicated to him by his mother, had entered the
convent of the Ursulines with the intention of taking
the veil, and *L'abbé* Viel had been ordered by his
Superior in the province to accomplish a certain mission in the fertile, but almost uncultivated prairies of
Attakapas, and to ascertain by what means the sparse
population of that extensive district, consisting of
whites, blacks, and Indians, could be best and most
speedily educated and civilized. As to Aubert Dubayet, he had departed for France in that very ship
which, with the *abbé* Viel, he had visited on her arrival, and which had brought him welcomed letters
from Calandro and Lakanal. There are times when,
for individuals as for nations, changes and revolutions
chase each other with the fleetness of a race-horse.
What was the day before, is not to be found, or recognized, on the next morning; something has passed

over it by which it is obliterated or transformed; events are often accelerated in their march and crowded together, as if fate itself was in a hurry to accomplish its decrees, and was subject to fits of impatience and precipitation.

Aubert Dubayet reached safely the shores of France. Without a moment's delay he went to Versailles, and asked for an audience of the Minister of War, Marshal Rochambeau, to whom he was distantly related, and to whom he had a letter of introduction. The marshal received him kindly, and inquired whether he could do anything for his service. " Much," replied Dubayet, gloomily. " I wish for the opportunity of being killed. Send me to the battle-field, and you will have done for me what I most desire."

The marshal looked at him fixedly, and, taking his hand, which he pressed, said in a tone not devoid of sympathy, although a slight smile was perceptible on his lips: "Bah! nonsense! What misfortune could, on the threshold of life, have been so serious and so irreparable as to make it hateful to you? You have not lived and suffered enough, to have the right and the wish to die so soon. Your adolescent grief, on whose chin beard has not had time to grow, will pass off like a spell of fever. Stir up, stir up, put spurs on your heels, serve your king and country, and do not mope like an owl in a corner. All that you need is occupation for mind and body—a purpose—an object in life—a career—action—action! Well, let me be your physician, and I shall cure you. The king sends a body of troops to the assistance of the North Americans, who are struggling for independence against Great Britain. The expedition will sail from Brest in six days. I advise you to join it.

2

If you consent, I offer you a commission of second lieutenant in the regiment of Agénois, commanded by the marquis of Autichamp, a brave officer."

"I accept with gratitude," replied Dubayet.

"Very well," said the marshal, "I compliment you on your decision." After having signed the commission and handed it to the new lieutenant, he added: "When we meet again I expect, young man, to see you with a higher grade." Aubert shook his head with an expression of profound dejection.

"Pshaw, pshaw!" said the marshal. "You mean that you will seek death. That is the very reason why you will not meet it. We know that, we veterans, who have faced it so often. Death and Dame Fortune are very capricious. That's one thing which they have in common. Be of good cheer; you may yet rise to be what I am. I remember that I, too, was once inconsolable. But gun-powder is an excellent cordial. It soon exhilarated and cured me; it will have the same effect on you. Good-bye, and success to your maiden sword. I will not lose sight of you, and I expect from your colonel a favorable report of your gallantry at the first battle that shall be fought in America."

CHAPTER II.

THE CONCERT GIVEN TO ROYALTY—THE PRINCESS DE LAMBALLE—IS THERE ANYTHING IN OMENS, PRESAGES, AND PRESENTIMENTS?

ON his leaving the marshal de Rochambeau, Dubayet hastened to look for Augustin Calandrano. The meeting of the two friends was warm and genial. Tintin Calandro (to call him by the name under which he was generally better known) was found in a state of intense excitement. There was to be, on the evening of that very day, at the *Hotel de Toulouse*, where resided the princess de Lamballe, a great concert, and the king and queen were to honor it with their presence. Tintin being the chief of the musicians of the princess, the whole responsibility of the entertainment rested on him. " I want you there," he said to Dubayet. " I will have a seat for you in the orchestra, not to admire my music, of course, but to enjoy the brilliancy of the audience. You will see our good and excellent king, our lovely Queen Marie Antoinette, the worthy daughter of the Cæsars, and above all, you will see the princess de Lamballe, the gem of the illustrious house of Savoy, the paragon of all the excellencies of which the earth is susceptible."

" Take care," said Dubayet, smiling. " You talk like a Romeo and betray your love."

" Betray ! I am ready to proclaim it on the housetops," replied Tintin. " Why should not a man openly worship the star that twinkles in the distant firmament? What can be more harmless? I love the princess as I love all that is most exquisite in the fine arts; I love her as I love beauty, eloquence, heroism, the royalty of intellect, the royalty of birth, and the rarest endowments of the heart and soul. I love all these things united in the embodiment of what may be deemed by others ideal perfection, but which to me is actual reality. My love is the love of seraphic innocence, that kind of love which must be the all-pervading fluid of paradise and the music of the celestial spheres. I lose sight of earth, my friend, when I look at the princess, and nothing of earth remains in me. I will introduce you to her, and you will understand my feelings, when you shall witness the halo which encircles her brow."

"I shall hardly have time," said Dubayet, "to avail myself of the honor which you offer to me, in utter forgetfulness of what I have already told you—that I depart the day after to-morrow for Brest, with the grade of lieutenant, to join an expedition which sails for the shores of the colonies of Great Britain in North America."

"True, I had forgotten it. But, nevertheless, you shall at least see the princess this evening, although at a distance. The effulgence which beams from her person will reach you, and will be sufficient to warm your heart. I'll take no refusal. You will sup with me after the concert, and to-morrow we shall have Lakanal to dine with us. I will write him an invitation to that effect, for he has recently come to Paris from Toulouse, in whose academy he is a professor, as you know. These are vacation times for him, and he makes the most of it in Paris and Versailles, rubbing off, as he says, his provincial rust, and sharpening himself on the grinding-stone of civilization."

"Very well," said Dubayet, "I consent, with pleasure, to all you desire. Adieu, to meet again soon. In the meantime, I must be preparing and packing for my departure the day after to-morrow."

Dubayet, according to his engagement, attended the concert to which he had been invited by Tintin Calandro, and, mingling with the musicians, witnessed from among them the brilliant display made on that occasion by the most refined court in Europe. It exceeded all the glorious dreams in which his imagination had ever indulged. Here stood royalty in all its antique and hereditary splendor, and radiant with the proud consciousness of its secure duration. Here was the cherished incarnation of a traditional principle; and, to defend it, if threatened, who then doubted that the loyal sword of France would leap from its scabbard? Here the most polished gentlemen of Christendom, whose breasts glittered with stars, and whose heroic names had for a thousand years brightened the pages of history, were eagerly pressing round the queen. Surrounded by the most beautiful and elegant women of the kingdom, who courted her smiles, she herself seemed the representation of enthroned happiness.

A piece of music had been composed for the occasion by Tintin Calandro. At the end of the performance, the example being given by Louis, a whirlwind of applause rose from an audience composed of the gods of the earth, who were over-fastidious in their taste, and not prone to manifestations of enthusiasm. This time these exclamations could be heard bursting from the ambrosia-fed lips of the highest in high

Olympus: "How wonderful! What is this? There never was anything like it. How new! How original, how eccentric! But what genius in that eccentricity!" Tintin was summoned to the presence of the king, who complimented him graciously, and decorated him with the cross of St. Louis, as one of the most distinguished artists of France. The queen was profuse in her praises, and encircling a magnificent bouquet she held in her hand with a heavy chain bracelet of gold studded with diamonds, which she detached from her arm, presented it to the astonished musician. The princess de Lamballe, delighted with the success of the entertainment she had given to royalty, approached Tintin Calandro in her turn, and, in the sweetest tones of her silvery voice, expressed her acknowledgments to him. "My Orpheus," she said, "it would ill befit me to compete with the Majesties of France, who have to-day so munificently and openly honored you with testimonials of their appreciation. I shall, therefore, content myself with presenting a mere trifle to your acceptance. I am sitting for my portrait to a young artist, a man of genius like yourself. It shall be sent to you as soon as finished." Tintin had received with self-possession the compliments of the king and queen; but, on being thus addressed by the princess de Lamballe, his agitation was such that it could not be concealed from those who happened to have their eyes fixed on him. He bowed to the ground without being able to reply, and, when attempting to withdraw from her presence, seemed so exhausted from the excess of his emotion, that one of his colleagues of the orchestra stepped forward, and offering his arm, led him away.

An hour afterward, Dubayet and Tintin Calandro

were supping together. Tintin had invited no one else, as he wished to be alone with his college chum, whom he had so recently met, and from whom he was again to be soon separated. The conversation turned, of course, on the concert, the great event of the evening. "It was truly," said Dubayet, "a fairy scene, too dazzling to mere mortals like me—so much light that one could hardly have believed in the existence of darkness in this world—such gorgeousness of wealth as to exclude the conception of poverty—and such an overflowing of all those things which ought to constitute happiness, that it seemed to leave no room for the intrusion of that little drop of water which often falls from human eyes, and which is called a tear."

Tintin became agitated, as if these words had touched in him some secret spring of grief, or awakened some fearful apprehension, and buried his head between his hands. After a little while, he looked up, and said: "Aubert, you have heard of second sight, or some sort of mysterious gift, or curse, as the case may be, which goes by more than one name. Do you believe in it?"

"No," replied Aubert.

"I do," continued Tintin Calandro. "I know two men who belong to that sect whose members are called *illuminati,* and at whose visions the world laughs. One is named Cazotte, and the other Gassner. Cazotte is here; Gassner in Vienna. The skeptic may say what he pleases, but surely they are strange men, possessing unknown and terrible faculties. I know of certain predictions of theirs which make my flesh creep. Shake not your head. They have but too often proved to be true prophets."

"What are those predictions?" inquired Dubayet.

"I shall only mention two, which I wish to remain buried in your breast as in a tomb. It is almost treason to speak of them."

"I almost shudder in anticipation and on trust," said Dubayet, laughing and emptying a glass of wine.

"Alas," groaned Tintin. "Treat not so slightingly what I am going to divulge. As the great dramatic poet of England has said—

"'There are more things in heaven and earth, Horatio,
Than are dreamt of in your philosophy.'

But to the point. Gassner, to avoid persecutions which his visions and his religious doctrines had brought upon him in his native country, had fled to Vienna, when our present queen was still a child. He was presented to the empress Maria Theresa, who became fond of him and took a strange pleasure in listening to his wild revelations, although she sometimes ridiculed, or pretended to ridicule, them. 'Tell me,' she one day said to him, 'tell me, since you have the privilege of knowing the future, if my Antoinette shall be happy.' He became very pale, and did not answer. The empress insisted on a reply, and Gassner, daring neither to continue silent, nor to speak to the point, said evasively: 'Madam, there are crosses for all shoulders.' I met him, some years after the marriage of the archduchess of Austria with the dauphin of France, now Louis XVI., and having heard of the anecdote, I interrogated him about it. He burst into tears, and requested me never to approach him on that subject."

"And can you permit, my friend," asked Aubert, "the nonsensical imaginings of diseased brains to have any influence over your mind?"

"Nonsensical imaginings! But are not the pages of history full of portents, presentiments, and presages which did not turn out to be without a meaning, notwithstanding the sneers of what goes by the name of philosophy? I can not but be alarmed, when I remember that Marie Antoinette was born on the day of the earthquake of Lisbon—that never-to-be-forgotten disaster—and it is not a disconnected omen. At the precise moment when her wedding took place at Versailles, the sky, which had been pure and serene before, became dark with clouds, and the most dreadful storm burst out on a sudden, shook to its foundations the palace of our kings, and did infinite damage wide and far. A few days afterward there were public rejoicings in Paris to commemorate the royal marriage. What happened? A series of the most heart-rending accidents which caused the death of more than twelve hundred persons. Nay, more—the prime minister, the duke de Choiseul, who negotiated that marriage, was shortly after exiled by Louis XV., notwithstanding the entreaties of Marie Antoinette, duchess of Berri and dauphiness of France. But this is enough. I will not go over all the mournful and death-ringing links of the long chain of extraordinary presages concerning her."

"Bah!" said Dubayet; "can you seriously be affected by such things? Can you attach any importance to coincidences?"

"Certainly not, were I to take it for granted, like other people, that an accident, or incident, is the result of chance. But I do not believe that there is any room left for chance in the mathematical creation of the omnipotent geometrician. This little world of ours, as we understand it with our dim and con-

tracted intellect, apparently teems with accidents.
Our life looks as if made up of them. But there are
no accidents for God. They are incompatible with
His providence and prescience. The infinite universe
could not hold on one minute together, if any hole
in it, however small it might be, had been permitted
to exist, so as to allow an accident to creep in. There
would be an entire disorganization of the whole machinery. Hence, I do not see why what we call accidents and coincidences should not have a language
and a meaning, if in reality they are, as I think, preconcerted events, with mysterious connections which
we do not comprehend, but which have something to
do with our destinies."

"Very well, go on," said Dubayet. "I am not inclined to contradiction to-night, and shall take care
that our conversation does not degenerate into a misty
metaphysical discussion. If you have done with
Gassner, what of Cazotte? I like prophets, for I like
the supernatural. The world is so commonplace,
stale, and flat! The supernatural is the champagne
of the banquet of life. Let us have some of it by
all means. Off with the cork, pop, pop! The cup
of credulity is ready."   .

"Well, then," continued Tinto Calandro, "when the
present king ascended the throne there were great
festivities in Paris. On the *Place Louis XV.* there
was to be a grand display of fireworks, which the
king was to grace with his presence and that of the
queen. My father then occupied an apartment, the
windows of which opened on the *Place*, and commanded a full view of it. Cazotte had dined with
us, and we were all three gazing at the vast multitude
before us, when the king, the queen, and their suite

made their appearance, and ascended the platform which had been prepared for them. Cazotte fixed his weird looks intently on the prince and kept them riveted on him, until he was thrown into a sort of trance, during which he raved incoherently. 'Ah! Louis, ah! Louis,' he exclaimed, 'that is the very spot where your scaffold shall be erected, and where the public executioner shall cut off your head, and show it in triumph to a demon-possessed multitude.' He continued his horrible vaticinations amidst sobs and shrieks, until he fell into a complete state of catalepsy, in which he remained several hours, as if dead. If you knew Cazotte as well as I do, you would not think so lightly of this tale of mine, preposterously monstrous and evidently impossible as the prediction may sound."

"Preposterously monstrous, yes; but evidently impossible, no," said Dubayet. "Did not Charles Stuart die on the scaffold?"

"Oh!" replied Tintin, "that was in England. But in France!——Pshaw!"

"Revolutions are cosmopolites," said Dubayet, dryly. "Whenever and wherever they set society topsy-turvy, the king and the rag-picker are on a footing of equality, and when time-honored institutions are tumbling down on all sides by the shaking of an universal earthquake, when the world is playing at somersaults, and old chaos claims his own again, I would rather insure the rag-picker's head than the king's. I do not wish to be a prophet of evil like your Gassner and your Cazotte, but, methinks, I hear strange rumblings in the bowels of the worn-out European monarchies. Even on the other side of the Atlantic, in new-born and virgin America, I hear an

ominous shout, which may be re-echoed from pole to
pole.   Remember one strange fact.   In a few days I
shall, by the order of the descendant of a long line of
kings and under the lily flag of France, be on my way
to the relief of rebels, who have not only denounced
their legitimate sovereign and impeached him at the
bar of their own self-instituted tribunal, but also proclaimed, in the face of heaven and earth, that all men
are born free and equal. You who believe in presages,
what think you of that one?"

"Alas," replied Tintin Calandro, "there were bad
presages enough from the birth of the king to the
present time.   He was born at Versailles when the
king, his grandfather, was at Choisy. The messenger
who carried to that place the news of the increase of
the royal family, fell from his horse as he arrived, and
subsequently died in consequence of that fall.   Louis
became an orphan when still a child; he lost his
father and mother almost at the same time.   Bad
luck, bad luck, is it not?   On the death of his elder
brother, when he heard of his being heir to the throne,
he burst into tears and even lost his senses. Was it a
presentiment of coming evil?   And finally, when he
was informed of the king's demise and of his acces-
sion to the throne, he exclaimed: 'O God, what a
misfortune for me!' Was it again a presentiment?
And then his very name!   There hardly ever was a
duke of Berri who was not ill-fated.   How strange!"

Thus they communed until it was very late in the
night, when they separated after having made the engagement of meeting again on the next day, to dine
with their classmate, Joseph Lakanal.   On that day,
at six o'clock in the afternoon, the three friends had
come together at a private room bespoken for the

purpose in one of the most celebrated *restaurants* of
Paris. Tintin Calandro, to do honor to his two guests,
whom he was so happy to meet and to entertain, had
put on his best apparel. He wore a blue silk coat,
with a flowered satin under-vest, chestnut-colored
breeches, white stockings, bright gold buckles at the
knee, and still brighter ones, if possible, on his highly
polished calf-skin shoes. On his breast glittered the
Cross of St. Louis, which had been given to him by
the king on the preceding evening. His hair was
elaborately powdered, and the queue which fell back
over his collar had been artistically combed and tied
with a glossy, jet-black ribbon. Ruffles and shirt
frills of exquisite lace completed his studiously nice
toilet. A steel-hilted sword was suspended to his
left side, and a large diamond sparkled on one of his
prodigiously elongated fingers. It was a gala day for
him to meet his school friends, so that the princess
de Lamballe's favorite and petted maestro had been
tempted to indulge in some foppishness of dress.
Lakanal was habited as ecclesiastics were in those
days. His black gown had a harsh look, which cor-
responded with that of his face. Aubert Dubayet
sported with youthful grace the elegant uniform of
the regiment in which he had obtained a lieutenancy.
But a black crape, the badge of mourning, encircled
his left arm, and an expression of sadness dwelt on
his handsome features.

"My friends," said he, after having exchanged
greetings with Tintin Calandro and Lakanal, " I meet
you not in a convivial mood, for I have just received
a letter from *L'abbé* Viel, who informs me of the death
of my mother in Louisiana, from which I lately departed for a reason that brooked no delay. She was

in precarious health, and I feared what has happened.
The blow, therefore, was not unexpected, but it is not
the less painful. I have not allowed it, however, to
prevent me from keeping my engagement, as we part
to-morrow, perhaps never to meet again. I am now
alone in the world, with no other ties than those which
bind us together, and I have no desire to prolong my
existence. Probably an English bullet will soon carry
me off in Virginia, or in Massachusetts."

Tintin embraced him tenderly and said: "You will
live, I hope, to conquer all your sorrows, of whatever
nature they may be, and to serve your king faithfully
wherever he sends you. It is not a misfortune to
taste of sorrow early in life. Sorrow is, perhaps, the
strongest pledge and proof of the immortality given
to us by Providence. It matures the heart and de-
velops in it a keener and clearer sense of our duties.
Man alone, among all the created things of which we
have any knowledge, has duties to perform. Hence
sorrow may be said to be one of his normal attributes,
and the assurance of eternal life with eternal obligations to discharge. The ox, the horse, and all other
creatures moved by instinct have no duties imposed
on them, and are incapable of guilt and virtue. Man
only is a moral being, susceptible of sorrow and of
the knowledge of good and evil. This imposes responsibility, and responsibility to God implies immortality; for annihilation would put on the same
footing vice and virtue. I do not know but what
we ought to thank Heaven for what lacerates our
hearts when we are still in the vestibule of our earthly
career. It is a passport to a better life here and hereafter."

"Tintin," said Lakanal, "you were born a preacher,

and you have missed your vocation. It is your passion to be moralizing forever, even in this butterfly
dress of yours. Although more worldly-minded than
you are, notwithstanding my canonicals, I am as
much for the performance of duty as you may be,
whether it secures, or not, a reward in another world.
But it is a pity that men so often disagree about that
fine thing called duty, particularly duty of a public
and political nature. Our whole country will soon
. fall to loggerheads on the subject. You, for instance,
think that the king is France, and that France is the
king. You are an intense royalist. For me France
is everything, and the king nothing. I am an intense
republican. Hence, fill your glass and drink to Louis
and to his lieutenant Dubayet, whilst I drink to the
rebels of America and to all those who go to their
assistance, including, of course, our dear friend here
present."

"I fill to the brim," chimed in Tintin Calandro,
"and here is my sentiment: Success to the allies of
my royal master, be they rebels, republicans, or dev-
ils. Good, it is said, frequently comes out of evil.
What matters the utensil the cook has used, if a
palatable dish is brought out of it? Therefore, hurrah for the Americans and the foes of England!"

"I join in your libation," said Dubayet gravely,
"but without deciding between you. I am not in a
mood just now to care much for royalists or republicans."

The friends spent several hours together. Their
conversation was serious and argumentative; not a
jest enlivened it. Professor Lakanal, of the Low
clergy, represented the new order of ideas which were
developing themselves. Tintin Calandro, on the con-

trary, was the type of that *régime* which was passing away. Dubayet was indifferent, thoughtful, and expectant. He was uncertain of what he might or might not be, and careless of the future. This trio was a faithful representation of the three classes into which French society was then divided. Dubayet closed the convivial entertainment over which so much sobriety and gravity had presided, by proposing this toast: "Whatever the future may have in store for us and for France, may we ever remain friends!" They drank to this sentiment with deep emotion, and separated after repeated embraces. They retired to their respective lodgings, but not one of them went to bed that night. In the reciprocal exchange of their thoughts and feelings, there had been something which had produced on their minds an impression that defied sleep. Vague presentiments, instinctive apprehensions, the distant gleam of future events, weird and fantastic imaginings, flitted confusedly before them, casting lights and shadows over the mirror of their brain. Lakanal, when he reached his room, trimmed his lamp, and began writing a treatise on the republics of Greece and Rome which he intended for publication. Dubayet opened Polybius; and, after reading two or three hours, turned to a map of the thirteen revolted colonies of Great Britain, and became absorbed in its study. As to Tintin Calandro, after having prayed devoutly, he took his violin, and the most plaintive melodies floated away on the waves of the midnight air, softening into tears those whom they reached in their sleep, and who dreamed that they heard the harp of Israel weeping over the fall of Jerusalem. Tintin was a poet, and had also the fearful morbid sensibilities of those who are fatally entitled to that name. His conceptions, although not worked out in metrical numbers, but only in quavers and crotchets, were not the less poems of the highest order. The rod of his violin was his pen, and his soul-stirring instrument was the tablet on which his genius wrote its inspirations. His was the poetry of thought and feeling expressed in sounds; and, alas! like them, evanescent. It had not the advantage of being chiselled in those words that are more lasting than brass, and excite the admiration of posterity, long after he who uttered them has been chilled into the silence of death.

CHAPTER III.

WHEN the French troops of which the regiment of Aubert Dubayet was a part, landed in 1780 at Newport, in Rhode Island, under the command of Count Rochambeau, the condition of the thirteen revolted colonies of Great Britain was found by their new allies to be worse than it was expected. Washington had just written to Reed, of Pennsylvania: "We have never experienced a like extremity at any period of the war." The winter of that year had been intensely rigorous. It had brought famine to the camps of the revolutionary soldiers. "For a fortnight past," wrote their illustrious chief on the 8th of January, "the troops, both officers and men, have been almost perishing with want." The Americans, tried by a multitude of indescribable sufferings, were learning to their sorrow what it costs to indulge in the luxury of revolutions. The French, not long after, made the same experiment, and have since repeated it often, although one of them has propounded to the world this question: "Is it possible for anybody to be again cheerful, who has ever witnessed a revolution and its consequences?" He might find an answer in the saying of one of his compatriots, who asserts "that a revolution always demoralizes everybody without instructing any one." But, whatever be the effects of such political convulsions, the Americans had to meet them in the best way they could, and although the cold had been so unusual as to freeze the great bay of New York, yet it had comparatively very little to do with their distress and difficulties. The main cause was, that Congress had gone to war without adequate preparations for it—a defect which it had never been able or willing to remedy. Congress, under the articles of the confederation which bound the thirteen States together, was the most effete of all governments, if it deserved at all the name of government, of which it had not the most essential attribute—the power of levying taxes. That power remained with the States in their respective capacity. Hence it follows that it had not that which is the breath—the sustaining element of armies—money—since patriotism and courage can not live and thrive on thin air alone. Under the pressure of absolute and irresistible wants, and gasping for relief, it had yielded to the temptation of adopting the modern contrivance of issuing paper money, and the natural consequences had followed. The new-fledged States which were struggling for their independence from Great Britain, and which were loth to subject themselves to a strong central government, although it should be of their own creation, imitated the fatal example of the shadowy one which they had set up as their head and leader, and flooded the country with their own issues of paper money. All those different streams mingled afterward into one which was called "continental currency." It soon became of no value, for in 1780 it

had declined to such a degree that more than forty
dollars in paper were hardly equivalent to one in specie.
To correct the evil, Congress imagined to make these
rags a legal tender, at the nominal value of the currency, in discharge of debts contracted for gold. Thus
a national sanction was given to knavery; bad faith
was legalized, and patriots were invited to become
pickpockets. On that occasion, as on every other of
the same nature, it was shown that good never can
come out of evil, notwithstanding the common saying
to the contrary, and the condition of the country became worse. The commissary department was rendered incapable of getting supplies, and Washington
was compelled to have recourse to the cruel and dangerous resource of impressing, and giving drafts which
were to be paid on a future and uncertain day. Charles
Lee, the second in command to Washington, and who
had been very near superseding him, having been
made prisoner, had turned traitor, and had voluntarily
submitted to the British government, for the subjugation of the rebels, a plan which, if it had been followed, might have been attended with disastrous consequences. Arnold, one of the most distinguished of
the American generals, was reported to have "an itch-
ing palm," and by many was suspected of dissatisfaction, particularly after his marriage in Philadelphia
with a lady who had been a "toast" and favorite
among the British officers. Arnold was a man of
luxurious habits and excessive extravagance, and his
impatience to get rich amounted almost to a mono-
mania. There were misgivings and whisperings in relation to him, as he was known to be getting deeper
and deeper into debt—a fatal habit, particularly for
a public man, and one which will never fail to sum-

mon to the elbow of the future victim the arch-
tempter with his fiendish seductions.

What materially impeded military operations and
produced discontent in the army was, that the business and duty of supporting that body devolved on
the respective States and not on Congress, which
could only make requisitions. Frequently those
requisitions were only partially attended to, if not
disregarded altogether. It produced great inequality
in the condition of the troops, according to the means
and the degree of liberality evinced by the States to
which they belonged. Some of the troops were
abundantly supplied; others were ragged, shoeless,
and starving; and these contrasts, being side by side,
were the more striking and effective. Hence mur-
murs, envious comparisons, heart-burnings, and a
tendency to seditious combinations. Even feelings
of jealousy were entertained in Congress of the commander-in-chief. It was thought that his influence
was already too great; that even his virtues afforded
motives for alarm; that the enthusiasm of the army,
joined to the kind of dictatorship already confided to
him, put Congress and the United States at his mercy; and that it was not expedient "to expose a man
even of the highest virtue to such temptations."

To make matters worse, Arnold—who, for money,
would have sold himself to the foul fiend—was looking all round for a purchaser. He went to the
French minister, M. de la Luzerne,* and expressed
the desire to borrow from him a sum equal to the
amount of his debts; "intimating that it might be
to the interest of the king of France to grant the

---

* Irving's " Life of Washington."

favor, thereby securing the attachment and gratitude
of an American general of his rank and influence."
It was not necessary to be a very acute diplomatist
to understand such language. M. de la Luzerne, being a high-spirited man, was greatly shocked. He
nobly replied: "When the envoy of a foreign power
gives—or, if you will, lends money, it is ordinarily
to corrupt those who receive it, and to make them
the creatures of the sovereign whom he serves; or,
rather, he corrupts without persuading. He buys
and does not secure. But the league entered into
between the king and the United States is the work
of justice and of the wisest policy. It has for its basis a reciprocal interest and good-will. In the mission with which I am charged, my true glory consists
in fulfilling it without intrigue or cabal—without re-
sorting to any secret practices, and by the force alone
of the conditions of the alliance." This was striking
with the lance of Ithuriel the toad crouching in the
heart of the traitor; and, with a view to dislodging
the reptile, the French minister complimented Arnold on his past career of glory, and expressed the
hope that he would gather further laurels. But this
had no effect on the sordid soul of the venal soldier.
What he wanted was money, and not empty-handed
compliments. Arnold had probably ceased to believe in the success of the cause in which he had
enlisted, and was perhaps strengthened in that belief
by the discontent which he knew to exist in the army, and by the defection of several of the Connecticut regiments. So dark indeed was the horizon in
1780, that Washington himself wrote to the Executive of Pennsylvania: "Every idea you can form of
our distress will fall short of the reality. There is

such a combination of circumstances to exhaust the patience of the soldiery that it begins at last to be worn out, and we see in every line of the army features of mutiny and sedition. All our departments, all our operations are at a stand ; and, unless a system very different from that which has a long time prevailed be immediately adopted throughout the, States, our affairs must soon become desperate beyond the possibility of recovery."

But what discouraged Washington more than anything else was the lethargy that had come over the public mind. The spirit with which the Revolution had begun seemed to be dead. It looked as if the majority of the people were sick of the war and anxious to resume those avocations of life which gave them profit and comfort. Patriotism and the struggle for independence required too many sacrifices. This was so evident that Washington gave way to an unusual fit of despair, and thus expressed himself : " I have almost ceased to hope. The country is in such a state of insensibility and indifference to its interests, that I do not flatter myself with any change for the better." And again: " The present juncture is so interesting, that, if it does not produce correspondent exertions, it will be a proof that motives of honor, public good, and even self-preservation have lost their influence over our minds. This is a decisive moment ; one of the most—I will go further and say *the most* — important America has seen. The court of France has made a glorious effort for our deliverance, and, if we disappoint its intentions by our supineness, we must become contemptible in the eyes of mankind ; nor can we, after that, venture to confide that our allies will persist in an attempt to establish what, it will appear, we want inclination or ability to assist them in."

Congress also seemed to partake of the general fainting debility which pervaded the whole confederacy, and Washington made a powerful effort to rouse that body by thus addressing one of its influential members: "Certain I am," he said, "unless Congress speak in a more decisive tone—unless they are vested with powers by the several States, competent to the purposes of war, or assume them as matters of right, and they and the States respectively act with more energy than they have hitherto done, that our cause is lost. We can no longer drudge on in the old way. By ill-timing the adoption of measures, by delays in the execution of them, or by unwarrantable jealousies, we incur enormous expenses and derive no benefit from them. One State will comply with a requisition of Congress, another neglects to do it, a third executes it by halves, and all differ either in the manner, the matter, or so much in point of time, that we are always working up-hill; and, while such a system as the present one—or rather, want of one—prevails, we shall ever be unable to apply our strength or resources to any advantage. I see one head gradually changing into thirteen—I see one army branching into thirteen, which, instead of looking up to Congress as the supreme controlling power of the United States, are considering themselves dependent on their respective States. In a word, I see the powers of Congress declining too fast for the consideration and respect which are due to them as the great representative body of America, and I am fearful of the consequences."

Such was the desperate condition of the revolted

colonies of Great Britain when the French fleet arrived at Newport, in Rhode Island, on the 10th of
July, 1780. It was composed of seven ships of the
line, two frigates, and two bombs, convoying transports on board of which were upward of five thousand troops. This was the first division of the forces
promised by France. The second division had been
detained at Brest for want of transports, but might
soon be expected. The French were not slow in dis-
covering the true state of things, and concluded that
their government had undertaken a hard task when
assuming to secure the independence of the thirteen
rebellious colonies. Six days after the arrival of the
fleet, on the 16th of July, Count de Rochambeau's
first dispatch to Vergennes, one of the members of
the ministry, was couched in these terms: " Upon my
arrival here the country was in consternation, the
paper money had fallen to sixty for one, and even the
government takes it up at forty for one. Washington had for a long time only three thousand men
under his command. The arrival of the Marquis de
Lafayette and the announcement of succor from
France, afforded some encouragement; but the Tories,
who are very numerous, gave out that it was only a
temporary assistance, like that of Count D'Estaing.
In describing to you our reception at this place, we
shall show you the feeling of all the inhabitants of
the continent. This town is of considerable size, and
contains, like the rest, both Whigs and Tories. I
landed with my staff without troops; nobody appeared on the streets; those at the windows looked sad
and depressed. I spoke to the principal persons of
the place, and told them, as I wrote to General
Washington, that this was merely the advanced guard

of a greater force, and that the king was determined
to support them with his whole power. In twenty-
four hours their spirits rose, and last night all the
streets, houses, and steeples were illuminated, in the
midst of fireworks and the greatest rejoicings. I am
now here with a single company of grenadiers, until
wood and straw will have been collected; my camp
is marked out, and I hope to have the troops landed
to-morrow."

Notwithstanding this illumination and rejoicing,
Rochambeau was too far-sighted not to discover that
the public joy was somewhat hollow like a rotten
tree, and that there was a lingering feeling of disappointment at the bottom of the heart of the population who appeared to welcome him. The shrewd
Rhode Islanders calculated that the French troops
were not sufficiently numerous to make success a fixed
fact, and the possibility of failure damped the ardor
of the patriotic satisfaction which, otherwise, they
would have exhibited to exuberance. " The Whigs,"
wrote Rochambeau, " are pleased, but they say that
the king ought to have sent twenty thousand men
and twenty ships, to drive the enemy from New York;
that the country is infallibly ruined; that it is impossible to find a recruit to send to General Washington's
army, without giving him one hundred hard dollars to
engage for six months' service, and they beseech his
majesty to assist them with all his strength. The
war will be an expensive one; we pay even for our
quarters, and for the land covered with the camp."

If the French were made to pay rent for the very
ground on which they encamped, in consequence of
the extraordinary degree of acquisitiveness character-
izing those whom they had come to assist, they showed

great taste and judgment in the selection of the site of that camp. It was to the east of the town,* and extended nearly across that small island over picturesque hills and dales. The gallant and martial appearance of those troops excited much admiration, and it was acknowledged that their officers, by their refinement and elegance of tone and manner, were a splendid specimen of that old French nobility who had, during so many centuries, filled the world with the fame of their exploits. They bore resplendent historical names, and they were not unworthy of that advantage. Many had come to this new field of achievement, moved by a feeling of adventure and romance. "They had brought out with them," said Rochambeau, their commander, "the heroic and chivalrous courage of the ancient French nobility." Among them was a duke de Lauzun, as brilliant as his famous ancestor who had saved the wife of James the Second and the infant Prince of Wales from the grasp of a revolutionary usurper. What a contrast, however, between the actions of the two—between the Lauzun of the age of Louis XIV. and the Lauzun of the age of Louis XVI.—the one, carrying away in his arms, at the dead hour of night and in a pitiless storm, the royalty of England fleeing from rebellion—and the other, drawing the sword of hereditary chivalry to sever the bonds of that loyalty which binds subjects to their sovereign! Very little, however, did the French nobility thus assembled at Newport think of the political consequences of their adventure and romance. They danced, laughed, flirted, won hearts, amused themselves and others, notwithstand-

---

* Irving's "Life of Washington."

ing great privations, spent with a prodigal hand the
contents of fat purses, and became, therefore, very
popular with the puritan descendants of the followers of Cromwell, and of William, the Dutch re-
storer of the liberties of England. The Rhode
Islanders were in an ecstasy of delight, for they sold
prodigiously high what they had to sell and made
money by the bushel. As to the women, they were
all in love with the gay companions who seemed to
have no other object in life than to please their sex,
and take their hearts by storm, or regular siege. In
fact, Newport had become a miniature Versailles,
where, in spite of pinching circumstances, prevailed
the ease, frivolity, and seduction of court manners,
not unfrequently set off by an awkward imitation
that provoked ridicule and mirth. During continuous
revelries which kept Newport in a blaze of gleesome
excitement, there were hardly any, among those
scions of the noblest houses of France, who reflected
on the antagonism of the two flags that flaunted in
the breeze on the shores of Rhode Island, and were
entwined together on all occasions of festivity—the
one, emblematically maintaining that distinctions of
rank, rights, and position were the only true and solid
basis of society—and the other, proclaiming that all
men are born free and equal. Most of those gaudy-
feathered and belaced gentlemen of France had come
to America to gain fame, few to establish a principle.
The few succeeded, however; the principle triumphed,
and became a dogma called the sovereignty of the
people. The dogma matured into an article of faith,
which was imported into France, where it found a
congenial soil for its growth. It soon proscribed all
social distinctions, razed to the ground the castellated

dwellings of its imprudent and self-sacrificing advocates, and brought to the block the anointed head of the heir of a hundred kings, whilst it destroyed forever, to their very foundations, hoary and honored institutions that had defied the hand of time during fifteen centuries.

CHAPTER IV.

GLOOMY VIEWS AND FEELINGS OF WASHINGTON DURING THE WAR OF INDEPENDENCE — HIS APPEAL TO FRANCE.

AMONG that gay crowd of officers, careless of the future, but mindful of the enjoyments of the present, Dubayet had remained abstracted and gloomy, equally indifferent to the love of fame and to the pursuit of pleasure. His participating in their sports was but apparent, and merely to avoid eliciting unpleasant comments on the singularity of his abstention. He did not wish to expose the secret condition of his heart. He sympathized not with the cause of American independence, nor with anything else. In the spring of life he had withered under the touch of sorrow. A terrible blow had deadened the tree too soon, with all the freshness and honors of its early foliage. Although young in years he was old in feeling. There are some souls to which grief clings tenaciously; it is the ivy of the dilapidated wall. For such organizations time and action are the only physicians. He was, therefore, a cold and unconcerned spectator, and being of a reflecting and inquiring turn of mind, he earnestly sought for that kind of information which might lead to healthy action, in the hope of its ending in being a relief to his painful thoughts. What he saw, heard, and read was of such a nature that, in a letter he addressed to his friend

Lakanal, whom he knew to be intensely interested in any struggle of republicanism against monarchy, he took the most discouraging view of American affairs, and it is not astonishing that he came to such conclusions, for they were warranted by the following circumstances:

At the time when Congress was refusing to reorganize effectively the department of the quartermaster-general, Washington was thus exposing its derangement: " I am reduced to the painful alternative, either of dismissing a part of the militia now assembling, or of letting them come forward to starve; which it will be extremely difficult for the troops already in the field to avoid. Every day's experience proves more and more that the present mode of supplies is the most uncertain, expensive, and injurious that could be devised. It is impossible for us to form any calculations of what we are to expect, and consequently to concert any plan for future execution. No adequate provision for forage having been made, we are obliged to subsist the horses of the army by force, which, among other evils, often gives rise to civil disputes and to prosecutions, as vexatious as they are burdensome to the public." In that pressing emergency he was compelled to consume all the provisions which had been concentrated at West Point; but this afforded only a temporary relief, and, on the 6th of September, 1780, Washington complained that his army had been entirely destitute of meat for three days. In such circumstances armies never fail to plunder even those whom they are called upon to defend and protect. " Such injury," wrote Washington, " to the discipline of the army and such distress to the inhabitants result from these frequent events, that my feelings are hurt beyond description at the cries of the one, and seeing the other." Such was the condition of things in the Northern States. It was sad enough, but it was made still more sad by events that had occurred in the South. On the 16th of August, General Gates, the conqueror of Burgoyne at Saratoga, had been crushed by Lord Cornwallis at Camden, in North Carolina, and the brave Baron de Kalb mortally wounded, whilst fighting with brilliant valor at the head of the Second Maryland brigade. On the next day, Sumter, surnamed the "game cock," had been surprised at the Catawba ford by the cavalry of Tarleton, and, after having been completely routed, losing between three and four hundred men, killed or wounded, all his arms and baggage, with two brass field-pieces, had galloped off, it is said, without saddle, hat, or coat.

On hearing of these disasters, General Washington ordered southward some regular troops enlisted in Maryland for the war. On the 12th of September, 1780, he wrote to Governor Rutledge, of South Carolina, "to raise a permanent, compact, well-organized body of troops, instead of depending upon an irregular army of effete militia, always inconceivably expensive and too fluctuating and undisciplined to oppose a regular force." Three days after, on the 15th of the same month, he sent to the President of Congress a still more urgent and explicit address: "Regular troops alone," he said, "are equal to the exigencies of modern warfare, as well for defense as offense, and whenever a substitute is attempted, it must prove illusory and ruinous. No militia will ever acquire the habits necessary to resist a regular force. The firmness requisite for the real business of fighting is only to be attained by a constant course of discipline and service. I have never yet been witness to a single instance that can justify a different opinion, and it is most earnestly to be wished that the liberties of America may no longer be trusted, in any material degree, to so precarious a dependence. In my idea of the true system of war at the southward, the object ought to be to have a good army rather than a large one. Every exertion should be made by North Carolina, Virginia, Maryland, and Delaware to raise a permanent force of six thousand men, exclusive of horse and artillery. These, with the occasional aid of the militia in the vicinity of the scene of action, will not only suffice to prevent the further progress of the enemy, but, if properly supplied, oblige them to compact their force and relinquish a part of what they now hold. To expel them from the country entirely is what we can not aim at, till we derive more effectual support from abroad; and by attempting too much, instead of going forward we shall go backward. Could such a force be once set on foot, it would immediately make an inconceivable change in the face of affairs, not only in opposition to the enemy, but in expense, consumption of provisions, and waste of arms and stores. No magazines can be equal to the demands of an army of militia, and none need economy wore than ours."

Washington was right. Nothing can be more inefficient and unavailable in the field than militia against regulars, and no magazines can be equal to the demands of an army of militia, particularly American militia, who, from their innate independence of spirit and the habits contracted in private life, are the most extravagantly wasteful of all armed

3*

bodies, and constitute the most all-consuming, all-devouring one which ever was known to exist. But regulars are not improvised; it takes years and the schooling of more than one campaign to form a good army, with the soul which ought to animate it, and that confidence which springs from traditions of glory, from discipline, gladiatorial skill, the proud recollection of past achievements, the consciousness of being able to surpass them, and of knowing how to use intelligently those materials and military appendages with which it can not dispense without impairing its strength. At the time when Washington expressed the sentiments that I have quoted, the forces which he had under his command, and which could have any pretensions to be called an army, had dwindled into what would hardly have constituted a brigade in Europe, and those forces were starving, discontented, and unequal to the task they had on hand. Hence the humiliating confession extorted from him, and which must have been so painful to his patriotic heart, that, "without a sufficient force from abroad," success was impossible. Such were the feelings, the views, and the apprehensions of the great leader of the American revolution, when, in the latter part of September, 1780, there came upon him, like a clap of thunder, the news of the treason and flight of Arnold, to whom West Point, one of the most strategic points for the Americans, had been confided. Well can we conceive the bitter agony with which he exclaimed, when putting the proofs of that crime into the hands of Knox and Lafayette: "Whom can we trust now?" It sounded like the dying exclamation of Brutus: "O virtue, thou art but a name!"

In these conjunctures of extreme distress, General

Greene, who possessed the friendship and confidence of Washington, was appropriately appointed to the command of the Southern department. At the end of November the army of the North had gone into winter quarters ; the Pennsylvania line in the neighborhood of Morristown, the Jersey line about Pompton, the New England troops at West Point and the other posts of the highlands. The New York line was stationed at Albany, to guard against any invasion from Canada. The French army remained stationed at Newport, excepting the Duke de Lauzun's legion, which was cantoned at Lebanon, in Connecticut. Washington's headquarters were established at New Windsor, on the Hudson. The commander-in-chief himself was weary of struggling on with such scanty means and such vast responsibilities. Commenting on the campaign which had just terminated, Washington wrote to General Sullivan : " We have been half our time without provisions and are likely to continue so. We have no magazines, no money to form them ; and, in a little time, we shall have no men, if we have no money to pay them. In a word, the history of the war is a history of false hopes and temporary devices, instead of system and economy. To suppose that this great revolution can be accomplished by a temporary army, that this army will be subsisted by State supplies, and that taxation alone is adequate to our wants, is in my opinion absurd, and as unreasonable as to expect an inversion in the order of nature to accommodate itself to our views."

At the South, notwithstanding the advantages obtained by Colonel Campbell at King's Mountain, Sumter at Black Stock Hill on the Tiger river, Colonel Washington at Clermont, and the incessant attacks of Marion, "the swamp fox," the situation of affairs was not encouraging. General Greene, on taking command of his department, found only a small, disorganized army, the one-half of which was militia, who had neither tents nor equipage, who were badly clothed and fed, and who had fallen into the habit of relieving their necessities by depredating upon their own countrymen. "The country is so extensive," wrote Greene to Washington, "and the powers of the government so weak, that every one does as he pleases. The inhabitants are much divided in their political sentiments, and the Whigs and Tories pursue each other with little less than savage fury. The back country people are bold and daring; but the people on the sea-shore are sickly and but indifferent militia. All the middle country is so disaffected that you can not lay in the most trifling magazine, or send a wagon through the country with the least articles of stores without a guard."

In the meantime, the campaign having ceased at the North, the commander of the British forces in New York was preparing to send to Cornwallis in the South all the reinforcements he could dispose of, "in order," as he said, "to strike a blow that would make the whole continent shake." As Washington beheld one hostile armament* after another winging its way to the South, and received applications from that quarter for assistance which he had not the means to furnish, it became painfully apparent to him, that the efforts to carry on the war had exceeded the natural capabilities of the country. Its widely diffused population and the composition and temper of some of its

---

* Irving's " History of Washington," p. 193, vol. iv.

people rendered it difficult to draw together some of its resources. Commerce was almost extinct; there was not sufficient natural wealth on which to found a revenue; paper currency had depreciated through want of funds for its redemption, until it was nearly valueless. The mode of supplying the army by assessing a proportion of the productions of the earth had proved ineffectual, oppressive, and productive of an alarming opposition. Domestic loans yielded but trifling assistance. The patience of the army was almost exhausted; the people were dissatisfied with the mode of supporting the war, and there was reason to apprehend that, under the pressure of impositions of a new and odious nature, they might imagine they had only exchanged one kind of tyranny for another. Hence, Washington urged upon Congress "that foreign aid in money and soldiers were indispensably necessary to a continuance of the war." That *indispensable foreign aid* had already been given by France, although not to the extent desired, and also by Spain, who had declared war against Great Britain, and had, in the West Indies and in the Southern part of the continent, produced a favorable diversion in favor of the Americans, for she had attacked and taken the possessions of that power in Florida and Louisiana, under the leadership of the gallant Galvez. But more was wanted to accomplish the independence of the revolted colonies.

The anxieties of Washington were greatly increased by the mutinous conduct of the Pennsylvania line hutted at Morristown, who marched on Philadelphia to obtain from Congress a redress of the wrongs of which they complained, and with whom it was found necessary to enter into a compromise, which threat-

ened to destroy the discipline of the rest of the army.
He was also much troubled by the failure of the combined American and French forces against Portsmouth,
where it was hoped to capture the traitor Arnold.
His disappointment and apprehensions are fully expressed in a letter to Laurens, the American minister
at Paris, who had been lately sent there on a special
mission, to obtain that assistance without which the
boasted Declaration of Independence issued by the
colonies was evidently destined to be a lamentable
abortion. "The failure of this expedition," said
Washington, "which was most flattering in the commencement, is much to be regretted, because a successful blow in that quarter would, in all probability,
have given a decisive turn to our affairs in all the
Southern States; because it has been attended with
considerable expense on our part and much incon-
venience to the State of Virginia by the assembling
of our militia; because the world is disappointed in
not seeing Arnold in gibbets; and above all, because
we stood in need of something to keep us afloat till
the result of your mission is known; for be assured,
my dear Laurens, day does not follow night more certainly than it brings with it some additional proof of
the impracticability of carrying on the war without
the aids you were directed to solicit. As an honest
and candid man, as a man whose all depends on the
final and happy termination of the present contest, I
assert this, while I give it decisively as my opinion,
that, without a foreign loan, our present force, which
is but the remnant of an army, can not be kept together this campaign, much less will it be increased
and in readiness for another. If France delays a
timely and powerful aid in the critical posture of our

affairs, it will avail us nothing should she attempt it hereafter. We are at this hour suspended in the balance, not from choice, but from hard and absolute necessity; and you may rely on it as a fact, that we can not transfer the provisions from the States in which they are assessed, to the army, because we can not pay the teamsters, who will no longer work for certificates. . . . . In a word, we are at the end of our tether, and now or never our deliverance must come."

CHAPTER V.

SUCH was the imbecility with which the conduct
of the war was managed by Congress, in spite of the
good advice and suggestions repeatedly laid before
them by Washington, that, although they had grand-
ly "resolved" to have in the field, in the beginning
of 1781, thirty-seven thousand men under arms,
Washington's whole force on the Hudson in the
month of May of that year did not reach seven thousand men, and of that number only four thousand
were effective. Congress was fond of adopting "resolves after resolves," grandiloquently significant of
its intention of doing wonders, but those "resolves"
were mere bags of wind, and Washington and the
country wanted something more. Fortunately at
this juncture, a French frigate arrived at Boston with
the cheerful intelligence that an additional armament
of twenty ships of the line with land forces had sailed
from France under the Count de Grasse for the West
Indies, and that twelve of those ships were to relieve
the squadron at Newport. After consulting with
Rochambeau, Washington determined to make a diversion and to transport the seat of war to the
South, where Greene had manœuvred with great
ability, and where the horizon had become some-

what brighter; for that general had succeeded, after
many trying vicissitudes, in regaining the greater
part of Georgia and the two Carolinas, and needed
only a little assistance from the North to complete
their recovery. If the British, thought Washington,
could be entirely expelled from the South, the effect
of the blow would be to crush them at the North.
In pursuance of the plan he had come to, he arrived
at Philadelphia on the 30th of August, 1781, but he
found a considerable difficulty on the very threshold
of his intended expedition. The Northern regiments were discontented at the idea of going South,
and Washington thought that a *douceur** of a "little
hard money would put them in a proper temper."
It was not easy, however, to procure that "little
hard money." Fortunately, Rochambeau accommodated him with a loan of twenty thousand dollars,
and a few days after, Colonel Laurens, returning from
his mission to France, brought with him two and a
half millions of livres, being part of a subsidy of six
millions of livres granted by the king. It was like
water to the lips of dying travelers in the parched
deserts of Arabia. It revived expiring patriotism
and stirred even despair into hopeful action.

On the 2d of September the American troops
passed through Philadelphia, followed on the next
day by the French, on their way to the South. On
the 5th, three miles below Chester, Washington
learned that Count de Grasse had entered the Chesa-
peake with twenty-eight ships of the line and landed
three thousand troops under the Marquis de St. Simon, who was reported to have opened a communi-

---

* Irving's " Life of Washington," p. 315, vol. iv.

cation with Lafayette at Williamsburg, then acting
against Cornwallis in Virginia. The British general
found it too late to evacuate Yorktown, where he
had been resting in fancied security. York river and
James river were blocked up by French ships, and on
land, Lafayette, Wayne, and St. Simon at Williamsburg prevented his hoping to retreat successfully in
that direction, for he had reconnoitered that post and
found it too strong to be forced. He was caught in
a trap, and all that he had to do was to strengthen
his works and defend himself until he could be relieved. On the 14th of September, Washington arrived at Williamsburg, and, by the 25th, most of the
American and French troops having reached that
place, preparations were made for an attack. The
town is situated on a peninsula on the south side of
York river, immediately opposite Gloucester Point,
and was fortified by seven redoubts and six batteries
on the land side connected by intrenchments, with a
line of batteries along the river. Besides, the town *
was flanked on each side by deep ravines and creeks
emptying into York river—their heads in front of the
town being not more than half a mile apart. Cornwallis had availed himself of these natural advantages
in the arrangement of extensive outworks, with redoubts strengthened by abatis, field-works mounted
with cannon, and trees cut down and left with the
branches pointed outward. This was a strong position, and it was occupied by more than seven thousand troops. The forces of the besiegers consisted of
sixteen thousand men, of whom 7,000 were French,
5,500 Continental, and 3,500 militia. Gloucester

* Irving's "Life of Washington," p. 327, vol. iv.

Point had likewise been fortified by Cornwallis—its batteries, with those of Yorktown, commanding the intervening river, in which British ships were also stationed, protected by the guns of the forts; and the channel was obstructed by sunken vessels.

On the night which followed the arrival of the combined forces before Yorktown, Washington bivouacked on the ground in the open air. He slept under a mulberry tree, a projecting root of which served for a pillow. Mounting guard near him were a few men taken from the American and French troops, the honor being thus divided. The French squad was commanded by Lieutenant Aubert Dubayet. The moon was full and brilliant, and its rays, passing through the foliage of the tree, would occasionally illumine, as with a halo of glory, the majestic face of the slumbering hero. The scene acted vividly on the imagination of Aubert Dubayet, and, whenever he spoke of it afterward, he mentioned it as having been more impressive than any one of those which he subsequently saw in his eventful life.

On that very night, Cornwallis, as if blinded, or intimidated, instead of determining to dispute inch by inch the approaches of the enemy through the position which he occupied, and which had been made strong by nature and art, inexplicably abandoned his outworks and cooped himself up within the town, notwithstanding the remonstrances of Colonel Tarleton, who earnestly dwelt on the advantages which he was throwing away. At daybreak, the American and French troops were not slow in availing themselves of the fault committed by the British commander. They seized upon the outworks thus abandoned and used them to cover the troops employed in throwing

up breastworks. On the 1st of October, the invest·
ment of Yorktown by land and by sea was complete,
and, on the 9th, Washington put the match to the
first gun which was fired against the town, after the
final establishment of the first parallel. At one time,
when he was superintending the works, a cannon shot
from the enemy struck the ground close by him,
throwing up a cloud of dust. A chaplain in the army, named Evans, was standing by the general and
was greatly agitated by the incident. In his alarm
he took off his hat, and showing it covered with sand,
he exclaimed in a tremulous voice: "See here, general, see!" Washington slightly bowed to him, and
said with gravity, although with a twinkle of humor
in his eye: "Mr. Evans, you had better carry that
home and show it to your wife and children." The
cannonade was kept up almost incessantly between
the besieged and the besiegers, and there were sorties
and rencounters, of which the most spirited was between the famous Colonel Tarleton and the Duke de
Lauzun, in which it was the fortune of the chivalrous
nobleman to unhorse that dashing officer, who scram-
bled out of the *mêlée*, mounted another horse, and
sounded a retreat. This was the last affair of the terrible Tarleton and of his legion in the Revolutionary
war.

On the night of the 14th, it was determined to
storm two of the redoubts which enfiladed the works
of the besiegers, and were supposed also to command
the communication between Yorktown and Gloucester. The one nearest the river was attacked by a
detachment of Americans commanded by Lafayette;
the other, by a French detachment led by the Baron
de Vioménil. Hamilton, who subsequently became

so famous as a statesman, was the first to mount the parapet by placing one foot on the shoulder of a soldier who knelt on one knee for the purpose, and the redoubt was carried at the point of the bayonet. The redoubt which was to be stormed by the French was more strongly garrisoned. They had, therefore, to proceed with less precipitation and according to rule. The soldiers stood still under a destructive fire, whilst the sappers were removing the abatis, and they suffered considerably. Whilst the French were thus patiently waiting for the order of assault, Major Barbour, Lafayette's aide-de-camp, came through the tremendous fire of the enemy, and informed the Baron de Vioménil that the marquis was in his redoubt, and wished to know where the baron was. "Tell your general," replied the latter, "that I am not in mine, but will be in it in five minutes." The word to assault was then given, and the French went to it with a rush. The Chevalier de Lameth was the first to mount the parapet, but, shot through both knees, he fell back into the ditch, and was carried away by his friend, the Count de Dumas. The Count de Deuxponts, leading on the royal grenadiers of the same name, was likewise wounded. The company in which Aubert Dubayet was a lieutenant, fought with exemplary heroism; two-thirds of the men fell, and almost all the officers were killed, with the exception of Dubayet. When the Baron de Vioménil stood in front of the few men at whose head Dubayet had placed himself to receive his commander, who came to inspect the taken redoubt, "Lieutenant," said the baron to the young officer, "I have heard of the conversation which you had with Marshal Rochambeau, when you applied for service in the army. You see that it is not so easy, as he predicted, to find death when seeking it, and that promotion presents itself in its stead. I salute you as captain."

Washington, notwithstanding his habitual self-possession, had, from the embrasure of the main battery, witnessed these assaults with intense interest. So much depended on their successful issue! Generals Knox and Lincoln and a crowd of officers were around him. The risk of a chance shot for their chief made those about him uneasy. One of his aides-de-camp ventured on the observation that the situation was very much exposed. "If you think so," replied he gravely, "you are at liberty to step back."

After the taking of these two redoubts, the besieged could not show a gun on the side of the works exposed to attack, without its being quickly silenced. Their provisions and ammunition were nearly spent; their works were tumbling in ruins under incessant cannonade, the garrison was reduced and prostrated by sickness, death, and constant fatigues; the place was no longer tenable; and Lord Cornwallis capitulated on the 19th of October, 1781; the officers, to retain their side arms, both officers and soldiers their private property, and no part of their baggage or papers to be subject to search or inspection. Cornwallis rendered the following testimony to his captors: "The treatment, in general, that we have received from the enemy since our surrender, has been perfectly good and proper; but the kindness and attention which has been shown us by the French officers in particular, their delicate sensibility for our situation, their generous and pressing offer of money, both public and private, to any amount, has really gone beyond what I can possibly describe, and will, I hope, make an impression in the breast of every officer, whenever the fortune of war shall put any of them into our power."

The joy of Congress was boundless. Thanks were voted to Washington,* to the Counts de Rochambeau and de Grasse, to the officers of the allied armies generally, and to the corps of artillery and engineers, especially. Two stands of colors, trophies of the capitulation, were voted to Washington; two pieces of field ordnance to Rochambeau and de Grasse; and it was decreed that a marble column, commemorative of the alliance between France and the United States, and of the victory achieved by their associated arms, should be erected in Yorktown. As to the British government, when Lord North, the head of the ministry, received at his office in Downing street the news of the surrender of Cornwallis, it was as if he had been struck with a ball in the breast, for he opened his arms, exclaiming wildly as he paced up and down the apartment: "O God! it is all over." It was, indeed, all over, and the independence of the United States of America was an accomplished fact.

---

* Irving's "Life of Washington," p. 356, vol. iv.

CHAPTER VI.

DISCONTENT OF THE ARMY—A CROWN OFFERED TO WASHINGTON.

THE allied forces separated shortly after the fall of Yorktown. The Marquis de St Simon embarked his troops on the last of October, and Admiral de Grasse sailed with his fleet on the 4th of November. Lafayette, seeing that the campaign had ended for that year, departed for Philadelphia to obtain from Congress leave to visit his family in France. Most of the American troops returned northward to winter in the Jerseys and on the Hudson. Count de Rochambeau was to remain in Virginia, and established his headquarters at Williamsburgh. On hearing of the capitulation of Cornwallis, the king of France promised a further loan of six millions of livres. It was the anxious wish of Washington to prepare everything for a vigorous campaign in the ensuing year. But the prevalent opinion was, that peace was at hand ; and, under that impression, the people were loth to make new sacrifices and to encounter a continuation of the terrible trials they had gone through. The respective quotas of troops which were expected from several States came dripping slowly like drops of water from a filtering stone, and still slower came the contributions in money. This condition of things produced great discontent in the army officers and men, for they were reduced to the utmost destitution without any hope of relief. There were days when they were entirely destitute of food, and their clothing was not sufficient to protect them against the inclemencies of the weather in that season. It was long since the officers had received any pay with which to support themselves and their starving families at home. Half pay had been decreed to them for a term of years after the termination of the war. But they began to fear, should that event happen, to be disbanded without any liquidation of their claims and without the fulfilment of the decree of Congress in relation to their half pay in the future. To be sent away penniless, when years of military life had unfitted them for the gainful pursuits of the civilian, was a prospect at which they looked with the utmost degree of anxiety.

Such was the state of affairs in America when Aubert Dubayet wrote to Lakanal the following letter:

" MY DEAR FRIEND :—This letter will be to you a shock which will awake you out of your republican dreams. The American army is on the eve of offering a crown to its commander-in-chief. Having obtained a furlough, I am on a visit to Colonel Lewis Nicola, a veteran officer, who honors me with his friendship and confidence. He has been for years on a footing of intimacy with General Washington and exercises a great influence over his companions in arms. As the organ of the suffering army with whose wrongs he keenly sympathizes, he has forwarded to the commander-in-chief a communication in which he strongly condemns the existing form of government, and attributes to it all the ills already experienced and yet to be anticipated by the army and the people at large. He considers that the idea of republican government rests on a sentimental and platonic theory,

which, in practice, would produce the most lamentable results, and is decidedly incompatible with the
permanency of stable institutions, such as are founded
on honor, dignity, and morality, and therefore exclusive of a lasting and reliable national prosperity. He
maintains that a mixed government like that of England is the best which has ever been devised by the
wisdom of man, and that it could be readily im-
planted here, if its many advantages and benefits
were properly pointed out and fearlessly advocated.
' In that case,' says he to the general, ' it will, I believe, be uncontroverted, that the same abilities which
have led us, through difficulties apparently insurmountable by human power, to victory and glory;
that those qualities which have merited and obtained
the universal esteem and veneration of an army,
would be most likely to conduct and direct us in the
smoother paths of peace. Some people have so connected the idea of tyranny and monarchy as to find
it very difficult to separate them. It may, therefore,
be requisite to give the head of such a constitution
as I propose some title apparently more moderate;
but, if all other things were once adjusted, I believe
strong arguments might be produced for admitting
the title of king, which, I conceive, would be attended
with some material advantages.'

" You shudder, my Brutus, but compose yourself
and listen to the magnificent answer of tempted ambition: ' With a mixture of great sorrow and astonishment,' says Washington to Colonel Lewis Nicola,
' I have read with attention the sentiments you have
submitted to my perusal. Be assured, Sir, no occurrence in the course of the war has given me more
painful sensations than your information of there

being such ideas existing in the army as you have expressed, and which I must view with abhorrence, and reprehend with severity. For the present, the communication of them will rest in my bosom, unless some further agitation of the matter shall make a disclosure necessary. I am much at a loss to conceive what part of my conduct could have given encouragement to an address which, to me, seems big with the greatest mischief that could befall my country. If I am not deceived in the knowledge of myself, you could not have found a person to whom your schemes are more disagreeable. At the same time, in justice to my own feelings, I must add, that no man possesses a more sincere wish to see ample justice done to the army than I do; and as far as my powers and influence, in a constitutional way, extend, they shall be employed to the utmost of my abilities to effect it, should there be any occasion. Let me conjure you, then, if you have any regard for your country, concern for yourself, or posterity, or respect for me, to banish these thoughts from your mind, and never communicate, as from yourself or any one else, a sentiment of the like nature.'

"You will no doubt, my dear Lakanal, on reading these lines, shout with enthusiasm, but patience—patience. Who knows what may yet turn up?"

On the 2d of August, 1782, Sir Guy Carleton and Admiral Digby wrote a joint letter to Washington, informing him that they knew officially that there had already commenced at Paris negotiations for a general peace, which would secure the independence of the United States. But these assurances found Washington very wary and distrustful. In one of his letters he says: "From the former infatuation, duplicity,

and perverse system of British policy, I confess I am
induced to doubt everything, to suspect everything.
Whatever the real intention of the enemy may be, I
think that the strictest attention and exertion which
have ever been exercised on our part, instead of being
diminished, ought to be increased. Jealousy and pre-
caution at least can do no harm. Too much confidence and supineness may be pernicious in the extreme." Under these impressions he wrote to Count
de Rochambeau, advising him to march his troops to
the banks of the Hudson and form a junction with
the American army. That junction took place about
the middle of September. The French army encamped on the left of the American, about two miles
from Verplanck's Point. The greatest good-will and
harmony continued to prevail between the allied
forces, but the Americans, in the raggedness of their
condition, had but scanty means to be hospitable to
their transatlantic friends. " Only conceive," wrote
Washington, " the mortification they must suffer, even
the general officers, when they can not invite a French
officer, a visiting friend, or a travelling acquaintance,
to a better repast than whisky hot from the still, and
not always that, and a bit of beef without vegetables,
will afford them."

Notwithstanding Washington's apprehensions, Congress acted as if they were already sure of peace, and
a contemplated reduction of the army was proposed
to take place on the 1st of January, 1783. Washington expressed warmly his feelings on that subject:
" While I premise that no one I have seen or heard
appears opposed to the principle of reducing the
army as circumstances may require, yet I can not help
fearing the result of the measure in contemplation,

under present circumstances, when I see a number of
men, goaded by a thousand stings of reflection on the
past, and of anticipation on the future, about to be
turned into the world, soured by penury and what
they call the ingratitude of the public, involved in
debts, without one farthing of money to carry them
home, after having spent the flower of their days,
and many of them their patrimonies, in establishing
the freedom and independence of their country, and
suffering everything that human nature is capable of
enduring on this side of death. I repeat it, that when
I consider these irritating circumstances, without one
thing to soothe their feelings, or dispel their gloomy
prospects, I can not avoid apprehending that a train
of evils will follow, of a very serious and distressing
nature. I wish not to heighten the shades of the
picture so far as the reality would justify me in doing
it. I could give anecdotes of patriotism and distress,
which have scarcely ever been paralleled, never surpassed, in the history of mankind. But you may
rely upon it, the patience and long-suffering of this
army are almost exhausted, and there never was so
great a spirit of discontent as at this instant. While
in the field, I think it may be kept from breaking into
acts of mutiny; but when we retire into winter quarters, unless the storm is previously dissipated, I can
not be at ease respecting the consequences. It is
high time for a peace." Well might Washington feel
ill at ease, for he had in his pocket, whilst he penned
these lines, the secret letter of Colonel Lewis Nicola,
and he knew that it contained the expression of the
sentiment of the army.

Among the papers of Lakanal has been found the

following communication which was addressed to him
in the month of March, 1783:

DUBAYET TO LAKANAL.

" MY DEAR FRIEND:—The French forces have
been for several months at Verplanck's Point, on the
Hudson river. I frequently visit the camp of the
American army, which is in our neighborhood, at a
place called Newburg, where General Washington had
established his headquarters for the winter, and where
they still remain, as the near prospect of peace prevents all military operations. I have already informed
you that the discontent of that army is very great.
The long inactivity of a winter camp has been but too
favorable to the fermentation of the leaven which was
but too ready to work. The soldiers brooded on their
wrongs and distresses. They had nothing else to do
but to discuss the neglect and injustice with which
they were treated, and lash themselves into anger.
Would the ' Resolution ' of Congress, granting half pay
to officers who should serve to the end of the war, be
carried into execution? Where would the funds be
procured? Is not the treasury of the confederation
an empty bag which is never to be filled up? Do not
the respective States show the utmost reluctance to
tax themselves? Can anything more be begged successfully from foreign sources? According to the articles of confederation, is not the concurrence of nine
States needed for the validity of any act appropriat-
ing public money, and is it not known that such a
concurrence has never been given? Will it ever be
obtained? Should scanty funds be collected with
laborious effort, will it not be said that there are more
pressing and imperious exigencies than our claim? Do

we not know that that claim, just and sacred as it is, stinks in the jealous nostrils of an ungrateful people? Who will care for us when we shall no longer be wanted? Shall we not be treated as drones who have no right to be fed at the public expense? Are not republics famous for their short memory of services rendered? Such were the questions which they put to themselves, and the more frequently they were asked, the higher rose the heat of their resentment. At last, Colonel John Armstrong, a young man of distinguished abilities, who is aide-de-camp to General Gates, and who, I am sure, will in the course of time rise to great eminence in his country, with the approbation of his chief, and at the request of a number of his fellow officers, applied the spur and the lash to the already too much goaded spirit of discontent, by causing to be circulated in the camp the following anonymous address, calling a meeting of the generals and other officers on the next day at eleven o'clock, to consider what means should be employed to obtain that redress of grievances which they had prayed for in vain :

" 'After a pursuit of seven long years,' said the writer, ' the object for which we set out is at length within your reach. Yes, my friends, that suffering courage of yours was active once; it has conducted the United States of America through a doubtful and bloody war; it has placed her in the chair of independency; and peace returns to bless—whom? A country willing to redress your wrongs, cherish your worth, and reward your services? A country courting your return to private life, with tears of gratitude and smiles of admiration, longing to divide with you that independency which your gallantry has given, and

those riches which your wounds have preserved? Is
this the case? Or is it rather a country that tramples
upon your rights, disdains your cries, and insults your
distress? Have you not more than once suggested
your wishes and made known your wants to Congress
—wants and wishes which gratitude and policy should
have anticipated, rather than evaded? And have you
not lately, in the meek language of entreating memo-
rials, begged from their justice what you could no
longer expect from their favor? How have you been
answered?

" ' If this, then, be your treatment while the swords
you wear are necessary for the defense of America,
what have you to expect from peace, when your voice
shall sink, and your strength dissipate by division;
when those very swords, the instruments and companions of your glory, shall be taken from your sides,
and no remaining mark of military distinction left but
your wants, infirmities, and scars? Can you then
consent to be the only sufferers by the revolution,
and, retiring from the field, grow old in poverty,
wretchedness, and contempt? Can you consent to
wade through the vile mire of dependency, and owe
the miserable remnant of that life to charity, which
has hitherto been spent in honor? If you can, go,
and carry with you the jest of Tories and the scorn
of Whigs, the ridicule, and, what is worse, the pity of
the world. Go, starve, and be forgotten. But if your
spirits should revolt at this; if you have sense enough
and spirit sufficient to oppose tyranny, under whatever
garb it may assume, whether it be the plain coat of
republicanism, or the splendid robe of royalty; if you
have yet learned to discriminate between a people
and a cause, between men and principles; awake, at-

tend to your situation, and redress yourselves! If the present moment be lost, every future effort is in vain; and your threats then will be as empty as your entreaties now.

" ' I would advise you, therefore, to come to some final opinion upon what you can bear, and what you will suffer. If your determination be in any proportion to your wrongs, carry your appeal from the justice to the fears of government. Change the milk-and-water style of your last memorial. Assume a bolder tone, decent, but lively, spirited, and determined; and suspect the man who would advise to more moderation and longer forbearance. Let two or three men, who can feel as well as write, be appointed to draw up your *last remonstrance*, for I would no longer give it the suing, soft, and unsuccessful epithet of *memorial*. Let it represent, in language that will neither dishonor you by its rudeness, nor betray you by its fears, what has been promised by Congress, and what has been performed; how long and patiently you have suffered; how little you have asked, and how much of that little has been denied. Tell them that, though you were the first, and would wish to be the last, to encounter danger, though despair itself can never drive you into dishonor, it may drive you from the field; that the wound, often irritated and never healed, may at last become incurable; and that the slightest mark of indignity from Congress now must operate like the grave and part you forever; that in any political event, the army has its alternative; if peace, that nothing shall separate you from your arms but death; if war, that, courting the auspices and inviting the direction of your illustrious leader, you will retire to some unsettled country, smile in your turn, and

4*

"mock when their fear cometh on." But let it represent also, that, should they comply with the request
of your late memorial, it would make you more happy
and them more respectable; that while war should
continue, you would follow their standard into the
field: and when it came to an end, you would withdraw into the shade of private life, and give the world
another subject of wonder and applause—an army
victorious over its enemies, victorious over itself.'

"Surely this was bold and eloquent, my dear
Lakanal, but it was dangerous; it meant mischief; it
meant more than it said, and it produced the effect
which was expected. The agitation in the camp became so intense, that Washington had to notice it.
He immediately issued general orders, in which he
reprobated as disorderly and seditious the anonymous
publication, and expressed his confidence that the
good sense of the people would prevent them from
paying attention to such an irregular invitation. He
went further; for, in order to counteract its effects,
which appeared to him exceedingly alarming, he requested that a meeting, fixed for the 10th of March,
should not take place, and convened another for the
15th, which delay would afford sufficient time to the
committee they had deputed to Congress to make
their report. But, the next morning, there appeared
another anonymous publication, subsequently discovered to be, like the first, by Colonel Armstrong,
the aide-de-camp of General Gates. With insidious
dexterity, it maintained that the step taken by General Washington was an approbation of the course
which the army had to pursue. ' That step,' said the
author, 'authorizes your meetings for redress, and
there is no doubt that our leader's private opinion

sanctifies our claims. Had he disliked the object in view, would not the same sense of duty which forbade your meeting on the third day of the week, have forbidden you from meeting on the seventh? Is not the same subject held up to your view? And has it not passed the seal of office, and taken all the solemnity of an order? This will give system to your proceedings and stability to your resolves.'

"Enough for the present, my dear Lakanal. This is the first act of the drama. It promises to be interesting, as you see. You may rest assured of my keeping you posted as to what is to follow."

CHAPTER VII.

DISBANDING OF THE REVOLUTIONARY ARMY—SUBLIMITY OF THE MORAL CHARACTER OF WASHINGTON.

" I WILL not attempt," wrote Dubayet to Lakanal a few days after, " to describe to you the intense interest with which I watched the results of the proceedings related to you in my last letter.   On the eve of the 15th, Washington, who, from the reports which had reached his ears, had serious misgivings as to the turn which the meeting would take, sent for the officers, one by one, in private, made a pathetic appeal to their patriotism, and represented to them in the most forcible language what would be the loss of character to the army, should they, in the meeting of the next day, adopt intemperate resolutions.   When they assembled on that day, General Gates was called to the chair. Washington had spent a sleepless night, and so keen had become his inquietude, notwithstanding, and perhaps because of, the personal interview which he had held with every officer, and in which he had had the opportunity of probing the condition of their minds and the excitement of their feelings, that he resolved to attend the meeting, and made his appearance there, to the astonishment of all.   He apologized for it, and said that such had not been his original intention when he had convoked the assemblage. But, as his sentiments had been misrepresented or misconstrued in anonymous writings, he had, after due reflection, come to the conclusion that it was proper that he should make his views clear to the army. Therefore, with the indulgence of his brother officers, he would take the liberty of reading to them the thoughts which he had committed to writing: 'If my conduct heretofore,' he said, 'has not convinced you that I have been a faithful friend to the army, my declaration of it at this time would be equally unavailing and improper.'

"He stopped after reading this first paragraph, made a short pause, looked round the audience with grave benignity, drew out his spectacles, and begged to be excused whilst he took time to put them on. 'My eyes have become dim,' he observed; 'I have grown gray in the service of our country, and now I find myself growing blind.' No studied burst of oratory ever produced, my dear Lakanal, the effect of a remark so natural, so unaffected, and so inexpressibly touching by the quiet manner in which it was delivered. Every eye became moist, every heart palpitated, and mine, for I had the good fortune to witness this scene, beat so loud that I fancied I could almost hear its throbs. Washington thus resumed his discourse: 'As I was among the first who embarked in the cause of our common country; as I have never left your side one moment, but when called from you on public duty; as I have been the constant companion and witness of your distresses, and not among the last to feel and acknowledge your merits; as I have ever considered my own military reputation as inseparably connected with that of the army; as my heart has ever expanded with joy when

I have heard its praises, and my indignation has arisen when the mouth of detraction has been opened against it, it can not be supposed at this last stage of the war that I am indifferent to its interests.' Here a deep sensation thrilled through the audience and found its vent in loud and prolonged cheers. Washington waved his hand, and silence was re-established. 'As to myself,' continued he, 'a recollection of the cheerful assistance and prompt obedience I have experienced from you under every vicissitude of fortune, and the sincere affection I feel for an army I have so long had the honor to command, will oblige me to declare, in this public and solemn manner, that for the attainment of complete justice for all your toils and dangers, and the gratification of every wish, so far as may be done consistently with the great duty I owe my country and those powers we are bound to respect, you may fully command my services to the utmost extent of my abilities.' There was another burst of applause, interrupted by a deprecatory gesture of the general.

"'While I give you these assurances,' he said, 'and pledge myself in the most unequivocal manner to exert whatever abilities I am possessed of in your favor, let me entreat you, gentlemen, on your part, not to take any measures which, viewed in the calm light of reason, will lessen the dignity and sully the glory you have hitherto maintained ; let me request you to rely on the plighted faith of your country, and place a full confidence in the purity of the intentions of Congress.' He went on assuring them that it was his conviction that complete justice would ultimately be done to them by that body. 'But, at the same time, let me conjure you,' he added, ' in the name of our common country, as you value your own sacred honor, as you respect the rights of humanity, as you regard the military and national honor of America, to express your utmost horror and detestation of the man who wishes, under any specious pretences, to overturn the liberties of our country, and who wickedly attempts to open the flood-gates of civil discord and deluge our rising empire in blood. By thus determining, and thus acting, you will pursue the plain and direct road to the attainment of your wishes; you will defeat the insidious designs of our enemies, who are compelled to resort from open force to secret artifice; you will give one more distinguished proof of unexampled patriotism and patient virtue, rising superior to the pressure of the most complicated sufferings; and you will, by the dignity of your conduct, afford occasion for posterity to say, when speaking of the glorious example you have exhibited to mankind : had this day been wanting, the world had never seen the last stage of perfection to which human nature is capable of attaining.'

" Now the general produced a letter which he had received from one of the most influential members of Congress, who assured him that, in spite of all difficulties and embarrassments, that body would, at all events, deal generously with the army. It was evident to me, my dear Lakanal, that this magnificent address had produced a revolution in the breasts of the audience, and that there would be no opposition to the wishes of the man whom they loved and venerated so much. The object of that love and veneration must also have been aware of the change he had operated, for, bowing kindly to his brother officers, he withdrew leaving them to their deliberations. As he

disappeared, I could not but exclaim: How sublime!
As I spoke these words, a hand pressed my arm, and
a sneering voice whispered in my ear, 'Sublime! aye
—a sublime simpleton in not availing himself of this
golden opportunity, and in believing in the duration
of institutions founded on that most mischievous of
all lies which proclaims that all men are born free
and equal.' I turned round and looked with astonishment at the speaker, who bowed slightly to me and
departed.   It was Colonel Aaron Burr, a man of iron
nerves, wonderful abilities, indefatigable industry, re-
morseless and unprincipled ambition, whom I have
met several times.   If I have read him well, my good
friend, let the new republic beware of him.

   " After General Washington had retired, the warm-
hearted Knox presented ' Resolutions,' seconded by
the rough and blunt General Putnam, which were in
conformity with the wishes of the commander-in-chief,
and were unanimously adopted.   One of those ' Resolutions' requested him to write to the President of Congress, and to earnestly entreat a speedy decision on
the late address forwarded by a committee of the
army.   In conformity to that request, Washington
thus addressed that high functionary :

   " ' The result of the proceedings of the grand convention of officers, which I have the honor of enclos-
ing to your excellency for the inspection of Congress,
will, I flatter myself, be considered as the last glorious
proof of patriotism which could have been given by
men who aspired to the distinction of a patriot army,
and will not only confirm their claim to the justice,
but will increase their title to the gratitude, of their
country.   Having seen the proceedings on the part
of the army terminate with perfect unanimity, and in

a manner certainly consonant to my wishes; being impressed with the liveliest sentiments of affection for those who have so long, so patiently, and so cheerfully suffered and fought under my immediate direction; having, from motives of justice, duty, and gratitude, spontaneously offered myself as an advocate for their rights; and having been requested to write to your excellency, earnestly entreating the most speedy decision of Congress upon the subjects of the late address from the army to that honorable body; it only remains for me to perform the task I have assumed, and to intercede in their behalf, as I now do, that the sovereign power will be pleased to verify the predictions I have pronounced, and the confidence the army has reposed in the justice of their country.

"'If, besides the simple payment of their wages, a further compensation is not due to the sufferings and sacrifices of the officers, then have I been mistaken indeed. If the whole army have not merited whatever a grateful people can bestow, then have I been beguiled by prejudice, and built opinion on the basis of error. If this country should not, in the end, perform everything which has been requested in the late memorial to Congress, then will my belief become vain, and the hope that has been excited void of foundation. And if, as has been suggested for the purpose of inflaming their passions, *the officers of the army are to be the only sufferers by the revolution; if, retiring from the field, they are to grow old in poverty, wretchedness, and contempt; if they are to wade through the vile mire of dependency, and owe the miserable remnant of that life to charity, which has hitherto been spent in honor*, then shall I have learned what ingratitude is, then shall I have realized a tale which will embit-

ter every moment of my future life. But I am under
no such apprehensions. A country, rescued by their
arms from impending ruin, will never leave unpaid
the debt of gratitude.'

" Do not believe, my dear Lakanal, that there was
not in these incidents a great danger to the republican institutions to be established. As a proof of the
temper of the army, let me tell you that, lately,
about three hundred soldiers of the Pennsylvania
line, with beat of drum and fixed bayonets, marched
to the State House where Congress and the Supreme
Executive Council were in session; that placing sentinels at every door to prevent egress, they next sent
in a written message to the President and Council,
threatening military violence if their demands were
not complied with in twenty minutes. Outraged at
being thus surrounded and blockaded for several
hours by an armed soldiery, Congress adjourned to
meet again within a few days at Princeton, in New Jersey, and in the meantime sent information to Washington of this mutinous outbreak, which was soon
quelled by him. You see, my dear friend, that armies
are the same everywhere, in every age, and in every
country. An army will never hesitate between their
leader and a legislative body, be it called Parliament,
Senate, or Congress. But this Washington is a hero
of Plutarch, or rather far above all those great men
whose memories have been handed down, embalmed
in the immortal pages of the Greek author. But will
there ever be another Washington? And should an
American army again offer the crown to their chief,
will it be refused?"

At last Washington was informed, in the spring of
1783, that a general treaty of peace had been signed

in Paris on the 20th of January, and that the independence of the United States had been secured. On that solemn occasion, that great man, great beyond all other men, thus addressed the governors of the different States: "We are the sole lords and proprietors of a vast tract of continent, comprehending all the various soils and climates of the world, and abounding with all the necessaries and conveniences of life; and the acknowledged possessors of absolute freedom and independency. This is the time of our political probation; this is the moment when the eyes of the world are turned upon us; this is the moment to establish or ruin our national character forever. This is the favorable moment to give such a tone to the Federal Government as will enable it to answer the ends of its institution; or this may be the moment for relaxing the powers of the Union, annihilating the cement of the confederation, and exposing us to become the sport of European politics, which may play one State against another, to prevent their growing importance, and to serve their own interested purposes."

On the disbanding of the army, which soon followed the conclusion of the treaty of peace, Washington issued a proclamation, which was a farewell address to his beloved and well-tried companions in arms. It was truly antique in its grand simplicity. "May ample justice," he said, "be done to you, and may the choicest of Heaven's favors, both here and hereafter, attend those who, under the divine auspices, have secured innumerable blessings for others. With these wishes and this benediction, your commander-in-chief is about to retire from service. The curtain of separation will soon be drawn, and the military scene to him will be closed forever."

Captain Aubert Dubayet witnessed with intense interest all the events which terminated the American revolution, and thus delineated some of the most impressive :

DUBAYET TO LAKANAL.

" I was present at a most affecting scene—the disbanding of the American army. No description of mine can give you an adequate idea of the painful circumstances under which it took place. Only fancy both officers and soldiers, obedient to the advice of their idolized commander-in-chief, and soothed perhaps by, but certainly not relying on, the empty ' Resolves' of Congress to pay and compensate them in such manner as the ability of the United States would permit, nobly consenting, although long unaccustomed to the affairs of private life, to be turned loose on the world to starve, and to become the prey to vulture speculators. Never can that melancholy day be forgotten by me—a foreigner though I am—when I saw friends, companions for seven long years in joy and in sorrow, torn asunder without the hope of meeting again and with only the terrible prospect of a miserable existence in the future. And they had arms in their hands, and they were masters of the situation ! But they had a Washington to deal with, and they were conquered by his moral sublimity !

" It has also been my good fortune, my dear Lakanal, to witness how that august personage closed his military career and resigned into the hands of Congress the almost dictatorial authority with which he had been clothed. On the 20th of December, he had written to the President of that body, requesting to know in what manner it would be most proper for him to offer his resignation. ' In a solemn audience worthy of the occasion,' was the reply, and the 23d of that month was selected for that purpose. At twelve o'clock, on that day, every inch of the floor of the hall of Congress which could be spared by the members, and the surrounding galleries ordinarily occupied by the public, were invaded by an eager crowd of ladies, by Federal and State functionaries, and other distinguished men. I remarked that the members of Congress were seated and had their hats on, when all the spectators stood up and were uncovered. On my inquiring for the reason of it, I was told that it was because they represented the sovereignty of the Union.

"Washington entered, and I assure you that there was in him a more commanding majesty than I can suppose to exist in any royal face. He was conducted by the Secretary of Congress, and took his seat in a chair appointed for him. After a brief pause, during which the whole assembly seemed to be awed into the deepest silence and the most breathless emotion, the President said: 'General, the United States, in Congress assembled, are prepared to receive your communication.'

"Washington rose, and, with an imposing dignity of which it is impossible to give you any idea, reviewed briefly the great events which had taken place, congratulated Congress and the country on their successful issue, offered his thanks for the assistance which had been so patriotically given him by all those who had co-operated with him in the execution of the trust committed to his hands, and concluded in these words: 'I consider it an indispensable duty to close this last solemn act of my official life, by commending the interests of our dearest country to the

protection of Almighty God; and those who have
the superintendence of them, to His holy keeping.
Having now finished the work assigned to me, I retire from the great theatre of action; and, bidding an
affectionate farewell to this august body, under whose
orders I have long acted, I here offer my commission,
and take my leave of all the employments of public
life.'

"The whole assembly was melted into tears, my
dear Lakanal, and it was with a voice almost choked
with emotion, that the President, after having received the tendered commission, attempted to bear testimony, in adequate terms, to the invaluable services
of that illustrious man. He closed his address in
these words: 'You retire, General, from the theatre
of action with the blessings of your fellow-citizens;
but the glory of your virtues will not terminate with
your military command; it will continue to animate
the remotest ages.'

"Washington arrived at Mount Vernon on Christmas eve, where he was welcomed to his cherished
home with bonfires and the warm greetings of his
friends and neighbors. Shortly after, he wrote to the
Governor of New York: 'The scene is at last closed;
I feel myself eased of a load of public care. I hope
to spend the remainder of my days in cultivating the
affections of good men, and in the practice of the
domestic virtues.'"

CHAPTER VIII.

WASHINGTON AT MOUNT VERNON — AUBERT DU-BAYET BECOMES HIS GUEST.

WHEN the French forces were recalled after the conclusion of peace, Aubert Dubayet obtained a furlough from his Government. His object was to sojourn some time in America, to see what use the former colonies of Great Britain would make of their independence, and also to sell his property in Louisiana, with a view of settling forever in France, the country of his ancestors. He was on a visit to General Knox, when the latter received and showed to him an interesting letter from General Washington written from Mount Vernon, and from which he was permitted to take the following extract: "Strange as it may seem," wrote the liberator of his country to his companion-in-arms, "it is nevertheless true that it was not until very lately I could get the better of my usual custom of ruminating, as soon as I waked in the morning, on the business of the ensuing day; and of my surprise at finding, after revolving many things in my mind, that I was no longer a public man, nor had anything to do with public transactions. I feel now, however, as I conceive a weary traveler must do, who, after treading many a weary step with a heavy burthen on his shoulders, is eased of the latter, having reached the haven to which all the former were directed, and from his house-top is looking back

(95)

and tracing with an eager eye the meanders by which he escaped the quicksands and mires which lay in his way, and into which none but the all-powerful Guide and Dispenser of human events could have prevented his falling."

At about the same time Lafayette received from the same source a letter which fully harmonized with the above expressed sentiments: " Free from the bustle of camp and the busy scenes of public life," wrote Washington, "I am solacing myself with those tranquil enjoyments of which the soldier, who is ever in the pursuit of fame—the statesman, whose watchful days and sleepless nights are spent in devising schemes to promote the welfare of his own, perhaps the ruin of other countries, as if the globe was insufficient for us all—and the courtier, who is always watching the countenance of his prince—can have very little conception. I have not only retired from all public employments, but I am retiring within myself, and shall be able to view the solitary walk, and to tread the paths of private life with heartfelt satisfaction. Envious of none, I am determined to be pleased with all; and this, my dear friend, being the order of my march, I will move gently down the stream of life until I sleep with my fathers."

In July, 1785, Aubert Dubayet wrote to Tintin Calandro: " My dear friend, although a republican is as hateful to you as water is to a mad dog, there is one in whom you can not but take an interest, because he is an honor to the human race, and it is of him, therefore, that I shall speak to you on the present occasion. Of course, you understand me to mean General Washington, without my naming him. I have the supreme honor of being a guest at his house on the strength of a letter given to me by General Knox. In the simple undress of private life he appears to me more admirable than when clothed in the purple mantle of the dictator. To-day he said to me: 'The more I am acquainted with agricultural affairs, the better I am pleased with them, in so much that I can nowhere find so much satisfaction as in those innocent and useful pursuits. While indulging these feelings I am led to reflect how much more delightful to an undebauched mind is the task of making improvements on the earth, than all the vainglory that can be acquired by ravaging it by the most uninterrupted career of conquest. How pitiful, in the age of reason and religion, is that false ambition which desolates the world with fire and sword for the purpose of conquest and fame, compared to the milder virtues of making our neighbors and our fellow-men as happy as their frail convictions and perishable natures will permit them to be!' I rode with him several times over his different farms, which extend over an area of four thousand acres. He seems to think of nothing but improving his grounds. Now he talks of curious and exotic plants which have been promised to him, now of grape-vines which he expects from France—but of public affairs, not a word. He keeps a minute diary of what he does as a farmer. In the spring of the year he was diligently employed in preparations to improve his groves and shrubbery; on the 10th of January, he noted that the white thorn was full in berry; on the 20th, he began to clear the undergrowth of his pine forest; in February he transplanted ivy under the walls of the garden; in March he was planting hemlock trees — a beautiful species of American ever-

5

green; in April he was sowing holly berries in drills.
He called my attention to the fact, that, of all the
trees fitted for shade in pasture-land, the locust, ma-
ple, black mulberry, black walnut, black gum, dog-
wood, and sassafras were those which, according to
his observation, did not materially injure the grass
beneath them. He delights in ornamental cultivation; he rides long distances in quest of young elms,
ash-trees, white thorn, crab-apples, willows, and lilacs;
he lays out winding paths and plants trees and shrubs
along them. Now he sows acorns and buckeye-nuts
selected by himself with peculiar care; now he opens
vistas through the pine groves; and now he twines
round the columns of his mansion scarlet honey-
suckles. I really think he takes more interest in conversing with his gardener than with anybody else.

"The world will hardly believe, my dear Tintin
Calandro, that the life of General Washington is a
sort of a Virgilian idyl, in which blooded horses, cattle, sheep, bees, and the like rural things perform a
conspicuous part. The other day he stopped before
a group of young horse-chestnuts, gazed at them with
a kindling eye, and said to me with an unusual degree of animation: 'Look at these trees, my young
friend; they make me young too, for they are from
Westmoreland, my native county, and the haunt of
my school-boy days. They were sent to me by Colonel Lee—he whom we call, as you know, *Light-
Horse Harry*.' He has retained his passion for hunting, and talks much of stocking his grounds with English deer. Yesterday, having accompanied him in
one of his walks, we came upon two of his negroes
who were struggling very hard and unsuccessfully to
remove a large log of wood which was in the way.

Washington took off his coat, and, using his shoulders, helped them to accomplish their task. I assure
you, my dear friend, that he appeared to me on that
occasion more grand than Louis XIV. would at Versailles with all his peacock court at his heels. Don't
threaten to eat me up in your anger, I beg you!

"Now that you have, as I suppose, curbed the rising
indignation of your loyalty, I will reward you for your
forbearance by giving you further details on the private life of that illustrious personage. It is in human
nature to delight in being informed how the immor-
tals sneeze, or cough. Know, then, that the active life
of Washington begins before dawn. Much of his correspondence, which is enormous, is dispatched before
breakfast, which takes place at half-past seven. After
breakfast he mounts his horse, which always stands
ready at the door, and rides out to different parts of
his estate, as he used to do to the various parts of the
camp, to see that all was right at the outposts, and
every one at his duty. At half-past two he dines, and
there is a social gathering in the evening at tea, which
is a sort of supper. If there is no company, he writes
until dark, or, if pressed by business, until nine o'clock;
otherwise, he amuses himself with a game of whist, or
reads—chiefly books on farming and gardening. One
of General Washington's guests at present is a Mr.
Elkanah Watson, a very intelligent gentleman, who
brought letters of introduction from General Greene
and Colonel Fitzgerald. This evening he was in my
room, and read to me a home picture of Washington
in his retirement. It is so graphic and so true that I
transcribe a part of it for your benefit:

"'I trembled with awe,' he said, 'as I came into the
presence of this great man. I found him at table with

Mrs. Washington and his private family, and was re
ceived with the native dignity and with the urbanity
so peculiarly combined in the character of a soldier
and an eminent private gentleman. He soon put me
at my case, by unbending in a free and affable conversation. The cautious reserve which wisdom and
policy dictated, whilst engaged in rearing the glorious
fabric of our independence, was evidently the result
of consummate prudence, and not characteristic of his
nature. I observed a peculiarity in his smile, which
seemed to illuminate his eye; his whole countenance
beamed with intelligence, while it commanded confidence and respect.

"'I found him calm and benignant in the domestic
circle; revered and beloved by all around him; agree-
ably social without ostentation; delighting in anecdotes and adventures; without assumption; his domestic arrangements harmonious and systematic. His
servants seemed to watch his eye, and to anticipate
his very wish; hence a look was equivalent to a command. His servant Billy, the faithful companion of
his military career, was always at his side. Smiling
content animated and beamed on every countenance
in his presence.

"'In the evening I sat conversing for a full hour
with him after all the family had retired, expecting to
hear him fight over some of his battles; but I was
disappointed, for he modestly waived all allusions to
the events in which he had acted so glorious and conspicuous a part. Much of his conversation had reference to the interior country, and to the opening of the
navigation of the Potomac by canals and locks, at the
Seneca, the Great and Little Falls. His mind seemed
to be deeply absorbed by that object, then in earnest
contemplation.

"'I had taken a severe cold in the course of my journey, and coughed excessively. The general pressed me to take some remedies, but I declined. After retiring for the night, my coughing increased. When some time had elapsed, the door of my room was gently opened; and, on drawing my bed curtains, I beheld Washington himself standing at my bedside with a bowl of hot tea in his hand. I was mortified and distressed beyond expression. This little incident, occurring in common life with an ordinary man, would not have been noticed; but, as a trait of the benevolence and private virtue of Washington, deserves to be recorded.'

"Having become, my good Tintin, acquainted with a learned bishop, who has lately passed through Mount Vernon, and who has long known General Washington, I expressed to him how much I was struck with the unassuming manners of a man who filled such a space in the world's eye. He replied: 'I know no one who is so carefully guarded against the discoursing of himself, or of his acts, or of anything that pertains to him; and it has occasionally occurred to me when in his company, that if a stranger to his person were present, he would never have known from anything said by him that he was conscious of having distinguished himself.'

"Washington, like all those who have a noble nature, and like Him who was of a divine one, is fond of little children, and apt to unbend with them. He is pleased to have them come to him. A charming young lady, named Miss Custis, who is a member of his family, has said to me: 'I have sometimes made him laugh most heartily from sympathy with my joyous and extravagant spirits, although he is habitually a silent and thoughtful man. He speaks little, generally; never of himself. I never heard him relate a single act of his life during the war. I have often seen him perfectly abstracted, his lips moving; but no sound was perceptible.'

"Hearty laughter, however, my dear Tintin Calandro, is rare with Washington, although he is said to have relaxed much of his thoughtful gravity of demeanor since he has no longer to answer on the battlefield for the fate of a nation. A few hilarious explosions are related, precisely because they have so seldom occurred. They were the result of some sudden and extremely ludicrous surprises. His general habit may be described as a calm seriousness easily softening into a benevolent smile. There is no doubt that he is generally approached and treated with reverential awe. There are exceptions, however, and I will mention one. Colonel Henry Lee—'Light Horse Harry'—who is a privileged favorite with Washington, and who is reported to take more liberties with him than anybody else, dropped in yesterday. Washington, at dinner, mentioned his being in want of carriage horses, and asked Lee if he knew where he could get a pair.

"'I have a fine pair, general,' replied Lee, 'but you can not get them.'

"'Why not?'

"'Because you will never pay more than half price for anything; and I must have full price for my horses.'

"This bantering reply set Mrs. Washington laughing; and her parrot, perched beside her, joined in the laugh. The general took this familiar attack upon his dignity in good part. 'Ah! Lee, you are a funny fellow,' said he; 'see, that bird is laughing at you.'

"I must mention that this reverential awe which his deeds and elevated position threw around this great man, is reported by those familiar with his disposition, to be a source of serious annoyance to him in private life, especially when he perceives its effect upon the young and gay. I had an instance of it last evening. Mrs. Washington had invited to a private and unceremonious dancing party the young men and girls of the neighborhood. All were enjoying themselves with the utmost glee, when Washington entered the room. The moment his majestic figure was seen, the buoyant mirth was checked; the dance lost its animation; every face became grave; every tongue was silent. He remained for a time, endeavoring to engage in cheerful conversation with some of the young people and to break the spell. When he found that it was in vain, I saw an expression of sadness steal over his face, and he retired to the company of the elders in an adjoining room, expressing his regret that his presence should operate as such a damper. After a little while, light laughter and happy voices again resounded from the ball-room; upon which he rose cautiously, approached on tiptoe the door, which was ajar, and there stood for some time a delighted spectator of the youthful revelry. How amiable and characteristic of what there is in that big soul! Will you not love such a man, O Tintin Calandro, notwithstanding the strength and the eccentricity of your prejudices; and, were you here, would you not, on your wondrous violin, O sublime musician, perform for him with as much inspired enthusiasm as you do for the princess de Lamballe and the majesties of France?

"On my expressing my intense admiration of such

a character to Mr. Lear, his secretary, that gentleman replied: 'Surely I am not astonished at your feelings, for after ten years' residence in this family on the most confidential footing, I must say that General Washington is, I believe, almost the only man of an exalted character, who does not lose some part of his respectability by an intimate acquaintance. I have never found a single thing that could lessen my respect for him. A complete knowledge of his honesty, uprightness, and candor in all his private transactions, has sometimes led me to think him more than a man."*

Aubert Dubayet spent a week under the roof of Washington, and used, in the subsequent years of his life, to speak of that circumstance as the event in it which he cherished and valued the most. He said that it had purified him from most of his earthly dross, and that he felt it was not in vain that he had been in contact with human perfection. From Mount Vernon he traveled over the Thirteen States, as he had determined not to return to Europe before making himself thoroughly acquainted with their resources, and particularly with the distinguished men whom they contained, and who would probably be leaders of their destinies. He visited James Warren, who had formerly been President of the Provisional Congress of Massachusetts. On that occasion, Aubert Dubayet, having spoken of the Arcadian felicity which he had observed at Mount Vernon, was greatly surprised when his host said to him: "You have de-

---

*Those who have read W. Irving's admirable "Life of Washington," need not be told how much I am indebted to him in my delineation of the character of that illustrious personage. Not being able to do as well, I have in more than one instance borrowed his very words.

ceived yourself. Washington's mind is, not without cause, full of anxieties. Although it has been his intention to bid farewell to public affairs, yet he can not but watch with keen solicitude the working together of the several parts of the great political machinery to the construction of which he has so powerfully contributed. Confederacies have never been harmonious and long-lived, and ours is unfortunately very weak in its original constitution. We have put up in haste a house to shelter us, but it is ill jointed, and the timbers are cracking on all sides. Washington sees it; we all see it. The bonds which kept us together under the pressure of external danger, have been relaxed by the gentle hand of peace. We are not a nation, but thirteen petty sovereignties which will soon quarrel like Kilkenny cats. See in what condition are our finances. Our confederate debts exceed forty millions of dollars, an enormous one for our present resources. Congress has devised a system of credit for the extinction of that debt and for the current yearly expenditure of the General Government. Congress might as well have legislated for the moon, for it has no coercive power. Some of the States have assented to those provisions, but neglect to act accordingly; others have rejected them. Each member of the Confederacy consults its local interests and prejudices, and ignores those of the whole. The steeple of each village towers higher than the cupola of the national capitol, whilst it should be the reverse. As to those treaty stipulations on the observance of which our credit abroad, our honor and our good faith must rest, they are slighted, West, North, and South, according to the dictates of sectional interests, and

5*

sometimes openly violated. The States seem to have no appreciation of their collective obligations."

"O God!" exclaimed Dubayet, "is it possible that you have already come to this, and does General Washington concur in this dismal view of your affairs?"

The Massachusetts statesman drew from his coat pocket a letter in the well-known handwriting of Washington, and read to his visitor the following passage:

"The Confederation appears to me to be little more than a shadow without the substance, and Congress a nugatory body; their ordinances being little attended to. To me it is a solecism in politics; indeed, it is one of the most extraordinary things in nature, that we should confederate as a nation, and yet be afraid to give the rulers of that nation (who are creatures of our own making, appointed for a limited and short duration, and who are amenable for every action and may be recalled at any moment, and are subject to all the evils which they may be instrumental in producing) sufficient powers to order and direct the affairs of the same. By such policy as this the wheels of government are clogged, our brightest prospects blasted, and that high expectation which was entertained of us by the wondering world, turned into disappointment; and from the high ground on which we stood, we are descending into the vale of confusion and darkness."

Aubert Dubayet was shocked and grieved to the core of his soul. His rose-colored dreams were assuming the dark hues of a nightmare. In a fit of despondency he shut himself up in his room, and thus wrote to Lakanal:

"Tell me no more of revolutions and reforms, my dear friend, you who, in conspiracy with the ghosts of Greek and Roman patriots, are always planning the overthrow of hoary institutions, to replace them with your pretended improvements, born out of the delusive creed of human progress and perfectibility. Here has been a successful revolution, in a virgin country, where there are no time-cemented obstacles in the way of contemplated innovations and experiments—a revolution of yesterday; and to-day, what is the result? *From the high ground upon which we stood,* says the hero of that revolution, *we are descending into the vale of confusion and darkness,*" and he related to his friend all that had passed between James Warren and himself.

From Boston Aubert Dubayet returned to New York, where he learned that Washington was earnestly advocating a stronger form of government. To one of the most influential men of the epoch, the general had written: "I have ever been a friend to adequate powers in Congress, without which it is evident to me we never shall establish a national character, or be considered as on a respectable footing by the powers of Europe. We are either a united people under one head and for federal purposes, or we are thirteen independent sovereignties, eternally counteracting each other. If the former, whatever such a majority of the States as the constitution points out, conceive to be for the benefit of the whole, should, in my humble opinion, be submitted to by the minority. I can foresee no evil greater than disunion, than the *unreasonable* jealousies (I say unreasonable, because I would have a *proper* jealousy always awake, and the United States on the watch to prevent individual States from infracting the constitution with impunity) which are constantly poisoning our minds and filling them with imaginary evils for the prevention of real ones."

Washington did not seem to entertain the most distant apprehension of the usurpation of power by the Federal Government, nor did he even seem to conceive the possibility of such an event.

CHAPTER IX.

REBELLIOUS INSURRECTION IN MASSACHUSETTS—
ADOPTION OF A NEW FORM OF GOVERNMENT
FOR THE UNITED STATES—VIEWS AND APPRE-
HENSIONS OF STATESMEN ON THE SUBJECT—
DUBAYET RETURNS TO FRANCE.

IN New York Aubert Dubayet resumed his correspondence with Lakanal. " I have had the good
luck," he wrote, " to be introduced to John Jay, one
of the brightest luminaries of the revolution, and now
secretary of foreign affairs. He is also very uneasy
as to the duration and vitality of this new republican
form of government. Start not in dismay, dear friend
of mine. ' Our affairs,' he said, ' seem to lead to some
crisis, something that I can not foresee or conjecture.
I am very apprehensive, more so than during the war.
Then we had a fixed object, and though the means
and time of obtaining it were problematical, yet I did
firmly believe that we should ultimately succeed, because I as firmly believed that justice was with us.
The case is now altered. We are going and doing
wrong, and, therefore, I look forward to evils and calamities, but without being able to guess at the instrument, nature, or measure of them. What I most fear
is, that the better kind of people, by which I mean
the people who are orderly and industrious, who are
content with their situations, and not uneasy in their
circumstances, will be led by the insecurity of prop-

erty, the loss of public faith and rectitude, to consider the charms of liberty as imaginary and delusive. A state of fluctuation and uncertainty must disgust and alarm.'

"'Mr. Jay,' said I, 'as you have the kindness to enlighten me on the condition of a country and institutions for which I have fought, and in which I take the deepest interest as a Frenchman and al'y, will you permit me to ask if you have ever communicated these views to General Washington?'

"'I have,' replied the secretary of foreign affairs, and he took a letter from a table before him. 'Here is,' he continued, 'Washington's answer: "I coincide in your opinion that public affairs are drawing rapidly to a crisis, and I acknowledge that the event is equally beyond my foresight. We have errors to correct. We have probably had too good an opinion of human nature in forming our confederation. Experience has taught us that men will not adopt and carry into execution measures the best calculated for their own good, without the intervention of coercive power. I do not conceive that we can exist long as a nation without lodging somewhere a power which will pervade the whole Union in as energetic a manner as the authority of the State governments extends over the several States. To be fearful of investing Congress, instituted as that body is, with ample authorities for national progress, appears to me the very climax of popular absurdity and madness. Could Congress exert them for the detriment of the people, without injuring themselves in an equal or greater proportion? Are not their interests inseparably connected with those of their constituents? By the rotation of appointments must they not mingle frequently with the mass of the citizens? Is it not rather to be apprehended, if they were possessed of the powers before described, that the individual members would be induced to use them, on many occasions, very timidly and inefficaciously, for fear of losing their popularity and future election? We must take human nature as we find it; perfection falls not to the state of mortals." '

"What food for reflection, my dear Lakanal! Here is the secretary of foreign affairs for this new-born republic, intensely afraid that, by the 'insecurity of property, the loss of public faith and rectitude,' the people may consider the charms of liberty, their recently chosen bride, as 'imaginary and delusive'! Here is Washington himself declaring that they had *too good an opinion of human nature* when they formed their confederation! *If experience,* as he said, *has taught that men will not adopt and carry into execution measures the best calculated for their own good, without the intervention of coercive power,* how can it be maintained that they are capable of self-government? Whence is to come that *coercive power* which is to compel the people to pursue their own good and prevent them from going astray? If they are so stupid or prejudiced as not to see what is conducive to their own welfare, surely they can not have the sense to choose properly those rulers who are to coerce them into it. Are we, then, to go back to the doctrine of divinely-appointed governors and kings? This sadly perplexes me, dear Lakanal. It must seem very incredible that such a declaration should come from such a source, and it certainly would rejoice the heart of Tintin Calandro, the royalist and the loyal.

"But let us, my friend, return to Washington's let-

ter to Jay. 'What, then, is to be done?' he says.
'Things can not go on in the same strain forever. It
is much to be feared, as you observe, that the better
kind of people, being disgusted with these circumstances, will have their minds prepared for any revolution whatever. We are apt to run from one extreme to another. I am told that even respectable
characters speak of a monarchical form of government
without horror. From thinking proceeds speaking;
thence acting is often but a single step. But how
irrevocable and tremendous! What a triumph for our
enemies to verify their predictions! What a triumph
for the advocates of despotism to find that we are incapable of governing ourselves, and that systems, founded
on the basis of equal liberty, are merely ideal and fal-
lacious! Would to God that wise measures may be
taken in time to avert the consequences we have but
too much reason to apprehend!' What an admission,
O ye deities of high Olympus! Will, my dear Lakanal, your intense worship of the Phrygian goddess
who wears a red cap on her head, permit you to believe that the founder of this infant republic declares
that he has but too much reason to apprehend that it
may be changed into a monarchy? O the vanity of
human aspirations and calculations!

"'Retired as I am from the world,' Washington
further says, 'I frankly acknowledge I can not feel
myself an unconcerned spectator. Yet, having happily assisted in bringing the ship into port, and having been fairly discharged, it is not my business to
embark again on the sea of troubles. Nor could it be
expected that my sentiments and opinions would have
much weight in the minds of my countrymen. They
have been neglected, though given as a last legacy in

a most solemn manner. I then perhaps had some claims to public attention. I consider myself as having none at present.'

"Can there be anything more inexpressibly sad than this last paragraph? What mournful dejection! Was this to be expected at the end of such a career? What discouragement there must have been in such a heart, when these lines were penned! And let me tell you, my dear Lakanal, that there are good causes for it, inasmuch as, according to my observations, I can safely assert, I think, that now, as during the war, the population of this country is about equally divided into Tories and Whigs—that is to say, between royalists and republicans. In Massachusetts, that famous land of the pilgrims, which claims to be the cradle of the revolution, there is now a dangerous insurrection which threatens to jeopardize all that has been secured. General Knox, the secretary of war, who had been sent by Congress to inquire into this matter, thus reports: 'The creed of the insurgents is, that the property of the United States has been protected from the confiscation of Britain by the joint exertion of *all*, and therefore ought to be the *common property of all*, and he that attempts opposition to this creed, is an enemy to equity and justice, and ought to be swept from the face of the earth. They are determined to annihilate all debts, public and private, and have agrarian laws, which are easily effected by the means of unfunded paper, which shall be a tender in all cases whatever."

These events were transpiring in 1786, and were not of a nature to inspire Aubert Dubayet with much confidence in, and much sympathy for, the popular movements and manœuvres which the friends of change and liberty were beginning to inaugurate in his own country, much to the delight of his former college companion, Joseph Lakanal, who kept him regularly posted up as to what was going on in France. He saw that anarchy and demoralization were the result of a revolution in America, and he was afraid that such would be the case on the other side of the Atlantic, to a much greater degree and with much more frightful consequences. He saw that it was not enough to be the elected representatives of the people, in order to be, from that single circumstance, honest, virtuous, and enlightened, and besides, that the wisdom and morality of representatives were of very little avail when facing the folly or evil passions of constituents. He had a striking example before him. Congress was powerless, and did not even know what resolve to take. One of the distinguished members of that body, Colonel Henry Lee, was writing letters after letters to Washington, asking for his advice. He replied at last: "You tell me, my good Sir, of employing influence to appease the present troubles in Massachusetts. I know not where that influence is to be found, or, if attainable, that it would be a proper remedy for the disorders. *Influence* is not government. Let us have a government by which our lives, liberties, and properties will be secured, or let us know the worst at once. There is a call for decision. Know precisely what the insurgents aim at. If they have *real* grievances, redress them if possible; or acknowledge the justice of them, and your inability to give that redress at that moment. If they have not, employ the force of government against them at once. If this is inadequate, all will be convinced that the superstructure is bad and wants support. To delay one or other of these expedients is to exasperate on one hand, or to give confidence on the other. Let the reins of government, then, be braced, and held with a steady hand, and every violation of the constitution be reprehended. If defective, let it be amended; but not suffered to be trampled upon whilst it has an existence."

This was the firm and considerate advice of a statesman and soldier, but the effete Congress had not nerve enough to apply the remedy needed by the evil, which grew as it fed upon itself. On the 1st of November, Colonel Humphreys, one of Washington's former aides-de-camp, wrote to him from New Haven, in Connecticut: "The troubles in Massachusetts still continue. Government is prostrated in the dust, and it is much to be feared that there is not energy enough in that State to re-establish the civil powers. The leaders of the mob, whose fortunes and measures are desperate, are strengthening themselves daily; and it is expected that they will soon take possession of the continental magazine at Springfield, in which there are from ten to fifteen thousand stand of arms in excellent order.

"A general want of compliance with the requisitions of Congress for money seems to prognosticate that we are rapidly advancing to a crisis. Congress, I am told, is seriously alarmed, and hardly knows which way to turn, or what to expect. Indeed, my dear General, nothing but a good Providence can extricate us from the present convulsion.

"In case of civil discord, I have already told you it was seriously my opinion that you could not remain neuter, and that you would be obliged, in self-defense, to take one part or the other, or withdraw from the continent. Your friends are of the same opinion."

What a picture! A war of seven years, indescribable sufferings endured by the Americans, the richest blood of France freely spilt or exposed, her millions scattered without stint, to enthrone liberty instead of oppression, and to establish forever the doctrine that all men are born free and equal! These had been the objects aimed at. What had been obtained? The preceding pages show it. What was the prospect in the future? A civil war, and Washington leading Americans against Americans, or flying from his country to avoid such a dire necessity! Notwithstanding his almost superhuman fortitude, well may Washington have been driven to despair, and exclaimed, as he did: "What, gracious God, is man, that there should be such inconsistency and perfidiousness in his conduct! It was but the other day that we were shedding our blood to obtain the constitutions under which we now live—constitutions of our own choice and making—and which now we are unsheathing the sword to overturn! The thing is so unaccountable, that I hardly know how to realize it, or to persuade myself that I am not under the illusion of a dream." *

The extent of the existing evils and the trouble of mind which it produced in him are strikingly exhibited in his letters to Knox: "I feel, my dear General Knox," he says, "infinitely more than I can express to you for the disorders which have arisen in these States. Good God! Who, besides a Tory, could have foreseen, or a Briton predicted them? I do assure you that, even at this moment, when I reflect upon the present prospect of our affairs, it seems to me to

---

* Irving's "Life of Washington," p. 453, vol. iv.

be like the vision of a dream. After what I have seen, or rather what I have heard, I shall be surprised at nothing; for, if three years since, any person had told me that there would have been such a formidable rebellion of our own making, I should have thought him a bedlamite, a fit subject for a madhouse. In regretting, which I have often done with the keenest sorrow, the death of our much-lamented friend, General Greene, I have accompanied it of late with a query, whether he would not have preferred such an event, to the scenes which, it is more than probable, many of his compatriots may live to bemoan." What a terrible sentence! What a lesson to the pride of man, who sometimes thinks that he is doing wonders for his race, when in reality he is leading it to perdition! This letter was communicated to Dubayet, who sent a copy of it to Lakanal, with this observation: "If such things are possible in the golden age of this republic, which was intended by its authors to be a model one for the world, what will happen to it in its age of brass?"

So distressed was Washington that, to use his own expressions, "he allowed himself, contrary to his original intention, to be swept back into the tide of human affairs, and to abandon that ease and retirement which," he said, "were so desired by him and so essentially necessary." He exerted himself to the utmost to bring about a modification of the government, and to give the new one proposed more force and vitality. In connection with that subject, he wrote to James Madison: "How melancholy is the reflection that, in so short a time, we should have made such large strides toward fulfilling the predictions of our transatlantic foes! *Leave them to them-*

selves, and their government will soon dissolve. Will
not the wise and good strive hard to avoid this evil?
Or will their supineness suffer ignorance and the arts
of self-interested and designing, disaffected, and desperate characters to involve this great country in
wretchedness and in contempt? What stronger evidence can be given of the want of energy in our government than those disorders? If there is no power
in it to check them, what security has a man for life,
liberty, or property? To you I am sure I need not
add aught on the subject. The consequences of a lax
or inefficient government are too obvious to be dwelt
upon. Thirteen sovereignties pulling against each
other, and all tugging at the Federal head, will soon
bring ruin on the whole; whereas a liberal and energetic constitution, well checked and well watched, to
prevent encroachments, might restore us to that degree of respectability and consequence to which we
had the finest prospect of attaining."

Notwithstanding Washington, in a fit of despondency, said that his opinions and counsels were of little
weight with his countrymen, it was the reverse of the
proposition which was the truth; they had been
widely effective, and had contributed to induce the
legislative assemblies of the several States to adopt
the plan of a convention, to meet at Philadelphia,
and devise a better system of federation. Washington
was put at the head of the Virginia delegation. Before the time arrived for the meeting of the
convention, the insurrection in Massachusetts was
suppressed with but little bloodshed. It had appeared very formidable; there had been a great deal
of sound and fury; but when they had to come to
blows, the roaring lions turned out to be sheep, and

the leaders fled to Canada, leaving their followers to fare as best they could. True to his character, Washington recommended lenient measures, and advocated the policy of not alienating the people from their government by the severity of unnecessary punishment. But it is not in the nature of Puritanism to be merciful and chivalrous—so that the Legislature of Massachusetts disfranchised a large number of her citizens, and thereby deprived some of them of the means of gaining a livelihood. Political helotism, thus established in the lap of liberty, seemed to Aubert Dubayet a monstrous contradiction. He had been still more startled by the insurrection itself; for, during the war and after, he had associated much with Massachusetts people, and from their conversations and representations he had derived the impression that the inhabitants of that State were the most law-abiding, the most patriotic, the most disinterested, the most charitable, the most virtuous, the most enlightened community that had ever existed—constituting, in fact, the only thoroughly pure spot in this sinful world.

The convention of the delegates from all the States met with a quorum on the 25th of May 1787, and Washington was unanimously called to the chair as president. After discussions which lasted four months, the result was the formation of a new confederacy and constitution for the United States. This constitution was to be ratified by the States before it went into effect. "This instrument," wrote Dubayet to Lakanal, "meets with the most strenuous opposition from many quarters. Washington, however, is highly pleased. I heard him say: 'It appears to me little short of a miracle, that the delegates from so many

States, different from each other in their manners and
prejudices, should unite in forming a system of
national government so little liable to well-founded
objections.   Nor am I such an enthusiastic, partial,
or indiscriminating admirer of it, as not to perceive it
is tinctured with some real, though not radical, defects.
With regard to the two great points, the pivots upon
which the whole machine must move, my creed is
simply, first, that the General Government is not invested with more powers than are indispensably necessary to perform the functions of a good government ; and, consequently, that no objection ought to
be made against the quantity of power delegated to
it.   Secondly, that these powers, as the appointment
of all rulers will ever arise from, and at short stated
intervals recur to, the free suffrages of the people, are
so distributed among the legislative, executive, and
judicial branches into which the General Government
is arranged, that it can never be in danger of degen-
erating into a monarchy, an oligarchy, an aristocracy,
or any other despotic or oppressive form, *so long as
there shall remain any virtue in the body of the people.*
We are not to expect perfection in this world.   Nothing but harmony, honesty, industry, and frugality are
necessary to make us a great and happy people.'

" This is the sound of one bell, my dear friend, but,
having met Patrick Henry, the great Virginian
patriot, the Demosthenes of America, whose famous
shout of ' Give me liberty, or give me death,' rever-
berated across the Atlantic with such thrilling effect,
as you well know, he sounded the tocsin of alarm
when I communicated to him Washington's views.

" ' I am sorry,' he said, ' that I can not agree with
that good and great man.   He is so happy at the

prospect of escaping the confusion and misery which were rapidly coming upon us, that I am afraid his excellent judgment is warped. He sees on this occasion with the eyes of hope, not with those of experience and stern reason; his verdict is from the heart and not from the brain. We have not laid a lasting foundation for tranquillity and happiness. This instrument gives too much constructive power to the Federal Government. Washington uses too often the word, *national;* I always say, *federal.* We are not a nation, but a federation of sovereignties. I am afraid that this will be forgotten in the end. I, for one, am a Virginian, and nothing else. That satisfies my ambition. I think that I read but too clearly into the future. Swelled by that mighty tide of emigration which, like the waves of the ocean, will beat incessantly upon our shores, the population of the United States, whose territory, in the course of time, may extend to the frontiers of Mexico, and perhaps beyond them, will exceed fifty millions in a century hence. It is, then, probable that we shall become the greatest commercial, agricultural, and manufacturing people in the world, and, therefore, the richest. The Federal Government, thus gigantic in its proportions, will hold the purse and the sword of that Titan under its absolute control. Will it not, then, be omnipotent? Who will gainsay its construction of its own powers? Give me the purse and the sword of a nation, and I am Cæsar in fact, no matter by what name you may call me, and no Cæsar is a respecter of rights secured only by paper guaranties.'

"I ventured here to interrupt him, and to express the hope that his fears were imaginary.

"'Imaginary!' he exclaimed. 'Has not our pres-

6

ent government begun in strife and insurrection? Is
not the new one proposed the object of angry opposition? What country ever had such a diversity of
interests, not to say anything of that antagonism
which must be irrepressible and irreconcilable between
slaveholding and non-slaveholding States; for, the
few slaves still existing on the north side of Maryland
are bound to be soon emancipated, or, rather, to be
sold to the South, where alone they can be profitable
to their masters. The late insurrection in Massachusetts will be imitated and "bettered by the instruction." On that occasion it was a mere rebellion
against that State. The like event in fifty years will
probably be termed a rebellion against the National
Government, as it will then be called, when its origin
is forgotten; and there will be disfranchisements decreed by Congress, as sweepingly as those which were
recently decreed by the Legislature of that State. But
what a difference, and with what awful consequences!
Were I to live a century longer, I should not be astonished to see half the people of the United States arrayed
in war against the other half, as it was lately very near
occurring, when we thought that he whom we call the
Father of his Country would have to take side, and to
choose between his fellow-citizens divided into two
hostile camps, or leave the continent to avoid being
forced into civil war. But should in after years that
war break out, it will no longer be between Whigs
and Tories. Probably it will be between the North
and the South, the Cavaliers against the Puritans, the
lordly owners of black slaves against the white slaves
of the wheel and spindle.'

"'I can not, however, but admire,' said I, 'the profound wisdom which has equally divided the powers

of the new government between the judiciary, the
executive, and the legislative department. It is a
skillful contrivance of checks and balances, which
must prevent many of the evils you apprehend.'

"'Powers equally divided!' said he. 'Those
checks and balances are as nugatory and deceptive
as shadows assuming the semblance of substances.
In times of high excitement, should the Supreme
Court of the United States dare to oppose Congress,
that body will legislate it into non-entity, nullity, or
insignificance. As to the President, should he thwart
a House and Senate composed of unscrupulous partisans elected by a passion-moved multitude, as all
multitudes are, they will either impeach and remove
him, or so fetter him in his office as to compel him
to be inactive, or follow them passively in leading-
strings. Then will be inaugurated the rule of a parliamentary oligarchy—the worst of all despotisms,
because it has no personal responsibility. Then will
the States be provinces and the Governors procon-
suls. As to myself, I am not for the splendor of consolidation, nor for the cohesion of public plunder and
demoralization in a vast American empire, imposing
on its subjects the chains of a gilded servitude. I
prefer small independent States, with moderate
wealth and power; but rich in virtue, patriotism,
and frugality. This is more conducive to the happiness of men. Give me a galaxy of stars self-ponder-
ated and supporting one another by mutual attrac-
tion in the atmosphere of liberty and equality, rather
than the radiant supremacy, gorgeous as it may be,
of the monarch of the day, who, when he appears on
the horizon, does not permit any other rival luminary
to shine in that firmament where he reigns in solitary
grandeur.'

"There are many, however, my dear Lakanal, and among them is Alexander Hamilton, who would have wished for a stronger government than the one which Patrick Henry thinks too strong. Such are the conflicting views of men! It is as difficult to make them agree as clocks; Charles V. found that out. Posterity alone will be able to decide correctly on this question of the merits of this new constitution of the United States, when tasting of its fruits."

That new constitution having gone into operation, Washington was elected President without opposition, and was inaugurated in the city of New York on the 30th of April, 1789, amidst the enthusiastic rejoicings of the people. A few days after having witnessed that august ceremony, Aubert Dubayet departed for France and landed safely at Bordeaux, where he found Lakanal, who, having been apprised of the probable time of his arrival, had hastened to meet him. After the friends had exchanged greetings—

"What news in our dear France?" said Dubayet.

"The news is," replied Lakanal, "that you have seen the end of one revolution, and that you arrive just in time to see the beginning of another."

"May we, then," exclaimed Dubayet, "have a Washington at our head to lead us through the terrible ordeal!"

"Amen!" ejaculated the priest and professor of belles-lettres.

"And our dear Tintin Calandro? How fares he?" inquired Dubayet.

"He fiddles," replied Lakanal with a sneer, "whilst Rome is burning."

CHAPTER X.

AUBERT DUBAYET had inherited considerable
property in Louisiana. Before departing from the
United States, to the formation of which he had contributed, he had ordered the whole of this property
to be sold and the amount remitted to him in Paris,
so that, on his arrival in that city, he found a large
sum at his disposal. He invested in a dwelling-house
in Grenoble and in farms near that town, where his
family originated, and where he still had many relatives. He soon acquired much influence in that
province, then called *Dauphiné*, and subsequently the
Department of Isère. In consequence of the peculiar condition of the public mind at that epoch, in a
country where great radical changes were desired and
probable, all persons connected with the American
revolution, which had so recently been accomplished,
and particularly those French officers who had taken
part in it, were objects of lively interest. Hence Aubert Dubayet became the lion of the locality and a
sort of political authority. Old and young turned
their eyes to him inquisitively, as if they hoped that
he had brought from the new world, and from the
cradle of its infant republic, some knowledge or experience by which they might profit in settling those

questions that threatened to convulse the nation. In fact, without aiming at any such distinction, Aubert Dubayet, by the mere force of circumstance, was gravitating toward the position of a leader of the people. The man who had been in contact with Washington, Lafayette, Franklin, and the other great patriots of America, and who had contributed in laying the broad foundations of the empire of freedom in the wilderness discovered by Columbus, was invested with a character which commanded respect and excited curiosity. In social circles he was eagerly listened to when he related some of the incidents of the struggle which he had witnessed, and described the new people, the new institutions, and the new country he had carefully examined. The population of the province where Aubert Dubayet had established himself, was soon intensely agitated by the convocation of the States-General of the kingdom. This was an assembly composed of the nobility, clergy, and *tiers état*, or commons, deliberating in distinct bodies and in separate chambers, as the representatives of the nation, and which used to be reluctantly convened by the royal authority, and then, only on occasions of the most vital importance. The French people were not accustomed to elections, and the present one was conducted with indescribable violence of party feelings. Aubert Dubayet had been solicited to participate in it, but had persistently refused, on the ground that his coming among them had been of too recent a date to permit him to acquire a sufficient knowledge of the country and of its wants. He contented himself, therefore, with being a spectator of the contest, but by no means an unconcerned one.

In the neighboring province, so well known in history and poetry under the name of Provence, there was a man destined to great celebrity, who was a candidate for the honors of a seat in the States-General. His name was Honoré Gabriel Riquetti, Count de Mirabeau. The bearer of that name, which was to become so famous, had already acquired an unenviable notoriety by the vices which he really possessed, and by those which were attributed to him. He had early yielded to the unrestrained indulgence of passions uncommonly fierce. His whole life had been but one perpetual storm, during which he seemed to have delighted in braving the thunderbolt of law and authority, and in setting Heaven itself at defiance; for he was bold enough to have repeated the exclamation of the younger Ajax: " I will escape from this wreck in spite of the gods." His eloquence was reported to be resistless, so much so that, on one occasion, his father, having caused him to be incarcerated in a state prison for some delinquency of which he was accused, refused to allow him the hearing that he claimed in self-defense, and gave this reason for his refusal: "I know that I am right, but were I to afford him the opportunity to speak for himself, he would convince me that I am wrong."

Being called to Aix on some private affair, Aubert Dubayet, in the evening of the day following his arrival, saw the streets filled with people who were hastening in a particular direction, and who seemed greatly excited. He inquired what was the matter, and was told that the public square in front of the cathedral was to be illuminated, and that Mirabeau, the candidate for the States-General, would address the people. The meeting was to take place at eight o'clock. Through the influence of a friend, Aubert Dubayet managed to secure a seat not far from the platform which had been prepared for the occasion. When the orator made his appearance he was received with a whirlwind of applause, mixed with shouts of derision and abuse. The object of these boisterous demonstrations was a man of ordinary size, but very robust. His shoulders were broad and square, and his swelling chest gave promise of a powerful voice; his bushy hair, carefully powdered and combed back, made more salient a high and heavy forehead of the Olympian cast, streaked with large blue veins. His eyes, gleaming under his arched brows, were a mirror that reflected all the emotions of which the soul is susceptible. His voice was superb in all its keys; his gestures were few, but worthy of the most consummate actor. His whole face was furrowed with deep lines; it looked as if made up of seams. A terrible disease had marred it, pitting the skin, thickening its texture, and enlarging his naturally harsh features into repulsive coarseness. His lips tightly pressed together, when he was silent, seemed purposely closed to check the explosion of feelings and the flow of thoughts crowding at the gate, and too eager to burst forth before being arrayed into the proper order that judgment required. When contemplating such a countenance it was impossible not to think that it was ugliness itself, although the sublimity of genius was visible through the horrid mask. This personage, who looked about forty years old, stood awhile with his arms folded over his broad chest, and with his massive head haughtily thrown back. Surveying leisurely the multitude before him with an ill-concealed air of superiority and self-confidence which seemed to say: Only hear me, and you will see if I am not your master—he waited until the

tumult occasioned by his presence had entirely sub-
sided.

"I know," he said, "that I have here both friends
and enemies. Before my friends applaud, and my
enemies hoot, I hope they will do me the favor to
listen. To those whom I wish to represent, it is necessary that I should be known physically, intellectu-
ally, and morally. Well, here I stand with all the
blushing honors of my far-famed ugliness. Although
it is rumored that more than one Venus has smiled on
me, I am no Adonis, as you must now rest assured from
actual inspection. Judge for yourselves on that point.
To a lady who wanted a description of my person, I
once wrote : 'You have only to imagine the face of a
lion just recovering from the most malignant attack
of small-pox.' Another thing, as accidental in me as
my ugliness, is my birth, which is noble. I am the
legitimate issue of Victor Riquetti, Marquis de Mirabeau, and of Louise de Caraman. Most of my ancestors were birds of prey, who used the sword as the
eagle uses its beak. There was but one exception in
the line—that of Riquet, the engineer who constructed
the canal of Languedoc. He, for one, did something
really useful. I wish that I could also mention, as
another exception, my own father, one of the chiefs
of that philanthropic sect called the 'Economists,'
who have formed a society to make every peasant
rich, and who have only succeeded in ruining all those
that have followed their precepts. That father of
mine has published a book entitled 'The Friend of
Man,' in which he speaks with delirious enthusiasm
of the charms of liberty, and in which he shows how
all men can live free and happy, without carrying between their teeth the curb and bit imposed by heaven-

6*

born rulers, and particularly without the soothing and moralizing influence of the rack and of the dungeon. But the ' Friend of Man ' having been the harshest of despots under his own roof, and having solicited and obtained fifty-four *lettres de cachet*** against members of his own family, I give him up with respectful regret, and can not say that I have much to brag of, as to that particular link in my hereditary chain of ancestry.

" I had received from nature a robust constitution, volcanic passions, an ardent imagination, a wonderful facility and aptitude for study, and a prodigious memory. In the hands of a mentor, and under the salutary influence of a judicious and well-regulated education, I might have avoided many errors. But it was attempted to rule the boy with the strong hand of paternal despotism. The boy spurned and broke the rod, thus giving promise of the man who is the sworn and implacable foe of arbitrary power wherever it raises its insolent head. I was born, I say, with an impetuous temper, but susceptible of generous sentiments. The gentle hand of a skillful pilot would have led me safely through those storms by which I have been wrecked more than once. Unfortunately, I was treated with extraordinary harshness from my infancy, and was irritated and goaded into excesses. Now that experience has taught me lessons by which I have profited, I repent, as a son, that I was sometimes rebellious; for paternal authority is the only one which is of divine right, even in its abuses, and against which insurrection can not be justified. But, setting this aside, what have I done that

---

* Arbitrary orders of arrest issued in the name of the king by one of his ministers.

ought to stamp on my brow the seal of Cain's curse? What have I done that has not been done by many other young men of the same social position, with impunity and without reproach, whilst every one of my delinquencies has been visited with extreme reprobation and punishment? Permit to the necessity of self-defense a short review of my life. I think that I can show that I am better than my reputation, and that my faults and sins have been exaggerated and distorted by the malignancy of my enemies.

"My early youth was intrusted to the care and tuition of an excellent and learned man, called Poisson, who still lives. He can tell whether I was born that monster I am represented to be. He can tell whether I was not the most studious and docile of pupils, and whether my progress under him was not so rapid, that, when I was withdrawn from his hands at the age of fourteen, I was already master of all the classics, and animated with the desire of acquiring a larger stock of the wealth of knowledge. Were these the indications of an evil nature? At the age which I have mentioned, being destined by my father to the profession of arms, I was placed at a military school, where I studied mathematics for two years, and obtained some proficiency in the arts of drawing and music. Tormented with the ambition of being one day a celebrity and the pride of my country, I wrote and published, before beard had grown on my chin, a eulogy of the Great Condé, and several pieces of poetry. Were these the signs of the beast, and ought not one, who thus began his career, to have been encouraged and assisted, instead of being thwarted, hated, oppressed, and slandered at that time of life when the soul feels so keenly such outrages, par-

ticularly when they come from a quarter where love,
or at least justice, is expected? When at school, a
friend surprised me in my chamber declaiming with
ardor: 'Oh! oh!' exclaimed he, 'are you rehearsing
the part of Demosthenes?' 'Why not?' I answered.
'We may, before I die, have the States-General in
France.' Well, fellow-citizens, my presentiment did
not deceive me; we shall have the States-General in
a few days." Here he paused, and lifting up his
hands toward heaven, he thundered forth these words:
"And should I be destined by the Almighty, in those
States-General representing the rights and majesty of
the nation, to be the Demosthenes of France even
for the brief space of two years, followed by the sad
death and the immortality of the Athenian, I ask no
more, and accept the decree of fate with enthusiastic
gratitude." This was said in such a manner that it
struck the vast assembly like an electric shock, and
this time there was heard but one unanimous shout
of acclamation.

"Pardon me," continued the orator with a voice
which had become composed, "pardon me the ego-
tism of these details. But I am here on my defense,
as you must remember. I am here to refute those
calumnies which are circulated with effrontery to defeat my election. I resume, therefore, the biographical sketch of my life. At seventeen years of age I
entered the army as a sub-lieutenant. Shortly after,
I had a love intrigue, unfortunately accompanied with
circumstances which gave it more notoriety than generally waits on affairs of this kind. What would most
of the fathers here present have done? Taking into
consideration the extreme youth of their son, they
would have gently reprimanded him, and by affec-

tionate advice guarded him against the repetition of such folly. But my father obtained against me a *lettre de cachet*, and had me locked up in the fortress of the Island of Ré, like a felon of the worst character. That was not all. He had determined to send me to the Dutch colonies of India, where the climate is almost certain death to Europeans, and it was with considerable difficulty, and only through the earnest and persistent entreaties of friends, that he was prevented from accomplishing his purpose. When I came out of the dungeon of Ré, did I, like young men of my rank, indulge in the excesses of an effete and corrupt life? No. I obtained permission to make the campaign of Corsica as a simple volunteer —a permission which was the only one I ever procured readily—probably on account of its affording the chance of my being killed. I distinguished myself so much in that campaign, that I rose to be a captain of dragoons. Let me here hasten to say, that I repented afterward having been an instrument in a war the object of which was to extinguish the liberties of a people; and, to expiate the fault that I had committed, I wrote a memorial in which I exposed and denounced the oppressive conduct of the Genoese invaders, who subsequently sold that island to France. That memorial I submitted to my father, who thought proper to destroy it.

"Reared with the prejudices of my race and of the class to which I belonged, and sharing their predilection for military service, I wished to continue in it. I thought that I was qualified for that profession. Five years of my life had been devoted to its study in all its branches, and there was not one single book treating of war, in any living or dead language, that

I had not read. My robust constitution permitted
me to endure any hardship and fatigue. I was full
of ardor and daring, and at the same time, phlegmat-
ically cool. Of this I gave proof in all the dangers
to which I found myself exposed. I felt, besides,
that I was gifted with an excellent and rapid *coup
d'œil*. Boiling all over with ambition, it was natural
that I should dream of becoming a marshal of France.
Why not? Stimulated by that hope, I urged my
father to purchase for me, according to usage, the
colonelcy of a regiment. He replied tauntingly:
' Duguesclin and Bayard did not thus begin.' I was
deeply wounded; I renounced in disgust that profession to which my father himself had destined me, and
in which, however, he refused to give me any assistance. He had changed his mind, it seems, and now
wished to bury me in the obscure labors of the administration of his estate. I obeyed him, and Heaven
only knows what it cost a man of my temperament
to consent to such a sacrifice of my tastes and aspirations! Was that the act of an undutiful son and of
a bad man? Thus I became a farmer to please my
father, and what was not so creditable, I became a
pettifogger, for I had to play a part in innumerable
lawsuits which he contrived to have with his neighbors and his tenants.

"In these conjunctures, having been sent on business by my father to this city, I fell in love with
Emilie de Marignane, whose family you all know.
Was it wrong in me to wish to be married? Was it
not a proof that I wished to escape from my licentious habits? My father refused, on the ground that
I was too bad a subject for matrimony. The marriage took place, however, and, as neither the family of

my wife, nor my own, supplied us with the means of living according to our rank, the consequence was that I became involved in debt, and conjugal difficulties and quarrels ensued in our pinched household, as it generally happens in such cases. My father, had he entertained any compassion for my youthful inexperience, could easily have extricated me from my troubles. What did he do? He obtained a *lettre de cachet* against me, and had me exiled to the chateau de Mirabeau, and subsequently to the town of Manosque. While thus exiled, and confined by order of the government within the limits of a small town as a prison, I ventured on a temporary absence from it, which I hoped would not be noticed. It was an imprudence, but surely it was not a crime. What was the cause of that imprudence? Was it anything for which I have to blush? No. I had gone to the neighboring town of Grasse to see a cherished sister, Madam de Cabris, who happened to be there on a visit. Whilst I was with her, she was insulted. I challenged the offender, who had the cowardice to refuse to meet me. I caned him. The fellow brought suit against me, and obtained an order of court to have me arrested and tried criminally. What did my father do? Did he sanction my attempt to defend the honor of his daughter and family? No. He procured against me another *lettre de cachet*, and had me locked up in the chateau D'If. Mr. d'Allègre, the commandant of that fortress, interested himself in my behalf as soon as he knew me. After a little while, he wrote to my father a letter, in which he commended my resignation and good conduct, and solicited him to set me free. What was the result of an application which did honor to the heart and judgment of the gentle-

man who made it? My father, far from listening
with favor to my praise, but in order to remove me
from the atmosphere of kindness and consideration
which he supposed I had secured for my comfort, had
me transferred to another fortress, that of Joux, near
Pontarlier.

"There again my deportment so captivated the good-
will of the Count de St. Maurice, who commanded
the fortress, that he permitted me to have Pontarlier
for a prison, and he himself introduced me into the
best society of that town. I then wrote to my wife to
come to me with my son, but there had been between
us, as I have already said, when I was laboring under
financial distress, some of those differences which,
under such circumstances, frequently visit the conjugal roof. I was still miserably poor, and it is not
astonishing that she refused, under different pretexts,
to share my fate. I do not blame her. Heroic devotion and sacrifices are not things to be expected in
the common run of human affairs. She probably
acted wisely; but bear in mind, however, that I invited her to come to me, and that she refused. It
was then that I became acquainted with the Marquise
de Monnier, a charming young woman who had been
forced into the arms of a septuagenarian husband.
What happened is but too well known. The marquis
instituted against me a criminal prosecution for having seduced his wife; and my father, according to
his chronic habit of treating me harshly, solicited a
lettre de cachet to have me confined in the citadel of
Dourlens. Under the pressure of such dangers, I
fled to Switzerland, where the marquise soon joined
me. From Switzerland we went to Holland, where
I hid myself and assumed the name of St. Mathieu.

In the meantime, on the complaint and at the request of the offended husband, I was condemned to death in France by default, executed in effigy, and all that I possessed was confiscated. I had hoped to be forgotten in Holland, where, to earn a precarious living for the object of my love and for myself, I worked without interruption in a garret from six o'clock in the morning until nine in the evening. I was a miserable drudge hired by booksellers, and I manufactured books according to their directions. I was even preparing to embark for free America, when my father, armed with the authority of one of those *lettres de cachet*, of which his pockets were always full, caused the law of nations and the sanctity of a foreign and independent territory to be violated, and, having procured my arrest through the instrumentality of some French police officers, had me incarcerated in the dungeon of Vincennes, where I remained four years!

"When I was restored to liberty, what did I do? I was poor and without a friend, and Sophie, Marquise de Monnier, who had suffered so much for me, was a prisoner in a convent. In our joint interest I went to Pontarlier to cause to be revoked the sentence pronounced against us, condemning her to reclusion in a cloister, and me, to lose my head on the scaffold. On the day of the trial, I appeared before the tribunal with a lock of her hair on my breast to inspire me, and a dose of active poison in my pocket, to put an end to my existence if I failed to have us both re-established in our civil rights. It was not even possible for me to secure the services of one single member of the bar. I stood before my judges without that professional assistance which is always

vouchsafed to the accused, and I confronted my enemies alone, penniless, friendless, and in chains. It is
reported, however, that I pleaded my own cause with
stupendous eloquence and energy. I struck terror
into my adversaries, I melted a prejudiced audience
into tears, and the result was, a compromise between
the Marquis de Monnier and myself, by which all
the proceedings against me were withdrawn and an-
nulled, and his wife obtained the restitution of her
dowry and her liberty. Was this the conduct of a
cowardly monster? I had been, it is true, the author
of a great scandal, but did I not cruelly suffer for it?
And did I not try to repair it as much as was in my
power? After having acted toward Madam de
Monnier as it was my duty to do, I turned to my
wife, and again made repeated efforts to bring her
back to my arms. 'Eight years have elapsed,' I
wrote to her, 'since we were separated. They have
sobered my evil passions, ripened my judgment, and
improved my morals. It is with difficulty that I
shall believe that eight years of incessant adversity,
which would be a sacred title to the compassion of
any kind and benevolent heart, have driven me from
yours.' My wife, however, resisted all the appeals that
I made to her, but so anxious was I to resume those
conjugal duties which, in better days, I had sworn
and failed to fulfill, that I applied to the tribunals of
the country to compel Madam de Mirabeau to return
to my domicile and protection. My efforts were vain,
it is true, and a final separation was pronounced between us. But then, let it be no longer said that I
have not done all that I could to repair the wrongs
of which I had been guilty.

"The greater portion of my life has been spent in

captivity and in sorrow, in incredible destitution and
intense labor. I am one of the most prolific writers of
the age, although I have reached only the meridian
of life. I spare you the long list of my publications.
Those of my works which treat of financial, historical,
and political subjects, and in which, under the eye
and within the hearing of despotism, I have been
the boldest advocate of liberty and liberal institutions, have gained for me a reputation of which I
may well be proud."

"And your infamous novels!" cried a voice from
the crowd. "What do you say of them?"

Mirabeau paused, and looking at the point in the
assembly from which the interruption had sprung,
said with a tone and a gesture of dignified courtesy:
"Whoever he may be, who has thus apostrophized
me, I thank him for it, because it gives me a fit opportunity to denounce and reprobate those works
which he rightly denominates infamous. I wish I
could efface with my blood every line of them. To
have composed them, is the only act of my life of
which I am disposed to repent in ashes and sackcloth.
There is no justification for it; but there may be an
excuse, or rather a sort of palliation. She who had
sacrificed so much for me was starving without a
murmur in a foreign land; and the tempter, in the
shape of a bookseller, said to me: 'Here is bread;
but, in exchange for it, you must give me licentious
and sensational novels which will sell.' You have the
whole story, on my honor; and you have also the assurance of my sincere contrition and repentance. I
hope that I shall make amends for my guilt by the
services which I have the consciousness of rendering
one day to France and to humanity."

Mirabeau paused again, and seemed to look thought-
fully back into the depths of his memory, to ascertain
if he had forgotten any one of the many accusations
brought against him, and then resumed his discourse
in these words: " I believe that I have made to you
a full confession, on which I invite you to pass judgment, and to decide whether I am too depraved to
be your representative in that great assembly which
is soon to convene, and on which will hang the destinies of France. When the nobles of Provence met
to deliberate on the choice of their delegates to the
States-General and on the instructions to be given to
them, being one of their order, I thought that it was
my duty to join their meeting, to show myself among
my peers, with the intention of urging them to a
course of action which would have been conducive
to their own interests and to those of the people at
large, of whom they could easily have become the benefactors, instead of being the oppressors. I wanted to
tell them that the patience of the people had held out
during centuries, but that it was now exhausted to the
last drop. I had intended to recommend the voluntary abolition on their part of the absurd and hateful
privileges which they possess, and which are incompatible with the progressive civilization of the age.
But they spared me the trouble; they declared that
I was too immoral and too much of a free-thinker to
be admitted and recognized as one of their immaculate body. Very well! I accepted their decision.
But, if I had ceased to be a nobleman, what was I?
Surely they could not have made me a mere non-
entity. I was a sentient being, and entitled as such,
I thought, to be something appertaining to human
nature, however humble and insignificant that some-

thing might be. If no longer Count de Mirabeau, I remained at least Mirabeau the man—Mirabeau the plebeian. I, therefore, acted immediately in accordance with my new position in society. Opening a shop in your city, I wrote on its front: ' Mirabeau, Draper,' and casting aside the purple mantle of the patrician, I stand before you, in the garb and character of a cloth merchant, a candidate for your suffrages, with the hope, if I obtain them, of being acknowledged before long and proclaimed the tribune of the people in the States-General of France.

" I will now sum up, in conclusion, this review of my life which I have laid before you without concealment. I think that, judging of it impartially, I can say: no doubt my youth was a stormy one. I have, through the fault of others, and particularly through my own, committed many errors. Few men, in their private life, have offered a fairer opportunity and more plausible and abundant pretexts for calumny to seize upon their acts, and add darker shades to their dark sides; but I dare assert here, that no one who aspires to be a public man, has a better right than I have to claim the possession of courageous sentiments, disinterested views, stern independence of character, and uniform inflexibility of principles. My errors, my qualities, and my defects, my reverses and my successes, have equally contributed to fit me to be the champion of liberty. I have learned, practically and theoretically, to love her and to hate despotism, in the dungeon of Vincennes and in the different fortresses where I was arbitrarily confined so many years. I challenge all and every one here to designate, if they can, one single act, line, or speech of mine, when either free or in captivity, which does not show a grand and energetic love of liberty. And could it be otherwise ? I count fifty-four *lettres de cachet* issued during my lifetime against members of my family, of which seventeen were to my address. But if the love of liberty has been to me the source of more than one keen and deep-felt enjoyment, I must confess that it has also inflicted exquisite torments, which it is now neither the proper place nor the opportune time to explain. Such as they are, I have cheerfully accepted them. It is not to-day that I have to learn that he who aspires to benefit the human race, must be prepared, in secret, or in public, for the agony of inevitable martyrdom.

" One reproach to me, fellow-citizens, I must notice. It is said that I am proud. Aye, I am proud—proud of the consciousness of my courage, of my strength, of the rectitude of my intentions—proud even of the injustices and persecutions of which I have been the object ; and I confess that I am but little humiliated by my innumerable faults and defects, because they do not, after all, in any way cast a stain on my honor.

" The nobles who rejected me as unworthy of belonging to their body, now call me the *plebeian count.* I accept the title ; and, so help me God, I will make them remember it forever. Let them know that the exile they have cast off like a wandering beggar, has found hospitality and fraternity among those hewers of wood and drawers of water who are the objects of their contempt, and that no Coriolanus will ever have shown himself a more valuable and grateful guest to those whose tents afforded him shelter ! Let those nobles know that, henceforth, between them and me there is an impassable gulf ; for the king is their master, and the people are mine ; let them send to the

States-General the best and the proudest knight they can find in their ranks, as the representative of their privileged class! I will meet him there without fear, as the representative of the unprivileged masses, and fling at the feet of despotism the gauntlet of liberty." Here he was interrupted by a hurricane of clamorous' applause. When it died away, " Fellow-citizens," he said, " in all countries and in all ages, the aristocrats have implacably hunted down the friends of the people; and if, by some fortunate and unaccountable circumstance or accident, there arose one out of their own privileged order, it is he at whom they have struck with more vigorous hatred, thereby showing their eagerness and avidity to inspire terror by the selection of the victim whom they deemed it sound policy to immolate to the necessity of self-defense. Thus died the last of the Gracchi from patrician hands. But, having fallen under the mortal blow, he grasped a handful of the dust of the ground on which his noble form was prostrate, and, flinging it toward heaven, he invoked the vengeance of the gods. Of that dust was born the plebeian Marius—Marius! less great for having exterminated the Cimbri, than for having crushed in Rome the aristocracy of the nobility." Peals after peals of thundering acclamations proved to the orator that he had struck the right chord.

" Fellow-citizens," he continued, " I am informed that the governor of this province, the Marquis de Caraman, a dear kinsman of mine, by-the-by, at the request of the nobility, who think that they see in me a second Marius, intends to have me secretly kidnapped and carried to the East Indies. Let him dare ! "

"Let him dare!" shouted the infuriated multitude, with ferocious gesticulations. "Down with all the nobles!"

A grim smile flitted over the lips of Mirabeau. "He will not dare!" he said; "resume your composure. I have no more to say beyond giving you the assurance that, if you think me worthy of being your representative, and send me to the States-General, I, Honoré Gabriel Riquetti de Mirabeau, nicknamed the *plebeian count*, solemnly pledge myself before God and man, that, following the example of Marius in Rome, I will level to the ground in Versailles the aristocracy of France; that I will wipe out every vestige of feudality from the fair bosom of our mother-land; and that I will establish the equality, fraternity, and liberty which we all desire, on the broad basis of national prosperity." There was a rush of the people toward the platform with a roar like that of the ocean. The orator was taken up in their arms, carried in triumph all round the public square, and then to his residence. Not only was he elected by the city of Aix, the old capital of Provence, but also by Marseilles, which the echo of that eloquent voice had reached, and he had to choose between the two. It was Aix—the scene of his first triumph.

Before leaving Aix, Aubert Dubayet had the good fortune to be introduced to Mirabeau, who seemed to take great pleasure in conversing with him on American affairs. Dubayet complimented him on his oratorial success and expressed his admiration. "Pshaw, pshaw!" said Mirabeau; "it was all nonsense and clap-trap. But come to Versailles, wait until I have taken my seat in the States-General, and then you will hear something worthy of being remembered."

CHAPTER XI.

REPUBLICANISM AND ROYALISM—THE RED CAP AND THE BASTILE.

A SHORT time after this interview with Mirabeau, Aubert Dubayet went to Versailles to witness the inauguration of the States-General. The first man he met was Lakanal, who had hastened from Toulouse to be present at the accomplishment of that great event. The two friends embraced each other tenderly. "What news?" asked Lakanal. "What news from America in particular? For I know that you keep up an active correspondence with that country."

"Well," answered Dubayet, "they are going on as smoothly as might be expected under a new and untried form of government. Many look forward to unparalleled prosperity and liberty with the most buoyant confidence. Many, on the other hand, have doubts and apprehensions."

"Incredible!" exclaimed Lakanal. "I have read and closely studied their federal constitution. It seems perfection itself."

"To you, no doubt, my friend, with your imaginative and ardent temperament," said Dubayet. "Besides, distance lends enchantment to the scene. But the Americans are a practical, sagacious, and coolheaded people. Remember that the constitution, about which you think there can be but one opinion, has met with violent opposition from a host of those

7

who were to live under its protecting shield. It became the subject of the fiercest discussions in the general assembly which framed it and in the State conventions. Do not forget that only three insignificant States, New Jersey, Delaware, and Georgia, accepted it unanimously, and that several of the most important States adopted it by a mere majority; five of them under an expressed expectation of specified amendments or modifications, while two States, Rhode Island and North Carolina, stood aloof a long time."

"Good God! What can be the objections?" exclaimed Lakanal.

"It would be too long to enumerate them," replied Dubayet. "Suffice it to say, that some feared that the Federal Government would have too little control over the individual States, and that their political connection would prove too weak to preserve order, prevent civil strife, and insure the duration of the republic; whilst others thought that it would be too strong for their separate existence, and would tend toward consolidation and despotism. Such diametrically antagonistic opinions are, as you see, entirely irreconcilable. Time will show which is right."

Lakanal shook his fist with wrath. "I am disappointed in the Americans," he said. "If they had chopped off the heads of a few leading traitors, it would have been a salutary warning to the rest, and things would have worked more harmoniously. But, on the contrary, they have encouraged those aristocrats by bestowing on them some of the highest offices within their gift. I, in their place, would have cut off the heads of Alexander Hamilton and John Adams."

"Softly, softly," interposed Dubayet. "To cut off men's heads is not the best way to convince them of their errors. It is rather a strange sort of eccentricity to kill people in order to teach them how to live and to improve. Surely, this is not what you will presume to call Christianity and republicanism. Besides, you are unjust to Alexander Hamilton and to John Adams. Both are staunch lovers of liberty and inflexible advocates of the rights of man, although not so incandescent and so ultra as you are. It is true that, in the Philadelphia convention, Alexander Hamilton held up the British constitution as a model to be approached as nearly as possible, by blending some of the advantages of monarchy with the republican form. It is true that he thinks that the constitution finally adopted is too low-toned; it is true that he fears it may prove feeble and inefficient ; but still, as a great statesman, which he undoubtedly is, he voted for it as the best attainable under existing circumstances, advocated it in the convention of his own State, and supported it in a series of essays, written conjunctively with Madison and Jay, and collectively known as the ' Federalist '—an admirable work, which, by-the-by, I advise you to procure and to study attentively. You must also bear in mind that it was mainly through his efforts, as a speaker and writer, that the constitution which you appreciate so warmly was ultimately adopted. I admit that many still consider him a monarchist at heart, and suspect him of a design to substitute royalty for the present form of government; but I think that in this supposition they do him injustice. He may doubt the healthful realization of republican theories, but I am convinced that he wishes to give them a fair trial, as long as there may be any chance of success."

"Very well," said Lakanal, "but I hope that you

will at least give up that uncouth compound of the plebeian born and of the would-be patrician—that puritanic worshipper of aristocracy — yclept John Adams. Have I not read with my own eyes his advice to Washington as to the stately forms which he wishes to be introduced in the performance of the functions of President? Does he not talk glibly of chamberlains, aides-de-camp, masters of ceremonies, and the like gilded gewgaws?" And he drew from his pocket a journal from which he read : " ' The office of President,' thus writes John Adams, ' by its legal authority defined in the constitution, has no equal in the world, excepting those only which are held by crowned heads; nor is the royal authority in all cases to be compared to it. The royal office in Poland is a mere shadow in comparison with it. The dogeship in Venice and the stadtholdership in Holland are not so much. Neither dignity nor authority can be supported in human minds collected into nations, or any great numbers, without a splendor and majesty in some degree proportioned to them. The sending and receiving of ambassadors is one of the most splendid and important prerogatives of sovereigns, absolute or limited, and this in our constitution is wholly in the President. If the state and pomp essential to this great department are not in a good degree preserved, it will be in vain for America to hope for consideration with foreign powers.'

" This is the impeachment I bring against him," continued Lakanal. "I now wait for your defense of the culprit I have arraigned."

"Go on," said Dubayet, "and read in the same journal that part of the writing in which Adams ingenuously confesses that 'his long residence abroad may have impressed him with views of things incompatible with the present temper and feelings of his countrymen,' and it is not, therefore, astonishing that Jefferson should have said of that great son of Massachusetts, 'that* the glare of royalty and nobility, during his mission to England, had made him believe their fascination a necessary ingredient in government.' But this does not prevent him from retaining the confidence of the people, and his merits are such that some allowance may well be made for trifling errors of judgment. Some irregularities of movements are observed even in the celestial bodies which adorn the vault of heaven, and yet do they cease for all that to be those luminous orbs at which we gaze with so much wonder?"

"The man to my taste," said Lakanal, "is Thomas Jefferson. He is a true patriot and republican. I heard him say: 'The terms† of Excellency, Honor, Worship, Esquire, should forever disappear from among us. I wish that of Mr. would follow them.' This I thought worthy of the best days of Rome, and I suggested that there should be no other prefix to names than that of citizen : 'Citizen Brutus, citizen Cassius, and citizen Jefferson.' He tapped me on the shoulder approvingly."

Aubert Dubayet smiled. "I have no doubt," he said, "that citizen Jefferson will contrive in due time to be President of the United States."

"Amen !" responded Lakanal, and the two friends parted.

Aubert Dubayet called on Tintin Calandro, who,

---

* Jefferson's Works, vol. ix., p. 97.

† Letter to Mr. Carmichael, Jefferson's Works, vol. iii., p. 88.

to his utter amazement, received him with some asperity of manner. "What is the matter?" inquired Dubayet, with tears in his eyes. "How can I have offended you?"

"Excuse me," said Tintin. "I am laboring under the effect of intense indignation. I can hardly forgive you for the part you have taken in establishing this new republic of America, which will become for the whole world worse than Pandora's box. Like the simoon, it will wither and level to the ground all that is noble and respected. What do you think I heard last night? The princess de Lamballe had the kindness to lend her musicians to Thomas Jefferson, the minister plenipotentiary of the republic, to perform at a festival which he gave. During one of those intervals when the orchestra was not called to play, I sauntered into the garden of the mansion, and I happened to be behind an arbor when the minister came with his secretary of legation, Colonel Humphreys, whom he was sending to Washington as bearer of dispatches, and who was to depart at day-break. He stopped near the spot where I was, and I heard him say, among other things, to the colonel, on dismissing him: 'Tell* our friends at home to besiege the throne of Heaven with eternal prayers to extirpate from creation this class of human lions, tigers, and mammoths, called kings, from whom, let him perish who does not say, good Lord deliver us.' What do you think of that? Saint Louis was a tiger; Isabella the Catholic and Blanche of Castile were hyenas; Titus and Marcus Aurelius were lions, and our own magnanimous Henry IV. a mammoth, because Provi-

---

* Jefferson's Letter to Colonel Humphreys.

dence destined them to be kings, emperors, and queens. They ought to have been exterminated to make way, I presume, to such blessings as this sacrilegious demagogue would shower upon the world; and all those who do not agree in opinion with this precious apostle of a new political religion ought to perish. So says Thomas Jefferson, the immaculate and the infallible, and the whip-in-hand democratic driver of a gang of poor black slaves who toil and breed for his exclusive benefit! Here is humility, humanity, and liberty for you with a vengeance! Accursed be that whelp of Satan! Accursed be that fiend, drunk on the fumes of his own ferocious and inordinate pride! I wish I could chain him forever at the bottom of the deepest and darkest dungeon of Christondom!"

"Alas!" exclaimed Dubayet, pressing his incensed friend in his arms, "what a future I foresee for France! I have just left the republican Lakanal. He talks of nothing but cutting off heads, and you, a royalist, would doom your opponents to the tender mercies of a Bastile. You are both the striking types of a population whose one half seeks liberty without knowing what it is, and whose other half strives to retain what it would be but justice and good policy to abandon."

CHAPTER XII.

LOUIS XVI. opened the States-General at Versailles on the 5th of May, 1789. But the nobility, the
clergy, and the commons, of which they were composed as three distinct orders, refused to meet as prescribed, and failed to work harmoniously. The commons, who were the most numerous and felt themselves the most powerful, determined to proceed with
their task without the other orders, should these refuse to meet them in a one and single assembly.
They further resolved to adopt another name than
that of States-General, which, in their opinion, was
no longer applicable. Mirabeau proposed that they
should call themselves "representatives of the people." This word *people* was the object of acrimonious
discussions.

"I care very little," said Mirabeau, on that occasion, "about the signification of words in the absurd
vocabulary of prejudice. I have tried to speak here
the language of liberty, and I relied on the example
given by the English and the Americans, who have
always honored the word *people*, and who have always consecrated it in their declarations of rights, in

their laws, and in their political institutions. When Chatham condensed into one word the charter of nations and said : ' *The majesty of the people*'; when the Americans asserted the natural rights of the *people* in opposition to the trashy disquisitions of superannuated publicists, they acknowledged and proclaimed all the signification, all the energy of that expression, to which liberty gives so much value. Are you afraid that it may be construed into the meaning of the Latin word *vulgus*, instead of *populus*, or the English word *mob*, or what, in our own language, all aristocrats, whether noble or not, insolently call the *canaille?*

"Representatives of the people, will you deign to answer me this question? Will you go back to your constituents and tell them that you have repudiated and ostracised the name *people*, which belongs to you all in common? Will you confess that, if you have not been ashamed of them, you have tried, however, to elude an appellation which is too low for your acceptance? Will you declare that you covet a more brilliant denomination than the one which they have conferred upon you? Do you not see that the name of 'representatives of the people' is necessary to you, because it endears you to the people—that imposing mass without which you would only be individualities and fragile rods that would be broken one by one? Do you not see that you need the name *people*, because it will make it known to the people that you have indissolubly bound your fate to theirs, and because it will teach them to look on you as the sole objects of their thoughts and their hopes?

"More skillful than we are, the Batavian heroes who won and established the liberty and independ-

7*

ence of their country, took the name of *beggars.*
They wanted no other name, because their tyrants
had contemptuously pretended to degrade them with
it, and that name, endearing them to that immense
mass which aristocracy and despotism loved to vilify,
was at the same time their strength, their glory, and
the guaranty of their success. The friends of liberty
choose the name which serves them the best, and not
the one which flatters them the most. They will call
themselves *malcontents* in America, *cowboys* in Switzerland, and *beggars* in the Low Countries. They will
adorn themselves with the injurious designations with
which they are reproved by their enemies; they will
thus deprive those enemies of the power of humiliating them with expressions which they will know how
to change into titles of honor!"

These sentiments were received with shouts of derision and disapprobation from several sides of the
Assembly, and from many of the spectators in the galleries. "Down with the demagogue!" cried one.
"Send him to harangue in the fish market," cried another. Vociferations followed vociferations, and the
confusion reached its height. "Silence!" thundered
Mirabeau, in the commanding tone of a master.
"Silence! Learn to discuss with calmness and with
freedom, if you wish to be free. I assume the whole
responsibility of what I have said. If there is any
guilt in my speech, welcome be the trial, the judgment, and the punishment! I will write down, sign,
and leave recorded on the desk of the President of
this Assembly every word that has fallen from my
lips."

After several days of stormy debates, the Third
Estate, or Commons, adopted the name of "National
Assembly."

The proceedings of the Assembly were thought by the king to encroach on the royal prerogative, and he ordered them in person to vacate the room which they occupied, to cease to call themselves the "National Assembly," and to form themselves, in conjunction with the nobility and clergy, into the States-General originally convened, each order deliberating and voting in separate chambers. The king was listened to in profound silence. On his departure, some members of the nobility and clergy who had joined the assembly followed him, but the true representatives of the people, the commoners, remained motionless and calm in their seats. The Marquis de Dreux Brézé, grand master of ceremonies, amazed at their disobedience, approached the President and said: "Gentlemen, you have heard the intentions of the king." Mirabeau rose, and replied with an inimitable dignity of tone and manner:

"Yes, Sir, we have heard the intentions which have been suggested to the king. But you, who can not be his organ before the National Assembly, you who have here neither a seat, nor a vote, nor the right of speech, are not qualified to put us in mind of the royal address. Nevertheless, to avoid all equivocation or delay, I declare to you that, if you have been authorized to make us leave this hall of our deliberations, you must ask for orders to employ force. Go, and tell your master that we are here by the power of the people, and that we can be driven hence only by the power of bayonets."

"Such are the sentiments of the Assembly," spontaneously shouted all his colleagues.

"Gentlemen," said the *abbé* Sieyes, "we are to-day what we were yesterday. Let us proceed with our deliberations."

From that solemn hour Mirabeau was the leader of
the Assembly and the most conspicuous man in
France. He became the idol of the people and the
terror of the court. One after the other the pillars
that supported the ancient monarchy went down
under the thunderbolts which he hurled with an un-
sparing hand. His eloquence was irresistible, his industry indefatigable. On the 8th of July, he de-
manded the formation of a national guard, and, on
the 9th, he caused to be adopted by the Assembly an
address to the king for the removal of the troops who
surrounded the legislative hall—which address was
pronounced to be a master-piece of composition, and
to possess all the excellencies of the highest order of
style. A few days after, the Bastile was taken by the
populace of Paris, and a revolution inaugurated. On
the king having notified the Assembly of his intention
to visit them, Mirabeau rose, and said in his most impressive manner: " Let a mute and mournful respect
be the welcome given to the monarch ; let kings find
a lesson in the silence with which they are met by
their subjects." On the 16th, he proposed an address
to the king asking for the dismissal of his ministers.
On the 25th, he spoke with much warmth of feeling
against the post-office violation of letters, " whatever
might be the authority which ordered or sanctioned
an act so infamous." Those who knew the Sardan-
apalian excesses in which he never ceased to indulge,
even in the midst of his intense labors, did not understand where he could find the time, and how he
could retain sufficient strength of body and mind, to
perform the Herculean task he had assumed. For
him there seemed to be no rest and no sleep ; from
the lap of voluptuousness he was always prompt to

spring up for action, fully equipped, never enervated by his orgies, and ever ready to bear down any opposition or obstacle with the club of his massive intellect.

Aubert Dubayet had been a constant attendant at all the sittings of the National Assembly. One day, when he was going out arm in arm with Mirabeau, "Well," said the latter personage, "what do you think of the tribune whom you heard for the first time at Aix?"

"I think," answered Dubayet, "that he has grown into the most formidable of Titans."

"Ah! ah!" exclaimed Mirabeau, evidently well pleased, "and that Titan will soon escalade Heaven. Such men as I am do not stop half way."

"Beware of Jove's thunderbolts."

"Pshaw! They are said, you know, to glance off harmlessly from laurels, and I shall take care to secure a sufficient supply of them to protect the mighty head which is destined to govern France. But, who is coming toward us? Is it not Mr. Gouverneur Morris, one of the ablest and most influential patriots of America, who has lately arrived here, bearing letters of introduction from Washington to distinguished persons in England, France, and Holland? I suppose that the President of the United States wishes to be correctly informed of what is passing on this side of the Atlantic, and has deputed, to that effect, an agent who enjoys his unlimited confidence. I am curious to hear what he has to say on our proceedings. You know him, of course; please to introduce me."

This was done as he desired. After a mutual exchange of civilities, Mirabeau said to Morris: "I hope, Sir, that like all Americans, you compliment us on our revolution."

"I hesitate, count," was the reply.* "Your nobles, your clergy, your people, are in motion. A spirit which has been dormant for generations starts up and stares about, ignorant of the means of obtaining, but evidently desirous to possess, its object; consequently active, energetic, easily led, but also easily, too easily misled. Such is the instinctive love of freedom which now grows warm in the bosom of your country. But I doubt whether you are not rushing too fast toward a state of things for which you are not prepared. Even Lafayette, prudent as he is, appears to me too republican for the genius of his country."

"Allow me to differ with you on this point," replied Mirabeau. "Lafayette is not too republican at present, I assure you. I know his views. He is now for a constitutional monarchy, approaching as near as possible that of Great Britain. But he is a weak man, too fond of popularity and newspaper flattery, and he may become too much of a republican in the course of time. He is not a leader, however, nor ever will be, whatever the appearances are to the contrary. Such men are made to follow; or, if they are followed, it is only after the fashion of an adopted flag; its value consists merely in its being emblematic."

"Lafayette and I," continued Morris, "are rather somewhat apart in our system of politics. He agrees better, I think, with Mr. Jefferson than with me, although he is not prepared to go as far as his friend in his democratic ideas. Still he, with all the other leaders of the liberal party here—for, with due deference to the opinion you have just expressed, I beg

---

* Morris' letter, 23d of February, 1789, to the French minister residing in New York.

leave to consider him a leader—is desirous, I say, of annihilating all distinctions of order. How far such views may be right, respecting mankind in general, is, I think, extremely problematical. But, with regard to your nation, I am sure it is wrong, and can not eventuate well."*

"I agree with you," said Mirabeau. "But those leaders you speak of shall not be allowed to have full sway, although I am sorry to say that they are urged on in their mad course by foreigners of distinction and influence who have but too much weight with them. For instance, that crack-brained and presumptuous fellow, Thomas Payne, who is now on a visit to your States, and your own countryman, Thomas Jefferson, who, by the by, is a man of a far superior calibre to that of his compeer in their partnership of demolition and Utopian reconstruction, are dangerous mischief-makers, and as active among our ultras as the most senseless of them all. This Thomas Payne has lately thought proper, forsooth, to pat me on the shoulder and approve some of my acts; and, by the way of encouragement, I presume, has sent me this extract from a letter addressed to him by Jefferson on the 11th of July, and in which this ambassador of yours reviews the proceedings of our Assembly. Permit me to read it; I happen to have it at hand:

"'The National Assembly,' says Jefferson, 'having shown through every stage of their transactions, coolness, wisdom, and resolution to set fire to the four corners of the kingdom, and to perish with it themselves, rather than relinquish an iota from their plan of a total change of government, are now in complete

---

* "Life of Gouverneur Morris," vol. i., p. 313.

and undisputed possession of the sovereignty. The executive and aristocracy are at their feet; the mass of the nation, the mass of the clergy and the army are with them; they have prostrated the old government and are now beginning to build one from the foundation.'"

Here Mirabeau paused, shook his bushy hair, squared his shoulders, swelled his chest, and threw his head back, as he was in the habit of doing when preparing to address an audience, and, striking his breast, said: "Mr. Morris, I, for one, as a member of the National Assembly, I, Honoré Gabriel de Riquetti, Count de Mirabeau, protest against such sentiments. I am too much of a Frenchman to set fire to the 'four corners of the kingdom and to perish with it,' rather than relinquish an iota from my plans. Far from calling it 'wisdom and coolness,' I would call it insanity, fury, and satanical pride. This is a kind of republicanism which I can not understand and do not appreciate. I would not, after the fashion and in imitation of Mr. Jefferson, desire to annihilate anybody, much less any considerable portion of mankind, for differing in opinion with me on morals, politics, or religion. I hear that there is a rumor of his being recalled by President Washington, and of his having a seat in the Cabinet. Should this be the case, I am much deceived if he is not destined to be a thorn in that great man's side, and if he does not sow in his native land the dragon's teeth, in the shape of social doctrines, which, producing a dead level of mediocrity, not free, however, from the heart-burnings of low ambition, envy, and malignity, will in the end produce anarchy and bloody struggles."

"I think," replied Morris, "that the good sense of

the Americans will preserve them against extremes, and that our free institutions may be relied on for centuries of existence without material modifications. But, although you may consider your revolution as achieved, although the authority of the king and nobility is completely subdued, yet I tremble for the new constitution you have in view. Instead of practical experience and soberness of desire, the French have all the romantic spirit and all the romantic ideas of government, which, happily for America, we were cured of before it was too late." *

"I have little respect," said Mirabeau, with his usual imprudence and haughty carelessness, "for most of the members of our Assembly. Some are fools, and many are knaves—poor stuff out of which to make proper charioteers for the Juggernaut car of revolution. But great national convulsions have always produced the man who is to end them. He will not be wanting to France."

"May it be so!" said Morris; "and if the French determine on a republic, may they have a Washington to conduct them through the experiment! By the by, as you have favored me with an extract from a letter, allow me to return you the compliment in communicating to you the views of men to whom you will concede some experience in revolution. It will show you how anxious your best friends and well-wishers are that you should behave with all the moderation, prudence, and foresight which this great crisis demands. I read from a letter addressed to me by General Washington :

---

* Gouverneur Morris' Letter to Washington, 31st of July, 1789.

"'I am persuaded,' he writes, 'that I express the sentiment of my fellow-citizens when I offer an earnest prayer that the revolution in France may terminate in the permanent honor and happiness of her government and people. That revolution is of so wonderful a nature, that the mind can hardly realize the fact. If it ends as our last accounts predict, that nation will be the most powerful and happy in Europe; but I fear, though it has gone triumphantly through its first paroxysm, it is not the last it has to encounter before matters are fully settled. In a word, the revolution is of too great a magnitude to be effected in so short a space, and with the loss of so little blood. The mortification of the king, the intrigues of the queen, and the discontent of the princes and the *noblesse*, will foment divisions, if possible, in that National Assembly; and they will unquestionably avail themselves of any *faux pas* in the formation of the constitution, if they do not give a more open, active opposition. In addition to these, the licentiousness of the people on one hand, and sanguinary punishments on the other, will alarm the best-disposed friends to the measure, and contribute not a little to the overthrow of their object. Great temperance, firmness, and foresight are necessary in the movements of that body. To forbear running from one extreme to the other is no easy matter; and should not this be the case, rocks and shelves, not visible at present, may wreck the vessel, and give a higher-toned despotism than the one which existed before.'"

Whilst Morris was reading, Mirabeau had taken off his hat, and listened, or pretended to listen, as reverentially as a disciple of Islam would to a firman from the Prophet. After the reading was over, "No man," he said, "was ever more disposed, Mr. Morris, to bow lower than I am to the moral grandeur and virtuous superiority of that sublime being; but I confess that I did not give him credit for so much political sagacity and foresight. He truly predicts what may happen to the tempest-tossed vessel, should the right pilot be not at the helm. If I perish, Mr. Morris, the ill-advised king will be dethroned; from a shivered throne to the scaffold there is but one step, and then—a republic, and a Cromwell. But let us hope that I shall live to direct the storm and ride the whirlwind."

Morris, unaccustomed to the candor of Mirabeau's boasting and to his usual expressions of overweening belief in himself, could not conceal a slight degree of astonishment, and smiled at the ingenuousness of the gigantic presumption which did not hesitate to manifest so openly such sentiments of self-appreciation and confidence. He drew another letter from his pocket, saying: "This one is from Hamilton to Lafayette, who has submitted it to my perusal:

"'As a friend to liberty and mankind,' writes Hamilton, 'I rejoice in the efforts which you are making to establish it, while I fear much for the final success of the attempts, for the fall of those who are engaged in it, and for the danger, in case of success, of innovations greater than will consist with the real felicity of your nation. I dread disagreements among those who are now united, about the nature of your constitution; I dread the vehement character of your people, whom, I fear, you may find more easy to bring on, than to keep within proper bounds after you have put them in motion. I dread the interested refractoriness of your nobles, who can not all be gratified, and who may be unwilling to submit to the requisite sacrifices; and I dread the reveries of your philosophic politicians, who appear in the moment to have great influence, and who, being mere speculatists, may aim at more refinement than suits either with human nature, or the composition of your nation.'" *

"I flatter myself," said Mirabeau, "that we shall not justify the apprehensions of our friends. In the meantime, Mr. Morris, allow me to thank you for the gratification and information which I have derived from this interview. I am happy to have made your acquaintance, and I beg leave to cultivate it to my profit." The gentlemen bowed and separated.

Morris had hardly departed, when there came by the brilliant equipage of one of the most popular actresses of the epoch. When she saw Mirabeau, she ordered her coachman to stop, and beckoned to him and to his companion. They both walked to the carriage door. Mirabeau introduced Aubert Dubayet. "Count," she said to Mirabeau, "you have not forgotten, I suppose, that we dine to-day at the Duke of Orleans'? But before we meet at the *Palais Royal*, I have something strictly private to confide to you; step into my carriage, with your friend's permission." Then, addressing Dubayet, she said, with the sweetest of smiles: "I hope you forgive the liberty I take. I am spoiled, and used to all sorts of liberties. But I'll not apologize now; I'll wait for another occasion—for instance, on Friday next, when you must sup with me. The count will accompany you; I take no refusal. *Au revoir*"; and the equipage, with its four splendid English bays—a present of the Duke of Orleans—dashed away, with a full load of beauty and eloquence, but, alas, with very little of virtue for ballast.

---

* Hamilton's Works, vol. v., p. 440.

CHAPTER XIII.

THE SUPPER OF THE ACTRESS—A SCENE BETWEEN MIRABEAU AND THE DUKE OF ORLEANS.

LEFT alone, Aubert Dubayet was crossing the garden of the Tuileries, when he met Lafayette. "Whither are you going?" inquired the marquis.

"To dinner," replied Dubayet.

"Then it shall be at my house. Come, let us go."

On the way, Dubayet related to Lafayette a part of the conversation he had just heard between Gouverneur Morris and Mirabeau. "So," said Lafayette, "Morris thinks that I and my friends are too republican for France."

"And I confess," observed Dubayet, "that I somewhat agree with him."

"You are both in error," continued Lafayette. "You and Morris have only witnessed the surface of things; it is for me to explain the interior. Mirabeau is right: I am for a monarchy, not for a republic. The object which is aimed at by the Duke de Larochefoucauld, Mr. Condorcet, myself, and some others, who consider themselves leaders, is to obtain for France a constitution nearly resembling that of England, which we regard as the most perfect model of government hitherto known. To accomplish this, it is necessary to diminish very essentially the power of the king; but our object is to retain the throne, in great majesty, as the first branch of the legislative

power, but retrenching its executive power in one
point, which, though very important in the British
Crown, we think is needless here. The peerage of
France is already so numerous that we would take
from our king the right of creating new peers, except
in cases where old families may become extinct.*
To all this, the king, who is one of the best of men,
and sincerely desirous of the happiness of his people,
most freely and cordially consents."

" How would you constitute your house of peers ? "
said Dubayet.

" We wish a house of peers," replied Lafayette,
" with powers of legislation similar to that of England,
restricted to one hundred members, to be elected by
the whole body of the nobility from among themselves, in the same manner as the Scotch peers are in
the British Parliament."†

" And the plebeians—the great mass of the people," inquired Dubayet, " what of them ? "

" We wish also," continued Lafayette, " as the
third branch of the legislative body, a house of representatives, chosen by the great body of the people
from among themselves, in such a ratio as shall not
make the house too numerous ; and this branch of
our project meets unanimous approbation. ‡

" How happy I am," exclaimed Dubayet, " to hear
that such a plan is feasible ! "

" Feasible, yes," remarked Lafayette, " but will it
be carried into execution ? Unhappily, there is one
powerful and wicked man, who, I fear, will destroy
this beautiful fabric of human happiness—the Duke

---

* Colonel Trumbull's Report to Washington.
† Ibid.   ‡ Ibid.

of Orleans. He does not, indeed, possess talent to carry into execution a great project, but he possesses immense wealth, and France abounds in marketable talents. Every city and town has young men eminent for abilities, particularly in the law, ardent in character, eloquent, ambitious of distinction, but poor.¹ These are the instruments which the duke may command by money, and they will do his bidding. His hatred of the royal family can be satisfied only by their ruin. His ambition, probably, leads him to aspire to the throne." *

" And do you suspect Mirabeau to be one of the tools of the duke?" was the question asked by Dubayet.

"No," replied Lafayette; "it is the duke who is the tool of Mirabeau, whilst the duke thinks he is using that extraordinary man to his own profit. They are now acting together, but their league will not last long. I have heard Mirabeau say that the duke had talents, but had not the consciousness of right and wrong, so absolute was his depravity. A creature, whom Mirabeau thinks so vile and for whom he has so much contempt, can not really exercise influence over one who, although corrupt himself, yet is susceptible of enthusiasm for all that is noble and virtuous. Such is Mirabeau. He will not trust the duke, and they will quarrel. Should, then, the king or queen tempt his ambition, I believe that they will secure his mighty support ; for Mirabeau is an aristocrat at heart, and is for a constitutional monarchy whose Chatham he will aim to be."

" I have heard the duke accused of being, with

---

* Colonel Trumbull's Report to Washington.

Mirabeau, the instigator of the late riots and mas-
sacres. Do you believe it?" inquired Dubayet.

"I am certain of it, so far as regards the Duke of
Orleans. As to Mirabeau, considering his present
relations with that personage, I am afraid that he is
not free from all responsibility, for he needs anarchy
to make himself necessary, and to have the merit of
re-establishing order at the opportune moment. You
saw the other day, in the mob, men who were called
les Marseillais, les patriotes par excellence; you saw
them particularly active and audacious in stimulating
the discontented artisans and laborers, who composed the great mass of the mob, to acts of violence
and ferocity; those men are, in truth, desperadoes,
assassins from the south of France, familiar with murder, robbery, and every atrocious crime, who have
been brought up to Paris by the money of the duke,
for the very purpose for which you saw them employed, of mingling in all mobs, and exciting the passions of the people to frenzy." *

"Good God!" exclaimed Dubayet, "this is horrible. What will be the end of it?"

"This is the first act of the drama," continued Lafayette. "The second will be to influence the elections, on the dissolution of this Assembly, which is
already talked of, and to fill the next one with ardent, inexperienced, desperate, ambitious young men,
who, instead of proceeding to discuss calmly the details of the political plan of which I have given you
the general outline for the establishment of a permanent constitutional monarchy, and to carry it quietly
into operation, will, under disguise of zeal for the

---

* Colonel Trumbull's Report to Washington.

people and abhorrence of the aristocrats, drive every measure to extremity, for the purpose of throwing the affairs of the nation into utter confusion, when the master spirit may accomplish his ultimate purpose." *

A few days afterward Mirabeau took Aubert Dubayet to supper at the house of his friend, Mademoiselle Guimard, according to the invitation which that actress had given. There were assembled most of the celebrated artists who belonged to the fair sex; and, on the masculine side, there was a gathering of nobles, of literary and scientific men, and of some members of the National Assembly. Mirabeau, with ineffable ease, as if a matter of course, and in the exercise of an indisputable right, took hold of the conversation, to which he gave the lead. All the honors of the evening were for him. He burned at random, with a profuse hand, coarse and delicate incense and perfumes for the women, and he showered upon them such pearls from his intellectual casket as he thought suitable to their tastes. He made love to them all in turn, and amused them with the most piquant anecdotes on the most renowned beauties of ancient and modern times, drawing largely on his imagination when historical truth failed him. With the men he skipped from subject to subject, frivolous or austere, but remaining always equal to himself and superior to all. It seemed as if, by a tacit consent, every one talked merely to draw him out. It was past midnight, when, leaving the supper-table, the guests moved to the brilliantly illuminated saloons, where parties who had dropped in as visitors in the course of the evening,

---

* Colonel Trumbull's Report to Washington.

8

were engaged in different kinds of game whilst expecting the fair hostess and her guests. Mirabeau was not one of the least eager to try his luck at the most hazardous of the games. He betted heavily and lost accordingly, but with the most superb indifference, notwithstanding the natural impetuosity of his temperament, and although he was evidently heated by wine. One would have supposed that he had the Indies at his disposal. He had at last a lucky run. One of the opera queens of the day happened to approach him. "Ah! love," he said, "is that you at my elbow? How splendid you were last Thursday in the part of Cleopatra! It was true to the life; the illusion was complete. Allow me to present this to you (pointing to the large glittering pile of gold before him) in the name of Marc Antony, that stout warrior and boon companion whom I love, because he had vices which were very much like my own."

At that moment, the Duke of Orleans was announced. He entered with a flushed face, and with the appearance of having just risen from one of his habitual orgies. He bowed to the right and left with a sort of haughty carelessness, after having kissed the hand of *La Guimard*, as she was called, and walked to Mirabeau. "Count," he said, "we had some difference together the other day. It has lasted long enough, and I have come to make it up. With the permission of our gentle hostess, pray, do me the favor to grant me the pleasure of your company in a private room. I have no doubt that a few minutes' conversation will be sufficient to re-establish harmony between us, and that we shall be able to proceed in our great undertaking of reform in France, with a mutual friendly understanding, as in the past."

Mirabeau rose, and with an ominous scowl on his brow followed the prince. " Let us station ourselves near the door of the apartment," said Mademoiselle Guimard to Dubayet. "I am afraid of the consequences of this interview in the condition in which both are. The duke and the count quarrelled violently the other day; and since, Mirabeau has told me that the prince was too rotten and too unreliable to be trusted; that it was disreputable, as he found out, for him to be connected with such a character, and that he would wash his hands of him."

La Guimard and Dubayet sat on a sofa that was near the folding doors behind which the two great personages had disappeared. After a little while it seemed evident to them that there was an angry altercation going on inside. The voices became louder and louder, and even assumed a threatening tone. Greatly alarmed, the actress opened the door; and, standing on the threshold with Dubayet, said: "I beg your royal highness, and I beg you, count, to pardon me for having intruded on your privacy. But I come to warn you that, if you do not beware, your conversation will be overheard."

" By the living God ! " exclaimed Mirabeau, " I care not a pinch of snuff, if what I have said, or intend to say, is heard by the whole world ! On the contrary, I should be glad of it. Therefore, walk in, both of you ; walk in, by all means. Know ye that this prince has been reproaching me, forsooth, with being a disobedient slave—a slave whom, as he fancies, he has bought with five hundred thousand livres which he presented to me a few days ago, and which I have already squandered. Ha! ha! a rich idea! Such a man as I am may condescend to take such a sum for services rendered, or to be rendered, but does not stoop to be sold. You forget that, *Monseigneur.* Mirabeau is Mirabeau, and ever remains his own master. I might think it worth while to spend your whole fortune to further your own purposes and mine, but after my own fashion, be it understood. Does your royal highness imagine that all your millions concentrated into one heap and offered to me, could make Philip of Orleans, first prince of the blood, master of Honoré Gabriel Riquetti, Count de Mirabeau? If you do, you have yet to learn that there is a royalty of intellect and of soul, which is better entitled to command than any authority derived from the divine right of kings." This was said with great vehemence, and with a contemptuous sneer.

The prince, who was evidently trying to regain his self-possession, which he seemed to have lost in this interview, said calmly: " You know, Mr. de Mirabeau, that these titles of prince and royal highness are no longer accepted by me, because they do not agree with the position which I have taken as the inflexible advocate of liberty, equality, and fraternity among men. You know that it is long since I have ceased to blush to acknowledge as my father Montfort, the coachman."

At these words, Dubayet felt as if his blood froze in his veins, and La Guimard uttered a smothered shriek. Mirabeau measured the prince with a withering glance from head to foot; and, turning round to the two spectators of this scene, said: " You have become pale, Dubayet; and you, dear Guimard, are near fainting. But keep up; keep up, and do not believe what this man says. In the name of all honest wives and mothers, I tell him that he lies. The truth is, that having ceased to fawn on Louis and on Marie Antoinette, who repudiate his homage, he has become a courtier, or rather a valet, in the ante-chambers of that new sovereign—the people—whose reign has been lately inaugurated, and in whose court he thinks that it would be·held a higher degree of nobility to be the son of a coachman, than of a royal duke. But it is a sheer pretence—a princely joke—that is all. Like his ancestor, the Regent, he is fond of boasting of more vices and crimes than have fallen to his share, although he is bad and infamous enough to satisfy himself in that respect, Heaven knows."*

The face of Orleans, which was already inflamed by his too liberal potations, became purple with shame and rage, and his eye, which had naturally a sinister expression, assumed the deadly look of an infuriated basilisk.

" Mr. de Mirabeau," he said, " such insolence would well deserve the whip."

Mirabeau struck three times his athletic and sonorous chest. "The whip to me! *Monseigneur*," he exclaimed ; " to me, the real king of France by the consecration and anointment of the people, whose majesty and power are incorporated in me as their representative ! This is another of your jokes, but a silly one, decidedly. Leave the whip to your pretended father, the coachman. It is the sword that befits your royal hand ; but I forget that you never had the courage to use one. There was in France but one prince who ever dared to use the whip. He was the greatest of the House of Bourbon, and named himself Louis XIV. It was on a grand occasion ; it was

---

* Jules Janin.

when, starting for the chase, in the pride of youth
and power, he drove before him, whip in hand, a disobedient parliament.   But the times have changed,
and the whip has passed into the hands of the nation.
It wields it, *Monseigneur*, with a firm and rough arm,
and, should it please God, you will feel it one day,
with a vengeance!   Already, if my memory serves
me right, it has been laid rudely across the face of
your royal race ; for you certainly can not have forgotten to whom the handsome and irresistible Lauzun
used to say: 'Louise D'Orleans, pull off my boots.'
I pray, therefore, your royal highness no longer to
speak of the whip.   Perhaps there remains yet a fortnight of respite, during which you may be permitted
to threaten your lacqueys with such punishment.
Lose no time in availing yourself of the opportunity,
and hasten back to the enjoyment of that luxury in
your palace."

The duke seemed petrified with astonishment.
Mirabeau, turning away from him, took two or three
rapid strides through the room, to and fro, from one
end to the other, like an angry lion in a cage.   Then,
suddenly halting, he said to La Guimard and to Dubayet, whilst he pointed at the prince with an insolent gesture which was natural to him: "It is strange
that this man should claim the right to change his
hereditary name, when he has sufficiently degraded it
to suit his taste!   It is strange that he should presume to lay aside his father to take up another, as I
would doff my coat!   It is strange that he should
arrogate the right to defame an honest coachman who
has done him nothing to deserve such treatment!   It
is passing strange that he should insult the memory
of his mother in our presence, as he has insulted his

wife, that woman so accomplished, so virtuous, so
chaste, so thoroughly a Christian, whom he forced to
appear, terrified and crossing herself, amidst a profane assembly of Freemasons! Perhaps it is due to
a certain old habit of princes—the habit of offering
insults, in the way of fun—a habit which time has
not yet corrected, it seems, and of which I hope that
we have seen, to-night, the last exhibition. Hence,
let us have patience."

The Duke of Orleans must have stood in absolute
need of Mirabeau, for he suddenly put on an air of
cordiality and said: "Bah! Bah! Genius has its
privileges and its infirmities, which must be respected.
Genius has its fits of insanity, and this is one of them,
but it claims the privilege to be forgotten, and it shall
be. Come, come, let us be friends, Mirabeau. Besides, we need each other for the good of France,"
and he tendered his hand.

Mirabeau stepped back. "Touch me not," he said,
"if you really are the adulterous son of a coachman;
know, Sir, that I am, and never will cease to be, of
noble birth, and that there can be nothing in common
between the bastard of Montfort and the legitimate
descendant of a hundred gentlemen."

After this explosion of wrath, he rushed out, followed by La Guimard and Dubayet. He was walking rapidly toward the entrance door of the house,
apparently to leave it, when he met one of his friends
of the National Assembly, who, on seeing him, exclaimed: "Thank Heaven! I find you at last. I
have been looking for you in all your accustomed
haunts, and I am out of breath. I have been dispatched in haste to tell you that the Assembly has
resumed the discussion of the projected decree re-

pudiating the national debt and proclaiming the bankruptcy of France. Notwithstanding your repeated efforts to prevent it, and the irrefutable arguments which you have already presented, it is believed that the measure will be carried. They will take the vote in less than an hour."

" O, the incorrigible jackanapes !" exclaimed Mirabeau. " Is it thus that they avail themselves of my absence to perpetrate all sorts of mischief ! Can I not allow myself a moment of relaxation ? Guimard, my dear, take me to your toilet room. Let me wash my face and remove the traces of my having enjoyed too much your exquisite supper. I have, I am afraid, been too partial to your rare wines. By-the-by, who is your purveyor? I must patronize him."

La Guimard took his arm, and, whilst leading him to her boudoir, whispered to him with all the signs of the utmost terror: "Mirabeau, you have mortally offended the duke. Beware of assassination."

"Pshaw! I fear him not," replied Mirabeau, contemptuously. "He, assassinate ! No, he can not rise up even to that. But,"——and after a pause, he added : " He is not above using the poison of the Borgias. That is low enough to reach his level."

After he had finished his ablutions and emptied a vial of perfume, he said to Dubayet : "Let us go; come with me; let us show to that assembly of asses the tusks of the wild boar. It is time."

Whilst Mirabeau's carriage was rattling toward the National Assembly, he said to Dubayet : "The fools! They are for a general bankruptcy, and do not see that in so doing they would cut their own throats and smother the revolution and liberty. Far from declaring France in a state of bankruptcy, far from wiping out the public debt, we must nurse and naturalize that blessing. The present deficit in the treasury is the germ of our intended constitution. No debt—no revolution—no constitution. Should the public debt be repudiated, the working classes—and they constitute the bulk of the nation—will be relieved and will rejoice at it. They will gain everything by it and lose nothing. They will clap their hands at the fate of the financiers and creditors of the State, whom they consider as blood-suckers, and who will be ruined. But the condition of the people will be greatly ameliorated, because the taxes will be much reduced, and prosperity will revive in every department of industry; there will be no longer any embarrassment in the way of the government, and France, free from its crushing burden, will start anew in the arena, like a spirited horse, well fed and refreshed. But then the National Assembly will cease to be a necessity. It will be dissolved, and what will become of the projected constitution and of the sovereignty of the people?"

"And of the sovereignty of Mirabeau?" added Dubayet, tapping him on the shoulder.

"True," replied Mirabeau, "I had forgotten that. France must have a constitutional government like England. Louis must continue to be a good-natured, honest drone on the throne; Marie Antoinette—who, by the by, is the worthy daughter of Maria Theresa, and has all the energy of a man—must be contented to be the queen of fashion; and Honoré Gabriel de Mirabeau will be the constitutional Richelieu of the monarchy, with an obedient parliament at his feet. Therefore, down with repudiation, and long live the national debt!"

8*

CHAPTER XIV.

THE TRIUMPH OF ELOQUENCE—A GLANCE AT THE FUTURE OF THE UNITED STATES BY MIRABEAU.

IT was about three o'clock in the morning when Mirabeau entered the hall of the National Assembly, which was unusually silent. The debates had ceased, and the members had agreed to cast a final vote on the vital question of national bankruptcy, which had kept them so long in a state of intense excitement. They looked exceedingly fatigued and broken-down ; some of them were sleeping in their seats, and leaning against the shoulders of their neighbors. The lights were burning dim, as if the oil which fed them was giving way. The clerk, slowly arranging and putting in order the papers on his desk, was languidly preparing to call the names and ascertain the votes. In the galleries occupied by spectators, males and females, there seemed to be prevailing a sort of torpor, the result of extreme exhaustion and *ennui*. When Mirabeau appeared, an instantaneous transformation of the dull scene took place. It was as if a current of electricity had suddenly struck every human being there present—first, a low, confused murmur ; then a general movement, followed by a wild burst of acclamation. "Ho! ho! here is Mirabeau!" was heard on all sides. "Hurrah for Mirabeau!" shouted the galleries. "Down with him!" shrieked some voices.

"Long live our dear gossip, our * little mother Mirabeau!" cried a troop of queans of the fish market.
"Come to us, gossip dear, we want to kiss you."
"Champion of the people," roared a butcher with
bare arms, shaking with fury his enormous fist, "we
have our eyes on thee. Welcome, and at work; we
are impatient. When wilt thou send to the shambles
the royal ox with the rest of the blooded cattle that
follow his heels?" The President of the Assembly
in vain endeavored to re-establish order. One of the
members, with a magnificent head on shoulders belonging to a monstrously large body which looked as
if it weighed five hundred pounds, rose in a fit of uncontrollable anger. "Silence, stupid multitude," he
shouted. "Respect your betters, *vile canaille*. Long
live the king! Down with the rag-pickers!" One of
his colleagues in front of him muttered something
which was imperfectly heard. "Sir," said the colossus,
"if you are not satisfied, I shall be happy to give you
any satisfaction you please." Then raising his head
defiantly and looking at some one in the galleries
above, who was vociferating: "Down with the Austrian hag, Marie Antoinette," he shouted, pointing at
the man: "Sergeant-at-arms, fetch me here that cook,
I want to cut off his ears and pin them to his dirty
apron." During all this uproar, Mirabeau, who
seemed to take no notice of it, was slowly moving
toward the tribune, passing between the benches on
which sat the members, bowing right and left, shaking
hands, and sometimes stopping to say a few words.
When reaching this mountain of flesh who was in a
state of volcanic eruption and who stood right in his

---

* Notre petite mère Mirabeau.

way, and blocked it, as it were, Mirabeau greeted him cordially, saying: "Good-morning, Viscount, you seem to be very mad. What is the matter?"

"Yes, I am angry with you and your worthy friends, and I really don't see how it can be otherwise," replied Mirabeau the younger. "Faith! What a rare collection of tatterdemalions of both sexes! I compliment you, brother, on your refined taste. Truly, you must be very proud of your alliance with shoemakers, tailors, and cooks; you, the eldest and the head of the Riquettis! I have the right to protest, I think, and I do protest in the name of an indignant family."

"Hush! hush! dear brother, be calm. I am astonished to see you irritated against shoemakers and tailors, whom you never condescend to pay, and against cooks, whom you generally appreciate so highly. One of them must have given you to-night a very bad supper which has soured on your titanic stomach."

"Count," retorted the other, "if we had not come out of the same maternal womb, I would certainly beg you to afford me the opportunity of slitting your conspicuous nose."

"Pooh! pooh! Boniface, are you not ashamed? You must be drunk, as usual. Shall I forever have to reproach you for that unbecoming vice?"

"By the holy rood! How unjust and niggardly you are, Gabriel!" replied the viscount with a chuckle. "Do you grudge me one single vice, when you have taken all the others as your inheritance, by virtue, I suppose, of your right of primogeniture?"

Mirabeau turned to the by-standers and said, cynically: "Gentlemen, I am sorry for the viscount. He pales before me, and is envious. In any other family he would have been a scapegrace and a genius. In ours he is an honest man and a fool."

There was loud laughter and clapping of hands all round at this keen encounter of wits between the brothers, but it was immediately followed by a silence as profound as that of the tomb. Mirabeau had ascended the rostrum. He remained motionless for a while, with his arms folded over his breast, and his massive head bent down as if in deep thought. Then, looking at the president, and from the president turning his eyes to the now stilled crowd, which he surveyed as if studying his ground, he said : " O, representatives of the people, must I again address you on a subject on which I have repeatedly spoken, and which I thought exhausted ? " At first, he seemed to seek for ideas and words; his utterance was slow and measured, and accompanied with no gesticulation whatever. There was hesitation in his manner, and something which indicated a lassitude of mind and body, not unpleasant in its effect on the audience. It elicited sympathy, for every one felt that deep and true must be the convictions of the orator, who, in their defense, entering the arena when evidently unprepared, risked his fame in his anxiety for the triumph of his principles, and who, forgetful of self, thought only of the great cause which he advocated. But soon inspiration came, the waters gushed from the rock, and Mirabeau made against the proposed decree of national bankruptcy a speech, which was considered by those who heard it, one of the grandest efforts of human eloquence. The Assembly rose to their feet spontaneously, and almost unanimously rejected the measure which, one moment before, they

Molé, the first actor of Paris, was present. He had come at the head of a deputation of comedians to present a petition. Attracted by the importance of the debate, he had determined to see it out, and had remained the whole night at the Assembly with a party of friends. He was intensely excited by the speech of Mirabeau. In a fit of enthusiasm he rushed to the spot where the orator stood in the midst of a crowd who were complimenting him, and exclaimed : "O, count, you are the prince of eloquence. What an oration ! With what exquisite and perfect emphasis you delivered it ! How dramatic you are ! How sub-lime is your voice ! What variety, what pathos in its intonations ! You have missed your vocation ; it was the stage. You should have been one of us." The actor had hardly paid this tribute of admiration, when he became aware of its singularity. He smiled, blushed, and looked a little confused. But Mirabeau was evidently very much pleased ; for it was in his nat-ure to hunger and thirst after praise of any kind. One of his friends, who had remarked that food of this qual-ity, administered largely, or sparingly, thin, lean, or fat, delicately or coarsely cooked, was always accept-able to his greedy appetite, had, one day, quaintly said to him : " Mirabeau, you would breakfast on an elephant and sup on a flesh-worm, if presented in the shape of flattery."

" Come on; day begins to dawn," said Mirabeau to Dubayet. " I have brought you here ; I must take you to your home. You will give me a light break-fast, a cup of coffee, one egg, and a toast. I feel ex-hausted and must have some refreshment ; for I have something yet to do which will not permit me to go to bed before noon, and I must be up in the evening at six, as I have to meet an important personage at seven."

The two friends were soon seated at the breakfast-table. "Well," said Mirabeau, "how do you like my speech of last night, fresh from La Guimard's toilet-room? I hope it did not smell of it, and was not that clap-trap, would-be imitation of eloquence which puts me in mind of the thunders and tempests of the opera, where that great actress reigns in undisputed supremacy. I hate all that is not genuine."

"By Jupiter, it was real thunder, and one of your most splendid efforts. You have trampled bankruptcy under your heel, saved French honor, and consolidated the national debt. I wish that you had been heard by the whole Congress of the United States, for they are quarrelling about assuming, or not, on behalf of the General Government, the debts contracted by the several States in the revolutionary struggle. The contest waxes so hot that there is some apprehension of a dissolution of the newly-formed Union."

"Already! I did not expect it so soon, whilst their honeymoon still shines on the horizon," said Mirabeau, dropping a lump of sugar into his coffee. "Do the sovereignty of the respective States and that of the Federal Government experience some difficulty in fusing together, like this sugar and coffee which now form a most delicious whole, truly?" and he sipped complacently the smoking beverage, while his eye glanced at Dubayet with a rather ironical expression.

"The accord would be perfect," answered Dubayet, "if the opposite parties listened to the wholesome advice given to them by Washington. I call your attention to this newspaper which I have just received from America. It contains an interesting letter from him to one of his friends, Dr. Stuart, of Virginia. But, before you peruse it, let me give you some explanation about the bone of contention.* Hamilton, the secretary of the treasury, in his official report, has urged the assumption by the General Government, of the separate debts of the States, contracted for the common cause, and recommends that a like provision be made for their payment as for the payment of those of the Union. They were, he says, all contracted in the struggle for national independence, not for the independence of any particular part. No more money would be required for their discharge as federal than as State debts. Money could be raised more readily by the Federal Government than by the States, and all clashing and jealousy between the States and federal creditors would thus be prevented. No doubt there was a reason which had great weight with him, though he did not bring it into consideration in his report, for fear, probably, of offending the jealousy of State sovereignty, dormant, but not extinct, and which was, that it would tend to unite the States financially, as they were united politically, and strengthen the central government by rallying capitalists around it, subjecting them to its influence, and rendering them agents of its will. He recommends, therefore, that the entire mass of the debt be funded, the Union made responsible for it, and taxes imposed for its liquidation. He suggests, moreover, the expediency, for the greater security of the debt and punctuality in the payment of interest, that the domestic creditors, if not the foreign ones, submit to an

---

* W. Irving's " Life of Washington," p. 53, vol. v.

abatement of accruing interest. This plan is opposed
with great earnestness, especially the point of assuming the State debts, as tending to consolidation, as
giving an undue influence to the General Government, and as being of doubtful constitutionality. The
financial union of the States is strongly reprobated,
not only on the floor of Congress, but in different
parts of the Union, as fraught with political evil. The
Northern and Eastern States favor the plan, but the
Southern States, with the exception of South Carolina, manifest a determined opposition, because it is
supposed that the funding of the State debts would
chiefly benefit the Northern States, in which is the
entire capital of the country. A letter to Washington from his friend, Dr. Stuart, whom I have already
mentioned, spoke with alarm of the jealous belief
growing up in Virginia, averring that the Northern
and Eastern States were combining to pursue their
own exclusive interests. Many, he observed, who had
heretofore been warm supporters of the new government, were changing their sentiments, from a conviction of the impracticability of the union with States
whose interests were so dissimilar. Now for Washington's reply."

Mirabeau took up the journal which had been
placed before him by Dubayet, and read aloud: " I
am sorry such jealousies as you speak of should be
gaining ground and possessing the minds of the
Southern people ; but admit the fact which is alleged
as the cause of them, and give it full scope, does it
amount to more than was known to every man of information before, at, and since, the adoption of the
new constitution? Was it not always believed that
there are some points which peculiarly interest the

Eastern States? And did any one who reads human
nature, and more especially the character of the Eastern people, conceive that they would not pursue those
interests steadily by a combination of their force?
Are there not other points which equally concern the
Southern States? If these States are less tenacious
of their interest, or if, while the Eastern move in a
solid phalanx to effect their views, the Southern are
always divided, which of the two is most to be
blamed? That there is diversity in the Union, none
has denied. That this is the case, also, in every State,
is equally certain; and that it even extends to the
counties of individual States, can be as readily proved;
instance the southern and northern parts of Virginia,
the upper and lower parts of South Carolina. Have
not the interests of these always been at variance?
Witness the county of Fairfax. Have not the interests of the people of that county varied, or the inhabitants been taught to believe so? These are well-
known truths, and yet it did not follow that separation was to result from the disagreement.

" To constitute a dispute, there must be two parties. To understand it well, both parties, and all the
circumstances, must be fully heard; and, to accommodate differences, temper and much forbearance are
requisite. Common danger brought the States into
confederacy, and on their union our safety and independence depend. A spirit of accommodation was
the basis of the present constitution. Can it be expected, then, that the Southern or Eastern parts of
the empire will succeed in all their measures? Certainly not. But I will readily grant that more points
will be carried by the latter than the former, and for
the reason which has been mentioned: namely, that

in all great national questions, they move in unison, whilst the others are divided. But I ask again, which is most praiseworthy, those who see and will steadily pursue their interests, or those who can not see, or seeing, will not act wisely? And I will ask another question of the highest magnitude in my mind, to-wit: if the Northern and Eastern States are dangerous in *union*, will they be less so in *separation?* If self-interest is their governing principle, will it forsake them, or be restrained by such an event? I hardly think it would. Then, independently of other considerations, what would Virginia, and such other States as might be inclined to join her, gain by a separation? Would they not, most unquestionably, be the weaker party?"

After having read, Mirabeau, dropping the paper on the table, said: "Very sensible indeed, and practical——in Utopia. But in this world of ours, constituted as it is, it will be the voice in the wilderness. Washington, when he founded his model republic, forgot to reckon with the passions of men. These are their rulers, and not cold-blooded reason, or virtue. Before the American confederacy is one hundred years old, there will be separation, or an attempt at separation."

"Why?" inquired Dubayet.

"Because, as Washington admits, their interests are at variance in a vast territory, where they are far more irreconcilable than in a small one, and because, as Washington again admits, the Southern States are weaker than their associates. If they are weaker, they will be oppressed; and, being oppressed, they will try to resist, and redress their wrongs, if they are high-spirited people, as I suppose them to be; and if they use force, as they will probably be tempted to do, they will be crushed."

" Why ? "

"You ask me why again. Washington tells you: because they are the weaker party."

" What then?" said Dubayet.

"When the Southern States are crushed," continued Mirabeau, "the confederation will become consolidation and centralization. The States, although they may be allowed to retain nominally their sovereignty, as a bauble for their childish vanity to play with, will in reality be mere provinces ruled by an omnipotent central government. Then the deluge, my friend, and good-bye to liberty. A government of majorities, under which there is no protection for minorities, except such as is granted according to the good pleasure of king numbers, is the most frightful of all despotisms. Everything, of course, will continue to be done in the name of liberty, as, under the Cæsars in Rome, the will of the imperial master was manifested in the name of the Roman Senate and people. But *vale ;* I see that you look drowsy. You need rest ; go to bed, you are not like me, a man of iron. By-the-by, do not forget, the day after to-morrow, to be at midnight at the National Assembly. It is the hour I have chosen to speak in opposition to those who wish to have no other church in France than the Roman Catholic. Antiquated nonsense ! As if religious toleration was not the universal cry of the age ! A fair field, and a free fight—every man for himself—God for all—and the devil take the hindmost !" He ran down-stairs laughing, and the chariot of the man of iron, as he called himself, was heard rattling away furiously, as if he had some precious time lost to regain.

It must not be taken for granted that the disaffec-
tion to the new-born republic of the United States
was imaginary, or confined to a few ; for Jefferson, who
had just returned to America, thus communicated
his impressions to a friend: " Being* fresh from the
French revolution, while in its first and pure stage,
and, consequently, somewhat whetted up in my own
republican principles, I found a state of things in the
general society of this place which I could not have
thought possible. The revolution I had left, and that
we had just gone through in the recent change of our
government, being the common topic of conversation, I was astonished to find the general prevalence
of monarchical sentiments, in so much, that in maintaining those of republicanism, I had always the whole
company on my hands, never scarcely finding among
them a single coadvocate in that argument, unless
some old member of Congress happened to be present. The furthest that any one would go in support
of the republican features of our government, would
be to say : ' The present constitution is well as a beginning, and may be allowed a fair trial, but it is, in
fact, only a stepping-stone to something better.' "
Had this letter of Jefferson been published in France
in 1790, it would have created profound astonishment,
and might have checked the enthusiasm of some of
the republicans of the day.

It had been proposed in the National Assembly that
all modes of worship should be tolerated in France,
but that the Catholic, Apostolic, and Roman Church
should be the predominating one and the representative of the religion of the state. Aubert Dubayet,

---

* W. Irving's " Life of Washington," p. 57, vol. v.

according to the invitation which he had received from Mirabeau, did not fail to be present when that question came up, and arrived just at the time when Mirabeau was ascending the tribune.

" I do not come here," said the orator, "to preach toleration. The most unlimited freedom of religious worship is to me so sacred a right that the word *toleration*, applied to it, sounds tyrannical to my ears, because, if the State can tolerate, it can prohibit, whilst no human legislation ought to interpose between man and his Creator. Religion is a conviction —a feeling—an opinion—and surely none here, in these days of national regeneration at the baptismal fount of liberty, will maintain that our convictions and our opinions must not be as free as the air which feeds our lungs."

" Admitting that," shouted the fiery *abbé* Maury, " it can not be denied that the manifestation of opinions may legitimately fall within the range of police regulations."

" So thought and spoke Nero and Domitian," retorted Mirabeau. " It was as a matter of police that they persecuted the Christians, and shed the blood of martyrs *to maintain public order*. That is the well-known phrase. But who is not aware that there is a *slang* for the imperial lips of tyranny, as well as for those of gutter-born demagogues?"

" The kings of France," exclaimed a deputy, interrupting him, " have always been proclaimed the eldest sons of the Church, and have gloried in the title. It is at least certain that, on the 25th of January, 1677, Louis XIV. solemnly swore in Cambrai to permit in that city the existence of no other worship than the Catholic, Apostolic, and Roman religion. I am a representative of Cambrai, and I claim the benefit of that royal oath."

"There can be no doubt, and it can not be wondered at," answered Mirabeau with the most imposing expression of calm dignity, "that, under a reign which was marked by the revocation of the edict of Nantes, and on which I refrain from passing judgment, a want of toleration in everything was the uniform policy of the monarch. I hope, however, that the acts of despots, in days of national servitude, are not to be presented to our recollection as precedents to be followed by the representatives of a free people. But, as a historical citation has been made in connection with the subject of our deliberations, I will take the liberty of making one in my turn." He paused. There was something in his manner, in his accent, in his look, which made the whole Assembly hold its breath.

"Remember, representatives of the people," he said, "remember that here, from this very tribune from which I address you, is to be seen the window of the palace at which stood, on a memorable occasion, a king of France, who, at the instigation of a faction of fanatic traitors serving their own selfish purposes in the name of the sacred interests of religion, fired, with a royal hand guided by them, the fatal arquebuse which gave the signal for the St. Bartholomew massacre."

This was said with a sweeping gesticulation that seemed to take in its grasp the whole Assembly and to carry them to the accursed window from which they could imagine that they saw the Huguenots fall bleeding and shrieking on the quays of the Seine in front of the Louvre. Every one looked spontaneously

in that direction, remaining motionless and pale as if
stunned by a thunderbolt.   This lasted but a minute
or two, and was followed by an enthusiastic burst of
applause.   Mirabeau had carried by storm the decree
for the freedom of all modes and forms of worship on
the broad surface of France.

"You have been sublime," exclaimed Dubayet,
when he could join the orator.

"Thank you," said Mirabeau, who evidently enjoyed to the utmost his splendid triumph.   "You
were born in Louisiana; you fought for the freedom
of the United States.   It is gratifying to me to accept
you as the representative of America.   Faith! It is
something, I think, that a voice from that distant
world should sweep across the ocean, and bring me in
your person a tribute of applause from the wilderness.
Well, well, I will reward you, child of the forest," and
he pinched playfully Dubayet's ear; "come to me
to-morrow, at five o'clock in the afternoon.   I want
to make a holiday of it and take a little rest.   You
will see Mirabeau *en deshabillé*, and then, to complete
the feast, I will take you to dine with Talleyrand at
seven o'clock.   He is the object of much obloquy, but
he is, after all, a princely fellow—by birth, and by
his own making.   I like him hugely.   *C'est un fort
grand seigneur et un démon d'esprit.*"

CHAPTER XV.

MIRABEAU IN HIS DRESSING-ROOM, *à sa toilette*—A VALET WHOSE HAPPINESS CONSISTS IN BEING BEATEN BY HIS MASTER.

AUBERT DUBAYET was punctual at the *rendezvous*. Mirabeau was then living in a splendid mansion, where opulence and taste had gathered all that could flatter the senses. It was filled by a host of lacqueys dressed in gorgeous livery; and a rich chariot, on which he sported conspicuously his antique coat-of-arms, was not unworthy of his blooded horses. None but Mirabeau could have dared to act as he did, and with impunity, but he was, at that time, the spoiled pet, the idol of the people. They forgave him, or did not care to notice, or to take amiss, what they looked upon as vagaries and eccentricities, to which they attached no offensive meaning. Careless of consequences, he who had opened a shop at Aix as a cloth merchant, to ingratiate himself with the people and become their representative in the great National Assembly, convoked by the king—he who had abdicated his nobility and apparently descended into the plebeian ranks—never forgot, never permitted others to forget, that he was a patrician. For his domestics, for his friends, for his enemies, for everybody, he was the *Comte de Mirabeau*. There were many who wondered how a man who had come to the National Assembly with nothing but debts, could find the means

9

of living like a Sardanapalus. Where was the source from which he drew all the gold that he scattered with such reckless profusion? Rumors were rife, and not to his credit, but still they did not affect his popularity.

When Aubert Dubayet called, he found Mirabeau in a loose morning robe of elegant blue velvet, spangled with gold, and slippers of the same materials, giving audience to a motley crew of men and women, of the lowest class. They had come to supplicate him to protect them against the *veto*, on which the National Assembly had been deliberating. The question was, whether under the constitution which they were framing, the king should have a *qualified veto*, or an *absolute* one, or *no veto* at all. Those who were in favor of the *veto* intended it as an indispensable check on the deliberative assemblies which would, in the future, legislate for France. What the *veto* was in reality, by far the greater number of the people could not understand. But it was, in their eyes, a sort of monster which assumed all sorts of imaginable shapes. It was sure to deprive them of shelter, work, bread, and everything else, if not devour them all. The less it was understood, the more terrific it appeared in its vague and indefinite form, wrapped up in mystery and gloom.

"*Monsieur le comte*," cried the ignorant wretches with tears of terror in their eyes, "you are the father of the people. You are bound in duty to save us, to defend us against those wicked traitors who wish to surrender us, hands and feet tied up, to the bloody rod of despotism. King *Veto* will destroy the National Assembly. All will be lost, and we shall be slaves." The "father of the people," as he was called, listened with much paternal patience to a good deal of this incoherent and absurd language. The terms and sentiments were frequently such as to provoke irresistible laughter. But Mirabeau looked grave and compassionate, and acted his part admirably. At last, with infinite art, and without committing himself to any course whatever, he, in a rather lordly but affectionate manner, dismissed the petitioners, satisfied with his indefinite assurances of protection. When these strange visitors had departed, Mirabeau threw himself upon a sofa, exclaiming: " Pho ! oh ! This is intolerable. My popularity has become a burden under which I am literally crushed." He rang a bell; a valet made his appearance. "Teutch," he said, " close my doors, I am not in for anybody," and, turning to Dubayet, he added: "You have no idea how I am besieged—a constant throng; my antechambers are always crowded to suffocation."

The whole scene had appeared extremely ludicrous to Dubayet, as he knew that Mirabeau had been in favor of giving an absolute *veto* power to the king. This question had come up in the National Assembly before they had decided one which ought to have taken the precedence—that is, whether the future legislative power of France, under the new constitution, was to be divided into two chambers, or not. If in two, an absolute *veto* was not so necessary to the executive, because it was to be supposed that the chambers might often disagree and not be led to act on all questions in common accord, so easily as a single one would. Hence a qualified *veto* might suffice. But if, in the future, the legislative branch of the government, like the present one, was to continue to be but one body, the absolute veto power could not be dispensed with as an appendage to royalty, which, without that protection, would be swept away like chaff, the real sovereignty being only in the Assembly. But even if armed with the *veto*, it was clear that the king would not be safe in the exercise of his authority, and would not be able to maintain his will against the will of the representatives of the people acting in a body. Hence Mirabeau, who desired the creation of two chambers, but who did not know as yet whether that feature would be inserted in the constitution, was, as a choice of evils, in favor of the absolute *veto*, which he intended as a temporary measure, and which he thought a necessary check on popular assemblies, until further developments in the work of political organization should enable him to see better his way. He had even spoken on the subject in the Assembly, but he had purposely been so obscure and diffuse, his discourse had been such a masterpiece of non-committal, that the public in the galleries had not understood his drift; but the National Assembly had discovered, through his sibylline language, equivocal and twisted in its meaning as it was, that he stood in favor of the absolute *veto*, and this had given great offense to the fanatics in what was called the party of progress. When the votes were taken on the question, he had deemed it prudent to be absent. Hence the people never could be made to believe, that he could be friendly to the bugbear or vampire which haunted their imagination. Mirabeau, being taxed by a friend with moral cowardice for having shirked the responsibility of his vote on that occasion, had replied: "Tut! man, those asses [meaning his colleagues of the Assembly] had brought the question prematurely. I can not afford yet to lose my popularity; I

must keep it to save those fools from their own blun-
ders. Believe me ; were I to die before accomplishing what I have in view, those senseless reformers
would bring the king and themselves to the scaffold."

Whilst Mirabeau was talking, Teutch was preparing all the necessary implements and ingredients for
the toilet of his master, which always lasted very long
and was very elaborate. Teutch had been a celebrated smuggler, and wonderful traits of daring and
of fool-hardy courage were related of him. He was
a sort of tamed lion whom Mirabeau had in his service, and of all sublunary things he loved and admired
his patron the most. " Aubert," said Mirabeau, " excuse me for a while. I must step into my cabinet,
where I have, besides my secretary, three men at
work in preparing materials for me. I'll be back in a
trice. I leave you with Teutch. Take care that he
does not eat you up, for he looks very fierce to-day ";
and he disappeared behind a heavy curtain in tapestry,
concealing a door which opened into another apartment.

" I have good reasons to be sullen," growled Teutch
between his teeth.

" What is the matter with you ? " said Dubayet.

" Ah ! Sir," answered Teutch, heaving a deep sigh,
" *Monsieur le comte* has been very reserved with me
for more than a week. He has not condescended to
give me the least sign of the friendly familiarity with
which he was in the habit of honoring me. It breaks
my heart ; I can not stand it any longer. But I will
soon put him to the test—this very day. Should he
continue to treat me so harshly, I will blow out my
brains in his presence ; for there is not a single member of his household who could live under his dis-

pleasure.   We all adore him, and would not hesitate
to die for one who is so good to us, and who is the
honor and the pride of France."

" I am glad to hear," said Dubayet, to keep up the
conversation with the faithful servant, " that you admire and love him so much."

" Admire him! Sir, who would not? I wish you
could see us peeping at him through every hole, and
from every nook, corner, and hiding-place, when he is
rehearsing."

" Rehearsing!"

" To be sure.   Thus he walks, to and fro, in that
large parlor where there are so many mirrors.   Thus
he stands before one of them, swelling his chest,
throwing his head back, making his adversaries talk,
and replying to them : ' Ha! you say so and so, Mr.
L'abbé Maury! Very well; and you, Mr. Barnave, are
these your sentiments? Go on, and explain them
fully ; *Mr. le comte* de Mirabeau will answer you as
follows.' That is the way he speaks of himself. It
is superb, Sir.   Sometimes, we are so transported with
admiration, that we can not refrain from betraying
ourselves by our applause, and he throws at our heads
everything that he can lay his hands upon."

Teutch was interrupted by Mirabeau, who returned
in a terrific fit of rage and shouted to him : " Rascal,
what have you done with those important papers
which, three hours ago, I ordered you to carry in haste
to my secretary ? "

" I have lost them."

" Lost them!" echoed Mirabeau with increasing
wrath; and seizing Teutch by the throat with one
hand, he knocked him down with the other. Teutch
picked himself up with a face beaming with satisfac-

tion, rubbing his hands in high glee and cracking his sides with laughter. "Thank you, *Monsieur le comte*," he said with a respectful bow. "I hope you will not neglect so long in the future to give me some proof of your kind regard. Excuse me if I have had recourse to a stratagem to compel you to notice your loving servant. Here are the papers," and he drew them out of his pocket.

Mirabeau looked at him with stupefaction. "Who on earth could believe this?" he said. "I must beat this odd fish to make him happy!" And then, seating himself before a table on which stood a beautiful Venetian looking-glass, "Very well, Teutch," continued he, "if you are so well pleased with the kindness which I have just now exhibited to you, return the favor by dressing my hair after your best fashion; bushy—bushy—the lion's main, you know. Do the most you can for this head of mine, whilst it is in this world; for, when it is gone, you shall not look upon its like again."

Teutch began to work at the august head intrusted to his care with as much solemnity as if it had been that of the Olympian God whose nod shook the whole vault of heaven.

"Now, dear Aubert," said Mirabeau, "whilst this honest fellow operates, do me the favor to relate something of interest. What have you been doing of late?"

"I breakfasted this morning with the Marquis de la Luzerne, General Lafayette, and Gouverneur Morris."

"Pray, give me a synopsis of their conversation, if it can be done without indiscretion."

"There can be no indiscretion whatever. The Mar-

quis de la Luzerne said to Lafayette: ' My dear general, I consider you as being at the head of the revolution; and, indeed, it is a very fortunate circumstance for the State that you are, but very little so for
yourself. Never has any man been placed in a more
critical situation. A good citizen, a faithful subject,
you are embarrassed by a thousand difficulties in making many people sensible of what is proper, who very
often feel it not, and who sometimes do not understand what it is.' *

" ' It is true,' replied Lafayette, ' but I hope that I
shall weather the storm. We have thus far advanced
in the career of the revolution without the vessel of
the State being wrecked against the rocks of aristocracy, or faction. In the midst of efforts, always re-
newing, of the partisans of the past and of the ambitious, we progress toward a tolerable conclusion.
At present, that which existed has been destroyed ;
a new political edifice is forming ; without being perfect, it is sufficient to assure liberty. Thus prepared,
the nation will be in a state to elect, in two years, a
convention which can correct the faults of the constitution. The result will, I hope, be happy for our
country and for humanity. One perceives the germs
of liberty in other parts of Europe. I will encourage
their development by all the means in my power.' †

" ' The time approaches when all good men must
cling to the throne,' put in Gouverneur Morris, who,
as you know, is no enthusiast with regard to the revolution, and who looks on its progress with a doubt-
ing mind. ' The present king is very valuable on ac-

---

* Marquis de la Luzerne's Letter to Washington.
† General Lafayette's Letter to Washington.

count of his moderation; and if he should possess too much authority, might be persuaded to grant a proper constitution. That thing called a constitution, which the Assembly have framed, is good for nothing. As to yourself, general, allow me to tell you frankly that your situation is very delicate. You, nominally, but not really, command the troops. Under present circumstances, I do not understand how you are to establish discipline among them; but, unless you can accomplish that object, you must be ruined, sooner or later. Besides, you have unluckily given in to measures, as to the constitution, which you do not heartily approve, and you have heartily approved many things which experience, I am afraid, will demonstrate to be injurious.' *

"'Washington gives me more encouragement than you do, Morris,' replied Lafayette. 'Thus he writes to me: "Happy am I, my good friend, that, amidst all the tremendous tempests which have assailed your political ship, you have had address and fortitude enough to steer her hitherto safely through the quicksands and rocks which threatened instant destruction on every side, and that your young king, in all things, seems so well disposed to conform to the wishes of the nation. In such an important, such a hazardous voyage, when everything dear and sacred is embarked, you know full well, my best wishes have never left you for a moment. Yet I will avow, that the accounts we received through the English papers, which were sometimes our only channel of information, caused our fears of failure almost to exceed our expectations of success." ' "

---

* Morris to Washington, 22d of January, 1790.

9*

"Aubert Dubayet," said Mirabeau, "the fears of Washington are not chimerical. Already has the Jacobin club of Paris sent forth ramifications throughout France; corresponding clubs are springing up by hundreds in the provinces, and everything is hurrying forward to a catastrophe."*

"I rely on Lafayette and his popularity," observed Dubayet.

"Bah! What virgin innocence!" replied Mirabeau. "Lafayette has no energy. He has some talent, I admit, but it is of a uniform mediocrity. He always possesses it and finds it ready at hand when wanted, but he never rises above its level. Is that enough? No. When the wind of revolution blows into a tempest, it is not the hand of mediocrity that will steer the ship safely into port. As to popularity! Whew! He who relies on it, reckons without his host, or rather attempts to ride and to guide the ever-changing wind. Remember that there is but one step from the capitol to the Tarpeian rock."

At that moment his secretary came in, and said to him: *"Monsieur le comte,* I regret that I am compelled to inform you, in my name and on behalf of the gentlemen employed with me, that it is impossible to do the work which you require of us within the time you specify."

"Impossible!" exclaimed Mirabeau, starting up. "Never use, when addressing me, that stupid word. Go back, Sir, and execute what I have told you, or I will do it myself, to show you that nothing is impossible."

By this time, Teutch had done dressing and pow-

---

* Irving's " Life of Washington," p. 73, vol. v.

dering Mirabeau's head. The great man rose, and, looking complacently at himself in the glass before him, said : " It is very well, Teutch ; this is exactly to my taste. Now, give me the coat that fits me the best ; you know which it is. Mind you, don't forget to sprinkle my handkerchief with the perfume which La Guimard sent me yesterday." Another look at the glass. " People say, Aubert Dubayet, that I am very ugly. But none but myself has any conception of the secret power of my ugliness. There is magic in it. By-the-by, Teutch, I am sorry that I omitted to fence with you this morning. It follows that I don't feel as well as usual. But I am always so much engaged ! I have so much to do ! What time have I for recreation, O God ! I assure you, Dubayet, that Teutch is the best swordsman in the kingdom, but he is no match for me, though. Teutch, give me a pair of gloves—one of that set which I won from my cousin, the Duchess de Guise. Are you fond of swimming, Dubayet ? "

" Not in the least."

" I regret it for your sake. It is so invigorating ! I swim better than Leander ever did. Do you like riding on horseback ? "

" Very."

" You are right ; it is a delightful exercise. When I was a captain of dragoons in Corsica, I was reputed the best horseman my companions had ever known— a real centaur ; and yet, I am a better shot than I am a horseman. I snuff a candle at forty paces. Have you been taught to use the brush of the painter, Dubayet ? "

" Yes, a little ; I have drawn landscapes."

" Well, Sir, I have missed my vocation. I should

have been a painter. I might have equalled Raphael. But my forte is music. The fact is, that nature has been pleased to exhaust her gifts on me. It is really singular—almost unique. The world, however, is very little appreciative in its taste, and very unjust often in its judgment. For instance, people talk of nothing else than my eloquence, as if I had no other merit. I assure you, Dubayet, that if I am anything at all, it is a musician. I am a genius in that line, and yet nobody gives me credit for it. I know but one man that is superior to me. It is Tintin Calandro, the chief of the troop of musicians in the service of the princess de Lamballe. But he is superhuman; he must have stolen his violin from heaven, as Prometheus stole the celestial fire. The princess de Lamballe did me the favor to lend him to me at the last concert which I gave, and of late he visits me often, and we play together. I have improved wonderfully under him. By-the-by, I understand that he is your friend."

"From boyhood; he is a college chum."

"They are the best friends. The next time you come to see me, Dubayet, I must find leisure to declaim for you some of the finest passages in Corneille and Racine. I shall show you hidden beauties in them of which you never dreamed. I could have been, if I had chosen, the greatest actor of the age. When starving in Holland, I was once tempted to appear on the stage. Fie! what an idea! A Riquetti, Count de Mirabeau, a stage player! My gorge rose at it. I felt instinctively that there would yet be another stage for me—the one on which I figure now." Pulling out his watch, "But I almost forget myself; it is time to go. Teutch, watch those fellows who are scribbling for me. Don't allow them to play truant when I am gone. Keep them at work, steady. Give them every hour a glass of iced champagne, followed by a cup of hot coffee; but no more, mind you. My enemies, Dubayet—and, of course, I have many, for I could not have blazed like a comet on the horizon of Europe, without having an innumerable pack of dogs to bark at me—my enemies, I say, reproach me with plagiarism, and maintain that I am indebted to others, whom I employ, for a good deal of the display of knowledge which I make. The fact is, that I have my masons to bring stones and mortar for the edifices I intend to erect. But I, alone, am the architect—the Michael Angelo. Teutch, see if my carriage is ready, and put my cloak in it."

"But really, count," said Dubayet, "I have scruples about accompanying you. I have not been invited by Mr. de Talleyrand."

"What of that? Do you not come with me? He will be delighted to see you, and you will be still more delighted to know him."

"I confess that I rather dislike the bishop of Autun. A priest should be a priest, and he is none."

"Better be no priest at all than a bad one. He will, before long, have himself secularized, I have no doubt. He was born for the world, and not for the cloister. Depend upon it, he is one of the shrewdest and strongest minds of the age. He will make his mark on it. Dubayet, it is advisable that you should cultivate him. He is one of those men who always contrive to be at the apex of the social pyramid."

" He has the reputation of being cold and haughty —absolutely repulsive."

" Pshaw! Mr. de Talleyrand in his intimacy is very

different from Mr. de Talleyrand in public. It is true that he never forgets his descent from one of the noblest and oldest families of France. His ancestors were sovereign counts by the grace of God, and reigned in their broad domains by the same right as that by which the Majesty of France reigned in his own kingdom. He retains, therefore, in his social intercourse, the dignity which befits his birth, but he has also the high-toned courtesy which is its inseparable appendage. Now as to his character. I must give you an insight into it. I have no doubt that it must have felt the influence of those circumstances which attended him from early youth. He was the eldest-born, but, as he was club-footed, his father compelled him to renounce his right of primogeniture and drove him into holy orders, for which he had no vocation. He could have been an ecclesiastic, only after the fashion of the cardinal de Retz, who had adopted a dagger for his breviary. Hated and ill-treated by his parents, under whose roof he had never been permitted to-sleep, he was, in his infancy, taciturn and sombre, and has grown up with that disposition. When at the seminary, he used to live apart, and within himself, and his habitual gloominess, which rendered him unsociable, had given him the reputation of being haughty. Condemned to be a churchman, he has neither adopted the sentiments nor the conduct that would have become his profession. He has even overstepped those broad limits which the indulgence of a lax society has allowed to high rank and youth. His morality is not clerical, but he is a strict observer of proprieties, and, whatever may be his habits and his way of thinking, no one knows better than he what may be spoken, and what not! He may perhaps be suspected of having somewhat the ambition of being impressive and imposing, by assuming that air of reserve with the aid of which some men will pass themselves off as being deep. But he needs no artifice of the kind, for he is by nature unfathomably deep. At first sight, he will generally be thought frigid. When among those with whom he is not familiar, he speaks little and listens with much attention. He keeps aloof, as it were, never exposes himself, and puts on a complete armor from head to foot. He has not apparently the social characteristics of the French, and does not exhibit their national vivacity, familiarity, indiscretion, and gaiety. His language is sententious, his politeness is cold, and the expression of his physiognomy that of a man who examines and studies those in whose company he finds himself. To shake off or punish indiscretion, or presumption, or to guard himself against any approach which he foresees and dislikes, he has the art of dropping a short sarcasm, or sentence, impregnated with prussic acid. It is instant death. So much for his behavior in the outside world, when moving in it."

"You frighten me," said Dubayet.

"There is no reason for it. Within the circle of his intimate society, and remember that it is into that circle I wish to introduce you, Talleyrand transforms himself into another being. He is cordial in manner, affable, and free in language. He takes a keen pleasure in conversation, in which he likes to perform an active part, and which he frequently prolongs to late hours in the night. On those occasions, he is familiar, even caressing, extremely and minutely attentive to please. He wishes to be amusing and amused; he is never in a hurry to speak, but, when he opens his lips, it is to give way to the purest atticism of language and sentiments. He never says anything which is commonplace or insignificant. There is depth of thought, piquancy of allusion, or the sharpest wit almost in every phrase which he utters, and yet so delicately veiled, as to be appreciated only by those who are accustomed to his manner and to the refined atmosphere of his intellect. But enough, let us depart ; come and see if this portrait is correct. I have already told you that I am a Raphael."

CHAPTER XVI.

AUBERT DUBAYET, introduced by Mirabeau, was received by Talleyrand with the most cordial urbanity, as predicted by his friend, and, in a few minutes, was made to feel as much at ease as if he had long been on a footing of intimacy with his host. The dinner was perfect, and most of the guests were men whose names will ever live in the pages of history. Talleyrand was particularly attentive to his new guest, as if he intended to make him understand that he was at once admitted into the privileged circle of those who had free access to his house, and encourage him to future intercourse. He asked him what were the news from America.

"None of very great importance," replied Aubert Dubayet, "save a sharp conflict in Congress about the creation of a national bank, which measure was urged upon them, as a matter of policy, by Alexander Hamilton in his annual treasury report. On one side, it is deemed that the constitution has not given to Congress the power of incorporating such an institution; on the other side, it is insisted that it is incident to the power vested in Congress for raising money. The question, after being argued at length and with great vehemence, was solved in the affirmative by both houses, who voted in favor of the expediency and constitutionality of the measure."

L'abbé Maury. "I consider the question of unconstitutionality, on that occasion, as of very little importance. All constitutions are baubles given to the childish multitude to amuse and cajole them into being docile under the guidance of their demagogue leaders. If the Congress of the United States derive from the grant of the power to coin money, that of creating a paper currency, which is the reverse of money, and which is only resorted to as a poor substitute when no money can be coined, what will they do, in the course of time, under that sweeping clause which says that they shall provide for the *general welfare?* That phrase, short as it is, puts me in mind of that small magic carpet of which I have read in some Arabian tale, and which, when laid down, covered only one foot of ground, but could be so stretched as to envelope the whole earth. Under that clause in the instrument to which I refer, and under the plea of necessity which is unavoidably connected with it, I am very sure it will be found out before long, that the boasted constitution of the model republic is of so light and flexible a texture, that despotism can drive through it in a coach and four with absolute ease. But, what side took Washington in that conflict? "

Aubert Dubayet. "Washington was fully alive to the magnitude of the question, and to the interest felt in it by the opposing parties. He requested each member of his Cabinet to give his opinion in writing. The Cabinet was divided. Jefferson and Randolph denied the constitutionality of the measure; Hamilton and Knox maintained it. After maturely weighing their arguments for and against, Washington sanctioned the measure, which was carried into effect."

Talleyrand. "I regret it; for I wish I could have used the authority of Washington to oppose it to Mr. de Mirabeau, who intends advocating in the National Assembly the emission of *assignats*, or paper money."

Aubert Dubayet. "You have Jefferson on your side, who, perhaps, will be of greater authority with a certain portion of the Assembly than Washington himself, for it was not alone on constitutional grounds that Jefferson was opposed to the creation of a national bank. It was also because he had always avowed himself inimical to banks as introducing a paper instead of a cash system, raising up a moneyed aristocracy, and scattering over the broad face of the country a locust host of greedy stock-jobbers and swindlers. He thinks that paper money may have some advantages, but that its abuses are inevitable, and that, by breaking up the measure of value, it makes a lottery of all private property. But he has other reasons which may be more urgent with him in the present instance.* He considers the bank as a powerful engine intended by Hamilton to complete the machinery by which the whole action of the Legislature is to be placed under the direction of the Treasury, and shaped to further a monarchical system of government. He affirms that Washington is unversed in financial projects, calculations, and budgets, and that his approbation of this measure was bottomed on his confidence in Hamilton, of whose schemes he does not see the drift. The fact is, that Hamilton and Jefferson, to use Mr. Jefferson's own words, are pitted in the Cabinet like two cocks."

Mirabeau. "Just as *L'abbé* Maury and myself are

---

* Irving's "Life of Washington," p. 80, vol. v.

pitted in the National Assembly. *Monsieur L'abbé*, I drink to your good health with this exquisite champagne. May you be a cardinal one day!" The *abbé* bowed in acknowledgment, with a smile which seemed to mean that, in his opinion, such an event was far from being an impossibility.

"In the meantime," continued Aubert Dubayet, "two political parties have formed themselves throughout the Union, under the adverse standards of these two statesmen. Both have the good of their country at heart, but differ as to the policy by which it is to be secured."

"Just like *Monsieur le Comte de Mirabeau* and myself," said *L'abbé* Maury, bowing slightly to that personage, who sat opposite to him. "My dear colleague, permit me to return the compliment which you have paid me. I drink to your health in this ruby-looking burgundy. May your shadow never grow less!"

"My shadow! *Monsieur L'abbé*," replied Mirabeau, laughing. "What do you mean? You forget that I am all light. But pardon us this interruption, Dubayet. Mr. *L'abbé* Maury and myself will never cease to be boyish. Pray, go on."

Aubert Dubayet. "The Federalists, who look up to Hamilton as their model, are in favor of strengthening the General Government so as to give it weight and dignity abroad, and efficacy at home, whilst guarding it against the encroachments of the individual States and a general tendency to anarchy. The other party, known as Republicans or Democrats, taking Mr. Jefferson's view of affairs, see in all the measures advocated by the Federalists an intention to convert the Federal into a great central or consolidated government, preparatory to a change from a republic to a monarchy."

L'abbé Sieyes (emerging from a sort of reverie, and talking, as it were, to himself in a fit of abstraction). " I am sorry that the Americans did not consult me. I should have greatly improved their constitution, and given them an unsurpassed declaration of the rights of man. For, political economy is a science which I have literally exhausted."

Mirabeau (nudging with his elbow Aubert Dubayet, next to whom he was seated). " Did you ever hear the like of it? I would rap him for it on the knuckles, were I not afraid of running foul of his implacable vanity. Mine, of which everybody talks so much, and which is·dwarfish when compared to the gigantic one of this man, is at least good-natured and sociable, whilst that of the *abbé* is as ferocious as a cannibal. Beware of him. *Habet fœnum in cornu.*"

Dupont de Nemours. " I have listened with great interest to what has been said on the United States. As we are advised to follow their example in their late revolutionary struggle, and, like them, to issue paper money to carry us through our own revolution, I beg leave to ask Mr. Dubayet if he knows for what sum, in continental money, I could procure a pair of boots in New York."

Aubert Dubayet. " Probably fifty thousand dollars."

Dupont de Nemours. " And what would cost such a dinner as this?"

Aubert Dubayet. " About five millions, I presume."

Dupont de Nemours. " What do you say of that, Mr. de Mirabeau?"

Mirabeau. " I say that, without the continental money at which you laugh, the Americans could not have achieved successfully what they have performed. That it should have become worthless is a great evil, but it would have been a greater one, if they had failed to shake off the yoke of Great Britain, and to establish their present government on the basis of the broadest liberty. I shall give in full my reasons in favor of the contemplated emission of *assignats*, when the question is discussed in the National Assembly. You will then have the opportunity to refute me."

Dupont de Nemours. "I will attempt it; in the meantime, I predict that the fate of the continental paper money of America will be that of all paper money to the end of time, and that, before the expiration of this century, you will not be able, Mr. de Mirabeau, to buy a truffled turkey with a million of livres in *assignats*."

Barnave. "The civilized world is emancipating itself from the thraldom of its old prejudices. It is getting rejuvenated, and youth, we know, must sow its wild oats and get into debt. The human mind now teems with new conceptions of hitherto unheard of improvements in political economy, in the science of navigation and war, in the mechanical arts, and in everything else. Nations have not the pecuniary means to carry into execution those discoveries which are daily crowding upon us; for, progress is a God who incessantly vouchsafes new inspirations to his worshipers. Hence nations must borrow, to keep pace with one another and to meet the exigencies of their epoch; they must establish credit as a national and fundamental institution, and they must draw on posterity, who must and will honor the draft."

L'abbé Maury. "Barnave is right as to the fact

that this is the present tendency of the world. Ere long, every nation, no doubt, will have its national debt and its national stocks, with their inevitable up and down movement, thus licensing public gambling and spreading universal demoralization. I predict that, before the expiration of the nineteenth century, all civilized nations will be so heavily saddled with their increasing debts, that they will be horribly taxed merely to pay the interests, and that, in the beginning of the twentieth century, the burden will be so crushing, that there will be a general repudiation."

Chamfort. " Why not ? I see no harm in it. Immense material improvements will be the results of those national debts, be they contracted for wars, or for peaceful purposes. When repudiation shall take place, the burden will be removed, but the benefit will remain. It will be all gain without any incumbrances attached to it."

La Rochefoucauld. " You horrify me. What ! Violate the national faith and reduce thousands to beggary ! "

Chamfort. " There is not a nation in the world, *Monsieur le duc,* which has not violated more than once, in every century, its public faith pledged in solemn treaties. Suppose that a national debt is so overwhelming that it can not be paid either in the present or in the future, because, under emergencies which are constantly recurring, it is forever increasing in bulk. The nation is perishing under the fatal incubus; excessive taxation destroys its agricultural, commercial, and industrial resources ; it loses its vigor, its rank among the powers of the earth, and can not support those armies which are necessary to

protect it against the ambition of its neighbors. Repudiate, I say, repudiate at once and without hesitation; for repudiation must come at last, since the
debt can not be paid; have the moral courage which
the occasion requires; cut off the cancer which
threatens life. *Salus populi, suprema lex;* the salvation of the commonwealth is the supreme law. Do
not nations go to war, as a matter of necessity, and
sacrifice often one million of men, who thus are lost to
productive labor? Why, then, hesitate to repudiate,
in case also of absolute necessity, or reduce the debt
to proportions which will not be necessarily destructive to the debtor, although it may impoverish the
same number of men that war would kill? Those
impoverished men would, at least, remain living and
active, and would find work and assistance in a community that shall have become suddenly rich and
prosperous by being freed from an indebtedness which
it was impossible to remove by payment. Surely the
sufferings inflicted by repudiation would not be equal
to those resulting from war. Suppose poor, oppressed, decrepit, and insolvent Spain, should, by one
bold stroke of the pen, expunge her national debt,
imposed upon her by rulers who went beyond the
powers constitutionally delegated to them, and ruined
the generous people who had confided in them.
There would be a loud clamor, senseless cries of
shame—shame! But, after all, what would be the
practical consequences? Some Spaniards would live
less comfortably, but none would perish from hunger,
I'll warrant; whilst the whole nation would spring up,
with the vigor of a giant, from the earth to which
she has been crushed down, and develop with un-
trammeled energy the wonderful resources with which

she has been endowed ; and should her example not
be followed—why, the Spanish genet, with no other
weight than that of its light saddle and nimble rider,
would soon distance in the career of prosperity the
heavy-loaded pack-horses of France, England, Italy,
and Germany, carrying with panting breath the grinding mill-stones accumulated on their cracked backs
by centuries of misrule and imbecility, or savage lust
and selfish ambition. As to the foreign creditors,
they could not complain, when put on the same footing with the natives."

La Rochefoucauld. "And the immorality of the
act ? "

Chamfort. "There would be no immorality in it.
Why should not a nation go honestly into bankruptcy, like a private individual, when her resources
are really and truly exhausted? If, in such circumstances, a man is not disgraced, why should a nation ?"

La Rochefoucauld. "Repudiation or bankruptcy
would immediately destroy public credit, which is
the life of a nation."

Chamfort. "It might increase it, because the resources of the State to pay future debts would be
greater, and capitalists, who are ever so anxious to
loan money securely and to own stocks, would feel
that such another act of bankruptcy would not be
probable, and would not become an absolute necessity
within several centuries. What mortal ken would
look through such a long vista of years, to anticipate consequences so remote ? "

Dupont de Nemours. "I beg leave, *Monsieur le duc,*
to deny, with due deference to your opinion, that
public credit is the life of a nation. Who ever heard
of the national loans of Rome, and yet Rome had

life in her, I presume? Who ever heard of th
Babylonian, Assyrian, or Egyptian loans being huck
stered about like crockery ware? Did those nations
who built magnificent capitals whose population ex
ceeded that of ours, issue bonds on papyrus, or oi
leather, or on wood, or brass tablets, or on any othe
durable materials, to carry on their eternal wars, o
to erect those stupendous monuments which excit
our wonder and admiration? Were their stock
quoted at the exchange-rooms of Nineveh, Babylon
Alexandria, and Rome, rising and falling according
to the thermometer of circumstances? Until recen
times, nations existed without manifesting that ex
istence by the creation of paper pyramids of nationa
bonds and national rag currency. We have latel;
witnessed the mighty struggle of little Prussia, witl
a population of five millions, against the combinec
forces of France, Austria, and Russia. She came ou
victorious without having had recourse to a loan, anc
therefore without a debt. Why can not we do lik
her, and like all the nations of antiquity?"

Mirabeau. "Because the complexion and face o
things have changed. Every age has its own peculia
spirit and its own peculiar destiny. The crusader
fitted the times they lived in, and Europe has eve
since passed through inevitable transformations. N
banker, for instance, could have been a minister unde
Louis XIV. Now, a banker, Mr. de Necker, is :
minister under Louis XVI., and the idol of the peo
ple. Be it for good or for evil, this is the age o
bankers, speculators, and stock-jobbers, of public credi
and national debt. They will have their phase o
allotted existence, and will pass away like everythin;
else. But, in the meantime, public credit will buil

cities, cover the seas with fleets, carry commerce and civilization to the extremities of the earth, and stim- ulate the mind of man into inventions and into the execution of works, before which those of past ages will be insignificant."

Talleyrand. "Mr. de Mirabeau takes a correct view of what is to happen. I have no doubt, from the signs of the times, that a sudden rage for material improvements will become epidemic, that the acqui- sition of wealth will be the ruling passion of the age, and that every one in Christendom will be eager to provide himself with an easy rocking-chair. I have no doubt that the day will come when, in the pursuit of every sort of wild schemes, generated by cupidity, every nation, every capital, every city, town, village, or corporation, as well as individuals, will have their irredeemable bonds, or promissory notes, floating on every sea in the tempest-torn boat of public credit."

L'abbé Maury. "What will be the end of this beau- tiful state of things?"

Talleyrand. "A crash."

Mirabeau. "Well, let it be a crash. Who is afraid of a crash? Was not the original fall of man a crash? Was not the deluge a crash? Was not the destruc- tion of the Roman empire a crash? The records of mankind are but the history of crashes. And yet, notwithstanding all those crashes, the world still moves on, affording more or less comfort to those who live in it."

Chamfort (with that bland intonation of voice which he always affected, when he intended to be otherwise than deferential): "You said, Mr. de Mira- beau, that what you call the age of bankers, stock-jobbers, and public credit, would pass away. Have you any idea of what will succeed it?"

Mirabeau. "Of course I have. Was I ever without an idea on anything? I think that the next mania will be about the abolition of marriage, of public credit, of national and private indebtedness, the amalgamation of all races, a chemical mixture of all religions, the promulgation of the doctrine of equality and fraternity, not only among men, but also between them and the lower animals; the creation of liberty—mutual—insurance companies among nations, and the emancipation of women, who will wear breeches and enjoy all the political, social, and other rights of man, now known, or to be discovered in the future. The abolition of marriage must certainly suit you, Mr. Chamfort, for you are always preaching against it; you best know why; and if perchance you should object to a woman being a politician, you might be glad to accept her as a physician. It is said, you know, that the lance of Achilles could cure the wounds which it inflicted."

This was a bitter retort; for Mirabeau was irritated at the familiar tone of levity with which he had been addressed. As to Chamfort, he became very pale and bit his lips. He had the misfortune of being a bastard, and was reported to have one of those shameful and incurable diseases which are the result of dissoluteness. Mirabeau's sarcastic allusions were understood by all, and a general titter, which could hardly be suppressed, increased the uncomfortable feelings of Chamfort. Fortunately, the archbishop of Aix, who was extremely dull, and who had been struck with the words, "a chemical mixture of all religions," said in a doleful tone: "I should not be astonished at the

sacrilegious attempt. For, what are we not coming
to in these days of portentous changes? Has not an
attack been already made in the National Assembly
against the collection of the tithe appropriated for
the support of the clergy?—the tithe!—that voluntary
offering of the piety of the faithful."

"True, the tithe!" said the Duke de la Rochefau-
cauld, with that air of simplicity and modesty which
was habitual to him, and which gave more piquancy
to his remarks, "the tithe!—that voluntary offering
of the piety of the faithful, about the payment of
which there are forty thousand lawsuits in France!"

This time there was a frank and unrestrained expression of hilarity, but *L'abbé* Maury came to the
rescue of the archbishop. "If we were only spoliated,"
he said, "of our prescriptive and time-honored right
to tithes, it would be comparatively nothing, for we
are threatened with being robbed even of our landed
possessions, which were royal or private donations,
or the fruits of our industry and economy, and to
which every century, as it passed, has affixed its
sacred seal with the sanction of religion and of the
State."

"There can be nothing sacred in what is oppressive," replied Mirabeau. "If this be true, it justifies
the abolition of tithes, for they are the most oppressive of burdens. For instance, suppose a piece of
ground produces twelve sacks of corn to a peasant.
If you deduct the rent, the cost of cultivation, the
wear and tear of implements, etc., there remains one-
half, to wit: six sacks, out of which three sacks are
to be taken to meet what is due to the king and other
official claimants. Thus the twelve sacks are reduced
to three. Is that all? No. Now comes the hand of

the priest, who, in the name of God, takes one sack, which represents, after having magnanimously thrown out a fraction, the tenth part of the gross produce; so that, out of the twelve sacks of corn which the laborer has extracted from the bowels of the earth by the sweat of his brow, he retains two for his subsistence and that of his family; and this is what is called the legitimate property of the clergy! I maintain that, far from being property, it does not amount even to possession. The tithe is merely a contribution, a tax for the support of public worship—which tax can be modified, changed, or abolished at will by the legislative power. It is a subsidy, a salary given by the nation to the professors of moral and religious instruction."

L'abbé Maury. "Bravo! bravo! This is worthy of the new era into which we are entering. I like the novelty of these expressions. Priests are no longer the apostles of Christ, the ministers of God, but the professors of moral and religious instruction for a stipulated salary. Go on, Mr. de Mirabeau; go on."

Archbishop of Aix. "For my part, I tell him not to go on. I protest against this word *salary*, applied to the *Church*—to the spouse of Christ."

Mirabeau. "I see, *Monseigneur*, that this word, *salary*, wounds your sense of sacerdotal dignity. I am sorry for it. But it is time, in the face of a revolution which has produced so many just and generous sentiments, and expelled forever so many gothic prejudices, that the pretensions of ignorant pride should be set aside. I know for man in society but three modes of existence. He must be a beggar, a thief, or a workman for a salary."

Chamfort. "What becomes of the proprietor? If

he is neither a beggar, nor a thief, he must be ranked, I suppose, among those who work for a salary, or wages."

Mirabeau. "To be sure. The proprietor must be classed among those who receive a salary. It is the law, and the law alone, which establishes and maintains property. The proprietor is a mere agent, or administrator, appointed or tolerated for the benefit of the social body. He pays, or must be made to pay, to the members of the community to which he belongs, a large proportion of the revenue of the property which that community allows him to possess, and in the possession of which it protects him. He pays it in the shape of expenses of all sorts for his living, for the gratification of his tastes or appetites, and in taxes. What remains is his salary for his taking care, in a special manner, of what, for the public good, has been intrusted to his administration, and belongs, after all, to the whole community. He has only been permitted to acquire it, and apparently to appropriate it to himself out of the common fund, as a sort of reward or social pre-eminence, granted to him for his labor, or the labor of the ancestors from whom he inherits it, and with a view to produce an emulation of industry. I know that this does not agree with the vulgarly acknowledged definition of property, but it does not follow that it is not the correct one, or the one, at least, which is in conformity with the enlarged views of the present day."

Archbishop of Aix. "Count, you must be joking. I would call this the sophistry of the devil, gentlemen, if it did not come out of the polite and Christian lips of Mr. de Mirabeau, who, I know, does not profess to be a heathen."

L'abbé Maury. "We must not be angry, *Monseig-neur.* I assure you that this doctrine is not of Mr. de Mirabeau, who can not claim, on this occasion, the rights of authorship or originality. It is the ingenious invention of that new-fangled philosophy which is embodied in the 'Social Contract' of Jean Jacques Rousseau, who, notwithstanding the title of his book, is the apostle of social disorganization. But you will permit the benighted like me, Mr. de Mirabeau, to cling to the Scriptural doctrine. It is not by any human law, nor by any social contract, nor by any assent of his fellow-beings, that man holds his title to property. He derives it from God himself. In the beginning of the world, the Creator gave to man dominion over the earth, over the fish of the sea, and the fowls of the air, and over every living thing. This is the foundation of man's property in the earth and in all its productions. Prior occupancy of the land which he cleared, and of the wild animals which he subjugated, gave to the first possessor the first property. To his own energy and industry he was indebted, under God, for it, and not to any imaginary contract with his fellowmen. The proprietor is not the steward of the State, but the steward of God. The State has no right to take a cent from his hard earnings, or from the accumulated hoard of his ancestors, to distribute it to the needy, and probably to the vicious. When the State says to me: 'Give half of your cloak to the poor, as the payment of a legitimate debt,' I rebel against the order, as the dictate of injustice and tyranny. But when God says: 'Give in charity half of what you possess, not because it is not your own, but because it is,' I obey cheerfully the mandate of justice and love, conveyed to me in the language of truth."

Talleyrand. "I have no doubt that the National Assembly will not only abolish tithes, but will even dispossess the clergy of all the property which they hold as religious corporations. I must confess that the clergy does not seem to me to be a proprietor after the fashion of other proprietors, because the property which they possess has not been given to them personally, and to subserve their private interests, but has been assigned to them as a body, or as the members of a body, to enable them to perform certain functions. What was the object of the donors? To provide for the poor, for the building and repairing of temples, hospitals, institutions of charity, and of public education, and for the expenses incidental to the keeping up of the religious worship approved by the nation. The clergy were bound to reserve for their personal wants only a small portion of those revenues. They were administrators or trustees. If the State assumes, as it is determined to do for the greater benefit of the nation, all the obligations imposed upon the clergy as conditions on which they hold the property given to them, and provides for their subsistence, surely it has the right to dispose of that property. The intentions of the donors have been fulfilled, and the clergy have no cause to complain. It can not be denied that corporations can only exist by the creation or permission of the State. If it can create, it can destroy its own work. If it can permit, it can prohibit. Therefore it can abolish at will all corporations on giving indemnities when just and necessary. This is the innate right of sovereignty. Without it, there would be no sovereignty. All that is within its sphere is subject to its action. There can be permitted to be no antagonism of existence within

10*

the circle of the national diadem—*no imperium in imperio.* It is true that the State could not abolish the whole clergy, because there can be no religion without a clergy, and a civilized State can no more exist without religion than the body without the soul. But, undoubtedly, the State can abolish, when necessary to its welfare, certain particular aggregations of the clergy which may, as corporations, have become too numerous and cumbersome—which may have outlived the purposes for which they were formed—and which may no longer be in harmony with the wants and ideas of the age. Governments have more than once destroyed religious orders, with the consent of the Pope. I need not recite all the instances of it related in history, and which will present themselves to your minds. That of the Jesuits, in the present century, is in point. Besides, it must be admitted that it is an intolerable evil, to have probably one-third of France held in mortmain by those innumerable monasteries and other religious corporations that have grown hoary and infirm on our soil, and are now of no more public utility than our old feudal towers. They must and will be struck down, on granting an indemnity which will be sufficiently ample to provide for their individual members. Their property must be thrown back into the general circulation from which it has been withdrawn. It will be bought with the paper currency issued by the State, and will thus contribute to its redemption. The national credit will be firmly established, and France saved from the awful calamity of bankruptcy. Surely the clergy are too patriotic not to make as many voluntary sacrifices as the nobility, to save their country from perdition."

L'abbé Maury. "If in the National Assembly the

absolute ruin of the secular and regular clergy has already been determined upon, if we have to struggle against the irresistible force of a fixed resolution, there is nothing left to us but resignation and silence. But if we are to be attacked only with the force of logic and the evidence of facts, we shall meet the contest with confidence. I am afraid, however, that the war undertaken against the clergy is a mere prelude to the one which is meditated against religion, forgetful, as all modern reformers are, that all the legislators who have preceded us, from the remotest antiquity to the present day, have uniformly recognized this unquestionable truth—that religion is the only basis on which society can be seated, because it is the only thing that can give morality to a people; because, according to the sound sentiments of a heathen philosopher and orator, the first duty of man on his becoming a partner in any human society, is to be religious. I hope that Cicero will be admitted here as an authority by my adversaries; for he was not a bigoted Catholic priest. But, before deciding if the clergy are to be stripped of all their possessions, is it not better to decide first, whether we are to have any clergy at all; and if we are to have a clergy, before determining whether that clergy shall be established and regulated by the Church, or by the assumed authority of the civil power, would it not be better to ascertain whether we are to have any religion at all? From the signs of the times I am inclined to believe that it is not impossible but what the existence of the clergy and of God himself will be simultaneously abolished by a national decree. God must be looked upon by the sages of the day as a great obstacle to those sublime reforms which are contemplated by human reason, and a stumbling-block in the way of the gradual march of our race toward perfection. What do I say? A march toward perfection! No. I take back my words, and beg pardon. We possess innate perfection; it is in the marrow of our bones, and, to be developed, it awaits only the *fiat* of the philosophy, benevolence, and omnipotence of matter. This question would, no doubt, be much simplified were God to be banished from the universe by a bold revolutionary stroke of the pen."

Mirabeau. "Allow me, *Monsieur L'abbé*, to point out to you that you are committing grave errors in chronology. There is no Satan here attempting to dethrone God in Heaven. We are in France, dealing with men, and not with angels and archangels; with the clergy, and not religion; with their temporal possessions, and not with their jurisdiction over souls and spiritual things."

L'abbé Maury. "Very well, *retournons à nos moutons.* Let us return to our sheep, which are to be fleeced without mercy. The main question then is, shall one hundred and fifty thousand Frenchmen who constitute the clergy, and on whom more than one million of persons are directly or indirectly dependent, be deprived of their possessions for what is called the patriotic regeneration of their country? Have I stated the question fairly, Mr. de Mirabeau? You nod assent. What is the meaning of that assent? It means that Peter shall be stripped naked to clothe Paul, that the clergy shall be spoliated, to facilitate the stock-jobbing operations of swindling Jews. It is substituting highway robbery for bankruptcy. What is the bankruptcy of national credit, compared with the bankruptcy of national honor and national justice? What would be thought of a man who, to pay his debts, should waylay travelers on the public road?"

L'abbé Sieyes. "Such are the French. They wish to be free, and they do not know how to be just."

L'abbé Maury. "It is not a little curious that the question of the suppression of monasteries and other religious institutions should have been made a financial one. Our holy altars are to be converted into counters, where the sellers of doves and money-changers, are to discount bonds bearing mortgage on church property. The value of stocks is to be the sole criterion of national prosperity, and the wealth of France is hereafter to lie in the portfolios of Jews, and not in her fertile soil ploughed by patient and honest labor. Surely, this can not be the true remedy for our ailments. On the contrary, it is poison and death. My opinion is, that, instead of this spend-thrift borrowing and of this consecration of robbery under the great national seal, we must develop our infinite resources by a wise and economical adminis-tration. We must renounce our luxurious habits; we must work, and not inscribe the name of France in Shylock's book. Instead of that, what is proposed? To pay our outstanding debts, we are told to issue State bonds, bearing interest. Well, how shall we provide for the payment of that new debt and its in-terests? By issuing other bonds! But will anybody have faith in those ever-increasing bonds, and will they be negotiated? Perhaps not. Therefore, let the clergy be robbed of their property, and let that property be the guarantee of the payment of the na-tional loan."

La Rochefoucauld. "There may be some abuses,

defects, and perhaps injustice to some extent, in the plan proposed to avoid the horrible calamity of national bankruptcy. But what plan could be free from similar objections? For my part, I do not see how, with the deficit which exists in the treasury, the Government can contrive to live, and can provide for its present and future necessities, without finding out the means of establishing a solid public credit, which, after all, is the only bank on which we can draw."

L'abbé Maury. "One would suppose that public credit, of which we hear so much, is the true treasure and the only salvation of the State. I confess that, in consequence of the past follies of France, we need credit, temporarily, to scramble our way up, out of the abyss into which we are gradually sinking. But, whenever the Government shall be administered with wisdom, public credit will no longer be what it now is : a necessary evil, a huge calamity, and the most terrible infliction which has ever befallen the nations of the earth. I lay at its door all our misfortunes; it has nourished the extravagant prodigalities of our kings, by which all our sources of wealth have been dried up; it has facilitated those wars which, very often, were undertaken for futile or criminal motives; it has equipped and fed those innumerable armies that have made war more fatal and more ruinous than it would otherwise have been—nay, it has perpetuated its image and its expenses in the midst of peace, by transforming Europe into a vast armed camp, always ready for action. It is credit which has engendered that long and complicated series of debts and taxes of all sorts under which we perish; it is credit which devours in anticipation the bread of future generations. When Francis I. issued for the

first time, in 1521, a loan guaranteed by the city of
Paris, he inaugurated a new era of calamities for Europe, by giving an example that was sure to be followed by his neighbors. He laid down the first stone
of that monstrous edifice which, now tottering to its
very foundations, threatens us with being crushed
under its ruins. The richest kingdom on earth has
not been able to stand up more than two centuries
and a half under that all-consuming system of con-
tinual borrowing, without even providing for the
punctual payment of interests, except with additional supplies of borrowed money. The capital of previous loans has been reimbursed only by the expedient of larger ones. Borrowing has been made the
most ingenious of arts, and the most skillful devices
have been imagined to fill the craving maw of an ever
empty exchequer. It has led us to bankruptcy, or to
the spoliation of one portion of the nation by the
other."

Chamfort (emptying his glass). "Well, let us
hope that good will come out of evil."

L'abbé Maury. "No, Sir, such a hope can not be
reasonably entertained. I predict that the confiscation of the possessions of the clergy will give no real
relief to the commonwealth. Their property will be
squandered ; for robbers are bad administrators ; and
the embarrassments of the treasury will remain what
they are. Such a confiscation would be worse than
an odious crime ; it would be a worthless and barren
one ; whilst I maintain that, as a matter of policy, a
territorial donation for the support of the clergy is a
precious institution for the State. Public worship
would be endangered and even annihilated, if it depended on a degrading and uncertain salary. An in-

fidel and rapacious government would soon be on the lookout for the cheapest form of worship, and it would be speedily discovered that it is still cheaper to have no worship at all. But, without any religious belief and without a respectable and independent clergy, the people, lacking that assistance, that check, that guidance which are so necessary to their moral and physcal infirmities and wants, would become lawless, and the world would again be taught the great political truth, too much forgotten nowadays, that public order reposes on religion, and that its ministers are the best guaranties which governments can have for the docility, submission, and good conduct of the people. It is by the giving of alms that the clergy have gained their hearts. How can the clergy, if poor, if receiving alms themselves and unable to relieve distress, retain that salutary influence? Reduce the clergy to beggary, make efficient charity an impossibility for them, confiscate monasteries, as was done in England, and you will soon have a poor tax, as in the country of Henry VIII. Besides, remember that a paid clergy is a slavish one. They will be tools, they will obey, instead of directing and controlling. In the name of that liberty which you preach, I ask why you should not allow us to be free?"

Mirabeau. "Who undertakes aught against your liberty?"

L'abbé Maury. "You, who are advocating the confiscation of what we possess. Without property, there is no liberty. Of all kinds of social property, liberty is the highest, for it makes a man proprietor of himself. Hence the necessity of property to insure liberty. Is it by making new victims that you wish to ameliorate the fate of the old ones? The

evils which we have to remove are nothing in comparison to those that are coming upon us. From the
palace of our kings to the humblest cottage, everything is in fermentation. What a spectacle does
France present! A king without power, and a people without liberty! For, already, you have been
compelled to prohibit popular meetings. Ha! Ha!
is it what we have gained by exchanging one master
for twelve hundred? Go on, gentlemen, go on, and
you will soon find out that the most terrific of all
despotisms is the one which wears the mask of liberty!"

Mirabeau. "We have had an eloquent speech
from *L'abbé* Maury. I will answer him in the National
Assembly, should he reproduce his sentiments in that
body. In the meantime I shall content myself with
saying, that blind indeed is he who does not see that
the time has come for the destruction of all those
religious communities which overshadow the land.
If it be a question of expediency, the State is certainly competent to decide upon it. As to the question of right, I think that it also appertains to the
same authority to pronounce on the subject. For
my part, I am convinced that corporations have no
self-derived existence, and are not created solely for
themselves. They are formed and preserved mainly
for the public good, and must cease to flourish at the
very moment when they cease to be useful. Your
religious corporations, *Monsieur L'abbé*, with the
ever-recurring donations made to them in the shape
of endowments or otherwise, by vanity, fear, or remorse, would in the end absorb all the capital of the
kingdom and all its territory. Hence the right of
the State to destroy them. They, on the other hand,

have no right to exist forever, because they once existed. If a tomb had been erected to every man who
lived in this world, it would unavoidably have been
necessary for the purpose of cultivation, to sweep off
those monuments in order to have land, and to rake
up the ashes of the dead to find food for the living."

Archbishop of Aix. "I am no debater or orator.
I will merely assert, as an article of faith with me,
that territorial possessions are as indispensable to the
clergy in every nation, as temporal power is to his
Holiness in Rome."

Mirabeau. "We have reached an epoch, *Monseigneur*, when, repelling dictation and deaf to the teach-
ings of questionable authority, the human mind will
arrive at its own conclusions on every subject. There
is no longer any implicit faith in anything, not even
in the infallibility of the Pope."

L'abbé Maury. "And pray, Mr. de Mirabeau, why
should there not be implicit faith in the infallibility
of the Pope?"

Mirabeau. "Because infallibility is the attribute
of the Deity, and because it is sufficiently hard to
believe that, to save the human race from perdition,
God became man, without exacting our assent to the
proposition that, for the same purpose, a man becomes God."

L'abbé Maury. "This is a glittering and witty
antithesis, but all that glitters is not gold, and all
that is wit is not always sense. The sober truth is,
that the Pope never had any pretension to be God.
He is only His delegate on earth to teach religious
tenets or dogmas, of which he is, therefore, the supreme exponent. That shallow minds should fling
their pointless shafts at the doctrine of his infallibility

might be expected. But such an intellect as that of
Mr. de Mirabeau should better understand a subject
which is worthy of his meditations, and which, when
understood, may command his assent, instead of
tempting him into a disrespectful sarcasm. The
Catholic, Apostolic, and Roman Church is an elective
monarchy. The Pope is a theocratic sovereign,
chosen without regard to birth, wealth, and nation-
ality, by electors appointed by his predecessors.
There can be no human society without government,
no government without sovereignty, no sovereignty
without supremacy, and no supremacy without infallibility, absolute or relative, real or fictitious. One of
the fundamental principles in the constitution of England is, that *the king can do no wrong.* This is a
declaration of infallibility. The King, the House of
Peers, and the Commons are omnipotent, when acting
in concert. That is admitted, I believe. Therefore
they are infallible; for political infallibility can not
be separated from political omnipotence, at least as a
legal and necessary fiction. Blackstone says in his
commentaries: 'The usurped power of the Pope
being destroyed, the crown was restored to its supremacy over spiritual men and causes.' Well, the Pope
claims no more for himself than Blackstone claims
for his Protestant King. The partisans of a republican form of government proclaim that absolute sovereignty lies in the people—that is to say, omnipotence, undisputed supremacy, or infallibility. *Vox
populi, vox Dei*—the voice of the people is the voice
of God. This has become an axiom in the school of
democracy. But, if an aggregation of men are the
organ of the Deity, why not twenty, or ten, or even
one single man? What is that proportion or degree

of aggregation which is necessary to constitute
supremacy or infallibility? Shall we forget that, if
we have often heard of the most wonderful wisdom
or virtue in individuals, we have never heard of it as
existing in the masses or millions, collectively?

" The Church asks no more for the Pope than what
temporal sovereignties ask for themselves—which is,
that infallibility or supremacy so indispensable to
the power of deciding without appeal; and finally,
the Church, I say, asks no more, although she has
over temporal sovereignties an immense superiority,
inasmuch as their infallibility is a mere human supposition or fiction, arising from the necessity of the
case, *ex necessitate rei*, whilst, in the Church, infallibility is the accomplishment of a divine promise.
England, which you admire so much, Mr. de Mirabeau, has put temporal and spiritual omnipotence in
her king and parliament, for they can establish and
prescribe what is to be the religion of the country.
If you have no objection to that, why then should
you blame the Church for placing spiritual supremacy
or infallibility in the Pope? Where is the absurdity?
Where is the unprecedented monstrosity? The
Church does not go as far as England, much less as
far as Russia, who has invested one single man, her
emperor, with spiritual and temporal omnipotence.
The fact is, that, for the government of the soul as
well as for the government of the body, there must
be a court of the last resort, and if so, it is sound
policy that the finality and infallibility of its judgments should go hand in hand. There is not one of
the Protestant Churches that does not claim to teach
the truth. That is logical; for if they were not sure,
in their estimation, to be free from error, how could

they assume the responsibility of teaching and enforcing the strict adoption and observance of their doctrines, under the penalty for their disciples to cease to belong to their respective denominations in case of dissent? Does not, therefore, the Episcopalian or the Presbyterian minister claim as much infallibility for his church, as the Catholic priest does for his own? For my part, I do not see why it is more difficult to believe in the infallibility of the Pope, than in that of synods, or presbyteries."

La Rochefoucauld. "Infallible or not, the Catholic, Apostolic and Roman Church is certainly the most wonderful human institution—viewing it only in that light—that the world has ever seen; for not only has it existed eighteen hundred years, but it has existed thus long without any material modification or alteration in its essence, and without any diminution of its vitality. No other of the institutions of men ever approached this duration."

L'abbé Maury. "Such an exemption from the fate of all human institutions proves that the Catholic, Apostolic and Roman Church has a supernatural character. If it is not human, it must be divine, and if divine, infallible."

Chamfort. "Religious questions have always been very perplexing to me. The relations existing between the human race and its Creator seem to have become obscure since our first disobedience, and seem to produce discontent on both sides. I wish the National Assembly would enlighten us on the subject. It has given us a declaration of the rights of man, which, I think, should be followed by a declaration of the rights of God."

L'abbé Maury. "Sir, the sneer that lurks in your

remarks is almost justified by the absurdity of that
declaration of the rights of man, which is partly borrowed from the famous document containing the declaration of independence of the United States. All
men born free and equal, forsooth! When has that
ever been seen since the deluge? In the first place,
we are not born men; we are born children, and we
remain in a state of tutelage until we are men; when
arrived at the age of manhood, we have to obey laws
which we have not made, and if we are then permitted to have a share in the legislation of our country, our wishes may be overruled by a majority that
may subject us to a government we detest, and thus
we are never free from the moment of our birth to
that of our death. As to equality among men, it is
a still more glaring absurdity. There is not a human
being who, at the bottom of his heart, does not repudiate such an assertion. Tell an honest cobbler
that he is the equal of anybody in the land, however
high, and that the distance between him and those
who are reputed his betters is a mere accident, the
folly of his pride may smile approvingly at the boldness of your flattery. But tell him that he is no better than the lousy beggar at the corner of the street,
and it is ten to one that he will knock you down. It
is a demagogic lie. There is no equality in the physical, moral, and intellectual departments of the world,
no equality among the trees of the forests, the beasts,
the insects, the birds, the reptiles, and the fishes.
Even geese would cackle in derision, if you told them
that one of their feathered tribe is as good as the
other, for they have a leader. The bees would sting
you for it; they have their queen and their drones;
the ants would bite you, for they have a nobility, the

distinction of classes, and even slaves. Man alone is stupid enough to listen to such barefaced falsehood. Woe to those who shall attempt to subvert the hierarchy which God has ordained in heaven and on earth! Woe to the mad architect who will attempt to make a pyramid repose on its apex! Woe to the social body which stands with its head down and its feet up! In that inverted and unnatural position, its liberty will be suffocated from the afflux of blood to the lungs, and even life itself will depart. The United States of America have been the first to proclaim this nonsense as an aphorism, and they will be the first to suffer from it. Equality among men demands equality of rights, civil and political; political equality means general suffrage, and general suffrage means the supreme power in the hands of the ignorant, the needy, and the vicious. When that fatal hour shall strike, our allies on the other side of the Atlantic may bid a long farewell to civilization."

Talleyrand. " My dear *abbé*, you are performing the part of Cassandra. I am afraid that you have not dined well. Forgetting the Americans and the wooden horse with which you threaten them, let us adjourn to the adjacent saloons, where coffee will be brought to us. We shall meet friends, for this is, you know, my reception evening."

CHAPTER XVII.

TALLEYRAND'S EVENING RECEPTION.

WHEN the party of guests moved from the dinner-table to the reception-rooms, they found in them from forty to fifty persons, most of whom divided into groups, some sitting, some standing, and some promenading, whilst engaged in animated conversation. Talleyrand courteously addressed every one of them in turn, saying some civil things to all. Not a single one was neglected. After that, he languidly sauntered a little while in a listless manner, with his eyes half closed, apparently inattentive to anything, when in reality nothing escaped his observation. Suddenly he approached Gouverneur Morris, the American minister plenipotentiary, took him by the arm, and leading him to a sofa, invited him to sit down on his right, whilst, beckoning to Lafayette, he made him take a seat on his left.

"I hope," said he to Morris, "that you have lately heard from General Washington, that he is well, and that your country is in a prosperous condition."

Morris. "General Washington writes exultingly * of the state of the country and of the attachment of all classes to the government. He says that, while in Europe wars or commotions seem to agitate almost every nation, peace and tranquillity prevail among us,

---

* Washington's Letter to Lafayette.

(240)

except in some part of our Western frontiers, where
the Indians have been troublesome, to reclaim or
chastise whom, proper measures are now pursuing.
He thinks that this contrast between the situation
of the United States and that of Europe is too striking to be passed over, even by the most superficial
observer, and he believes that it may be considered
as one great cause of leading the people there to reflect more attentively on their own prosperous state,
and to examine more minutely, and consequently
approve more fully of, the government under which
they live, than they would otherwise have done. But
he does not wish us to be the only people who may
taste the sweets of an equal and good government.
He looks with an anxious eye to the time when happiness and tranquillity shall prevail in your country,
and all Europe shall be freed from commotions, tumults, and alarms."

Talleyrand. "Such generous sentiments are worthy
of that great man. But, what are your own, Mr.
Morris, on our affairs? You are an impartial and
sagacious spectator, who has a full view of the stage
on which we are acting."

Morris. "I am sorry to tell you, Sir, that I take
but a gloomy survey of the spectacle which is before
me.* Permit me to say, with a somewhat rude but
well-meant severity, that your unhappy country, be-
wildered in the pursuit of metaphysical whimsies and
political utopias, presents to my moral view nothing
but a mighty ruin. Like the remnants of ancient
magnificence, we admire the architecture of the temple, while we detest the false god to whom it was

---

* Morris to Lafayette.

11

dedicated. Daws, and ravens, and the birds of night now build their nests in its niches. The sovereign, humbled to the level of a beggar's pity, is without resources, without authority, without a friend. The National Assembly is at once a master and a slave— the master of the king, and the slave of the populace. It is new in power, wild in theory, raw in practice. It engrosses all functions, whilst incapable of exercising any, and has taken from this fierce, ferocious people every restraint of religion and respect. Hitherto, my dear General Lafayette, you have performed a splendid part ; you stand as a rampart between royalty and democracy, and, thus far, you have prevented a frightful collision. But how long will it last? The king obeys, but detests you. He obeys because he fears. As to the people, they also obey you, because they trust and love him whom they consider as their champion. But, how long will they trust and love ?"

Lafayette. " I expect,* of course, to continue for some time to be tossed on an ocean of factions and commotions of every kind ; for it is my fate to be attacked with great animosity, on one side, by all that is aristocratic, servile, parliamentary—in a word, by all the adversaries of my free and leveling doctrine ; on the other, by the Orleans and anti-monarchical factions, and all the workers of disorder and pillage. It is doubtful whether I may escape personally from so many enemies, but the success of our grand and good revolution is, at least, thank Heaven, assured in France, and soon it will propagate itself in the rest of the world, if we succeed in establishing public order in this country. Unfortunately, the people have much

---

* Lafayette to Washington.

better learnt to overthrow despotism than to comprehend the duty of submission to law.   But we
must have patience and forbearance.   For my part, I
will, as a leader, pursue the course of moderation,
avoiding all excesses, and I have no doubt that all
will be right in the end."

Morris. "Moderation! Moderation in a revolution such as yours is destined to be! Revolutions
always rush to their extreme limits, General, and
leave moderation stranded far behind.   In the stormy
nights of popular commotions, it is better for a leader,
better for his followers, and better for the cause he
has espoused, that he should be a bold, cold-hearted,
ever calculating, unscrupulous, and iron-handed, but
far-seeing pilot, than a warm, generous, honest, and
impulsive one, with his organ of vision obstructed or
impaired by his sensibilities, or by illusions of his own
raising."

Lafayette. "If you apply this to me, my friend,
I assure you that I have no illusions.   I give you the
assurance that my conviction is, that our troubles will
not be terminated until our intended constitution is
thoroughly formed and established.   Nevertheless,
though our horizon is still very dark, we commence
to foresee the moment when a new legislature will
replace our Assembly: and, unless there come an intervention of foreign powers, I shall have resumed the
life of a peaceful and simple citizen." *

Morris. "Amen!   Better the shades of your
château de la Grange than the pangs of exile and the
horrors of a dungeon!"

Lafayette. "I see nothing, after all, justifying ex-

---

* Lafayette to Washington.

cessive alarms. The rage of party between the two different shades of patriots has gone very far, it is true ; but, as yet, with little effusion of blood. If, as I am willing to admit, animosities are far from subsiding, yet present circumstances are somewhat less menacing of a collision between the different supporters of the popular cause. As to myself, I am always the butt for attacks of all parties,because they see in my person an insurmountable obstacle to their evil designs.* In the meantime, what appears to me a species of phenomenon, my popularity hitherto has not been shaken."

Morris. "Alas, beware! Popularity, you know, is but the broken reed which pierces the hand that rests on it."

During this conversation, reclining in an easy posture against the back of the sofa, Talleyrand had closed entirely his eyes, which he habitually kept half shut. His face was expressionless, but a keen observer might have detected an almost imperceptible smile of irony occasionally flitting on his lips.

Mirabeau had approached the group. "Count," said Lafayette, "I have just told Mr. Morris that our troubles will not terminate before the constitution we are preparing is completed and adopted."

"An upstart constitution is but a poor panacea," replied Mirabeau. "A constitution of yesterday is too new for the evils of to-day, and too old for those of to-morrow. Give me a constitution which, like that of England, has been made by nobody living, but is the gradual and imperceptible work of ages— a constitution which has grown and expanded with

---

* Lafayette to Washington.

the nation, as the soul does with the human body—a constitution which, composed of traditions and precedents, is invisible and impalpable like the atmosphere of liberty in which it flourishes, but is felt through every pore of the commonwealth. Give me an elastic and easy coat that adapts itself to the enlargement or contraction of every limb, as it grows fat or lean, and impedes no unforeseen movement or action. But a written constitution is not worth the paper on which it is inscribed, although, by the force of circumstances, I am compelled to lend my aid to such an abortive creation. A written constitution is for a people what a strait-jacket is for a man. But, what will subdue the one, will be broken through by the other. It is attempting to chain a Titan with a cobweb. Pshaw! A written constitution is no better than an almanac; it will have to be changed every year. I have always wished to retain all that was good in our old *régime*, but most of my colleagues are opposed to it. I wished to engraft the sapling of the present on the sturdy oak of the past. But no, we seem determined to act as if we imagined that we are but one day older than creation. Everything is new; there is nothing that has preceded us, and with which we are bound to reckon. We forget that life is not self-generated, that it proceeds from anterior life, and, therefore, that we must connect harmoniously our present and future existence with that of the past. I think that we are introducing too much radicalism into our fundamental institution; and, as extreme radicalism is the root of all troubles, I am afraid, General, that we are not near the end of ours. Instead of using as a foundation the primeval rock of antiquity which God has given us, we pulverize it and fling it to the four winds of

heaven. Hence there remains but an abyss on which
to build the edifice which we destine for ourselves
and for posterity. But, excuse me, I see Cabanis and
Candorcet just coming in. I know that they have
something to say to me," and he turned on his heels,
with a slight bow to the company from whom he departed.

Morris. "Mr. de Mirabeau is more conservative
than I thought."

Talleyrand (inhaling a pinch of snuff). "And more
musical than you have any idea of. He has been, of
late, taking long lessons on the violin from Tintin
Calandro, the chief musician of the Princess de Lamballe, who is, as you know, the confidential and bosom
friend of the queen. Mr. de Mirabeau is a wonderful
man, Mr. Morris."

"Yes, a very wonderful man!" echoed Brissot, a
member of the National Assembly, who, at that moment, had come to salute Talleyrand, and who sometimes amused his colleagues by the uncalled-for bursts
of his excessive anglophobia; "but it is a pity that
he is so infatuated about the English constitution,
and that he wishes to assimilate ours to the one which
rules those thick-headed, pudding-eating islanders, with
whom we have nothing in common, either in thought,
feeling, or language, either in eating or drinking,
either in sleeping or waking. The constitution
of England! Whew! That constitution is the
cause of her ruin. Everybody knows that she is
lost."

"What!" exclaimed Talleyrand, with a comical
expression of dismay, " England is lost! When did
you receive such stupendous news, Mr. Brissot? By
what degree of latitude was she lost? How many

men, women, and children were saved from the wreck, or did they all perish?"

This was said in Talleyrand's inimitable way. It produced a hearty laugh, and Brissot was somewhat disconcerted. "But," continued Talleyrand, with a genial expression of kindness, "excuse this little bit of raillery. I never take such liberties except with my friends. Give me your arm, for you know I am somewhat lame, and, leaving General Lafayette and Mr. Gouverneur Morris together, who will be glad to talk of American affairs, let us join *L'abbé* Maury and Mr. de Robespierre, who seem to be engaged in an interesting discussion."

CHAPTER XVIII.

AN INTELLECTUAL PASSAGE–AT–ARMS BETWEEN L'ABBÉ MAURY AND ROBESPIERRE.

ROBESPIERRE was a sour-looking, undersized man, extremely spruce and rigidly neat in his dress, almost a dandy, but of too sinister an aspect for such a character. His unsteady look, which seemed always anxious to avoid meeting the look of any one with whom he conversed, the incessant nervous quivering of his eyelids, his receding narrow forehead, his sandy hair, the peculiar smile of his thin lips, his upturned nose, his ghastly complexion, his dogmatic and dry manner, the hissing intonations of his voice when he was excited, the occasional convulsive twitches of his limbs, produced the most disagreeable impression. It would have been impossible for a physiognomist not to feel uncomfortable in his presence. When Talleyrand and Brissot approached, he was saying to *L'abbé* Maury: " Nothing, in my opinion, Sir, can regenerate France but a republican form of government."

L'abbé Maury. " Aristocratic, or democratic ? "

Robespierre. " Democratic, of course."

L'abbé Maury. " Founded on the absolute sovereignty of the people ? "

Robespierre. " Undoubtedly."

L'abbé Maury. " Equality of political and civil rights for all Frenchmen ? "

(248)

Robespierre. "Certainly."

L'abbé Maury. "That implies general suffrage."

Robespierre. "A logical deduction."

L'abbé Maury. "I am glad to see that we may not be irreconcilable on all points. Thus, if I understand you, the people, in their collective capacity, are to assume, without opposition and deception, the control of their own destinies, and are to decide, whenever they choose, what is, or what is not, for their general welfare?"

Robespierre. "That is my doctrine."

L'abbé Maury. "Well, you are for a republic; I am for a monarchy. I propose that we refer the question to the people, and accept their verdict."

Robespierre. "Provided that the clergy, the nobility, the army, the navy, and all persons depending on them, and also all the employes, high and low, of the Government, with their dependents, be excluded. They could not be impartial."

L'abbé Maury. "This would be excluding half of the French people. But, proceed; I am in a liberal mood this evening, and I am willing to grant all you want. Let it be as you say, and let the populace of the cities and the peasantry be alone consulted."

Robespierre. "Not yet. They are still under the influence of the excluded classes. They are too ignorant. They must previously be educated into a proper knowledge of their rights."

L'abbé Maury. "Oh! oh! I understand. A few educators, philosophers, and philanthropists, like Mr. de Robespierre, will appoint themselves the representatives and tutors of the people. They will constitute a regency with unlimited powers, whilst paternally forming the heart and judgment of their confiding

11*

pupils, and qualifying them for the future sovereignty which they are to exercise. But you must admit that, in the meantime, it will be the government of a minority—which is anti-democratic. Thus your conclusions are at variance with your premises."

Robespierre. "Only temporarily. This minority will, in the end, swell into a majority, by educating the people and preparing them for liberty."

L'abbé Maury. "In the end! When will that end come? How long will it take?"

Robespierre. "I can not tell. It must be left to circumstances."

L'abbé Maury. "But, during that indefinite space of time, we shall be living in a republic only in name, not in reality. For, the minority, whilst educating the majority, will rule without consulting it."

Robespierre. "It will be a transient evil, to secure a permanent good. A republic must repose on virtue and universal education. Otherwise, it would soon perish. The people must be gradually prepared for the new condition to which they are destined."

L'abbé Maury. "You talk so fair, Mr. de Robespierre, that I am almost converted, and that I am tempted to hope that you will make the world see the day when the lamb shall lie in peace with the wolf, or rather, when all wolves shall be sheep. A government founded on virtue and general education! It makes my mouth water."

Robespierre. "Mr. *L'abbé* is disposed to jest, whilst I am in earnest."

L'abbé Maury. "Well, Sir, I shall be serious enough to please you. I suppose that you understand by education, that series of scientific and scholarly instruction and moral discipline which is intended to enlighten the understanding, correct the temper, and form the manners and habits of youth to fit them for usefulness in their future stations."

Robespierre. "I do not object to the definition."

L'abbé Maury. "But who is to prescribe and to impart that education? Not the one half of the people of France whom you have disfranchised, because, if they are too disloyal to vote, they are too dangerous to be permitted to teach; and not the other half, who are too ignorant to be trusted, as you think, with political power for the present. If they are too ignorant for self-government, surely they are too ignorant to educate others. Thus you alone and your friends, that is, a handful of men, regardless of what may be the will of an immense majority of your fellow-citizens whom you do not consult, after having determined what is the best form of government for them, are to settle what is the most efficient education to be given to the rising generation, in order to prepare it for the support of that very government. But pray, Sir, how are you to determine the various degrees of education which must be made to harmonize with the future stations of your innumerable pupils? What basis will you go upon? Will it be the accident of birth, or of social position, or the indication of intellect? How much of education will be allowed to the son of a tailor, a cobbler, a peasant, or a rag-picker? Will it be in reference to the probability of their pursuing the avocations of their parents? When and how will you acquire that knowledge? Will you consult their wishes or tastes, or will you make them conform to the better judgment of their teachers? At what period of the life of a student will a decision be taken on the qualifications which he may have for a future station, in order to direct his education accordingly?"

Robespierre. "My plan is much more simple. I am in favor of the same system and degree of education for all. I want no distinction. The proficiency of each child in his studies, and his qualifications as they are developed, will determine his future station in life. Let there be the same incubation for all the eggs of the nation, without presuming to ascertain in advance out of which shells will come the eagle, the buzzard, or the crow. Let there be public schools supported by taxation."

L'abbé Maury. "If poor parents say that they can not spare their children whom they need at home to work and make a living, if they refuse to send them to your schools, what then?"

Robespierre. "They shall be compelled."

L'abbé Maury. "Who will clothe and feed those children when they are at school? For you can not deny that, in our country, children, even in very early life, must help their parents by their labor."

Robespierre. "These are details into which the State can not enter. The State can not be expected to take the trouble of ascertaining who are, and who are not, the parents that can support their children, or what degree of support they can give them, without relying on the co-operative labor of those children."

L'abbé Maury. "Very well, I see how it will work. The poor who will say that they can not support their children at school, and who will refuse to send them there, will be fined, I suppose. If they do not pay the fine, they will be imprisoned, and, in that case, the State will have to support the parents in jail and the quasi orphans at school. Otherwise, they would not be educated at all, and for a very good reason, because they would starve—their parents being locked up. Pshaw! Is it not self-evident that it is an impossibility to disseminate education equally among all classes, even under the very best form of all governments—a French republic?"

Robespierre. "For a republic founded on fraternity, equality, and the acknowledged rights of man, an impossibility is merely a feasibility bristling with difficulties."

L'abbé Maury. "Sublime! I am so overpowered that I give up. I grant that the cup of classic lore, if not a dish of broth, can be brought to the lips of every poor child in France. But the rich?—the rich who shall pay for the education of the poor, whether they approve, or do not approve, of the tax and of the nature of that education, will, at least, be permitted, I suppose, to rear their own children after their own fashion? If so, one half of France will be educated very differently from the other. Here is at once a stab between the fourth and fifth ribs of that equality of which you dream in everything."

Robespierre. "This would be anti-republican. The rich and the poor must be fused and must matriculate together at the same public schools. There they will be born again, as it were, and will fraternally come out of the vast womb of the same motherly education."

L'abbé Maury. "What! All proprietors, or rich men, after having been heavily taxed to educate the children of those who own nothing, and therefore do not pay any portion of that tax, shall be compelled to subject their own children to a course of education which they may deem deleterious!"

Robespierre. "The State is the best judge of that. It will be an education preparatory and conducive to social equality, the greatest of all blessings. There will no longer be left an inch of ground for an aristocracy to stand upon."

L'abbé Maury. "Why not come at once to the tables in common of Sparta, where all citizens, high or low, ate together?"

Robespierre. "We may come to that in due time, for under the fraternal rod of equality there will be neither high nor low."

L'abbé Maury. "Admitting that there should be one day neither high nor low, and that society should have become as flat as the back of a bedbug, you will grant, I presume, that men who are on a footing of equality, have an equal and inalienable right to think for themselves?"

Robespierre. "Unquestionably."

L'abbé Maury. "Very good. You know that watches, however similarly constructed, never can be made to agree for any length of time. Charles V. found that out. Therefore, you can not expect unanimity of thought even among those whom your democratic education will mould into equals. From some quarter, perhaps the least suspected, there may come some fierce opposition to the continuance of your system."

Robespierre. "It would be treason against liberty, and such treason must be crushed without mercy."

L'abbé Maury. "O liberty, how much despotism there may be in a republic!"

Robespierre. "Permit me, *Monsieur L'abbé*, to put you in mind of certain words which fell from the lips of one who belonged to your holy order. *When I find obstacles in my way*, said Cardinal Richelieu, *I mow them down, and, covering them with my scarlet mantle, I step over.* Like him, I would mow down all my opponents with the scythe of progress, and, throwing over their corpses the red flag of liberty, I would move onward."

L'abbé Maury. "If you ever wield the axe of that wonderful man, may you have his genius to direct your arm! He assumed a frightful responsibility. But France, remembering that he made her great, has absolved him from the blood he shed. To him we owe, long after his death, the splendors of the reign of Louis XIV. Should you ever become a ruler among men, and should you ever spill blood like him, may you be able to make as good a defense as he before the tribunal of posterity, and may you, on the page of history, appear as grand a figure with your red flag of liberty, as the great cardinal with his scarlet mantle, which he spread as a protecting screen between the stability of anointed royalty and the turbulence of feudal anarchy, between the hereditary power of one legitimate sovereign and the selfish conspiracies of a thousand would-be usurpers of authority, who, ever changing and ever hungry, would devour the last crumb of the substance of the people!"

Robespierre. "Although I have quoted Richelieu, I am not ambitious to have anything in common with him. My model is Tiberius Graechus."

L'abbé Maury. "Cardinal Richelieu died quietly in his bed, forgiving his enemies, and with a conscience which he declared to be calm. Tiberius Graechus had the tragical fate of a revolutionist, of a flatterer of the populace, and died with imprecations on his lips. But allow me one more question in relation to your aphorism : *that a republic must rest on virtue and education.* What your intended plan of education is, I have been sufficiently informed. Thanks to it, I take it for granted that every man in France will, in due course of time, be as well read in polite literature and will possess as many scholarly attainments as yourself. But I am curious to know what system you will establish to secure the reign of virtue among the people. Virtue is based on morality, and morality rests on religion. Morality without religion is like a woman without chastity. Let temptation open the door, and sin will enter. I know that philosophists maintain that virtue may exist, distinct from religion. They say that the practice of moral duties, merely from motives of conscience, or from compulsion, or from regard to reputation, is virtue Surely this can not be your appreciation of it. What can be the solidity of that virtue which is based on convenience or compulsion? Let that convenience or that compulsion cease, and where is virtue? As to a mere regard to reputation, it is clear that it would not be a reliable foundation, because virtue, whenever sure of her reputation being protected by secrecy, might be seduced into some indecorous eccentricity of behavior. It is laughable to think of putting trust in that kind of virtue which, caring only for reputation, would grow weak or strong according to the probabilities of detection. Therefore, considering virtue and religion as inseparably connected, I beg leave to ask what religion would be taught in your schools."

Robespierre. " Every one has the right to worship his Creator, or not, according to his own free will, and in the form he pleases. No particular religion,

therefore, can be taught in the public schools in preference to another; and, as the teaching of all creeds
indiscriminately would produce confusion and the
most mischievous squabbles, it shall be prohibited.
The works of Plato, Horace, Virgil, Cicero, and such
other productions of human genius, ancient and modern, shall be read, but neither the Protestant, nor the
Catholic Bible, nor the Koran, nor any other religious
code."

L'abbé Maury. "Exactly what I expected. God
has become an obsolete piece of furniture in this
renovated and improved household of scientific doc-
tors and philanthropic reformers, and is to be cast
aside with what is called the remaining rubbish of
superstition."

Robespierre. "Not at all. Voltaire has said with
truth and pithiness of expression: *If God did not exist it would be necessary to invent Him.* Atheism is
aristocratic.* Nothing is more essentially popular
and democratic than the idea of a Great Being who
watches over oppressed innocence, and who punishes
triumphant crime. Therefore my republic would acknowledge Him by a national decree."

L'abbé Maury. "The Supreme Being would, no
doubt, feel highly complimented and be grateful for
the honor. The next step, I suppose, will be to proclaim the existence of the sun. Well, the world,
thanks to your republic, is informed that God exists.
But is that all? Will not the republic deign to do
something more for Him? Will He not have His
temples and His ministers?"

Robespierre. "His temple is the universe; all men
are His ministers on earth. Therefore His worship

---

* The very words of Robespierre in the National Assembly.

shall not be confined within the narrow limits of edifices erected by human hands, nor shall His altars be intrusted to any privileged set of Levites. But, on certain days during the year, there shall be grand national festivities in His honor. The people shall meet under the broad canopy of heaven to worship the Creator, and under the presidency of the State authorities everywhere. Hymns shall be composed by the most celebrated poets, and sung by the most melodious voices. There shall be imposing processions of men, women, and children, crowned with emblematic wreaths of flowers. The chief executive, for the time being, shall be the high-priest, and shall be represented in the same functions by the delegates of his authority throughout the whole extent of the republic. In the capital, for instance, a superb altar shall be erected on the most beautiful and the largest public square within its walls, where shall be enthroned the goddess of reason, as the visible representative of the invisible Deity."

L'abbé Maury. "Perfect! God having given man a partner in woman, man, in his turn, presents a goddess to God! This is a proper exchange of reciprocal civilities. But why should it be the goddess of reason, rather than any other divinity of the same sex?"

Robespierre. "Reason being that faculty of the mind by which it distinguishes truth from falsehood, and good from evil, and which enables its possessor to deduce correct inferences from facts and from propositions, must emanate from God alone ; and, emanating from God, it necessarily follows that it partakes of His essence, and is, by His will, incarnated in man. In worshiping it, we worship Him."

L'abbé Maury. "There is nothing more variable

and more fallible than human reason. How can reason, therefore, be the representative of divine infallibility? For instance, my reason makes me a monarchist; yours makes you a republican. Which is right?
What permanent form shall that Protean goddess of
reason assume? What vagaries of hers shall be our
religion? Is it on the virtue proceeding from such a
religion, whatever it may be, that your republic is to be
founded? I am afraid, Mr. de Robespierre, that your
system of universal virtue will be as abortive as your
system of universal education, and that these two pillars of your contemplated French republic will be as
brittle as glass."

Robespierre. "The experiment, however, is worth
making."

L'abbé Maury. "Well, let us suppose it made.
Equality, fraternity, and liberty are in the ascendant,
and shine like the Pleiads in the firmament of France,
shedding their sweet influences over her destinies.
Incense fumes over the numerous altars of the goddess of reason, the visible representative of God on
earth. So much for France. But what of her colonies, where two races confront each other as masters
and slaves, as whites and blacks?"

Robespierre. "If a republic should ever be proclaimed in France, on that day the chains of the slave
shall be broken wherever the flag of liberty will float,
and there shall be no political, civil, or social distinction between the white and the black race, or any
other race."

L'abbé Maury. "It would ruin our colonies."

Robespierre. "Perish the colonies rather than a
principle!"*

---

* Words attributed to Robespierre in the National Assembly.

L'abbé Maury. " Perish the colonies! Shall they be sunk to the bottom of the ocean ? "

Robespierre. " Yes, rather than tolerate, one single day, the institution of slavery, or any distinction of color."

L'abbé Maury. " To drown those poor negroes would be a prompt but unpleasant way to emancipate them. They might prefer their present condition to such a summary kind of introduction to freedom. Would it not be fair to consult them ? "

Robespierre. " No. The republic would consult principles, and not men."

Talleyrand. " I have been an attentive and gratified listener. But permit me, Mr. de Robespierre, to say that too much zeal often defeats the object it has in view. There must be moderation in all things. Equality and fraternity among men, liberty for all, and universal education, are excellent sugar plums, but let us not eat too much of them. It might give us a sick stomach."

L'abbé Maury. " Jean Jacques Rousseau, who certainly must be a strong authority in the eye of Mr. de Robespierre, has argued that the arts and sciences have been, in proportion to their development, fatal to the virtue and social happiness of nations. Prometheus stole the fire of civilization from Heaven, and lighted a torch which led man, on the road of progress, farther than it was intended by the Gods that he should go. Hence his punishment on the rock where he was chained for his crime, and where his entrails were devoured by the vulture-beak of eternal remorse. This is the tale of paganism, and therein lies a deep lesson. Satan said to our first parents: ' In the day ye eat the fruit of the tree of knowledge, then your eyes shall be opened, and ye shall be as Gods, knowing good and evil.' This is the tale of Christianity. If these are fables, or allegories, as is maintained by skepticism, they are the fables of wisdom and the allegories of truth. *Every man to his trade*, is the proverbial saying of the practical common sense of all nations. You must remember, Mr. de Robespierre, the words of Horace: *ne sutor ultrà crepidam.*"

Brissot. "Good God! Here is a Latin quotation. You know that I do not understand that barbarous language, and yet you see that I am listening with all my ears to your very interesting sentiments. You would not have distressed me more if you had spoken English. Pray, tell me in plain French what means your quotation?"

L'abbé Maury. "It means that the cobbler ought not to presume to rise above the shoe on which he is at work. But now, it seems, the cobbler must be as well-educated and refined as anybody, and anybody must be as good and as well-informed as any other body. I am sick of all this cant. There will ever be in this world the poor and the rich, the learned and the ignorant, the strong and the weak in intellect as well as in body, the virtuous and the wicked, just as there is always prevailing a certain proportion of rain and sunshine. Should it be otherwise, this world would not be what it is, and what it is intended to be. Let the scale of education correspond with the ascending steps of the ladder of society, and it will work well."

Robespierre. "No, Sir; let there be the same education for all, and the same opportunity to profit by it, or not. Why should not the whole French nation be a nation of gentlemen and ladies?"

L'abbé Maury. "I should have no objection, were it not that all washerwomen having become ladies, and all cooks and valets being gentlemen, I might run the risk of not having my clothes washed, my soup made, and my coat dusted."

Talleyrand. "It would be a dire calamity for such sybarites as the *abbé* and myself, Monsieur de Robespierre. You must excuse us if we have not your frugality, and if we could not be contented, like you, with occupying a small room above a carpenter's shop, dining at his table, and enjoying the company of such humble and uncultivated friends. But, so far as I am concerned, I will throw no impediment in the way of your experiment, although I am afraid that you are levelling down, instead of levelling up, and that, instead of raising scullions and rag-pickers to the standard of gentlemen, you will sink gentlemen to the standard of the former. Oh! oh! What do I see? Sir Samuel Romilly entering through yonder door. I am delighted. He must have lately arrived from England. Brissot, do me the favor not to bite him. Put your anglophobia into your pocket, as long as he is under my roof. Besides, remember that he is of French origin, and that it is the revocation of the edict of Nantes which compelled him to be born an Englishman. It is not his fault." Slightly bowing to the group which he left, he glided slowly toward his English friend, for he never was known to do anything with eagerness or haste.

CHAPTER XIX.

WARMLY greeting Sir Samuel Romilly, Talleyrand led him to the sofa where still remained Gouverneur Morris and Lafayette, to whom he introduced that distinguished member of the English bar. After an exchange of mutual civilities, he was earnestly requested to express with the utmost frankness his opinion on the works of the National Assembly, and on the possibility of giving to France such institutions as had secured the liberties, the prosperity, and the glory of England. Sir Samuel hesitated a good while, but yielding at last to pressing solicitations, he spoke in these terms:

"You have decided so abruptly on so many questions, that I do not know which of them I can take *first* into consideration. Besides, there is hardly a question which is completely isolated. Generally a question is so connected with others, that it is impossible to pronounce on it any sound judgment without examining it in relation to its surrounding satellites. The great fault committed, for instance, in your National Assembly, was to work separately on each portion of your constitution in utter forgetfulness of the other parts, and then to try afterward to dovetail them into one harmonious whole. The consequence

(263)

is, that you have produced an edifice which can not be expected to hang together. There is a conspicuous want of regularity and adaptation in its proportions. Some of the columns are too weak; others unnecessarily strong. It is an incoherent mass which will not stand the slightest shock. It is a gigantic structure, whose foundations, instead of being deeply laid, repose merely on the surface of the soil without any reference to the superincumbent weight. This is due to what may be called an organic defect in your national character. In an Assembly convened for the most important of all human purposes, there was in almost every member an extreme impatience to bring himself forward and to move faster than his competitors. There was no concert, no preparation in that body. Every one was for himself, and strove to surprise the Assembly by some novel and unexpected proposition. Everything was done under the whip and spur of the moment. Jealousies and personal rivalries, leading to acrimonious altercations, were the cause of a total want of preconcerted action. There was no pulling together to attain one object. But every one tugged separately at his own little rope, at the end of which was attached some favorite hobby, which was to be dragged on the stage without delay and at whatever costs. To shine exclusively was the aspiration of every heart. It became a war of *amour propre.* I can not see in the deliberations of the National Assembly any evidence of patient study or meditation, and of calm discussion. All the decrees of that body seem to have been carried at the sword's point, as if your orators had been the leaders of a storming party. Fury pulled down, and haste was the architect that built up. All had been levelled to the ground at once, without hesitation ; and, without pausing to reflect on the lessons imprinted on those ruins, a general and instantaneous reconstruction was attempted, in the mere wantonness of power, by the fanaticism of self-conceit. Such is the overweening opinion evidently entertained by the Assembly of their own wisdom and of the salutary comprehensiveness of their powers, that they would, no doubt, readily undertake the reconstruction, not only of France, but also of all the nations of the earth, if permitted to do so.

"Allow me to say that the predominating trait in the French character is self-confidence. With a few exceptions, which rather prove than disprove the general rule, there is nothing which a member of the National Assembly thinks that he can not do. It is impossible to imagine a body of men more sincerely convinced that they are all legislators of the highest order, and that their mission is to repair all the faults of the past, to extirpate from the human mind the very seeds of error, and to secure forever the happiness of unborn generations in future ages. It struck me, on a close examination of your proceedings, that, when venturing on grounds that required the utmost circumspection, you progressed with an assurance which showed that you were not checked, or even retarded, by the slightest doubt as to the perfect appropriateness of every one of your acts. The National Assembly seemed to assume for itself in temporal matters as much of infallibility as is claimed spiritually by the Church of Rome. Any opposition or protest, on the part of the minority, only increased the self-satisfaction of the majority. When the King ventured to send some modest remonstrances in relation to their mode of expressing their 'declaration of rights,' they were astonished at the audacity of those ministers who had gone so far as to hazard any criticism on any one of their acts, and Necker, who was the author of those remonstrances, began to lose favor with them.

" Being an Englishman, of French descent, I think that I can, better than anybody else, compare impartially the character of the two nations in a legislative point of view. I am, of course, very familiar with the proceedings of the British Parliament, and I have paid the most minute attention to all the doings of the National Assembly of France. There is nothing, in my sight, more striking than the timidity and modesty of the English in legislation, and the boldness and self-confidence of the French on the same subject. If one hundred persons were stopped at random in the streets of London, and if it was proposed to them to assume the direction of the government, I am certain that ninety-nine would refuse. But were the same question, under the same circumstances, put in the streets of Paris, I should not be afraid of betting that, out of one hundred, ninety-nine would accept the proposition."

These remarks seemed to afford infinite amusement to Gouverneur Morris. Sir Samuel noticed it. " Mr. Morris," he said, " I think that I am paying a great compliment to General Lafayette and to Mr. de Talleyrand. There are very few Frenchmen in whose presence I would venture to speak so frankly."

" Pray go on," replied Morris. " America loves France, and will not indiscreetly repeat the wholesome truths which you speak to her noble ally, who, it is to be hoped, would profit by your gentle and

well-meant castigation, if not confined within so narrow a circle of listeners."

"What is remarkable," continued Sir Samuel, bowing with a smile to Morris, "is, that so many of the
speeches and reports made in the National Assembly,
were manufactured outside of that body. Members
did not scruple to read speeches which they had not
composed, and to decorate themselves with borrowed
feathers, to the certain knowledge of hundreds. No
Englishman could have been found, disposed thus to
bask openly in the glaring light of public imposture.
No Englishman of any reputation whatever would
have stooped to perform the humiliating part of
mouthing as his own, before an audience, the composition of another. Were I to go to any one of your colleagues and suggest to him some glittering idea, he
would fling it at once from the tribune into the Assembly, without pausing one minute to consider the
consequences. Not so with an Englishman; he would
be afraid of exposing himself. He would carefully
study the subject, to enable himself to answer objections, and not to be easily beaten from the position he
might take. A Frenchman affirms with inconceivable
thoughtlessness. In general, he attaches very little
importance to an assertion. An Englishman reflects
before believing, speaking, and acting. Before inviting the judgment of the public, an Englishman will
dry up all the sources of information within his reach;
he will look for authorities by which to be backed,
and he will try to render himself master of all the
circumstances of the case which he makes his own.
A Frenchman thinks that *wit* alone will be sufficient
to extricate him out of all difficulties. He will readily
undertake that which is the most foreign to the nat-

ure of his capacities. Thus Mirabeau had himself appointed chairman of a committee on mines, when I know personally that his ignorance on the subject can not be surpassed. A Frenchman thinks that wit, not common sense, is the pass-key with which he can open every lock. An Englishman believes that knowledge and practice are indispensable to insure success. Once a French gentleman was asked, in my presence, if he could perform on the piano. ' I do not know,' he replied, ' for I have never tried ; but 'I will see what I can do.' This sounds like a comical exaggeration. But substitute the word *government* for the word *piano*, *legislation* for *music*, and, instead of one French gentleman, you will have twelve hundred."

Whilst this conversation was going on, in a distant corner of the room sat Mirabeau by himself, with a scowl on his brow, which, no doubt, warned many not to trespass on the solitary musings of the lion, when evidently in an unamiable mood. Aubert Dubayet was not deterred by it from approaching, and, sitting in an arm-chair next to him, said with an affectionate tone : " You do not seem to be well, Count."

" I am very unwell," replied Mirabeau. " My digestion has become bad. Ah ! my friend, when the first functionary in the establishment is disabled, it is time to close it up. But who could help being dyspeptic, when looking at many of those creatures who are parading here ? Chamfort, for instance, who affects to adorn with eccentricity what he calls the independence of his character, whilst he licks the heels of birth, wealth, and power. He wishes to pass for a misanthrope, but his misanthropy is nothing but wounded pride and manifests itself by epigrams, each of which it takes him two months to sharpen. He has the audacity to say that the knowledge of the world has bronzed his heart, as if the fellow ever had such an organ. His whole body is nothing but a' mass of diseased liver, secreting the worst kind of bile, and nothing else. He is a revolutionist, because he hates the superiorities which overshadow his little-ness. He talks like an austere moralist, when his very bones are rotting from corruption. Whilst others are attacking with the ponderous ram the colossus of despotism, he is scratching it with his satirical arrows. He is the Thersites of the revolution."

Robespierre happened to pass before them. " Look at that man, Aubert Dubayet," said Mirabeau. " His friends say that he is incorruptible. Better the thirst for gold than the thirst for blood. Beware of that compound of the vampire and of the Aristides. It is not that I do not appreciate integrity. On the contrary, I have always thought that, if probity did not exist, it would have to be invented as the best means of success in this world.* But this man smells of the charnel house."

" Many of those men here present are remarkable for their merit," said Dubayet.

" Yes," continued Mirabeau, " some there are ; but few that are not overrated. Most of them are sophists, who would discuss one month on syllables, and who would not hesitate to destroy in one night a mon-archy of one thousand years without knowing what to put in its place. Others there are who are rank cow-ards, and who, after having unchained the bull, are afraid of taking him by the horns. They are moles,

---

* Dumont's " Recollections of Mirabeau."

fit only to work under-ground and upheave it without being seen."

Camille Desmoulins bowed to them at a distance. "What of him?" inquired Dubayet.

"A man of unripe talent—very green for the present," replied Mirabeau. "He shoots always beyond the mark. If you told him to reward a lacquey with a glass of brandy, he would give him the whole bottle. One merit he has, however: it is to make a good many people admire him when he speaks of things of which he has not the slightest idea."

Aubert Dubayet. "I see Mr. de Lameth conversing with Mr. de Lafayette."

Mirabeau. "A well-matched pair. Lameth is one of those men who would constitute a monarchy without retaining in it a single monarchical element. He is a bag of wind. As to Lafayette——have you read the novel of "Clarissa" by Richardson? Well, if you have, you are acquainted with the ineffably stupid perfection of her lover, Grandisson. Now, you will understand why I call that man Cromwell—Grandisson. He wants to be both, and it will ruin him. There are times when virtue is out of place. A revolution is a pandemonium—it admits of no angel."

Dubayet. "Who is that man bowing so low to Mr. de Talleyrand?"

Mirabeau. "Do you not know him? It is Barriere de Vieuzac—a Gascon, who will pipe alternately for monarchy, or liberty, according to his pay. His natural disposition is to be mean, to fawn, and to flatter. He would, if he had anything to gain by it, write sonnets to the hangman in the impassioned style of a lover. There is no crime which he would not whitewash into the semblance of innocence. He would indite an idyl on the St. Bartholomew. Should he die, he would be appointed the poet laureate of the court of Pluto; he would address tender epistles to the Furies, soft madrigals to Proserpina, and become the Anacreon of hell."

Dubayet. " Barnave is taking him by the arm."

Mirabeau. " I am sorry for it. Barnave ought to have more respect for himself; for Barnave is a tree that is growing to be one day the mast of a ship of the line." *

Dubayet. " Target joins them. He is said to be a distinguished member of the Assembly for talent and eloquence."

Mirabeau. " Nonsense. He is swollen with words. His eloquence is dropsical. Tap it, and you will have nothing but water."

Dubayet. " Ho! Ho! Here is Volney, with his book on ' Ruins ' reflecting its sombre hue on his face. What an atrabiliary look! How thin and dry he is! He puts me in mind of some piece of parchment exhumed from Pompeii."

Mirabeau. " A thorough radical. He is one of those men who make me exclaim : What an admirable thing would democracy be, if there were no democrats! It is laughable to see him shake hands with *L'abbé* Lamourette, who is also an author, having published a book entitled ' Meditations of my Soul.' Pretty meditations they are ! He is such an apostle of moderation in everything that he recommends not to believe even in God more than is necessary. Ha! ha! I see *L'abbé* Sieyes, the would-be Mohammed of the revolution, retiring with D'Espréménil, the Crispin—

---

* Dumont's " Recollections of Mirabeau."

Catiline, and with Camus, the ultra radical, and ultra rigid Cato of modern times, who, on account of his incandescent nose, is well named the *red flag*. Goodnight to the worthy trio. Will you dine with me tomorrow, Dubayet?"

Dubayet. "I thank you, Count. I dine with Mr. de Necker."

Mirabeau. "Good. Study him, for he is a celebrity. You will find him to be a clock which is always behind time. He does not know the epoch he is living in. Such men are pigmies in a revolution. Mallebranche, the philosopher, saw nothing out of God; Necker, the banker and would-be statesman, sees nothing out of Necker. As to France, he has concentrated it into the stock-jobbing, financiering shops of *Rue Vivienne*."

Dubayet. "I am to meet at his house some of the other members of the Cabinet—Clavière, for instance."

Mirabeau. "I like him. He has the heart of a child and the head of a man. But he needs a regulator. Left to himself, he always varies."

Dubayet. "I am also to meet, I understand, the Count de Clermont Tonnerre, who is called the Pitt of France."

Mirabeau. "The appellation may be deserved. It is questionable, however, whether Pitt would be flattered to be called the Clermont Tonnerre of England. But I forget myself here. Dubayet, what time is it by yonder clock? As late as two in the morning! I must go; come with me; I'll drop you down at your lodgings. As to myself, I'll have to spend the rest of the night in correcting proof-sheets; for a pamphlet of mine must make its appearance to-morrow. By-the-by, Aubert, do you know that I am the first proof-reader in the kingdom, and yet nobody gives me any credit for it. May you, my friend, be better appreciated whilst living! Justice will be done to me only after my death."

12*

CHAPTER XX.

A PORTRAIT OF MIRABEAU BY HIMSELF—HE AN-
NOUNCES IN THE NATIONAL ASSEMBLY THE
DEATH OF FRANKLIN.

SEVERAL days had elapsed since Talleyrand's evening reception, and Aubert Dubayet had nowhere met
Mirabeau, who had not even made his appearance at
the National Assembly. He, therefore, rang at the
door of his illustrious friend and sent in his card. He
was instantly admitted, and found Mirabeau in his
bedroom, wrapped up in a loose morning-gown. He
looked much fatigued and worn out. Round his neck
were bloody bandages.

" I am glad to see you," he said to Dubayet. " I
had caused myself to be denied to everybody. Not
at home was the word; but an exception has been
made for you, my friend. You are not mixed up with
all our miserable intrigues and our halting, one-leg
ambitions, and there is something refreshing in your
honest nature that soothes my irritated nerves. Your
person must be impregnated with some charm borrowed from the virgin wilderness of your American
cradle. I wonder if all Louisianians are like you?
Ah! dear Dubayet, I am dying. You see that I have
been leeched copiously. My blood is inflamed; it
rushes up to my head, and affects my sight, which is
often much impaired. I am compelled to be bled frequently. If I believed in slow poisons, I should be

disposed to suspect that some drug of that sort has been administered to me. I am perishing by inches; a secret fire consumes me inwardly."

"Faith!" exclaimed Dubayet, "considering your way of living, you must be a salamander, not to be already consumed to ashes!"

"I will reform," replied Mirabeau. "I am sick of this abominable world. Before long, I will renounce ambition, kick away with my toe the temptation of sinful pleasure, which has become a burden to me, and live only for philosophy, agriculture, and friendship in a Tusculum of my own."

Aubert Dubayet smiled as he remembered the old saying:

> "The devil was sick; the devil a monk would be;
> The devil got well; devil of a monk was he."

Mirabeau went on: "That stupid National Assembly! I have an indigestion of them; they are killing me. The blockheads! They have assumed to govern the King, instead of governing through him. But soon neither he nor they will govern; a vile faction will seize on the government, and will cover the whole surface of France with a flood of horrors. Were I to descend into the tomb, my death would be the signal for factious pigmies to advance to the front rank. Robespierre, Pétion, and a multitude of others, who are mere shadows in the background as long as I remain on the horizon, will become great men if I disappear. There are in me inspired anticipations of the future; I feel at times that there is in my bosom something of the old spirit of prophecy. I assure you, without any presumptuous boasting—I assure you, because it is so—that there is in me a political

sagacity, a certain prevision of coming events, a knowledge of men and things, which amounts almost to a
supernatural intuition. I speak of myself as impartially as I would of a person dead a thousand years
ago. The secrets of the human heart lie open before
me; there is no mask which a glance of mine does
not penetrate. This infallibility of my second sight,
which is as sure as positive revelation, serves me better than would any multitude of spies in the camp
of the enemy. I tell you that those braying asses
whom I now check in their mad career, will ere long
inaugurate ferocious measures and butcheries, without even having the execrable honor of a civil war.
When I shall be dead, Dubayet, do not believe the
calumnies that will be circulated to blacken my
memory. Although vicious in many respects, I admire intensely what is good, moral, and pure. I have
the highest esteem for energetic and virtuous characters, a sort of enthusiasm for all that is grand, and
that enthusiasm has never been weakened by the consciousness that I have of my own imperfections and
errors. My soul is like a mirror, which may be mo-
mentarily tarnished by the breath of depravity, but
which soon resumes its bright and polished surface.
My conduct is often in contradiction with my profes-
sions, not because I am capable of the meanness of
falsehood, but because I am carried away by irresistible passions. My reason is luminous, but sometimes
clouded by the fumes of the evil instincts of the flesh.
The original elements of my nature were sound and
pure, but a tempestuous wind has occasionally swept
over them, lashed them into fury, and the ship in
which morality was embarked, broke more than once
her sheet-anchors. There is much of everything in

men; much that is good, and much that is bad. But is it not true, my friend, be it said without vanity, that no one can know me without being under the impression forever, and beyond the possibility of forgetfulness, that he has stood before the magnificent grandeur of the fallen angel—he that was once the brightest among the hosts of Heaven? Will it not be admitted, whatever may be said of me as a private man, that, as a public one, I was born to fill with my immense activity and personality any sphere, however large it might be, in which I could possibly be placed by the caprice of circumstance?"

Mirabeau paused, and his face assumed an expression of deep sadness. After a minute or two of silence, he said: "Much talk there is of my venality. If some people are to be believed, I have literally set myself up at auction, and the hammer of corruption adjudicates me to the highest bidder. If I have been so long in the market, it seems to me that I ought to have gained enough to have bought a kingdom, and I do not understand how it is that I have remained so poor, after having had all the kings of the earth and their treasures at my disposal. I admit that I have not been very delicate in money matters. But my pride has been at least a good substitute for honesty, if I lack the latter. I would at any time have flung out of my windows anybody who should have dared to make to me a humiliating proposition. Between you and me, I have lately accepted a pension from the King and from his brother, the Count of Provence, because I regard myself as an agent intrusted with their interests, and I take their money to govern them, but not to be governed. If Spain and England have bought me, as reported, what has be-

come of the immense sums which I must have received? How is it that I shall die insolvent? It is
true that I live in a state of opulence, but it is a political necessity, as much as a matter of taste with me.
If I am supplied with money by the King, I spend it
for his service. I can not, therefore, be deemed guilty
of the baseness of cupidity. I am nothing else, after
all, than the banker of the Crown."

"What!" exclaimed Dubayet, with undisguised
amazement, " you have been won over to the King?"

"Yes," replied Mirabeau. " It is time to stop the
red-hot wheels of the revolution. I am for the liberty
of the people, and not for their dictatorship. I am
for order, and not for anarchy. The monarchy must
be saved, or France, and even Europe, will be deluged
with blood. The constitution concocted by the National Assembly is a monstrosity. There is too much
of a republic in it for a monarchy, and too much of a
monarchy for a republic. It is neither the one, nor
the other; the king in it is a surplusage. In it the
semblance of royalty is visible everywhere; but where
is its substance and reality to be found? I want no
bastard government, no mongrel constitution."

"This new enterprise of yours," observed Aubert
Dubayet, "seems to me as difficult as if you attempted
to stop the Falls of Niagara."

"It is not demonstrated to me that I could not,"
replied Mirabeau. "I have not seen them; but I see
what is going on around me, and I know what I can
do. Let the King listen to me, and I will so shape
this revolution as to make it a blessing for the nation
and for himself."

Here his valet, Teutch, entered, and informed him
that a deputation of the people wished to address him.

"No," shouted Mirabeau fiercely. "Tell them that I am sick in bed"; and, turning to Dubayet, he said to him with a sardonic laugh: "It is no excuse, but the truth. I am sick of them, sick to death. By the immortal Gods, do those fellows imagine that, after having taken royalty by the throat, crushed it to the ground, and set my foot on its breast, I am to be the valet of king multitude! The impudent knaves! I can not but laugh at the idea. Haw! haw! haw! A good joke. Do you know the language of the populace to me—to me, in whose veins runs the blood of the Guises and of the Caramans? Hear how the gibbering monkeys talk: 'Speak loud, Mirabeau; say this, or say that, if thou wishest to be applauded and tapped encouragingly on the shoulder. Play the tragedian, Mirabeau; quick, ascend the stage; we want an explosion of wrath or hatred on thy part; if thou valuest our approbation wake up, Mirabeau; lash thy sides and roar like the lion, or scream like the eagle, or thunder like Jove; beg, weep, laugh, praise, or scold, act, or do not act, as our passions or whims command; uproot, break, and kill, or caper and blow thy nose at our beck like a child, if thou wishest to retain thy popularity.' I have enough of this, forsooth! I was not made to obey the hatless, shoeless, shirtless, and howling would-be master who issues his edicts from the gutters of the streets, and who thinks that he does me a favor, when he permits me to wear powder in my hair, to ride in a carriage, and to have behind that carriage a lacquey in livery. No, no; it is irrevocably settled in my mind. The Count de Mirabeau brings back his allegiance to the King, the knight swears fealty to the Queen, and the strong man flies to the rescue of the woman who claims his protection."

The American minister happened to be announced and was cordially received by Mirabeau.

"Count," said Morris, "I have just received bad news from America, and you are the first to know it. Franklin is dead."

Mirabeau jumped up from the arm-chair in which he had languidly seated himself, and rang violently. Teutch rushed in. "Order my coach, quick; powder my hair; give me my coat; haste, haste," said hurriedly his impetuous master. "I want to be the first to announce the death of Franklin to the National Assembly. You will, my friends, both of you, accompany me, I hope."

In a short time they entered the hall where sat that body. Mirabeau ascended the tribune. "How's that? How's that?" was heard on all sides. "Where do you come from so abruptly and unexpectedly? You have no right to speak; it is not your turn. You interfere with the order of the day. Order of the day! Order of the day!" vociferated the majority of the members, who evidently were not disposed to show at that moment any favor to the orator. Mirabeau remained at the tribune, calm and imposing. The tumult was increasing, when he said in his most imperious and stentorian tone: "Silence! and listen to me. Franklin is dead!" The silence of the tomb immediately prevailed, and Mirabeau continued in these words:

"Franklin is dead! That great man who gave liberty to America, and whose genius, by its discoveries, has shed such a flood of light on the progress of civilization in Europe, has returned to the bosom of the Deity.

"The sage whom two worlds claim as their own, who ranks as high in the history of sciences as in the history of empires, occupies unquestionably a most exalted position among the human race.

"Long enough have political and official notifications been given of the death of those who were great only in their funeral orations. Long enough has the etiquette of courts proclaimed hypocritical mournings. Nations ought to grieve only for the loss of their benefactors. Their representatives ought to recommend to their homage none but the heroes of humanity.

"The Congress has ordered that, in the fourteen Confederate States, a mourning of two months shall be observed for the death of Franklin ; and America, at this moment, pays this tribute of veneration and gratitude to one of the fathers of her constitution.

"Would it not be worthy of you, gentlemen, to join in this truly religious demonstration and to participate in that homage which is thus solemnly rendered to the rights of man, and to the philosopher who has the most contributed to their propagation on earth? Antiquity would have raised altars to that vast and powerful genius who, for the benefit of mankind, embracing the universe within the grasp of his mind, knew how to conquer tyranny on earth and subjugate to his will the thunderbolt of Heaven. Free and enlightened France owes at least a testimonial of souvenir and regret to the memory of one of the greatest men who ever served philosophy and liberty.

"I propose that it be decreed, that the National Assembly shall go into mourning during three days, for Benjamin Franklin."

This proposition was adopted by a unanimous acclamation.

A few days after, Aubert Dubayet, according to a pressing request which he had received, called on

Mirabeau, whom he found studying attentively the map of France, and marking with a pencil several points on its Northern frontier. "I need you," said Mirabeau, "as you must have inferred from the tone of my note. I have a most confidential communication to make to you, and a service to ask at your hands. But, before doing so, tell me if you have any political information to communicate."

"No," replied Aubert Dubayet. "I have nothing of special significance to relate. But I think that the sky is darkening. I have just been conversing with General Lafayette. He speaks of the multiplying dangers that menace the progress of reform in France. I inquired what were those dangers. He answered: 'The refugees hovering about the frontiers, intrigues in most of the despotic and aristocratic cabinets, our regular army divided into Tory officers and undisciplined soldiers, licentiousness among the people not easily repressed, the capital, that gives the tone to the empire, distracted by anti-revolutionary or factious parties, the Assembly fatigued by hard labor and very unmanagerable.' But he added: 'however, according to the popular motto, *Ça ira*, it will go on.'"*

Mirabeau shrugged his shoulders: "Poor Lafayette! Honest simpleton!" he muttered. "Will the scales never fall from his eyes? *Ça ira* will not do. *Ça ira* is not a popular motto, but, what is worse, is a popular song. Aubert, beware of popular songs in a revolution! The devil is always at the bottom of them all. Does not Lafayette know what are the words which come after *ça ira*? If he does not, I will tell him they are: *Les aristocrates à la lanterne.*† It

---

* Lafayette to Washington.
† The aristocrats to the lamp-post!

is there that he will dangle, if he does not take care. Does he not know that faction, at this very hour, is predominant in Paris, that liberty and equality begin to be the only watchwords of the people, and that the Jacobin Club has set up a journal which is spreading the spirit of revolt and preparing a scaffold *à la Stuart* for royalty?"

Dubayet. "Lafayette has lent me this letter recently received by him from General Washington, and which I have read with much interest. The President, who seems to be well informed of the condition of things here, is alarmed for the safety of his friend."

Mirabeau. "Well may he be! But let me hear what he says."

Dubayet. Reading: "I assure you," writes Washington to Lafayette, "that I have often contemplated, with great anxiety, the danger to which you are personally exposed by your peculiar and delicate situation in the tumult of the time, and your letters are far from quieting that friendly concern. But to one who engages in hazardous enterprises for the good of his country, and who is guided by pure and upright views, as I am sure is the case with you, life is but a secondary consideration.

"The tumultuous populace of large cities are ever to be dreaded. Their indiscriminate violence prostrates, for the time, all public authority, and its consequences are sometimes extensive and terrible. In Paris, we may suppose these tumults are peculiarly disastrous at this time, when the public mind is in a ferment, and when, as is always the case on such occasions, there are not wanted wicked and designing men whose element is confusion, and who will not hesitate in destroying the public tranquillity to gain a favorite point."

Mirabeau. "General Washington has a hundred times more sagacity, more common sense, and brains than General Lafayette."

Dubayet. "I have also been shown a letter from Jefferson, who says that the popular cause prevails only with a part of Washington's Cabinet. He expresses ardent wishes that the French revolution may be carried to its utmost results. He writes that the permanence of the American revolution leans, in some degree, on that of France, and that a failure here would be a powerful argument to prove that there must be a failure in America. He maintains that the success of the French revolution is necessary to stay up their own, and *prevent its falling back to that kind of half-way house—the English constitution.*[*] These are his very expressions."

Mirabeau. "Better the half-way house than the mad-house. Your Jefferson, were he here, would soon lead us to the latter, if permitted. You see, Aubert Dubayet, how fully justified I am in taking the step on which I have resolved. The monarchy must be saved. There is no time to be lost."

At that moment, a gentle tap was heard at a door that led into inner apartments. "Come in," said Mirabeau, and Tintin Calandro entered with his violin in his hand. He looked somewhat confused when he saw Dubayet, with whom, however, he shook hands cordially.

"*Monsieur le comte,*" he said to Mirabeau, "I see that you are engaged, and that the moment is not

---

* Irving's "Life of Washington," p. 91, vol. v.

opportune for our musical lesson. I will call again,"
and he turned to depart. Mirabeau sprang on him,
and, holding him by the arm, exclaimed: "Stop,
stop, man! Don't be in such a hurry. Drop all disguise at once; it is not necessary. Is not Aubert
Dubayet your friend? He is mine, and I trust him
entirely. I have even summoned him here, that he
may know all. He must help us; speak, then, without reserve. What says the Princess de Lamballe?
Does the Queen assent to all my conditions, and will
she grant me an audience?"

"Yes," replied Tintin Calandro. "She will meet
you secretly and alone, to-morrow night, at twelve
o'clock, in the garden of Versailles, at the foot of the
statues of Laocoon and his sons struggling against the
twin serpents. I am commissioned to bring back
your answer."

"Fly, then," said Mirabeau, "and tell the Queen
that nothing but death shall prevent my being in
time at the spot designated." Then, turning to Dubayet: "Dear friend, you must be my companion. You
alone I can trust on this momentous occasion. At
nine o'clock to-morrow evening, two horses, as fleet
as the wind, shall be in attendance outside of the
gates of Paris, at the most secluded place which I can
select, to avoid observation, and which I shall let you
know. Come armed to the teeth under your cloak.
We shall be masked, and must speed to Versailles
through by-ways. He who will attempt to penetrate
through our disguise must die."

CHAPTER XXI.

A MIDNIGHT INTERVIEW IN THE GARDEN OF VER-
SAILLES BETWEEN MIRABEAU AND THE QUEEN
—DEATH OF MIRABEAU.

AT twelve precisely, on the night of the following
day, a postern of the palace of Versailles opened on
the side facing the garden, and a woman, wrapped in
a long veil, came out. It was Marie Antoinette,
Queen of France. She was followed by two companions of her own sex; one was the Princess de Lamballe, and the other the Princess de Polignac. At a
short distance behind them walked a young man of
distinguished appearance. In his belt hung a pair of
silver-mounted pistols, and he carried in his hand a
sheathed sword, as if he held himself ready to draw it
at the instant it might be wanted. He was the Baron
de Vaudreuil, a descendant of the Marquis de Vaudreuil, one of the former Governors of Louisiana. His
romantic and respectful devotion for the Queen is
related in the memoirs of the epoch. The party
moved rapidly toward a round point or spot of small
dimensions, fenced in by a circular row of shrubbery,
to which led several alleys or avenues of dense hedges,
six feet high, from which emerged at regular intervals
some tall trees, like those towers which overtop the
walls of a fortified city. In the center of that round
spot rose a monument that commemorated the
tragic fate of Laocoon and his sons, as related in the

immortal verses of Virgil. It had been lately erected by one of the most celebrated sculptors of the time, who, with the permission of the good-natured King, had selected this place, where he thought his work would be seen to the best advantage. The pedestal was large, and apparently of massive Italian marble, from Carrara. The Queen alone entered this open spot. Her attendants disappeared behind a thick bush of roses and myrtles. Marie Antoinette had hardly reached the foot of the monument, when a man issued from behind the circular mass of foliage which enveloped the spot. He advanced slowly, hat in hand. When within a short but respectful distance from the Queen, after having bowed profoundly, he stood erect, calm, motionless, and evidently awaiting to be addressed. The Queen at first had lost her self-possession when facing the terrible Titan whose blows had almost destroyed a monarchy, the basis of which had been cemented by a thousand years. She blushed, then became deadly pale, and a visible shudder passed over her whole frame. She soon mastered her emotion, however, and said, in a voice that was but slightly tremulous :

" Mr. de Mirabeau, your services have been accepted, and, with the King's consent, I have granted the secret audience which you desired."

Mirabeau. "I am inexpressibly grateful, Madam, for your Majesty's condescension. I have anxiously wished for this opportunity to present to your Majesty the homage of a devoted subject, and to receive from the lips of the Queen the assurance that my services are accepted on the conditions which I have thought necessary to indicate, for the sake of the royal family, for the permanence of the monarchy, for the prosperity of France, and also in token of the confirmation by the court of the liberties of the people."

Marie Antoinette drew from her bosom a paper which she handed to Mirabeau, saying: "It is signed by the King and by myself, as you have stipulated." At this moment a sense of her humiliation seemed to have come over her, and to rouse her into a fit of uncontrollable passion. Her eyes flashed, she drew herself up, and, forgetful of all prudential considerations, she thus spoke, in a haughty tone: "And what guaranties will the Count de Mirabeau give to the King and Queen of France in exchange for those which he has exacted of his sovereigns? Shall we be satisfied with his word of honor as to the fulfilment of his obligations? Are his antecedents such as to forbid distrust?" All the wounded pride of her race had gathered on the brow of the daughter of Maria Theresa, and of a long line of imperial Cæsars.

"Madam," replied Mirabeau, "I understand and appreciate all the force of the reproach implied in your Majesty's question. There is nothing so terrible and so unjust as the exaggerations of the judgments of public opinion. There is nothing that could have subjected me to a more excruciating torture than has done the severity of that tribunal. I have long felt that, if I had enjoyed personal consideration for unblemished virtue, the whole of France would have been at my feet. There are times, and at this present moment more than ever before, when I would cheerfully pass through an ocean of fire to purify the name of Mirabeau. No language can express the agony which the allusions of your Majesty have inflicted on my heart. Alas! I but too cruelly expiate the errors of my youth!"

The eyes of Mirabeau became suffused with tears, and two big scalding drops ran down his lion face. Marie Antoinette saw his emotion, her woman's heart softened, and she said in a gentle tone: "Mr. de Mirabeau, the faults of the past may not be irreparable, and suitable amends may be made for them. We are assured that God forgives, when the prayer of true repentance rises up to His footstool. But let us only think of the present and of the future. I hope that, now at least, all your aspirations are noble."

Mirabeau. "I wish that your Majesty could read my heart. You would see that, if I destroy the absolute power which the King has inherited, it is not from base motives, but to make him a greater and happier monarch, satisfy the irresistible exigencies of the epoch, establish on a solid basis the just liberties of the people, and increase the glory and prosperity of France. My whole ambition is to be the trusted prime minister of the most powerful sovereign of Europe, reigning over a free and grateful nation."

Marie Antoinette. "I understand. You wish to be the Pitt of France."

Mirabeau. "I wish to be more than that, Madam. My most intense aspiration is to eclipse, if possible, all the past ministers of State. I feel myself strong enough to gather around me, without envy and without fear, the ablest men of France in a luminous phalanx. I wish to encircle my brow with a halo of such effulgence as to dazzle the whole world, whilst that brow shall still bow humbly to the throne of St. Louis."

Marie Antoinette. "Then, if I comprehend your views, Mr. de Mirabeau, your plan is to introduce into France the government of Great Britain?"

Mirabeau. "With such modifications as may be required. The tottering throne can only be made steady by resting it on a House of Commons, and a vigorous Peerage selected from our highest nobility. Oh! Madam, would to God that I could persuade your Majesty to give up absolutely all distrust of me, to enter frankly into the broad and straight road of reform, and set aside forever all the prejudices of the past! Is not the rank of the sovereigns of Great Britain sufficiently exalted? Is not their position far safer and more enviable than that of despots whom hidden perils ever threaten?"

Marie Antoinette. "You have in your possession the written assurance that your sovereigns bind themselves to follow you as their guide; and now, before we part, what advice do you give?"

Mirabeau. "The King, although apparently free, is in reality in a state of captivity. He must escape from such a position. Let him secretly prepare everything for his departure; let him go to Metz, or to some other strong place where he has generals who can answer for some faithful regiments. As soon as he shall have reached his destination, let him issue a proclamation making an appeal to France; let him publish to the world all that he has so benevolently done, and what he yet intends to do; and let him depict in strong language the crimes of the capital; let him annul all the decrees of the National Assembly, on the ground of their being contrary to the instructions given by the electors to their representatives, and founded on a manifest usurpation. Let him dissolve the Assembly, and order immediately new elections. Let him, at the same time, instruct all his military commandants to maintain their author-

ity at whatever costs, and the high courts of justice
to resume their functions and proceed with the trial
of all rebels. Let him make an energetic appeal to
the whole nobility and summon them together, around
him, for the defense of the throne. I will remain in
Paris, and watch the movements of the Assembly.
As soon as the royal proclamation shall have reached
us, I will move that all the supporters of a constitutional monarchy depart, to meet again, with his
Majesty's sanction, and until their successors are
elected, at the place where the King shall have chosen
his residence. Should a portion of the Assembly remain in session in Paris, and should the city support
their disobedience, all its communications with the
provinces must be interrupted, until it is reduced by
famine. The clergy, who have been stripped of all
their possessions, will, no doubt, exert all their
spiritual influence on the people, and the bishops
must be invited to meet and protest in a body against
the sacrilegious usurpations of the Assembly."*

Marie Antoinette. "This would be the signal for
civil war."

Mirabeau. "Permit me to say that your Majesty
is greatly in error. You see only the surface of
things, and you have no idea of the degree of attachment which the whole of France still retains for her
King. France is essentially monarchical. At the moment when the King shall be free, the National Assembly will be reduced to nothing. With him in their
midst, they constitute a colossus of strength; without him, they will be a mountain of sand. At the
instigation of the Duke of Orleans, there may be

---

* This was really at one time Mirabeau's plan.

some movements attempted at the *Palais Royal*, but they will be crushed in the bud. As to Lafayette, should he pretend to play the part of Washington, and put himself at the head of the national guard, he will deserve to perish, and his fate will soon be decided." *

Marie Antoinette. "I will faithfully, Count, carry your message to the King."

Mirabeau. "Will you, Madam, do me the favor to tell him further, that I have destroyed the paper which I hold in my hand, and that I humbly beg pardon for having asked any pledge to guarantee the sincerity of your Majesty and of the King." Suiting his action to his words, Mirabeau tore into minute pieces and flung away the sheet of paper which had been delivered to him by Marie Antoinette.

The Queen's face flushed with a deep feeling of gratification, and, looking benignantly at Mirabeau, she said with emotion: "It is nobly done, Count; it is nobly done. From this day forth, I have the most implicit confidence in your loyalty. Adieu; may God protect us all!" And, with a gracious smile, she presented her hand to Mirabeau. He knelt on one knee and kissed it reverentially. When he rose, she had vanished behind a cluster of jessamines and other odoriferous plants. Mirabeau appeared as if transfigured with hope and pride. He looked up to the lowering sky, where glimmered in the West one solitary star, and, shaking aloft his fist with enthusiasm, he exclaimed: "By yonder globe of fire which has witnessed this scene, and by my own good soul, I swear to save her, or die." As he uttered these words, and hurried away in the direction from which he had

---

* Dumont's "Recollections of Mirabeau."

come, the star had been smothered in a dark cloud which passed over its face. The vault of heaven, without the twinkling of one single ray of light, looked like a funeral pall, and the wind sighed mournfully through the deserted garden.

Hardly a minute had elapsed after Mirabeau's departure, when one of the marble slabs of the pedestal of Laocoon's monument slided inside on silent grooves, and two men came out. One was masked, the other was not, and presented the appearance of a shrivelled-up old man, with a pale and pinched face, and with small, round, dark eyes, sparkling with the most malignant expression of triumph. The man with the mask, pointing in the direction which Mirabeau had taken, said fiercely: "She shall not be saved, and you shall die, Mr. de Mirabeau."

"Amen!" ejaculated his companion. "What an excellent idea your Royal Highness had when you bribed that sculptor and obtained of him to erect his monument on this spot, to which leads a secret subterranean passage only known to few, and to construct this pedestal so as to make it a safe place of concealment and observation! Hidden in it, I have frequently made for you, *Monseigneur*, important discoveries, but none to be compared to the one we have procured to-night—and so, he shall die! When?"

"As soon as possible," replied his companion. "Have you, my dear Italian chemist, distilled one of those poisons which leave no traces?"

"Better than that. I have one which produces the effects of a well-known disease, and which therefore will give rise to no suspicion of foul play."

"Excellent! It is worth twenty thousand livres, and you shall have them."

The Italian grinned a horrid smile. Both re-entered the pedestal; the marble slab noiselessly resumed its place; the monumental serpents above, swelling with wrath and venom, seemed to tighten their folds around their expiring victims, and to lift over them more fearfully their hideous heads, with an expression of living reality.

On the day following this interview between the Queen and Mirabeau, Aubert Dubayet had been compelled to leave Paris for Grenoble in Dauphiné, where he had been recalled by his private affairs. He was absent only two weeks, but, when he returned, Mirabeau was dead, and the whole of France was in mourning. That fatal event had taken place on the 2d of April, 1791. The body of the great orator and statesman was opened, and the report of physicians was, that he had died of an abdominal inflammation produced by excesses. His sufferings had been terrible; the agony of the convulsions into which he was frequently thrown, was so intense, that he called and prayed for death. He said to his friends: "I will endure these torments as long as you may have the slightest hope of curing me. But, if you have not, why should you not have the humanity to put a term to tortures of which you can have no conception?" In those rare moments when he was free from the extreme pains which racked his body, his serenity and self-possession were admirable. He believed his end to be at hand and inevitable, and spoke of it calmly. He had affectionate and pleasant things to say to the anxious visitors who crowded his bedroom. His intense passion for glory never left him to the last. "I regret," he said, "that I shall not have the opportunity to deliver in the National Assembly a speech which I had prepared on the slave trade. There was a passage in it, which, I think, would have produced an immense effect. It began thus: 'O ye, representatives of a free people, advocates of the rights of man, and apostles of liberty throughout the world, cast your eyes on the almost endless expanse of water which separates America from Africa, and follow with me on the Atlantic that ship loaded with captives, or rather that long black coffin, in which a lingering death has assumed its most hideous form.'" To Tintin Calandro, who could not tear himself away from the death-bed of one whom he considered as the only hope of the throne, he whispered: "Tell the Princess de Lamballe, tell the Queen to fly with the King and royal family. Let them lose no time in providing for their safety. The monarchy is dead, and descends with me into the grave." Having fallen asleep, he was awakened by a great tumult in the street. He asked for the cause of it, and was told that the noise came from the immense multitude who had gathered before his house and in its environs, and who eagerly inquired how he really was. "Tell them," he said, "that I have always lived for the people, and that it is sweet to me to die in their midst and with their sympathies." Minute guns were heard. "What!" exclaimed he, "have the obsequies of Achilles already commenced?" When he lost the faculty of speech, he wrote on a scrap of paper: "Do not think, my friends, that the feeling of death is so painful." And, after a little while, he wrote again: "To sleep." This was the last act of Mirabeau's life—this, his last word on this side of the grave. Genius, passion, ambition—all restless things!—had suddenly gone to sleep forever—at least in this world.

His funeral was a gorgeous pageantry. The whole National Assembly attended it in a body; there was an immense concourse of national guards and of civilians. The procession was three miles long, and it took four hours to pass at any given point. The entire population of Paris was in the streets, at the windows, and on the tops of houses. Even trees were loaded with human beings. The National Assembly decreed for his body the honors of a tomb in the Pantheon, a building which had been consecrated to the memory of all those citizens who should deserve well of their country. Two years after, it was ignominiously torn away from its sepulchre by the same people, whose idol he had been when living, and who now desecrated the last remnants of the former object of their worship, on their suspecting that, shortly before his death, Mirabeau had determined to support the royal cause. O vanity of vanities! But who will profit by the lessons of history? Who ever remembers, when ascending in triumph to the Capitol, that there is, as Mirabeau himself had said: "but one step from it to the Tarpeian Rock"? Was it Lafayette, that other idol of the people, who fled from his own army to save his life, and surrendered for protection to the Austrians, of whose hospitality he had a taste in the fortress of Olmutz, from which the friend of Washington was so very near being successfully rescued by the courage and perseverance of two Americans, Dr. Eric Bollman, and Francis K. Huger of South Carolina?

"I envy you the consolation you had in attending our illustrious friend during his last illness," said Aubert Dubayet, the first time he met Talleyrand after Mirabeau's death.

"You would have admired," replied Talleyrand, "his consistency. He was true, to the last, to the character which he had always sustained. This is the privilege of strong men. He saw that he was an object of general attention, and he never ceased to speak and to act like a great and noble actor on the national theatre. He superbly dramatized his death. A short time before he died, conquering the intense torture which he suffered, he had his papers brought to him and selected one that contained a speech on testaments. 'This,' he said to me, 'is my last contribution to the labors of the National Assembly. I make you the depository of it. Read it from the tribune in my name, when I shall be no more. It is my legacy to the Assembly. It will be singular to hear a speech on testaments by one who made his own the day before.'

"What is quite as singular," continued Talleyrand, "is, that to my certain knowledge, be it said between you and me, that speech is the production of one Mr. Raybaz, and not of Mirabeau. It is written in a style which is not his, and it is really very remarkable that, even in death, he should have retained his mania to deck himself in borrowed feathers, when he must have had the consciousness of having acquired so much personal glory, and when his reputation was such that he could well have afforded to scorn to enrich himself with the spoils of others. But the world, after all, is nothing but a vast conglomeration of imposture."

Shortly after, Louis XVI. attempted to fly with his family, as advised by Mirabeau, and it is but too well known how he was brought back from Varennes, where he was arrested. The news of that event was

13*

received in the United States with antagonistic feelings on the part of many. Jefferson thought that the King had been guilty of a breach of faith, and all his innate hatred of royalty was aroused.

"Such are the fruits of that form of government," he wrote to Dubayet, "which heaps importance on idiots, and which the Tories of the present day are trying to preach into our favor. It would be unfortunate, were it in the power of any one man to defeat the issue of so beautiful a revolution. I hope and trust that it is not, and that, for the good of suffering humanity all over the earth, the revolution will be established and spread all over the world." *

Washington was differently impressed. Jefferson was the first to communicate to him that event, whilst he was holding one of his levees, and observed in the same communication to Dubayet: "I never saw him so dejected in my life." Washington himself declared that he remained for some time in painful suspense as to what would be the consequences of that event. Ultimately, when the news arrived that the King had accepted the constitution from the hands of the National Assembly, he hailed the event as promising happy consequences to France, and to mankind in general; and what added to his joy was the noble and disinterested part which his friend Lafayette had acted in that great drama. "The prayers and wishes of the human race," he wrote to the Marquis, "have attended the exertions of your nation; and when your affairs are settled under an energetic and equal government, the hearts of all good men will be satisfied."

---

* Irving's " Life of Washington."

Delighted with such a letter, Lafayette had handed
it over to Aubert Dubayet for perusal, who carried it
·home and who happened to be reading it, when Talleyrand dropped in.   Dubayet took pleasure in communicating it to his distinguished friend, who seemed
to enjoy its contents in a very particular manner ; for,
taking, with an appearance of luxurious satisfaction,
a sort of recumbent position on the sofa on which he
had seated himself, and resting his head against the
adjacent wall, he closed entirely his habitually half-
closed eyes, and indulged, to the intense surprise of
Aubert Dubayet, in a short fit of peculiarly dry and
cynical cachinnation—a rare circumstance in such a
man.   Mephistopheles could not have laughed otherwise.   "What is in that letter which can provoke this
hilarity?" inquired Dubayet.

"I beg to be excused, my good friend," replied
Talleyrand, resuming that composed and imperturba-
ble face for which, among other things, he became
famous, "but, in the secret history of men, there is
sometimes between appearances and realities something exceedingly ludicrous.   Now, listen.   This is
strictly between you and me.   I have been lately
ransacking the archives of the State Department, and
here is an extract which I have made of a letter addressed by our friend Lafayette, on the 18th of July,
1779, from Havre, to Mr. de Vergennes.   'The idea,'
he says to that minister, 'of a revolution in Canada
seems very attractive to every good Frenchman, and
should political reasons condemn it, you will confess,
Monsieur le comte, we can yield to them only by re-
sisting the first impulses of the heart.   The advantages and disadvantages of such a scheme would demand a larger discussion than I can enter into.   Is it

better to leave to the Americans an object of fear and jealousy in the vicinage of an English colony, or shall we set free our oppressed brethren, in order to find again and at the same time among them, our ancient supply of furs, our former trade with the Indians, and all the profits of our original settlements, without exposing ourselves as of yore to expenses and depredations? Shall we put in the scales of the New World a fourteenth State which will be always attached to France, and which, by its situation, would secure to us a great preponderance in the dissensions that will one day divide America? There is a great variety of sentiment on this subject.'

"Now," said Talleyrand, rising and smiling a sardonic smile, "methinks that the partisans of America were not exactly as thoroughly Americanized as they wished to appear, and not as friendly inwardly as they were outwardly, and that Washington, if he knew what conflict of opinions existed at the time among his allies, as to which thorn it would have been most to the interest of France to plant in the side of his projected republic, might allow his gratitude to cool down to a lower degree of temperature, and not take so deep an interest in our great drama, and in the establishment here of an 'energetic and equal government,' which he might in the end not find as pleasant to deal with and as 'satisfactory' as he expects. But he shall not know it," and deliberately folding the sheet of paper which he held in his hand, he put it in his side-pocket, and, after buttoning his coat over it, he bowed to Dubayet, and glided out of the room, saying: *"Au prochain revoir, mon cher."*

This incident added a darker shade to the habitual gloom of Dubayet's mind. He knew that Washington, who entertained such fervent hopes of the new government of France, was somewhat weary of the one he had established at home. There were irreconcilable and angry discussions in his Cabinet; some of its members threatened to resign; symptoms of dissatisfaction had lately shown themselves among the people, far beyond what he would have expected; and to what height those might arise, in case of too great a change in the administration, could not be foreseen. Jefferson, who never allowed the opportunity to escape, when he had a chance, to fling a stone at his great rival, Alexander Hamilton, maintained that those discontents were produced by the administration of the treasury department. "A system has been contrived," he said, "for deluging the States with paper money instead of gold and silver, for withdrawing our citizens from the pursuits of commerce, manufactures, buildings, and other branches of useful industry, to occupy themselves and their capitals in a species of gambling destructive of morality, and which has introduced its poison into the Government itself."

Aubert Dubayet, to whom these remarks had been addressed, communicated them to Gouverneur Morris, who observed: "Jefferson, in his fits of jealousy or spleen, may say what he pleases; but he has, notwithstanding, a keen appreciation of the sterling merit of Hamilton, for he once said to me: 'Hamilton is a man of acute understanding, disinterested, honest, and honorable in all private transactions; amiable in society and duly valuing virtue in private life; yet so bewitched and perverted by the British example, as to be under thorough conviction that corruption is essential to the government of a nation.'" *

"This puts me in mind," replied Dubayet, "of a conversation which I heard, when in America, at Jefferson's own table, between Hamilton and Adams, after the cloth was removed. Conversation had begun on other matters, and, by some circumstance, led to the British constitution, on which Adams observed: 'Purge that constitution of its corruption, and give to its popular branch equality of representation, and it would be the most perfect constitution ever devised by the wit of man.' Hamilton paused, and said: 'Purge it of its corruption, and give to its popular branch equality of representation, and it would become an *impracticable* government; as it stands at present, with all its supposed defects, it is the most perfect government which ever existed.'" †

---

* Jefferson's Anas.　　† Jefferson's Works, vol. ix., p. 96.

CHAPTER XXII.

THE National Assembly, having been dissolved, was succeeded by what was called the Legislative Assembly. Aubert Dubayet was elected to that body, and took an active part in its deliberations. One day, when his friend, Gouverneur Morris, was complimenting him on the wise and moderate course which he pursued in the Assembly, and particularly on his vigorous and able defense of General Lafayette, who had been violently attacked by the lovers of anarchy, he replied:

"I am passionately attached to France and to liberty, and I will do all that may be in my power to secure the glory and prosperity of the former, and the permanency of the latter. I believe, however, with Mirabeau, that the monarchy is dead, and that a republic will, ere long, be inaugurated. I have great doubts as to the possibility of maintaining such a form of government here. But I think that the experiment must be tried. It will be a curious spectacle to watch the progress of those twin sisters—the American and French republics. If they both fail, the human mind will no longer pursue what will be considered a political chimera—self-government. It will be a point settled; and the next wisest step to be taken, I suppose, will be to resort to constitutional monarchies, as a *pis-aller*—as the least evil."

"If a public debt, as Jefferson maintains, is incompatible with a republic," answered Gouverneur Morris, "then your future French republic is threatened with speedy dissolution; for your indebtedness is enlarging its proportions with mushroom growth. Take these American journals which I have just received, and you will see Jefferson's views on affairs on the other side of the Atlantic."

Aubert Dubayet, when he went home, perused those papers with great interest, and saw with what vigor Jefferson was launching out against the public debt in America, and against all the evils which he apprehended from the funding system, "the ultimate object of which was," said he, "to prepare the way for a change from the present republican form of government to that of a monarchy, of which the English constitution is to be the model." He concluded by pronouncing the continuance of Washington at the head of the Government, to be of the last importance. "The confidence of the whole Union," he wrote to the President, "is centred in you. Your being at the helm will be more than an answer to every argument which can be used to alarm and lead the people in any quarter into violence, or secession. North and South will hang together, if they have you to hang on." *

Thus it became evident to Dubayet that the Union was far from being considered as firmly established, even in the opinion of its founders. What! said he

---

* Irving's "Life of Washington," p. 115, vol. v.

to himself, if Washington were to disappear, "the
North and the South would not hang together!"
There would be "secession"! Of what value are institutions which depend on the life of a man? If the
American republic is not safely constructed, can we
hope to raise such an edifice on the volcanic soil of
France? His mind became filled with gloomy apprehensions. He resolved, however, not to waver in
what he considered his path of duty, and he went on
working with patience, dignity, and good intentions.
He rose to so much personal consideration in the Assembly that he was elected their president, and occupied that position for two weeks. But he soon discovered that, as a conservative, he was in the minority in all his political views and opinions, and he re-
joiced when the Assembly was dissolved. He determined not to incur the responsibilities of being a
member in any other; and to escape from a forced
participation in the excesses which he foresaw, he re-
entered the army; for war had been declared; and
from the grade of captain he soon ascended to be general of brigade. He was complimented on his promotion by Jefferson, who professed great esteem for him,
and who wrote to him in relation to American affairs:

"A sect has shown itself among us, who declare
they espoused our constitution, not as a good and
sufficient thing in itself, but only as a step to an English constitution, the only thing good and sufficient
in itself, in their eyes. It is happy for us that these
are preachers without followers, and that our people
are firm and constant in their republican purity. You
will wonder to be told that it is from the eastward,
chiefly, that these champions for a King, Lords, and
Commons come. They get some important associates

from New York, and are puffed up by a tribe of *agio-teurs* which have been hatched in a bed of corruption, made up after the model of their beloved England. Too many of these stock-jobbers and king-jobbers have come into our legislature, or rather, too many of our legislature have become stock-jobbers and king-jobbers. However, the voice of the people is beginning to make itself heard, and will probably cleanse their seats at the next election." *

With deep concern Aubert Dubayet saw the rancorous bitterness with which Jefferson expressed himself on Hamilton, when speaking of his own probable retirement from Washington's Cabinet.

" To a thorough disregard," he said, " of the honors and emoluments of office I join as great a value for the esteem of my countrymen ; and conscious of having merited it by an integrity which can not be reproached, and by an enthusiastic devotion to their rights and liberty, I will not suffer my retirement to be clouded by the slanders of a man, whose history, from the moment at which history can stoop to notice him, is a tissue of machinations against the liberty of the country which has not only received and given him bread, but heaped its honors on his head." †

Jefferson was also much excited against Gouverneur Morris ; he complained that the American minister falsely represented France as governed by Jacobin clubs, and Lafayette as having completely lost his authority by endeavoring to check their excesses. " He writes to the President," said Jefferson, "that were Lafayette, who is at the head of an army on the

---

* Jefferson's Works, vol. iii., p. 450.

† Irving's " Life of Washington," vol. v., p. 130.

frontier and facing the enemy, to appear just now in Paris, unattended by that army, he would be torn to pieces. I am impatient of these gloomy picturings, especially when I see their effect on the mind of Washington, who is exceedingly anxious about the fate of his friend and the condition of France. The fact is, that Gouverneur Morris, a high-flying monarchy man, shutting his eyes and his faith to every fact against his wishes, and believing everything he desires to be true, has kept the President's mind constantly poisoned with his forebodings."

Morris, however, was not so very far from the truth in his prognostications. Revolutions are swift-footed, and do not feed with milk those who seek food from their breast. Revolutions secrete blood, and nothing else. Hardly had Jefferson penned the lines above quoted, when, on the 9th of August, 1792, Paris was startled by the sound of the tocsin at midnight. On the next morning, the populace, yelling like demons, rushed pell-mell into the palace of the Tuileries, after having massacred the few Swiss guards who defended the hereditary abode of royalty. The King and Queen had barely time to escape and to fly to the Assembly of the representatives of the people for protection. That protection exhibited itself in the shape of a decree suspending the King's authority. This meant his dethronement, the annihilation of the constitutional party, and the commencement of the reign of terror. Lafayette was a constitutionalist, and, therefore, was proscribed. In the name of liberty, universal fraternity, and philanthropy, the Jacobins denounced him in the Assembly. He had the original sin of being born a Marquis, and, of course, every Marquis was bound to be a traitor to the people. His arrest was decreed, and emissaries were sent to carry the decree into effect. The first impulse of Lafayette was to seize these Jacobin envoys, or *sans culottes*, as they began to be called, and march on Paris to face his accusers. He soon discovered, however, that his army was disposed to fraternize with the *sans culottes*, or patriots without breeches, and he fled with a few trusty friends, intending to seek an asylum in Holland, or the United States. But he was detained a prisoner at the first Austrian post, and subsequently domiciliated in a fortress to reflect on the inconstancy of human affairs, as already related.

" Thus his circle is completed," wrote Morris. " He has spent his fortune on a revolution, and is now crushed by the wheel which he has set in motion. He lasted longer than I expected." It is hardly necessary to mention that Washington looked with a sad eye on this catastrophe.

Gouverneur Morris probably took a malicious pleasure in writing to Jefferson : " The reign of terror continues. We have had one week of unchecked murders, in which some thousands have perished in this city. It began with between two and three hundred of the clergy, who had been shot because they would not take the oaths prescribed by the law, and which, they said, were contrary to their conscience. From the streets, the *executors of speedy justice*, as they called themselves, went to the *Abbaye*, where persons of noble birth were confined. These were dispatched also, and afterward, these judges visited the other prisons ; and all those who were confined, either on the accusation or suspicion of crimes, were destroyed." *

* Morris to Jefferson, September 10, 1792.

Jefferson was stung to the quick by this letter, which he looked upon as casting a slur on the Jacobins, to whom he was much attached, and whom he considered as pure as any of the Roman patriots of old. Thinking that justice was not done to them, he, probably in a fit of indignation, wrote to Mr. Short,* an attaché to the American legation in Paris, a letter which was purloined by an unfaithful valet, a Jacobin himself. This letter was used in a manner which Jefferson did not anticipate, and which would have astounded him.

Dogs that have tasted blood want more of it. The Jacobins were wolves; and wolves, when they have lapped that liquid, are more greedy for it than dogs. Hence, one evening, in one of the suburbs of Paris, a large crowd of patriots had met in an immense cellar, a sort of cavern, dimly lighted, and ornamented with red flags and other decorations appropriately devised for the occasion. But all those things, remarkable and impressive as they were, could hardly be noticed, when there were such faces, to absorb all attention, as those of the human beings who composed the assembly. Their photographs would have commanded a high price in the fancy shops, duly licensed, of his Satanic Majesty's kingdom. Barrère de Vieuzac presided over the meeting, and, on taking his seat, stated in his mellifluous voice and in his peculiar phraseology: "that the tree of liberty, recently planted, was withering; that its roots needed more irrigation; and that its head expected a refreshing fall of heavenly dew." What that dew was, every one present understood. Hence the sentiment was

---

* Jefferson's Works, vol. iii., p. 501.

vociferously applauded. Then the assembly took up the famous song of the epoch, *ça ira, ça ira, les aristocrates à la lanterne.**

"It will be a mercy to them," shouted a shirtless and half-inebriated wit; "but they are so hopelessly blind that they will not see any better for it."

This sally was a success, and Pandemonium yelled with delight. At that moment there appeared a personage who was greeted with a deafening demonstration of enthusiasm. He was a deformed dwarf, with a monstrously large head and hideous features, decayed teeth, and a coarse mouth extending almost from ear to ear. His dress seemed to be affectedly dirty and seedy. His name was Jean Paul Marat, a Swiss by birth and a physician by profession. Starving in his country, he had come to France in search of bread, and had established himself as an empiric and a strolling quack, who sold medicinal herbs, and a panacea which cured all diseases. Notwithstanding the possession of that miraculous nostrum, he had continued to remain in the most abject destitution. To emerge from it, he had imagined to become an author. His first production was the translation of an English publication, of very slender merit, entitled "The Chains of Slavery." Having failed to coin the "Chains of Slavery" into money, he launched out a more aspiring and voluminous work with this title: "Man, Principles and Laws which Govern Him; Influence of the Soul on the Body, and of the Body on the Soul." It seems, therefore, that Marat believed, or pretended to believe, in the soul. He had also given to the press several other compositions on anatomy,

---

*The aristocrats to the lamp-post.

optics, and electricity. Notwithstanding all these attempted displays of learning, Marat had remained
obscure and miserably poor, and had ended in gladly
accepting the humble situation of horse doctor in the
stables of the Count of Artois, a brother of the King.
He was performing these functions when the revolution broke out. In a storm which convulsed society
to its foundations, and brought its dregs to the surface, Marat could not but become prominent. He
immediately established a journal called *The Friend
of the People*, in which he daily advocated, openly or
impliedly, the commission of every one of the crimes
prohibited by the decalogue. It very naturally followed that he acquired an immense popularity. His
paper was read with avidity, and approvingly com-
mented on with delirious violence in all the sinks of
the capital. The horse doctor, the quack who cured
with his Swiss balsam all the ills that flesh is heir to,
obtained the honor of being elected a representative
of Paris in the National Convention.

As soon as the plaudits which had greeted his entrance into the Jacobin Club had ceased, Marat ascended a sort of platform, or tribune, that stood in
front of the president, a little lower than his seat, and
said with his harsh, croaking, discordant voice:

"Citizens, the country is still in danger, but be not
alarmed; I am on the watch tower. The country requires new doses of the most powerful drastics, and
copious bleedings, to recover robust health and per-
petuate the duration of its liberties and franchises.
We must continue with steadiness the wholesome
medical treatment which we have begun to admin-
ister. The jails of Paris are now vacant, in consequence of the purging which we recently gave them.

We must fill them again, and again make them vacant. But this will not be enough. We must do the same in all the provinces. All the prisons in France are gorged; it is a dangerous plethora. They must be relieved from it, and be made to vomit into the grave the indigestible food with which their maws are loaded. I have calculated with minute exactness the quantity of blood required for the safety of the people. The head of the King must fall, and with it the heads of three hundred thousand aristocrats and traitors."

Marat continued in this strain, becoming more and more extravagantly atrocious in his insane ravings, which were accompanied with epileptic gesticulations, until the very excess of his ferocity produced a reaction in the assembly, thoroughly steeped in cruelty and all alive with evil passions as it was. Reprobating cries of "Oh! oh! that is going too far. You will make the very name of Jacobin a word of shame and horror!" were heard in different parts of the vast dingy room. The orator paused in astonishment at this manifestation of unexpected and unusual disapprobation. But he was not put out of countenance.

"What is this? What do you mean?" he exclaimed with unabashed assurance. "Have you become chicken-hearted? Jacobins, you need not be ashamed of what you have done; go on, and do not lose your well-earned reputation for stern and honest patriotism. I will demonstrate to you that the course which we have pursued, and which I wish you still to pursue, is approved by the very highest authority on earth. Is not the republic of America our model? Can we have better guides than those sages who established it for the benefit and example of mankind? You all venerate the name of Jefferson, now a member of the

Cabinet of General Washington. You know how he encouraged us in all our plans, when he was here. I have in my pocket a letter addressed by him to a friend in Paris. Listen to what he writes. He begins with saying that he does not find fault with our acquiescing for a time in the experiment of retaining a hereditary executive, but that, as we have ascertained that it would ensure the re-establishment of despotism, he considers it absolutely indispensable to expunge that office. Thus he and I agree in the premises, as you see. What is the sequel? I quote his very words. Open your ears, you, my friends, who think proper to make asses of yourselves, this evening, and who presume to think that I go too far."

Wiping his perspiring forehead with a coarse and filthy-looking rag which he used as a handkerchief, Marat went on:

"Thus citizen Jefferson expresses himself: *'In the struggle which was necessary, many guilty persons fell without the forms of trial, and with them, some innocent.'* I deny, of course, the latter part of the assertion. *'These I deplore,'* he says, *'as much as anybody, and some of them I shall deplore to the day of my death. But I deplore them, as I should have done, had they fallen in battle.'* Admirable! The great patriot is tender-hearted; and, at the same time, firm as a rock and unswerving as fate. *'It was necessary to use the arm of the people, a machine not quite as blind as balls and bombs, but blind to a certain degree. A few of their cordial friends met at their hands the fate of enemies. But time and truth will rescue and embalm their memories, while their posterity will be enjoying the very liberty for which they never would have hesitated to offer up their lives. The liberty of the whole earth was depending on the issue of the contest ; and was ever such a prize won with so little innocent blood ?'* Now, Jacobins, what do you say to that? What our enemies call murders and butcheries, Jefferson calls '*a necessary struggle.'* Our breaking into all the prisons of Paris and killing in them thousands of men, women, and children, he considers to be '*a battle in a good cause.'* He says that we were right in assuming that many were guilty, and in destroying them without any forms of preparatory trial to ascertain the fact. I agree with him in this, but I disagree when he asserts that you massacred some of your '*cordial friends,'* and approves of it. You never did so, and I would never sanction the perpetration of such an act. A cause which requires for its success the assassination of cordial friends, is bad and must be abandoned. I am not afraid of being disavowed by you, citizens, when I proclaim that the people shall be without mercy for their enemies; but, at the same time, shall always consider their friends as sacred objects, and shall never have the cowardly selfishness to sacrifice any one of them to any of the exigencies of the time." Great applause.

After a pause, during which he surveyed the assembly with a gratified look, Marat thus resumed his discourse:

"You will observe, Jacobins, that Jefferson says that there never was such a prize won with so little innocent blood. '*Little blood !'* Do you hear? Hence am I not justified in asking for more, to confirm us in the possession of that prize! But I deny that there was innocent blood shed. I would not approve of it, as he does. It was guilty blood; and it is a larger quantity of that guilty blood, which I desire at your hands, to secure that liberty, equality, and fraternity which it is our mission to spread over the whole earth. Should one of you here be disposed to think that enough of it has been spilt, I now call his special attention to this last paragraph of Jefferson's letter: ' My own affections have been deeply wounded by some of the martyrs to this cause, but rather than it should have failed, I would have seen half the earth desolated; were there but an Adam and Eve left in every country, and left free, it would be better than as it now is.' * Well, citizens, that beats me, you must admit. I am overwhelmed with the grandeur and heroism of a sentiment for which I can not have too much admiration, but I dare not go so far. I only insist on having three hundred thousand heads."

In one of the corners of the room, in the background, and unnoticed by anybody, sat a youth, who had been an attentive observer and listener. He rose, and walked deliberately to an open space running from the entrance door to the seat of the president, and serving as a passage for the members of the club and for the public, as they came in and took their seats on the right and left. There he stopped, drawing himself up to his full height, which measured about six feet, and exhibiting as fine a specimen of humanity as the eye loves to rest upon. He was pale, not from fear, but from the intensity of some feeling which he had evidently determined to keep under control, if possible. Surely there was, there could be, no fear in the breast of that man. His flashing eyes would have forbidden such a supposition; they were those of a hero. There was in his

---

* Letter to Mr. Short. Jefferson's Works, vol. iii., p. 501.

manner and look something so expressive, that he riveted at once the attention of the whole assembly. All turned toward him, and the silence was profound. It is astonishing what rapidity of intuition there is, sometimes, in a crowd of men! Every one present felt at once and sympathetically, that something striking and unexpected was to take place.

" Mr. President," said the unknown, with a voice which sounded like the bold and stirring blast of a clarion, " I am from Brittany. The son of an honest peasant, I disregarded his remonstrances and the entreaties of a pious mother, in a moment of folly, to come to Paris, and witness the wonders which the nation hoped for, under the new order of things that was to be established. Thanks to the priest of my village, I have received some education, and I have delighted to read with him the history of the heroic days of antiquity. I loved to dream of the republics of Rome and Greece, and I had come to the capital to participate in the inauguration of one superior to those of past and pagan ages, because born in the bosom of Christianity. But I have heard and seen enough. The cries of your victims have appalled my ears, and I shall never forget the streams of blood which I have beheld. My illusions are gone. I look with horror on the infidel and heartless republicanism of America and France, as typified by Jefferson and Marat. What will become of America with such sentiments and principles as are professed by leaders of that stamp, I do not know, and care not. I know, however, but too well, what you will make of France. I curse the day when I called myself a republican. Brigands, I will never associate with you any more. I am a royalist now, from head to foot, body and soul.

Long live the King! I am off for La Vendée. My name is Cathelineau, and, God helping, I hope, ere long, to make it ring in your ears."

He rushed out of the room and disappeared, be-fore the assembly, taken by surprise, had recovered from the stupor of amazement into which they had been thrown by so bold a speech.

CHAPTER XXIII.

CHARLOTTE CORDAY—ASSASSINATION OF MARAT.

ON the next day after this nocturnal assembly of the Jacobins, Marat, relying on the importance which he derived from his being one of the representatives of Paris in the National Convention, appeared in the midst of that body, followed by a band of patriotic bandits and liberty-loving cut-throats, who tumultuously occupied the galleries and lobbies and all the other places reserved for the public. Tormented by his insatiable thirst for blood, that insane monster ascended the tribune, and with the gesticulations and rage of a maniac denounced that part of the assembly called the *Girondists*, which was composed of the élite of its members. "The aristocrats," he shouted, "say that those precious colleagues of ours are the only statesmen of whom this assembly can boast, and that the rest of us are braying jackasses, or hungry tigers. Ha! ha! Is it so? Well, *I* call those men traitors. They are a dangerous faction of conspirators against the liberties of the people. I ask for the heads of that faction of pretended statesmen. I also ask you to decree the massacre of two hundred and seventy thousand partisans of the old *régime*—I have counted them—the sum total is correct—and I further ask you to reduce to one-fourth the members of this National Convention, which, after this epuration, will be composed only of the well-tried and well-known friends of the people, such, for instance, as Danton, St. Just, Robespierre, and myself. I ask that one hundred thousand of the relatives of the *émigrés*—I can not spare a single one of them—it makes a round number—be imprisoned as guaranties for the conduct of those rebels who have fled to foreign territories."

"And *I* ask in my turn," exclaimed the impetuous Barbaroux, rising in his seat and interrupting the orator—Barbaroux, one of the deputies of Marseilles, who, by his eloquence, his real enthusiasm for liberty, and the wonderful beauty of his person, was one of the most conspicuous among the Girondists—"I ask in the name of common sense, in the name of the outraged rights of humanity, in the name of justice, dignity, and respect for ourselves, that this disgusting foreigner be kicked out of this hall of our deliberations which he pollutes by his presence; that he be whipped by the hangman, and then confined in a lunatic asylum, or rather in some house of correction, for there is more malignity in him than madness." There followed an indescribable scene of confusion that brought on a death struggle between the different parties dividing the Convention—which struggle, after days of the fiercest contention, ended in the destruction of the Girondists. They were all outlawed; some were arrested and incarcerated; others, among whom was . Barbaroux, fled from Paris to the provinces. This was Marat's last triumph; his mission was at an end. Providence has marvelous ways of her own to get rid of those agents of evil who, for a little while, are permitted to run their unchecked course through the apparent chaos of human affairs.

There lived at that epoch, near the village of St.

Saturnin, in Normandy, a young woman of noble birth. Her name was Marie Anne Charlotte Corday D'Armans. Damsels of her rank, in those days, were generally educated in convents. She had been no exception to that almost universal rule. But, at the age of fifteen, she became, on the death of her parents, the ward of an uncle, a Knight of Malta, who had retired from active service in consequence of his numerous wounds, and of those infirmities which announce the approach of the winter of life. Louis Corday D'Armans, having installed himself in the feudal manor of his niece with a maiden sister, only two years younger than himself, determined, after due consultation with that venerable spinster, to assume the responsibility of giving a home education to Charlotte, and withdrew her from the religious institution where she had already been several years. The old uncle and aunt thought that the monotony of the solitude in which they lived, would be much relieved by the companionship of their young niece. The aunt would take care to initiate her into the mysteries of housekeeping, and the uncle would while away many of the hours that hung heavy on his hands, by teaching his ward to love those classic works of antiquity which he himself idolized. Thus the fate of Charlotte was fixed. She was taken away from the convent, and an important historical event was the consequence of her guardian's somewhat selfish resolution.

Louis Corday D'Armans, Count of Séez, and Knight of Malta, although a military man and a man of the world, was a scholar of considerable attainments, and one of those free-thinkers who had been the fashion since the beginning of the eighteenth century. It was not strange, therefore, that he should be one of those nobles who thought that monarchies were the effete things of the past, and that the regeneration of mankind required a fraternity of nations and a universal system of republics all over the world. He was a fanatical admirer of antiquity, and would have wished to substitute the institutions of Athens and Rome for those which had prevailed so long in his own native country, although it certainly would have puzzled him, if he had been called upon to reconcile the democracy of Attica with the aristocracy that had built the imperial city on the banks of the Tiber. His ideas were rather nebulous on the subject, but he had no doubt that, under a proper and skillful manipulation, his Gallic countrymen could be turned into a glorious compound of the Greek and Roman, that would astonish the world by the exhibition of a material and intellectual progress hitherto unknown to the human race. He had traveled and resided a long while in Italy and Greece, and cherished for the memory of what they were in the past, a feeling which amounted to almost a sort of religious worship. He had brought home from those classic lands a large collection of curiosities, objects of art, engravings and paintings which reproduced with exquisite accuracy the monuments and picturesque scenery of those favored regions. There was not a Greek or Latin author whose productions were not to be found in his library. He had become passionately attached to his niece, to whom he had succeeded in communicating all his tastes. In that hall on whose walls were sculptured the armorial bearings of feudal barons, and wherein had feasted a long line of Norman knights, there were to be seen no other statues

14*

or busts than those of the heroes of Plutarch; and
the battles of ancient Greece were more frequently
alluded to than those which had been fought by all
the chivalry of Europe.

Wrapped in studies which grew upon them with
delightful fascination, the Count and his niece lived
in utter seclusion—and in an ideal world of their own.
Apart from a few and rare visits from neighbors, to
which they rather submitted with courteous resignation, than assented with any degree of complacency,
they had no other diversion they liked than that of
the chase.   With a view of strengthening the constitution of his pupil, the Count had insisted on her accompanying him when he hunted, not only the timid
deer, but even the wild boar and the ferocious wolf.
He had achieved his purpose; for the glow of health
was on the cheeks of his lovely kinswoman, and the
vigor of manhood was harmoniously blended with
the delicacy and softness of her sex. She could swim
like one of the water-nymphs of ancient mythology,
and the Gods themselves would have admired the
skill, grace, and activity with which she engaged in
the favorite pursuit of the chaste Diana. She had
become a bold rider, and self-reliant even in the presence of danger, although she retained all her feminine
attractions, which were made still more attractive by
her look of exquisite modesty, by the natural elegance of her figure, and by the perfect symmetry of
such features as those we find chiselled on antique
cameos by the hand of a master. Under the guidance of her uncle, this wonderful young woman, gifted with a soul to which all that was pure, elevated,
and sublime was congenial, had so identified herself
with the poetry, the history, the philosophy, the

manners, usages, religion, and feelings of Greece and Rome, that she was more of a Grecian or a Roman than a Frenchwoman. She was a self-consecrated vestal in the temple of antiquity, keeping up in all its brightness the sacred fire which was the object of her worship.

When the French revolution broke out, both the uncle and the niece followed with intense interest all the phases of that momentous event. They had read with enthusiasm the declaration of the rights of man, and had looked on Mirabeau as the Demosthenes of France. All their dreams were now, at length, to be realized, and the virtues of the best days of Greece and Rome were to be revived on the fruitful soil of those heroic Gauls who had so long deserved to be free, and to be purified from those prejudices which, during so many centuries, had clouded their intellect and riveted the chains that encumbered their limbs.

The title of King which Louis and Charlotte Corday hated as deeply as the Romans had ever done, had just been abolished, when the Knight of Malta died of a severe cold caught in hunting; and his highly imaginative and classically-educated niece, who felt with acute sorrow the loss of her kind guardian, was left to the sole and uncongenial companionship of her aunt, whose mind was exclusively engrossed by household cares. The aged dame took no interest in the history of the past, and very little in that of the present. She was a woman of few words. When occasionally the prospect of the adoption of republican institutions was forced upon her attention, she would say with an ominous shake of the head: "I do not see how what is not good for a family, can be good for a nation. There must be but one ruler in

every house. If you suppress the head cook in the
kitchen, the scullions will quarrel, and the broth will
be spoiled. What is everybody's business, is nobody's." The utterance of these wise saws was all
that could be extracted from her on that subject. It
is at least doubtful whether her theory of government
was not as correct as any other. The fact is, that she
daily carried it into effective practice, for she never
allowed any one to interfere with her management of
her niece's establishment, from the garret to the cellar. It was as beautiful a specimen of autocratic administration as could be desired, and it was quietly
acquiesced in by the person who alone had the right
to dispute her authority.

At dawn, one day, not long after the death of Louis
Corday D'Armans, Count of Séez, there stood a
young woman on the brow of a hill which rose almost
to the dignity of a mountain, about three miles from
the village of St. Saturnin. It was Charlotte Corday.
In one hand she held a riding-whip, and in the other
a book—that wonderful book in which still lives the
Republic of Plato — the utopia of genius, wherein
dimly shone the half-luminous shadow of the coming
light of Christianity. She wore on her head the traditional bonnet of Normandy, white as snow, with
flaps hanging down on either side of her cheeks to
her neck. This helmet of lace was so adjusted as to
leave uncovered the rich edge of glossy hair, that
from a noble forehead streamed down in curling
locks to shoulders over which were thrown the folds
of a woolen tissue, pinned to her black dress. A
groom with two horses was in waiting at a short
distance. A steep path, three feet wide, cut in the
rock, wound along the crest of the mountain on one

side, and, on the other, yawned an abyss five hundred feet deep.

There Charlotte Corday had alighted from her horse, to admire the magnificent view which spread far and wide before her. The sun, just rising above the horizon, was tipping every object in the valley below, one after the other, with its golden rays. But, for her who gazed at the scene, it was not the luminary that science has nailed in the vault of Heaven; it was Apollo in his chariot of light, urging his immortal steeds through their prescribed career. The gentle wind which sported with her locks, was not a current of air, but an amorous zephyr who had been permitted to woo the beauties of nature, whilst his tempestuous brothers slept in the cavern of Eolus. To her imagination, yon stream which meandered through the valley was the far-famed Eurotas, or the still more famous Tiber. That edifice which loomed on a distant hill, took the Corinthian proportions of a Temple of Minerva. On her left, the smoke that rose from the midst of a cluster of trees, proceeded, no doubt, from the altar of some deity to whom a sacrifice was being offered. On her right, that rosy cloud ascending to the empyreal sphere, was Venus returning to the abode of the Gods above, from a visit to the Nereids who dwell in the depths of the sea where she was born. The flute which greeted her ears must have been that of Pan summoning his sylvan court to his presence. In front of her the horizon closed with a range of precipitous hills, between which she could discover only a narrow passage. Surely such must have been the immortal Thermopylæ. She fancied that she saw the glittering arms of the three hundred, and the crowns of flowers with which they had decorated their brows for the feast of death in a noble cause. But her reveries were disturbed by a sudden noise which awoke the dreamer to the realities of life.

A shot had been fired at a man who was seen running up the narrow path that led to the spot where she stood. He seemed exhausted, and his pursuers, half a score in number, were evidently gaining ground upon him, although the distance which separated them might be a quarter of a mile. At that sight, the groom in waiting, fearing some danger, had approached his mistress, and presenting the bridle of her horse, was urging her to mount. Whilst she hesitated, the fugitive, who had rallied all his strength for a supreme effort, bounded to her side. "Lady," he said, with panting breath, "whoever you may be, save my life. I am no wretch hunted for any crime, but a representative of the people—a member of the National Convention, one of the Girondists outlawed by Marat and his assassin compeers. My name is Barbaroux." It would not have been in the heart of woman to resist the supplicating look of this Antinous of modern times. But it was not that which moved her whom he addressed. Prompt as thought she pointed to one of the horses. "Take him," she said, "and give him the reins. The faithful animal will carry you to a castellated building in a secluded spot. When at the gate, knock with confidence, ask for Grandchamp, the steward; show him this ring for your authority, and tell him to hide you in that place which is known only to him and to me." Away, away flew the horse with his charge, and he had almost disappeared, when the men who were in pursuit confronted the young woman who had calmly awaited their coming. "We have seen, damsel, what you have done," said the commandant in a threatening tone. "How dared you assist the flight of the guilty from justice? Who are you?"

"One who loves liberty, and hates tyranny most when hypocritically committing crimes in that sacred name."

"That fugitive," continued the officer, "is an enemy of the people, and his life is forfeited by a decree of the National Convention. I will arrest you and bring you before that body to answer for yourself."

"I am willing to follow you. My answer is ready. I will fearlessly plead guilty of an act of humanity. I know what will be my fate before such judges as Marat and Robespierre. But, before I ascend the scaffold, I promise to ask them one favor—which is, not to forget to give you the price of blood that you will have so well deserved. How much is my head worth, citizen, and at what sum will you assess it? Speak."

The officer's face crimsoned. "Soldiers," he said, turning to his men with an affected smile, "my mother has always told me to be blind to the faults of women. Yours did probably the same. What do you say? Were our mothers right?" "Aye, aye," was the reply.

"Then, right about face and forward—march. We shall move down this confounded hill with more ease than we came up. When at headquarters, I will send men in every direction after the fugitive. He shall not escape. For the present, we can not, on foot, catch one who is on horseback. As to the *citoyenne* here, we will not report her. She is no aristocrat, for she has told us that she loves liberty and hates tyranny.

Three cheers for liberty!" And they departed, shouting with all the strength of their lungs for what they so little understood in its political and practical application.

For several weeks after this event the whole province of Normandy had been thoroughly scoured by the emissaries of the National Convention, and the manor of Charlotte Corday had been twice searched, without any discovery being made that could lead to the arrest of Barbaroux. Finally, there came a report, generally believed to be true, that he had safely reached the sea-coast and embarked for England. The pursuit ceased, and the inhabitants of the district suspected of having harbored the fugitive became free from domiciliary visits. The human bloodhounds had been withdrawn, and probably sent elsewhere after other victims. All this while, however, Barbaroux had remained concealed in the place where he had found a refuge. Old Grandchamp, the steward, had watched with the utmost solicitude over the safety of the guest who had been intrusted to his care, not that he took the slightest personal interest in him, but because his arrest, where he was, might have endangered the life of her by whom he was sheltered. That gray-haired servant had been the trusty esquire and secretary of Count Louis Corday D'Armans during forty years, his inseparable companion in all his campaigns, and a sympathizing participator in all the trials of his life.

It is difficult, nowadays, fully to understand the relations which still existed at that epoch, between gentlemen and those of their domestics who approached the nearest to their persons. Grandchamp was a specimen of those family attendants who commanded the confidence and friendship of those to whom they had attached themselves with hereditary fidelity, and who boasted that their fathers had served the ancestors of their masters. He had always been ready to sacrifice himself for *Le Comte mon maitre*, as the *Comte* should have been to die for *Le Roi mon maitre;* and that a Corday should have been a republican and have failed in his allegiance to royal authority, was the most portentous and inexplicable event of which old Grandchamp's imagination could dream. *He*, at least, would follow his mission on earth, which was to be true and cling forever to the family under whose roof his cradle had been placed by Providence, and to perish, if mote be, with the last representative of that race—a calamity which, he doubted not, would soon happen. For, what were the signs of the times? Had not the highest nobility of France renounced and sacrificed their titles, their honors, and even their historical names on what they called the altar of patriotism? Were not some of the former magnates of the land at the head of low-born and ignorant demagogues, who had destroyed a glorious monarchy consecrated by a thousand years of existence? Had not a prince of the blood, a descendant of Saint Louis, boasted of being the adulterous son of a coachman? Were not such monstrosities and horrors the indications and forerunners of the coming end of the world? Had he not been ordered, he, Grandchamp, to conceal a regicide under the roof of a long line of knights who had perished in the defense of those ideas and affections which the last heiress of their name and blood had repudiated? But he had obeyed, hard as it was to his loyal heart. It was not for such as he to question the deeds or the motives of those he was bound to love and to serve; and, if they courted self-destruction, it

was none of his business to oppose them. His duty
was to follow them whither they went. Theirs was
the responsibility; that was enough for him. Forlorn
sentinel of the past, when all changed around him, he
would die at his post. Such were the feelings of that
humble and generous soul. Such was the strange up-
side-down of all things on the revolutionary soil of
France. Nobles had become democrats, and valets
had remained aristocrats!

During his concealment, Barbaroux had been favored, always in the evening, when there was less danger
of being seen, with several interviews with Charlotte
Corday. They took place in the library, to which he
obtained access through a secret passage cut in the
thickness of the walls. Grandchamp, on such occasions, had never failed to be present. He was a man
of tall stature, of military mien, with a bronzed face,
harsh features, rough voice, and a few locks of white
hair straggling over a bald and osseous head, which
formed a striking contrast with his very dark, heavy
brows and thick moustaches. Under this rugged ex-
terior there was hid a soul full of gentleness and susceptible of unlimited devotion. At all these meetings
of Charlotte and Barbaroux he had attended in obedience to her special request. Stationing himself near
the wall of the apartment between two bookcases,
there he stood like a statue with his arms folded on
his breast, while the fugitive and his kind protectress,
seated near a table in the center of the library, conversed together. Barbaroux was only twenty-five
years old, of the same age with Charlotte Corday. He
was a man of considerable abilities and had some of
the gifts of the orator. His eloquence was impetuous
like his temper. He was more vehement than logical,

more bold than tenacious of purpose. He readily produced a favorable impression by his brilliant qualities and his manly beauty, which is reported to have been extraordinary. He was possessed of elevated sentiments, but deficient in that maturity of judgment which is in most men only the fruit of experience. His patriotism was sincere and ardent, and he ingratiated himself with all those who approached him, by the amiable frankness of his character. He had a poetical mind, and there is still extant an ode by him on volcanoes, that contains some passages of great literary merit. He had delivered in the National Convention several speeches full of vigor; he had made excellent reports on matters of administration and legislation, and written, in a style worthy of commendation, several fragments of instructive memoirs on certain events of the revolution which required elucidation. But his career was destined to be short. He had attacked Marat and Robespierre; and, being deemed by them a dangerous adversary, they had resolved to remove him from the tribune of the National Convention to the platform of the guillotine.

It is not astonishing that such a personage, made still more interesting by the touch of adversity, should have produced the most vivid impression on Charlotte Corday. She loved to listen to his picturesque descriptions of the struggles he had witnessed and in which he had shared, and of the celebrated men who occupied the attention of the world. What a gigantic drama! Was there ever one more replete with awful and sudden turns of fortune? She never tired of interrogating him on what he had seen, heard, felt, and hoped. He threw light on many of those wonderful events which had stood before her like dark and impenetrable shadows. As to Barbaroux, the better he became acquainted with her, the greater was his astonishment, and the more intense the admiration he felt for her character. He could hardly realize the moral phenomenon which was revealed to him. He had accidentally met a young and highly-educated woman, as foreign as the Coliseum and Parthenon to the age in which she lived. It seemed as if in her the spirit of antiquity had been revived in all its grand and pristine simplicity, and had incarnated itself with all its intellectual chastity of taste, its sublime thoughts, its exalted sentiments, its self-sacrificing and all-absorbing patriotism, and its heroic philosophy, such as glow in the pages of Plato and Plutarch. By what incantation had this beauteous being been evoked from her marble tomb, and made again a thing of life, such as she was centuries ago, when she moved, no doubt, and breathed like a goddess in the porticoes of Athens or Rome? Under the spell which she had thrown over his soul, he felt that his faculties had expanded, that his heart palpitated with nobler aspirations, and that his ambition had been hallowed as if by a purifying flame from heaven. He had but one thought— one burning and all-engrossing thought—to do some great thing for his country and mankind, and then say to her: "Am I worthy of your love?"

Barbaroux, with the assistance of Charlotte, Grandchamp, and the groom whose horse he had taken on the day of his escape from his pursuers, had maintained constant communication with his friends, and had been informed that they had levied a small army, with which, under the leadership of some of the outlawed Girondists, they had taken a stand at Vernon, on the banks of the Seine. Their intention was, if backed by Custine, who had the command of the army of the North, to march upon the Convention in Paris and arrest those members who constituted what was called "the mountain." But the co-operation of that General had failed them, and, attacked by superior forces, they had been totally routed, at the very time when Barbaroux was preparing to emerge from his hiding-place and join their ranks. Defeated in his hopes in that quarter, he had resolved to make his way to Bordeaux, where he relied on finding warm partisans of his cause, and from that city to proceed to Marseilles by moving along the Mediterranean coast. "There," he had said to Charlotte, "I shall be in my stronghold, and if it come to the worst—if we must give up the rest of France to tyranny and sanguinary misrule—there we will erect the standard of a true republic. That old city of the Phoceans has lungs in good condition to breathe the genial air of liberty, and enough of stubborn courage to maintain her independence. She once knew how to resist the Carthaginians, jealous of her commercial prosperity, and did not succumb to the Athenians when attacked by their intrepid hosts. Nay, three centuries before the Christian Era, she had become the Athens of the Gauls. Her municipal administration was praised by Cicero as a fit model for imitation. Her government was republican under the auspices of six hundred senators. After many disasters which could not crush her, she remained an independent republic under the protection of Rome, recovered her commercial importance, and became famous for her schools. After her annexation to the French monarchy, she had preserved, even under Louis XIV., many privileges and franchises, which could not have been taken away by that despot without the most desperate resistance. She has retained her instincts of liberty and the recollection of her past splendor when she was free. She can, therefore, be relied upon. There, at all events, being supported by numerous friends throughout the rest of France, we can make a long stand, until Marat and Robespierre, who are the sole obstacles to her regeneration, shall be swept away, as soon as their nefarious designs are better understood by the masses whom they deceive." Cherishing such hopes, he had begged Charlotte Corday to prepare everything for his secret departure, and to provide him with the means of reaching Bordeaux as speedily as circumstances would permit. After several days, during which she had cautiously planned the execution of his contemplated design, Charlotte sent word to Barbaroux that all was ready, and that she would meet him in the library at the usual hour. When it struck, she entered the room with Grandchamp bearing in his hands a large bundle.

"My poor prisoner," she said to Barbaroux, "I have been successful in accomplishing your wishes. You will soon be on the wing with the lark. Before daybreak, a wagoner will meet you at the small gate of the park. Grandchamp will take you to him. You will find in this bundle all that is necessary for a complete disguise of your person. The wagoner can be trusted, and is a man well known on the roads from Normandy to Bordeaux, on which he frequently travels. You will pass for his nephew, whom he has lately associated in business with himself."

Barbaroux returned his acknowledgments, and begged, as they were to part perhaps forever, that she would be pleased to prolong, as much as possible, an

interview which was to be followed by a painful separation. Graciously assenting, she beckoned him to a
seat, and took one for herself, whilst Grandchamp occupied his post as usual between the two bookcases.
Never had Barbaroux been more interesting in the
expression of his views, feelings, and hopes. Never
had he with more sympathetic and contagious ardor
spoken of that future which he saw so glorious for
France and for himself. The soul of Charlotte Corday responded to his with all the enthusiasm of her
nature, which had been made more vehement by her
peculiar training under her uncle's supervision. Two
young and generous hearts they were, full of noble
illusions and high resolves, dreaming, alas, of impossi-
bilities and of things which are not of earth. Let them
enjoy the flitting hour which was never to return ; for,
near them, although invisible, yawned a bloody grave !
In a delightful interchange of congenial aspirations,
they were unconscious of the flight of time, when the
announcement of midnight came solemnly to their
astonished ears from the belfry of the neighboring
village. Startled at the sound, Charlotte rose from
her seat.

"Barbaroux," she said, " I have lingered too long.
We must part. Farewell ! " and she tendered her
hand to him, which he took eagerly, and on which he
imprinted a respectful kiss, in token of such profound
homage as a loyal subject pays to his sovereign.

"Dear Charlotte," he replied with emotion, "you
have saved my life and periled yours for my sake.
This has established between us such ties as author-
ize me to use the word which I have coupled with
your name, and which bursts from a more than grateful heart, for I am a lover—but one whose love is

so strangely mixed with sentiments akin to what must be felt toward an object of divine worship, that I can not address you in the ordinary language of commonplace passion. I will only say: permit me in the presence and with the sanction of that venerable servant of your house, who watches over it with hereditary devotion, permit me, ere we part, to pledge to you my faith, which I hope soon to redeem in more auspicious times," and he knelt at her feet.

A slight blush overspread the beautiful, serene face of Charlotte Corday, but it vanished like the flash of the lightning. "Rise, my noble friend; rise, I beseech you," she said in gentle tones. "I thank you for the honor you do me; I thank you for not addressing me with the expressions of vulgar passion. There is no mortal lover whose vows Charlotte Corday could accept. I am wedded—start not—wedded," continued she, with a smile, "to one of those heroes of antiquity among whom I have always lived. Choose which you please—it matters not. I long to join those sublime beings who dwelt in the distant past, and whom my imagination cherishes as realities of the present. Hence the seclusion and solitude of my existence. I have always felt as if in a state of widowhood. Seek not to kindle love in my heart. My love is buried under the ashes of ages. My friendship you have. If you value it, go on in the path of glory. Save France from tyranny—think not of woman when your country calls you to the rescue; be a modern hero; let that be your mission; I have mine. It is to co-operate with you as much as may be in my power. You shall know in time what I meditate. Farewell again. Grandchamp, I commit him to your care. Do not leave him until he is safe on the way. Farewell,

Barbaroux; farewell, my dear friend." And they parted, never to meet again on earth.

Four weeks had elapsed, when a trusty messenger delivered to Charlotte a scrap of paper which contained these words:

"BORDEAUX, *July*, 1793.

"NOBLE AND DEAR FRIEND:—I found the reign of terror prevailing here as in Paris. The whole population is paralyzed by abject fear. I am in the hands of the emissaries of Marat, the butcher of France. Before long I shall die on the scaffold. May we meet in the Elysian Fields among your favorite heroes of antiquity. BARBAROUX."

She kissed the note, and put it in her bosom; then she walked to the library, and, taking down from one of the shelves the "Phedo of Plato," in which the question of the immortality of the soul is so luminously and eloquently discussed, she read it attentively, until her eyes straying from the book and her mind lapsing into a state of abstraction, she remained a long while motionless—the statue of meditation. At last, she raised her head, and her looks fell on the bust of Brutus. She rose and approached the sculptured image. "No, Brutus, no," she exclaimed. "It is not true, what thou once didst say. It is not true, that virtue is nothing but a name, for it lived in thee, it has lived ever since, and it is because it will live forever, an ennobling and consoling reality, that thy memory has ever been honored, and that thy example shall ever be followed, as long as man shall deserve to be free. With despair in thy heart, thou hast perished for Rome. With hope in mine, I shall die for France." She rang a bell; the old steward made his appearance, and stood before her in the attitude of a soldier waiting for the command of his superior. "Grandchamp," she said, "I depart this evening for Paris. You will hasten to Sécz, and secure for me a seat in the public coach."

"Alone?" inquired Grandchamp, looking fixedly at her.

"Alone." •

"It is well. Has *Mademoiselle* informed her aunt of her intended departure?"

"No. It would give her unnecessary alarm. I could not explain to her the important business which calls me away. It is a secret. Give her what excuse you please for my absence. I commend her to your care."

"The will of the last of the Cordays be done in all things!" ejaculated the old man, with an air of solemn resignation, and with his harsh voice, now become slightly tremulous, as if from some sudden emotion. Charlotte looked at him with inexpressible tenderness. "Grandchamp," she said, "let me embrace you," and she threw herself upon his breast with tears and sobs. The aged servant folded her in his arms, kissed her brow, and muttered, in broken accents: "The will of the last of the Cordays be done in all things!"

When Charlotte Corday arrived in Paris, she was informed that twenty-one Girondists had been seized and were in prison, awaiting their trial. All knew what in those days a trial meant. It was a mere formality, rapidly gone through, previous to passing the sentence of death. It was a sort of mechanical operation—the stamping of victims for the scaffold as letters are for the post-office. Charlotte attended the sessions of the National Convention, and found that the scenes which she witnessed were far more horrible than those of which she had heard or read. Once she saw Marat in his seat, and the hideousness of the monster strengthened the resolution which she had taken. He affected to speak in the vilest jargon used by the populace, and to dress like the lowest of those whom he represented. A round hat, shorn of its brim, much torn, and battered into an almost shapeless form, covered his enormous head, which looked as if it would crush the body of the filthy dwarf. His greasy and uncombed black hair was tied round his temples by a piece of coarse twine, that strove in vain to confine his disheveled locks. He sported a rough, shaggy overcoat, with multitudinous stains, and with a discolored velvet collar. He had on leather breeches; his gray woolen stockings fell over his heels, and his heavy, iron-nailed shoes were remarkable for the ingenuity with which so many patches on them were made to hang together. He was several days, however, without showing himself again, and it was rumored that "the Friend of the People" was exhausted by the excess of his labors, and would remain for awhile at home to recuperate, before reappearing at the tribune to ask for the heads of the incarcerated Girondists.

Charlotte wrote to Marat the following note: "Citizen, I arrive from Normandy. Your love for your country makes you desire, no doubt, to know what events have taken place in that section of the republic. I will present myself at your lodgings, with your permission, at one o'clock. Be so kind as to receive me. I will enable you to render a great service to France." This application was not answered; another was sent, and met with the same fate. Shortly after, she addressed him a third letter, in which she spoke of "important secrets which she had to reveal," and called herself in person a few minutes after she had ascertained that it had been delivered. She asked for admittance: it was refused by two women whom she met in the ante-chamber, and who opposed her efforts to go farther. One of them was Marat's concubine. He was just coming out of a bath, and, judging from a few words which he overheard that it was the person who had written to him, he ordered her to be introduced. He was wrapped in a loose morning gown, and, with cynical carelessness, left his shaggy breast exposed. The conversation was short.

"What do you want?" said Marat roughly. "What are the secrets to be revealed?"

"The mayors and other administrative officers of Caen and Evreux," she replied, "are aristocrats. I come to denounce them."

"Who are they?" and, with fiendish glee, he wrote down the fictitious names which were given to him. "You may be sure that they shall die. What next?"

"As a reward for what I have done, will you grant me the lives of some of the Girondists? I have a friend among them."

"No!" answered Marat, chuckling. "All that I can do is to give you their heads as keepsakes. Choose your friends better."

"If I make known to you," continued Charlotte Corday, "one who is ready to assassinate you, will you grant the lives I sue for?"

"No!" shouted Marat, with mixed anger and fear. "Not one life shall I spare. But I will have you arrested instantly."

"Then die, tyrant !" she exclaimed, and she buried in his heart, up to the hilt, a dagger that she had concealed about her person. "Help, my dear," cried Marat, calling to his concubine in the next room. That was all he could say. The blow had been so well struck that he died instantly. The two women who had heard his voice, rushed in. Charlotte made no effort to escape. She stood motionless, pressing the bloody dagger to her breast, and with her eyes lifted up to Heaven, as if thanking the Gods for her success. Charlotte Corday was soon in the hands of an officer of justice.

As to Marat, his death was cruelly avenged by the sacrifice of hecatombs of victims, and extraordinary honors were granted to his memory, as if he had been the best and the greatest citizen of the new republic. Triumphal arches and provisional mausoleums were erected on the principal public squares of Paris ; and on the one called *Le Carrousel*, between the Tuileries and the Louvre, a pyramid was constructed, in which were exhibited his bust, his bath-tub, his inkstand, and his lamp. It was guarded by sentinels day and night. His corpse was carried to the Pantheon, the last asylum reserved for the illustrious dead—the pagan Westminster of France. His bust was solemnly installed in every public edifice throughout the republic, and, in many private ones, was conspicuously exhibited as the image of some household god.

There could not be discovered a single moment of weakness in Charlotte Corday during all her trial before the revolutionary tribunal. There was in her deportment no sign of affectation, no trace of exaggeration. Throughout the examination she had to undergo, her answers were simple, concise, and sweet·

tempered. Once, observing that somebody was drawing her portrait, she turned toward him to afford a better view of her person. If she wished merely to oblige, it was wondrously kind under such terrible circumstances; if it was to have her features transmitted to posterity, was it exceptionable in the woman and in the heroine? She was provided by the court with a counsel for her defense; his name was Chateau Lagarde. His defense of his client was marked with Spartan brevity. "I believe," he said, "that I have read the soul of the accused, and that it stands revealed to me. Understanding, I am sure, how she wishes to be defended, I have only to declare in her name that she confesses what she has done, and avers that it was a homicide long premeditated, matured with care, executed without fear, and remembered without remorse!" That was all, and he sat down. The accused thanked him with noble simplicity and infinite grace of manner for having comprehended her so well. She added: "In my turn, I wish to show you that I understand your soul as you do mine. As a proof of it, considering that all my property will be confiscated, I do not hesitate to request you to pay the small debts which I have incurred in my prison." She listened with calm fortitude to her sentence of death. In the cart which took her to the scaffold, she showed the same sublime serenity. On that day, the most humiliating spectacle, because the most disgraceful, was exhibited in one of the largest cities of civilized Europe. A woman, abandoned by all, having no other support than her own soul, no other comforter than the conviction of having done her duty, entitled to all the interest which her sex has a right to claim, endowed with surpassing beauty, blooming with all the freshness of youth, manifesting a degree of heroism which, if misconceived, had never been excelled, might surely have been thought worthy of enthusiastic admiration. And yet, what happened? More than twenty thousand men pursued her with clamorous insults, whilst as many looked at her in cold blood and with stupid indifference, or heartless curiosity. But she noticed them not—no, not one instant. She passed between them like an impassible apparition from a purer sphere. Perhaps, with her mind's eye, she saw gathered round her as an encouraging escort, and waving their laurel crowns to their future companion, disembodied spirits with the halo of immortality on their brows. The only emotion which she showed was that of offended modesty, when the public executioner removed the kerchief covering her bosom and the neck on which his ax was to fall. Let it be recorded, to the honor of humanity, that four men dared to publicly praise Charlotte Corday shortly after her death. Three were executed for it. One of them, who had caused to be printed a eulogy of that heroine, and who had proposed to have a statue erected to her memory, with this inscription, "Greater than Brutus," exclaimed, when he was brought to the block: "I am happy to die for Charlotte Corday, and on the same scaffold."

True, she was greater than Brutus, for she was a woman, and her motives were probably purer and more disinterested. She was a beautiful specimen of pagan, but not Christian heroism. To murder, even for a noble purpose, is not sanctioned by the ethics of the Gospel. It is impossible, however, not to take pleasure in admiring her magnificent self-sacrifice, notwithstanding the stern admonition of Montesquieu, who says: "It is that heroism which is destructive of morality that excites the most our admiration."

CHAPTER XXIV.

THE LAST BANQUET OF THE GIRONDISTS.

"BLOOD will have blood," is a phrase which has become axiomatic, and history informs us that political assassinations never answer the purpose for which they were perpetrated. The blow which Brutus struck at Cæsar in the Senate of Rome, rather consolidated tyranny than re-established liberty, and the death of Marat by the dagger of Charlotte Corday, instead of saving the Girondists, was a pretext for Robespierre to send them to the scaffold, and adopt measures of proscription that gave rise in France to that condition of things which will ever be known in the annals of that country as being emphatically "the reign of terror." About three months after Marat had perished, and been put among the new gods of the republic after the mythological fashion of Rome and Greece, twenty-one Girondists had been brought before the revolutionary tribunal of justice and sentenced to be executed the next day. At that epoch, a prison was called "the ante-chamber to the guillotine." Those who were taken to that ante-chamber, generally did not wait long for an introduction to her ladyship. She administered an expeditious mode of death, which was said to be less painful than any one previously practiced by public executioners, and which could not be disgraceful, since it was inflicted on the *élite* of the nation merely because it was the *élite*. It is, therefore, singular that so many persons, when arrested, should have resolved to escape by suicide the easy and honorable death awarded by the guillotine. But, to imitate antiquity was the prevailing mania, and, as suicides were deemed heroic deeds, every man thought himself a Brutus, or a Cato, if he blew out his brains, or opened his bowels. It was a pagan custom worthy of being followed—the more so, perhaps, because it was reprobated by the Christian religion, which the republicans, philosophers, and progressists of the day, like Julian the apostate, wished to set aside by the revival of the superseded worship of the gods and goddesses. Thus Valazé, one of the Girondists who had been put on their trial, when sentenced to the guillotine, struck himself to the heart with a concealed weapon and fell dead in court. It was thought dramatic and sublime. It certainly was sensational. The corpse was carried back to jail with the surviving twenty, and there a scene took place which could have happened only in France, and which shows, more impressively than anything else, the moral condition of the people at that time. The Girondists were admitted to be the most high-toned among the members of the Convention, and yet, on the eve of death, how did they prepare themselves to meet their Creator and close a life that entailed, on some of them at least, a responsibility from which, if properly conscious of it, stouter hearts might have shrunk with terror? Their last and engrossing thought seems to have been to take striking attitudes before the world like actors on the stage, and to dramatize their end. With the corpse of one of their companions lying in a corner of the room, they conceived the idea of

15*

having a final exit banquet, in which, although death might be said to be seated at the board, they would, notwithstanding his grim presence, enjoy the flitting hours, and not only prove themselves philosophically unconcerned about their fate, but even show more gaiety, wit, and eloquence than on ordinary occasions. As they entertained different and antagonistic opinions and feelings, some toasted the republic, and others, royalty. They drank to their wives and mistresses, among whom were some of the most notorious courtesans of the epoch, who were mentioned by name, such as the "brunette Gabrielle" and the "giddy Illyrine." Wives and mistresses toasted together in festive association! The parade of worldly sentiments and of skepticism in sight of the scaffold, and at that awful moment which summons us to a separation of soul and body, with its unknown consequences! And these were some of the men who had the pretension to establish forever the "virtuous republic" announced by Robespierre, and who had thought themselves capable of being the leaders of a great nation! It is singular that every French writer who speaks of that supper of the Girondists, treats it as one of the most impressive and sublime scenes on record. Thus the historian Thiers says with an evident feeling of complacency: "They took in common their last repast, in which they were alternately gay, grave, eloquent." Twenty patriots carousing gaily and talking wittily and eloquently, not only over the graves that expected them, but even over the grave of that liberty which they cherished so much, as the greatest blessing their country could obtain! And under what circumstances? When that country was a volcano, torn by its internal throes, when foreign armies were threatening it on every side, when cartloads of women and men were butchered every day, when they themselves left their families in utter destitution and in the agonies of despair, and when such horrors were perpetrated in their capital as no civilized society had ever seen before! No, their hearts were not, could not be, in it. To act as they did is not in human nature, and it is not to be supposed that there is a peculiar French nature which is an exception to it. They were acting a part—acting like madmen, more intoxicated with the fumes of an excessive vanity than with those of the wine they drank. Their hearts were misled and their minds crazed by the extraordinary moral disease which, for more than half a century, had possessed itself of that once glorious and Christian nation—glorious still, but now skeptic in everything and pitied by those who loved her the best, at the very moment when, in her fatal convulsions and illusions, she thought herself the light and the guide of the world.

I shall give a mere sketch of that celebrated banquet, leaving out of sight all that is impure, and presenting only the side view which is the least objectionable. That last banquet of the Girondists was a mere bravado offered to God and man, which is no more like the sublimity of true moral courage than the vaporings of Orlando Furioso are like the serene intrepidity of a Christian martyr. If we, Americans, wish to form a correct estimate of the exhibition made by the Girondists on that occasion, we have only to fancy that England had triumphed in that war for independence carried against her by her revolted colonies; that Washington, Franklin, John Adams, Thomas Jefferson, Alexander Hamilton, and others of the great men of our revolution are sentenced to death, and that, a few hours before their execution, they are feasting together in their prison, drinking madeira, sherry, and champagne, cracking jokes at each other, toasting their wives and mistresses, or some of the belles of New York, Philadelphia, or Boston, saying smart and pithy things about forms of government and other matters, making a parade of stoicism, wit, and erudition, whilst entirely forgetful of their God, their souls, and their country! Could any conception so absurd, or execrable, spring up in the brain of any American? Is there not even something ridiculous in the bare idea of the possibility of such a scene? But let us go back to the Girondists and listen to them whilst seated at table, and, to use their language, making their last libation to the Gods —that is, if they believed in any god whatever.

" I drink," * said Mainvielle, " to all and every one of our colleagues among the Girondists who are still free, and I wish them success against Robespierre and his acolyths."

Ducos. " I drink to the republic, one and indivisible."

Vergniaud. " The republic! I give it up. It is a phantasma of the brain—an idle chimera—a bauble for the enthusiastic imagination of youth to play with. Remember the words of Barbaroux, who, like us, had lost all faith in that which he once worshiped. ' If I could recommence life,' he said, ' I would consecrate it entirely to those noble studies which raise the thoughts of man above the goods of the earth, and I would not venture on attempting to give free institutions to a

---

* Charles Nodier's " Girondists."

people destitute of all morality. The howling and maniac populace of France is no more worthy of a philosophical government than the lazaroni of Naples and the cannibals of the New World.' Barbaroux spoke the truth. A man, if he is wise, may, in his leisure hours, indulge in dreaming of the republican utopias of Plato, Thomas Morus, and our dear Madam Roland, who knew at last, when at the foot of the scaffold, what crimes can be perpetrated in the name of liberty, but he does not seriously think of realizing shadows. We have all been insane, and we shall soon be cured by the guillotine. Let us sacrifice a cock to Esculapius.

Gensonné. "Decidedly, Vergniaud, you seem to believe no longer in liberty."

Vergniaud. "If liberty were a goddess descending among us with her hands full of blessings, I would worship her; but I execrate the fury who makes men drunk and then devours them. Altars would never have been erected to the sun, if it had always appeared escorted by tempests and desolation."

Fonfrède. "Has not nature herself prescribed social equality, or is it but a vain word?"

Vergniaud. "Who ever heard of social equality among the Greeks and Romans, of whom we talk so much, and whom we are so anxious to imitate? As to social equality being prescribed by nature, it is a cant phrase, like many others by which simpletons are deluded! There is not the slightest vestige of equality whatever in anything which nature produces. If social equality could exist—which I consider an impossibility—it would be the most odious and most unendurable of all tyrannies. Have you not heard of Procrustes? That monster had contrived an iron bed with which he accommodated all travelers who claimed his hospitality. He stretched and dislocated those who were shorter than the bed, and mutilated those whose limbs protruded beyond it. That is social equality."

Brissot. "Fraternity and social equality might be established among men who, acknowledging the errors and miseries of civilization, have returned to the innocence of primitive tribes."

Vergniaud. "Abel and Cain were primitive enough, God knows, and yet what a specimen of fraternity!"

Brissot. "I will, in dying, address to the republic a salutation full of regret and hope."

Vergniaud. "And I also will address her a salutation—the salutation of the vanquished gladiator to Cæsar. But I shall carry with me in my mourning heart the image of that sublime revolution which my mind had conceived. Thus, what remained of the monarchy died with Mirabeau."

Brissot. "Let us hope that Vergniaud, dying, has only seen the cradle of Hercules."

Vergniaud. "Pshaw! Hercules in his cradle strangled serpents, and did not vomit them."

Brissot. "We have legislated like Moses, in a tempest. Let us flatter ourselves, however, that our republic, like his laws, will live forever."

Fauchet. "Moses! His laws came from Heaven, tempestuous as it was; yours, from the abyss below."

Vergniaud. "There is in decrepitude a sterility which prevents old nations from giving birth to youthful institutions. The idea that a monarchy of one thousand years can be successfully transformed into a vigorous and long-lived republic is absurd. Too much must be destroyed to operate the change.

It can not be done without a general conflagration. What would be the result? Nothing but ashes— two fathoms deep of ashes over the whole bosom of France! Well, we know that nothing comes out of ashes, except the phœnix. But it is from its own ashes that the eternal bird springs into regenerated life. Shall a new monarchy, phœnix-like, come out of the ashes of the old one which has been consumed? I doubt it. I am afraid that posterity will see republics constructing monarchies—monarchies reconstructing republics—and then chaos."

Brissot. "The English monarchy is not chaos. It presides over the civilization of two worlds. Much as I detest those islanders, I must make this admission."

Vergniaud. "The present English monarchy was born yesterday—born of a republic—and there is no telling how soon it may end in one. Who can foresee what it will be?"

Brissot. "The North Americans are not a new people—their civilization is borrowed from Europe, and yet they have established a prosperous republic."

Vergniaud. "The monarchy of France gave birth to that republic, and lost her life by it. But what will become of the child, is a question to be solved by time. That republic, with the co-operation of France, was born out of the womb of an abstract idea, as the statue of Pygmalion was born of marble. To that creation of genius, life was granted by the goddess of beauty, at the invocation of love, but no soul, and it was denied the power of reproduction. It never had a mother, and never was destined to be one. The United States have no ancestry, no poetical past, nothing for the imagination to dwell upon.

Hence they can have no real and deep-rooted patriotism. It is a sentiment which springs from the heart
alone, and the heart is not warmed by reason, which
is as cold as ice. Nothing durable can ever be founded simply on moral ideas. The principle of life which
is indispensable to social or political creations is not
the doctrine of the philosopher, or the erudite experience of the legislator; it is imparted by the nymph
of the poet and the fairy rod of the romance writer.
Homer did more to inspire Greece with patriotism
than all its Solons and Lycurguses. Even the institutions inspired by the wisdom of Numa would not
have been adopted by the Romans, if not sanctioned
by Egeria. Besides, the young transatlantic republic, having no neighbor to check her expansion, will
evidently extend over the whole continent of North
America. It will be a new kind of patriotism, that
which will have to spread over an area of thousands of
miles! Probably it will have no more strength than
a bottle of this generous wine here would possess, if
diluted in the ocean. My conclusion is, that in a vast
country destined to be enormously rich, a republic
without intense patriotism is an impossibility."

Duchatel. " My heart was sick of the long errors
and miseries of so many brutish and enslaved generations. Like yours, it aimed, in its blindness, at impossible ameliorations which have already cost too
many tears and too much blood. The lovers of Pene-
lope were not more bitterly deceived than have been
the lovers of liberty. There are days and nights for
the intelligence of nations as for the physical world,
and during the hours of darkness, what had been done
during the hours of light, is frequently undone."

Fauchet. " The French are a people without religion, and therefore incapable of establishing any solid institutions. A nation may do the masonry of an edifice, but God alone must be its architect; otherwise it will be a tower of Babel. Civilization is the serpent that leads ungodly societies to the foot of the tree of knowledge, and when they pluck its fruit, it is only to learn that they are doomed to death, because of their infidelity. Ah! gentlemen, our revolution came from that fruit which hung on the tree of knowledge spoken of in Genesis. The eating thereof produced one in Paradise."

Ducos. "Citizens, we are getting too prosy and dull. Fill up your glasses to the brim. We are not preaching here like monks, but feasting like the companions of Leonidas, before passing from the battlefield to an immortal life. Let us rejoice and be merry; let us pour perfumes on our heads and put on crowns of flowers. By-the-by, I regret that, whilst we were in power and voting decrees by the bushel, I forgot to propose the indivisibility of the head and shoulders like the indivisibility of the republic."

Viger. "I am a military man. Permit me to speak with the frankness which characterizes my profession, and without offense to most of you who are lawyers. You talked too much in the Convention. No orator, no sophist ever founded or preserved social order. The sword is the only agent of civilization and government which is worth a cent. Robespierre, who is fond of listening to his own voice, will end as we do. France will be saved by one who will not talk, but act. There is nothing like the eloquence of artillery and the logic of the sword, to argue the lovers of anarchy into orderly conduct. It is not in the gangrened heart of a large and impure city that it is possible to gather the elements of a sound republic. A populace feeds on the entrails of the social body, as ravens and buzzards on the offals of the slaughter-house. The regenerator of France will come out of the army."

Duperret. "I agree with Viger; and, if you had seconded us, as we frequently proposed it to you, his sword, or mine, or the sword of some other military man, would have cut the Gordian knot of the revolution."

Fauchet. "A sword will cut it yet."

Gensonné. "That of Cromwell?"

Duchatel. "Of Monk?"

Viger. "Who knows? France is at war with Europe, and war alone produces those men who are capable of governing powerful States."

Duperret. "Yes, men who save a nation from its own excesses, after having protected it against a foreign foe."

Vergniaud. "Like Pelopidas."

Carra. "All the events of the future being the unavoidable repetition of the past, it seems to me true in principle that a sword must inevitably close the revolution."

Duprat. "You put me in mind of what I heard a young captain of artillery say, when I was supping with him more than a year ago. It produced an impression on me, and I remember his very words. Speaking of the present leaders, he said: 'They will march in the midst of revolutions without knowing how to profit by them. They will frame constitutions and violate their own work. They will make themselves odious to the people and to mankind by excesses which had disappeared from history since Sylla and the triumvirs. Then a man will come, with a halo of glory, and, guided by fortune and victory, he will say to them : "You had laws, and you now have none, for you have trampled them under your feet. What have you done with the blood of those brave legions which was uselessly shed for their country?" Thus he will speak; and, with the mere waving of his sword, he will drive them out of sight and power.'"

Vergniaud. "That young captain may be the man of destiny whom the future keeps in reserve. *Heu ! Marcellus eris.*"

Mainvielle. "I know who it is. He is a Corsican, an undersized man, with a luminous and penetrating gray eye, a lean body, a long and thin profile, a vast forehead, an olivaceous complexion, hair combed flat and falling down to his shoulders. He speaks little ; his language is picturesque and sententious. His thoughts come out—abrupt and brief—as if they were orders. His name is, I believe, Napoleon Bonaparte."

Fonfrède. "Tossed about between an imbecile aristocracy who dream of nothing but the past, and frantic demagogues who have no other instincts than those of destruction, rapine, and assassination, the French, one day, will be perhaps but too happy to have a master."

Vergniaud. "There are epochs of dissolution, when it is no more possible for tyranny to establish itself among a people, than it is possible for liberty. Where the tempest of revolution has passed, it leaves behind in its track an oscillation which prevents stability—a dangerous flux and reflux. What the tide had deposited on the shore, the ebb carries back. All powers which are not grafted on ancient and necessary institutions, identified by long usage with the national character, are structures without a reliable basis. Under the sirocco breath of skepticism the whole surface of France has become but one quicksand where nothing can take root. I am afraid that, henceforth, despotism and liberty will be but transitory things in our country, and will alternately succeed each other at regular intervals."

Duchatel. "This will undoubtedly happen, unless the country should shelter itself under one of those powers that you have just defined as resting on ancient institutions and usages, and it is no other than that monarchy which you have destroyed, and which, by a salutary re-action, will be re-established and founded on a constitution, or fundamental law, that will be a guaranty against the evils of despotism and of too much liberty. O my friends! in a moment of insanity, you have voted the death of Louis. Thank God, I have not. But the planks of the scaffold did not drink the last drop of that noble blood of the Bourbons, which has never been shed without carrying a thrill of horror to the very entrails of France."

Here he was interrupted by loud cries of "Long live liberty!"

Vergniaud. "Yes, long live liberty, but liberty must permit the freedom of opinions, particularly in front of the scaffold. Therefore, fill up your glasses. Let us drink to whatever we please, each according to his own fancy, and then, let Duchatel go on."

After silence had been re-established, Duchatel rose again, and said: "Long live the King and liberty!"

Fauchet. "And religion!"

Duchatel. "Yes; and religion. Long live the King, liberty, and religion! They harmonize beautifully, and

are essential to one another. The ancient charters and
constitutions of the French monarchy, which I have
studied too late, and which we ought to have modified, and not destroyed, contained a thousand times
more of the elements of liberty than will, in the
course of many ages, ever come out of the caverns of
your republic. Hence, I shout again: Long live the
King!"

"Long live liberty, and down with Kings!" shouted in their turn most of the Girondists. Several remained silent and pensive—among others, Vergniaud. After a little while, he said: "I have proved
that I love liberty, since I perish for having attempted
to establish an impossible republic in France. I must,
however, confess that Duchatel may be right after all;
for if the happiness and prosperity of a people depend on the virtue of those by whom they are governed, it follows that a monarchy is preferable to an
aristocracy, because there is a better chance to find
one virtuous man than a hundred; and an aristocracy
is preferable to a democracy, because there is a greater
probability that one hundred virtuous men can be
found than twenty thousand. But why trouble ourselves with the forms of government? In our situation, we had better discuss the immortality of the soul.
It is the only question which should be made the
order of the day."

Le Hardy. "For me it is not a question. Creation
can not be imperfect, because it comes from God. It
must, therefore, be perfect, which it would not be
without morality, and it would have none, were not
the good to be rewarded and the bad punished."

Fonfrède. "That question is answered by nature.
It has made man the only intelligent being in whom

exists, as an instinct, the desire, the hope, and the want of resurrection. The instinct would not have been given, were it not to be satisfied."

Brissot. "It is answered by human reason, which manifests itself in its highest degree of excellence in the philosophical works of Plato. I look for the accomplishment of the promise made to me by that sage in the name of the great Architect of the universe."

Fauchet. "It is answered by faith, which is more learned and more faithful to its promises than Plato with all his conjectural investigations, and which makes the Christian more certain of the future existence than the philosopher."

Duprat. "My friends, we are getting to be as solemn and gloomy as a cathedral seen by the dim light of a half-clouded moon. I protest against it. Let us adjourn this metaphysical discussion to the moment when, our heads being in the market-basket of the republic, the question of the immortality of the soul will be solved *ipso facto*—by actual demonstration. For the present, let us drink, eat, and be merry. We have no time to lose. Look at this huge bowl of punch. I am going to set fire to it. Fill up your glasses. You shall have a bacchanalian song which would heat the cold blood of Robespierre himself."

From that moment the banquet took a character which would cease to be interesting or acceptable to such readers as I choose or hope to have. At last, Vergniaud pulled out his watch. "Four o'clock," he said, "it will soon be day—our last day! We have but two or three hours left that we can call our own. It is not too much for thinking, writing, making our final arrangements with the world which we leave behind us, and sleeping a little."

Mainvielle. "So far as I am concerned, I have nothing to settle with the world. Let it settle its own concerns to please itself. I never cared for it, and now less than ever. As to thinking, my brain never fatigued itself with such an operation. Writing is a bore; and as to sleeping, I shall before long do nothing else."

" My dear colleagues of the National Convention," said Vergniaud, striking the table with the handle of his knife, " our sitting is at an end. We adjourn *sine die*." Five minutes after, the room was vacant. No —it was still occupied ; there was remaining in a corner the corpse of Valazé.

The prisoners departed, escorted by the jailers, the turnkeys, and their subordinates—some bearing torches, and others carrying lanterns. When Gensonné arrived at the door of his cell, the man in whose charge he was, instead of pushing him in and turning the key, walked in with him, and looking steadfastly at the prisoner, whose face seemed to inquire for the cause of this unusual proceeding, said, in a voice which nature had made harsh in its intonations : " Citizen Gensonné, you are the intimate friend of Barbaroux, are you not?" "Yes." "Very well. I have a mission to accomplish on your behalf. I was an old servant of the noble damsel, Charlotte Corday D'Armans. My mistress said to me, before she went to. the scaffold: 'Grandchamp, it is probable that Barbaroux has perished at Bordeaux. We can do nothing for him ; but his friend, Gensonné, is in great danger in Paris. Watch over him.' Before she thus spoke, I had determined to die with her, for she was the last of her race. I had no longer anything to do on earth. But, as she chose to give me an order, of course I had to live and execute it. So, I turned Ja-

cobin, as I foresaw that it would offer me the opportunity of being of service to you. I frequented their
clubs and became somewhat popular. When you
were arrested, I contrived to be appointed one of the
turnkeys of this prison. Now, be quick; let us exchange clothing. Take mine; I'll take yours. We
are fortunately of the same size. Make my broad-
brimmed hat hang low over your face, as I habitually
wear it. The prison is dimly lighted, and the guards
are getting drunk over the wines which you left. I
have been given an errand by the chief jailer. Here
is the order in writing which permits me to go out.
Show it to the man at the outside gate. As to the
inside doors, here are the keys; they are all num-
bered—one, two, three, four—to be used as you go
on. You can not make a mistake." And he began
stripping himself.

"Stop," said Gensonné, almost paralyzed with astonishment. "What have I done for you, that you
forfeit your life to save mine?"

"You have done nothing," replied Grandchamp.
"I care not for your life; you will owe me no obliga-
tion. I was told to watch over you, and to save you,
if possible. I obey the order. That's all."

"But, if I fly, you will be butchered in my place."

"Exactly what I want," growled Grandchamp.
"My mission being at an end, I am free to act as I
please. But, hurry, hurry; take off your clothes as
I do mine. Otherwise, it will be too late."

Tears of admiration came into the eyes of Gensonné, and he pressed warmly in his hands those of
Grandchamp. "You are the noblest and most generous of men in your heroic simplicity," he said.
"Would that all the French were like you!"

" If they were," answered Grandchamp, " France would not be a republic. I am a royalist of the deepest dye. But, make haste."

Gensonné. " My friend, keep your clothes on, and answer me frankly one single question, as I know you will; for you have sufficiently revealed your nature to me. We are capable of understanding each other. Were you in my place, would you desert your companions and fly ? "

" No !" replied Grandchamp, firmly and unhesitatingly.

Gensonné. "Your answer prescribes what I have to do, and precludes all further solicitations on your part. Thanks to you with all my heart for your attempt to save my life, and—farewell ! Any further stay would expose you unnecessarily."

Grandchamp. " Is it your last word ? "

Gensonné. " The last."

Grandchamp. "You are what you should be." And it was his turn to shake cordially Gensonné's hands. " It is time to part," he continued. " But we shall meet again at the foot of the scaffold." And he retired, muttering between his teeth : " Those republicans, after all, are not so mean and rascally as I thought."

On the next day, the Girondists were piled up in a large and long cart and carried to the place of execution, where an immense crowd awaited them. There they all acted dramatically, and uttered pithy and brilliant sentences, destined to produce stage effect, and to be duly recorded for posterity. Some joked, some laughed, some even perpetrated puns. Others hummed the *Marseillaise*, or an opera tune. Every one showed his contempt of death in the way which he thought would be most striking. Several of them shouted : "Long live the republic!"—in which they did not believe, and which was tyrannically slaughtering them without any cause, or reason, or pretext whatever, to palliate the atrocity of the deed. There was an incident which moved the multitude. When Duchatel ascended the scaffold, a bouquet of daisies and immortelles, to which was attached a paper, and which was thrown by an unseen hand, fell at his feet. It was picked up by the public executioner. "Read it! read it!" cried the crowd. The executioner read it in a distinct voice :

" FOR MR. DUCHATEL :

"My heart had responded to your love, dear Duchatel, and yet I did not express it to you, because there could be no possible alliance between us on earth. To-day you die ; in a few days it will be my turn, for I have just been arrested, and I am soon to be tried. You will not long precede me to the bridal chamber. Prepare it for me, dearest. My heart and hand are yours throughout eternity.

" LUCILE."

Duchatel looked up to Heaven with a radiant face, and after his head had fallen, his features had retained an expression of joy.

The last who perished was Gensonné. "Long live the republic!" he exclaimed with a mocking tone and attitude. "Long live the republic!—which you have not, and which you will never have."

It was eleven o'clock when this massacre began, and, "Thirty minutes after," says a French writer, "twenty of the judges of the King of France had appeared before the Eternal Judge."

When the last of the Girondists had ceased to exist, a tall and rugged figure ascended the scaffold with slow and measured steps, and, when on the platform, looked calmly but austerely at the astonished multitude, whom he seemed disposed to address. It was Grandchamp. That address was not long. Stretching himself up to his full height, and expanding his breast, he shouted : " Vile and blood-thirsty *canaille*, I hope that you will one day receive the punishment which you deserve. I defy you all. Long live the King! Long live the memory of Charlotte Corday, and down with your republic of demons!" There was but one vast clamor of: "Off with his head! Off with his head!" Grandchamp smiled in approbation, and, after waving his hand as if returning thanks, adjusted himself his neck in the guillotine. The "off with his head" was more vociferously repeated by thousands of voices. "Citizens," said the public executioner, "I have no authority to do it ; I am without orders ; I can not incur the responsibility." "I will assume it," exclaimed a man frantic with rage, who jumped upon the platform, and touched a spring that kept suspended the fatal ax. It descended with a hissing sound, and Grandchamp's head was the twenty-first which, by its fall on that day, gratified the eyes of a ferocious multitude. Thus perished one of those faithful domestics of whom so many of the households of France could boast under the old *régime*, and who, henceforth, will be looked upon as an impossible type of beings, whose chronicled devotion and honesty seem more compatible with those fictions which grace legendary traditions, than with the sobriety of history and its truth-sifting investigations.

CHAPTER XXV.

DEMOLITION BY A DECREE OF THE NATIONAL AS-
SEMBLY OF THE CHATEAU DE CHANTILLY,
THE HOME OF THE GREAT CONDÉ — THE
VISION IN THE LAKE.

WE have lost sight of Tintin Calandro. What had
become of him, since he brought to Mirabeau the
grateful news that Marie Antoinette had granted him
the interview which he so desired, to save, as he
hoped, the monarchy of France, and since he had received from the dying orator his last message to royalty? We must retrace our steps to the epoch when
the King was still nominally on the throne, after his
return from Varennes, where he had been arrested in
his flight and brought back to Paris, whilst the friend
of the Queen, the Princess de Lamballe, had succeeded in finding a safe asylum in England, which she was
preparing, however, to abandon; for she had determined to come back and share in all the dangers of
her royal mistress. At that time, the National Convention was passing the most severe decrees against
those nobles who had emigrated from France, among
whom were all the members of the House of Condé,
a prince of the blood. Lakanal, who had obtained a
seat in that Assembly, and who had ceased to be a
Catholic priest, like other similar *progressists*, had
been instructed to take possession of Chantilly, the
famous residence of the prince, where one of his an-

cestors, the Great Condé, had given to Louis XIV. those marvelous entertainments described in the letters of Madam de Sévigné, and in more than one of the memoirs of the seventeenth century. The *château* was to be demolished; all the gold, silver, copper, and lead, and all the other valuable materials there to be found, were to be appropriated to public purposes.

Immediately after receiving this commission, Lakanal had departed for Chantilly without any attendant. He wished to examine the extent of the work to be done, and ascertain what number of men he would have to employ. He had other reasons to desire to be alone when applying to get possession of the building he was to destroy. Although he had occasionally met Aubert Dubayet, he had been, since he had begun his revolutionary career, sedulously avoided by Tintin Calandro, and this man, whose heart was as hard as adamant, and who, to achieve his fanatical purposes, would without emotion have sent to the block all the kings, queens, and nobility of Europe, shrank from meeting a poor musician, once his school companion. In his memory, blooming at times with all the freshness of youth, there lived again two boys who had often been locked in each other's arms, who had gamboled together on the green-sward, and one of whom had been saved by the other, when the angry waves of a torrent were carrying him away. The joyful laugh of childhood still rang in his ears; the sight of a bright, candid, confiding face, budding into adolescence, still greeted his eyes; and into that stern heart of his a softness crept which he could not subdue. He had heard that the Princess de Lamballe, previous to her flight, had provided for Tintin Calandro, and had caused him to be appointed keeper of the *Château de Chantilly*, with a good salary. .Would he, Lakanal, attempt to drive him away? He knew Tintin Calandro but too well; he expected resistance, and resistance to the will of the National Convention was death! Would he kill Tintin Calandro? No! no! He had laughed, he had sneered at him—that he could do—but dig his grave! Never! That life at least was safe in his hands. He would not yield it to any exigency; he would battle for it like a man; he would watch over it with a woman's tenderness. Such are the mysteries of human nature. Thus in barren deserts travelers will meet a green spot and a gushing spring from some blasted rock.

As we see, Lakanal had his own special reason for encountering Tintin Calandro without a witness. He had prepared himself for the first burst of indignation of his sensitive friend; he would coax and soothe him; he would persuade him to succumb gently to resistless fate, and to accept his protection. Encouraged by these thoughts, Lakanal summoned all his resolution, and, on the clear evening of an autumnal day, entered the park of Chantilly on foot. A herd of tame deer glided by him, and were soon lost among the trees and in the darkening shades of the departing twilight. A milk-white fawn, with a gilt collar on her neck, had detached herself from the rest, and, after circling round and round the stranger in frolicsome coquetry, displaying her beauty and grace, approached him with her nostrils distended, her soft eyes beaming with the expectation of familiar caresses, and with her head and neck stretched to receive some dainty bit of food. Charmed with the sight, Lakanal stood motionless, not to frighten the timid animal. The fawn turned around him, smelling his clothes and hands, and, suddenly showing all the signs of extreme terror, uttered a plaintive cry and bounded away, as if she had been chased by a famished wolf. He sighed, and went on. He walked in alleys shaded by tall oaks whose aged limbs spread over his head. The wind moaned through their leafy crowns, and dismal howls, far distant, were wafted to his ears. Lakanal was a man of strong nerves, and entirely destitute of imagination; and yet he could not but feel, now and then, a creeping of the flesh, as he fancied that he heard near him some strange noise, and that he had indistinct glimpses of mysterious forms which scowled at him and melted into the rising mist. As he proceeded, a shower of leaves kept falling on and about him, and he shuddered when to his eye every leaf, as it reached the ground, seemed to assume the appearance of a large drop of blood. He hastened his steps, and when at last he stood in front of the stately edifice of which he was to be the destroyer, perspiration streamed from his forehead, notwithstanding the keenness of the night air. He stared at the palace for a moment with something like a feeling of awe. The silence and solitude were appalling; no sign of life was visible; every door and window was closed, not a light was to be seen. With a trembling hand he knocked at the main entrance. After a little while, steps were heard approaching, bolts and bars were withdrawn, and Tintin Calandro, with a lantern in his hand, and an enormous dog of the Mount St. Bernard breed by his side, stood on the threshold. The dog, as soon as he saw the stranger, was about to spring upon him with a ferocious bark, when, " Down, Norlingue, down!" from

Tintin Calandro, brought him crouching to his feet but still growling, and keeping his fierce eyes riveted on the unknown visitor.

"My dear Tintin," said Lakanal, in a deprecating tone, "you are no doubt surprised at seeing me," and he presented his hand to greet his former school companion. Tintin did not take it, and replied, with freezing gravity: "I am not surprised at anything. Walk in"; and he led Lakanal through a long suite of apartments. The pale light of the lantern now and then fell on the grim figure of some warrior painted on the wall, or reproduced in sculptured marble, that seemed to frown upon him. He grew almost indignant with himself. He was not superstitious, and he attributed the illusion to fatigue and an over-excited mind which, for the first time, he could not control. At last they reached a door before which Tintin Calandro stopped. "This is my apartment," he said, "step in." The dog had followed, keeping close to Lakanal, growling all the time, and showing signs of increasing anger—so that Tintin had to put him out. "How strange!" he muttered to himself. "That animal has never before been ferocious and disobedient. What wonderful instinct! He must know, as if intuitively, that an enemy of the house has crossed its threshold."

When he returned, Lakanal was warming himself by a large fire which burnt cheerfully in an antique chimney. The apartment itself was vast and gloomy. "This room is very cold," said Lakanal, rubbing his hands and spreading them open to the flames.

"For mortal man, it is always cold in the presence of spirits," replied Tintin, in a solemn tone, "and spirits dwell here."

Lakanal felt colder, and approached closer to the fire. A dead silence ensued. No sound was heard except the monotonous, heavy tick of a large clock in the corner and the chirping of a cricket on the hearth. Was it a funeral dirge sung by the little insect to the departing hour? It had a saddening effect on Lakanal's already depressed mind. But, bracing his nerves, he said: "I have a message from the National Convention to the keeper or warder of the *Château de Chantilly.*"

"Ha! ha! Is it so? Well, then, this bed-chamber is not a proper place for its delivery," said Tintin Calandro, with bitter irony. "Let us walk to the reception hall. The ambassador of the National Convention must be treated with due respect"; and, taking his lantern, he conducted Lakanal, who followed him mechanically and almost in a state of bewilderment, to a lofty and immense apartment, where every object was indistinct, for the feeble light of the lantern only served to make "darkness visible." Lakanal had gone through unusual emotions that evening, and began to feel really sick—almost fainting. He tottered to a large gothic arm-chair which was not far from him. He was in the act of dropping into it, when Tintin Calandro pushed him violently aside. "Not there, not there!" he cried fiercely. "This is a sacred relic. It was the favorite seat of the Great Condé. In my presence, none but one of his race shall sit in it. By the living God, man, it is fortunate that I put out that sagacious dog. He would have throttled you in an instant, without my being able to prevent it. Take that other chair; and now, speak. But let me put this lantern between you and me, so that we may see each other's honest faces."

16*

This rude treatment recalled Lakanal to his habitual sternness of character, and almost roused him to anger. "Sir," said he firmly to Tintin Calandro, "the Prince of Condé having emigrated, this property is confiscated. To-morrow, I will demand possession. Here is the decree of the Convention, and here are my credentials. The *château* is to be razed to the ground."

Contrary to Lakanal's expectation, Tintin replied, calmly: "It shall be done as you desire. You and your colleagues of the Convention are but the tools of Providence. I am prepared, for I knew that all this was to happen."

"How?" said the astonished Lakanal.

"You shall see. Not far from here, and appertaining to this domain, there is an old structure, called the *Château de la Reine Blanche*, because it was the favorite residence of Saint Louis and of his pious mother, Blanche of Castile. It is beautifully situated on the bank of a small sheet of water named the Lake of Commelle. Shortly after I came here as keeper of Chantilly for the Prince of Condé, I heard of what you would have treated with contempt, as a ridiculous superstition. I was told that, for several centuries, it had been implicitly believed among the peasantry of this locality that if, on Christmas night, at twelve o'clock, the moon being full, one should dare to row to the middle of the lake, and, after addressing a short prayer to his patron saint, should cast a stone into the water, saying, 'Blessed be Queen Blanche,' he would see the revelation of some future event clearly conveyed to him, by looking steadfastly at the placid surface of the lake. You know what a passion I have always had, since my boyhood, for all such legends and traditions of the middle ages. It so happened that, on the first Christmas eve I spent here, all the circumstances required by the tradition presented themselves. The temperature was unusually mild, the weather magnificent, and I determined to have a pleasant rowing excursion on the lake, to enjoy a view of the castle and of the surrounding scenery by moonlight, whilst indulging in dreamy reveries on Saint Louis, Blanche of Castile, and the ancient knights of France and Spain. But, whilst rowing along the romantic banks of the lake, there came on me an irresistible temptation to try the incantation scene, and test the truth of the legend. Obedient to the oar, my boat was soon in the middle of the lake, and, just when I heard the bell of the town of Chantilly strike twelve, I muttered a prayer to St. Augustin, my patron, and flung a stone into the water, saying: 'Blessed be Queen Blanche!' Circles within circles spread to the shore; next, to my surprise, the water around the boat hissed and foamed, and was convulsed as if a storm had swept over it. But it passed away, and the bosom of the lake became as smooth as a glass. I gazed at it with intense curiosity, and I saw this noble structure reflected with the utmost distinctness, as if in a mirror. It seemed to bask in the rays of the setting sun, and its two stately towers never had appeared so majestic to me. Suddenly, dark clouds gathered round them, with lightning and thunder. I looked up; the moon shone undimmed in a serene sky. I looked down again; the clouds had grown darker and the lightnings more vivid and threatening, when one of the towers was struck, fell, and disappeared. In its place, I saw the ditch of a fortress, which looked like Vincennes. In

that ditch was the body of the Duke D'Enghien, shot
dead by a platoon of soldiers. Whilst I shrank with
horror from the ghastly spectacle, the other tower
was also crushed by a thunderbolt, and I saw nothing
but a bed-chamber, in which an old man had been
hung to the fastening iron bar of a window. It was
the Duke de Bourbon. Two murders! and a race of
heroes was extinct! But this was not all. There
came a man with a red cap and a red jacket, and a
spade in his hand. He dug a large grave, and buried
the two corpses, father and son, side by side. Do
you want to know who that man was? It was you,
Lakanal. Do you now understand how I was prepared for your mission here? Public executioner, do
thy duty. In God's name, raze this glorious manor
to the ground, since there will soon be no Condé to
be sheltered under its roof."

At that moment the shutters of a window were
thrown open with violence, as if by an irresistible gust
of wind, and there floated on the silent air, fearfully
distinct, the prolonged wailings of a female voice. It
was expressive of intense grief and agonizing in its
tones. It sounded as if coming from afar—far away.
There was a sort of musical modulation in those
mournful accents, as they struck the ear like a wild
melody from the harp of despair. "Listen," said
Tintin Calandro, turning deadly pale, "listen. What
this is, I do not know. But thrice in my life have I
heard this voice of unearthly misery, and thrice it was
on the eve of a frightful calamity." This was too
much for Lakanal, after all the shocks he had received.
He shivered in all his limbs, and his teeth chattered.
"I see," said Tintin, "that the cold you complained
of has increased. Come to your room, where you will
find a good fire. It is next to mine. You need rest."

Three hours had elapsed since they had parted for the night. Tintin Calandro, who could not sleep, was pacing his room in sad meditation, when a terrific shriek was heard in the next one. He rushed in with a light, and found Lakanal sitting upright in his bed, and still asleep, but under the spell of some horrible dream. He had not undressed himself; and, wrapped in his traveling cloak, he had sought repose on the couch. His face expressed the wildest terror; his eyes were open and glaring at some dreadful object. " Enough, enough," he shrieked, tossing his arms about as if to guard himself against the approach of something he feared. " Enough! Why this interminable procession of the dead, each one, as his appalling form glides by, inflicting on me a more exquisite torture? And thou, O Prince, the greatest of thy race, spare me! I can not help it, I must execute my mission. I have sworn an oath which no mortal man dares disobey. Thou knowest what it is, and to whom I have pledged my faith. Strike me not again with that blade which has flashed on so many battle-fields. Its touch burns me like intensified fire." And putting both his hands on his eyes as a screen against what they saw, he fell groaning on his pillow, and gradually grew more quiet.

" O Heaven!" exclaimed Tintin Calandro. " If such is the sleep of the wicked, then retribution begins in this world. I will not wake him. May the chastisement which he finds in his own conscience be a timely warning, and arrest him in his career of evil!"

On the next morning the pale, wan, wasted look of Lakanal spoke of the night which he had passed. It made an appeal to the heart of Tintin Calandro. He was mollified by the sight, and it was not without a certain degree of kindness that he urged his unwelcome guest to take some refreshments, of which he evidently stood in need. When they were seated at the same table, the recollection of better days and of ties which had been painfully dissolved, came upon him with a force which he could not resist. "Lakanal," he said, "it is hard to think that, being once so closely bound together, we are now so wide apart. Our broken friendship is one of the lesser ruins of that hateful revolution which, alas, will leave so many mightier ones in its fiery track of desolation. We are now irreconcilable in thoughts, feelings, and convictions. Between us there is a mortal antagonism."

Lakanal. "I deplore it as much as you do. But the revolution was no work of mine, although I lend a helping hand to its development. It is the work of ages of oppression and abuses. There are no revolutions where the people are happy."

Tintin Calandro. "Better be unhappy than criminal. But what do you want as a substitute for what you repudiate?"

Lakanal. "A patriarchal government."

Tintin Calandro. "Then you must raise up again what you have pulled down. What is a patriarchal government, if not the absolute one of the father and ruler of a family by divine and natural right? Abraham, Isaac, and Jacob were the despotic chiefs of their tribe, whose property they disposed of as they pleased. They had slaves, and their authority was supreme over their own children even in matters of life and death, with no other responsibility than unto God. What nonsense, therefore, are you talking to me?"

Lakanal. "I may not have been correct in the use of the word, if taken in its strictly historical meaning. I merely wanted to convey the idea that we, the party of reform, desire to establish society on a basis of equality for all men, by virtue of which no one shall be forever at the foot of the ladder, and another at the top."

Tintin Calandro. "The shortest way to accomplish your purpose would be to prohibit ladders altogether. But the question is, whether you could get along without ladders. For instance, it would be difficult to build without them; and civilization, you know, is choice in her tastes, and requires a rather stately edifice for a shelter."

Lakanal. "Ladders are indispensable in the social state, and can not be looked upon with distrust, or displeasure, if, among their occupants from top to bottom, there is a rotation by which they will frequently change their respective positions."

Tintin Calandro. "Perhaps it would not work well. The one who hands up the stone at the foot, might not, if at the top, know how to cement it in its proper place with the required skill. The stone might tumble down and break the skull of somebody. But why not simplify the matter? Instead of having rotation among those who occupy the different steps of the ladder, why not give that rotatory movement to the ladder itself? Let it revolve on an axis like a wheel. Thus there could be no permanent *up*, and no permanent *down*. The only difficulty would be, that such a ladder might batter to the ground what it might come in contact with, and be an instrument of demolition, rather than construction."

Lakanal. "This is sarcastic rather than argumentative."

Tintin Calandro. "I do not agree to that. There may be a good deal of condensed argument in a sar casm. But, since your colleagues and yourself are such wonderful architects, let me hear further of your plans, before I pass judgment. First, explain to me the reasons why you want to make a clean sweep of what is already in existence, instead of modifying and improving it, and thus saving materials?"

Lakanal. "Look at the condition of the world. Have not the masses, ever since nations existed, been working for the benefit of the few? The masses, composed of mere beasts of labor and burden, toiling incessantly for their masters! The masses, made up of the innumerable poor, starving to give more luxuries to a handful of rich oppressors! Should not this be changed, if possible? See what are the chances in life for the children of the disinherited *many*, compared with the chances favoring the children of the chosen *few*. Are they equal? No! Why should this be so? The source of all evil in civilized societies is the unequal division of the goods of the earth. All the crimes, all the miseries which afflict mankind, are attributable to the struggle eternally going on to acquire wealth for personal use, or abuse, and for distinction. Let there be no individual wealth, and the struggle ceases, and with the struggle will also cease the crimes and miseries. But how is this to be done? How are the opulent to be reached? They are protected by all monarchical forms of government. Down, therefore, with all monarchies! It is a necessity, and it will be an economy. Within the range of the shadow of every church there is a conservative influence exercised on behalf of the throne and the hoardings of Dives. Down, therefore, with the church! It is another necessity, and will be another economy. Down with the cross! It is the emblem of resignation and patient endurance; it must not be kept before the eyes of the masses, who are called upon to spurn Cæsar and pay no tribute but to their own treasury. Down with the Gospel, good as far as it goes in some of its parts! But in the whole it is insufficient; it preaches only to the soul; we must also have a Gospel for the body; we are composed of spirit and matter. Man must be his own god and master. Surely, by this time, he is old enough to take care of himself."

Tintin Calandro. "What will you put in the place of the crown and church?"

Lakanal. "A republic of free-thinkers, of course, with no salaried ministers of religion, and with no endorsement or recommendation of any particular creed. Every man will be his own priest and will worship the Creator of the universe, when, how, and where he may please. The French republic being once established, all the monarchies of Europe will crumble into dust before it, and there will be universal fraternity among all the nations of the earth. Then, standing armies will be abolished — another necessity of the future, and another great financial economy. Besides, a standing army is a hierarchical body, and is in the way of all leveling systems. When there shall be no monarchy, no church, and no standing army, then the rich and the poor will stand front to front without any intermediate shield or barrier, and when they shall grapple for the final contest, methinks that, which will be uppermost in the end, is a question easily to be answered."

Tintin Calandro. "Aye, aye,—the beginning of wholesale robbery."

Lakanal. "It would be no robbery--it would be taking back what had been selfishly appropriated and

abstracted from the common treasury of nature in
violation of her laws. The rich have no right to be
rich, because it is always at the expense of somebody
else. Civil society is nothing but a copartnership
between all its members on an equal footing. Every
one of them must bring to the general fund all his
physical and intellectual powers; and the results of
the collective labor and industry of each must be distributed faithfully among all the partners, for the
purpose of promoting their individual comfort and
happiness. It will be a mutual insurance company
against the dangers of life and the vicissitudes of fortune. But what do I say? There would be no vicissitudes of fortune. A nation would be a family of
brothers. Its head, father, or patriarch, would be the
government established by that family. It is, by-the-
by, what I meant when I used the word *patriarchal*
at the beginning of this conversation."

Tintin Calandro. "But this government, father,
or patriarch, who is to prescribe what every one, according to the measure of his capacity, is to do in
your community of socialists, and who is to distribute among the mass, in person, or through his delegates, the fruit of the labor of its component parts,
will be a supreme authority. Where there is authority and therefore superiority on one side, there must
be obedience and inferiority on the other. Hence,
where will be your equality?"

Lakanal. "There will be no individual superiority, but a collective one. It will be the authority of
the mass exercised by its representative. It will be
like the volition of man making his fingers or feet act
at his pleasure for the service of his whole organization. Besides, the delegation of authority will be
transient and rotatory."

Tintin Calandro. " Enough of this farrago; I see what you are driving at. A man will have no property, no wife, no children, no family of his own."

Lakanal. "Why not? Let there be but one family—the national family."

Tintin Calandro. " This will lead to a degree of demoralization and servitude never heard of before."

Lakanal. "To secure to man the means of gratifying all his physical wants can not lead to demoralization. To suppose it, is a slander against nature itself. It is the reverse of the proposition which is true. Man, being made easy on that point—the satisfaction of his physical wants—will be left free to attend to his moral and intellectual improvement. So much for the demoralization you apprehend. As to what you call servitude, if servitude at all, it will be like the servitude of the universe to God, its central point; it will be the servitude of man in his individuality to man in the aggregate—of the human fraction to the nation of which it is a part."

Tintin Calandro. " These are high-sounding words, which, no doubt, will elicit shouts of applause from the multitudinous and ignorant rabble; but, when you shall attempt to carry into practice your theoretical plans in all their details, I am sure that you will meet with insurmountable obstacles of which you have not thought."

Lakanal. " No! We have not thought of those details and those difficulties. It is not time yet. First, we must do away with the monarchy, the church, and the army—next, we must inaugurate a republic—and then, when in a republic, the rich alone shall remain to be disposed of, I am sure that the poor will find some way to establish practically, on a solid foundation, that liberty, fraternity, and equality

which they require, and will work out effectively
some plan to maintain forever the duration of that
new system which appears to you so monstrous, and
impossible in its execution. But, to the business of
the hour. I beg you to lead me to some public house
in a neighboring town or village, where I shall establish my headquarters whilst executing my mission.
We shall return with the mayor, in whose presence I
shall take possession of the *Château de Chantilly* and
relieve you of your responsibilities."

Tintin Calandro took his hat and cane, and said:
" I am ready."

On their entering the town of Chantilly, they were
met by a boy in rags, who, in a whining tone, begged
for himself and his starving mother at home. As no
attention was paid to his doleful story, he pertina-
ciously followed the two gentlemen, until Tintin Calandro stopped in front of a butcher's stall. " Lakanal," he said with caustic playfulness, " I think that
you have too long turned a deaf ear to your little
brother, and that you ought to share with him some
of the coin which you, no doubt, have in your human-
itarian pocket. It would not be an uncalled-for application of your doctrine of an equal division of the
goods of mother earth."

Lakanal replied not, but bought a loaf of bread and
a few pounds of beef, which he gave to the little beggar, who, instead of going away with the provisions,
seemed to hesitate and to look with apprehension
toward the extremity of the short street in which
they were. "What is the matter?" inquired Lakanal, "and why don't you run fast, to satisfy the
hunger of your starving mother?"

" I am afraid," answered the boy.

" Afraid of what ? "

" I am afraid of big Joe, whom I saw just now behind yonder wall. He will beat me and take away
all that you gave."

" I think," said Tintin Calandro, laughing, "that
you ought, Lakanal, to lose no time in preaching in
your best style to big Joe; for he seems disposed not
merely to share liberally in what others have, but even
to take it all to himself. I fear that you will need a
little patriarchal flogging and hanging in your new
republic, to help moral suasion in enforcing the observance of universal communism and fraternity."

When they reached the only tavern which the
town possessed, Lakanal noticed that its sign was a
sword with this inscription : " *à l'épée de Condé*." He
frowned, and, after having bespoken an apartment,
he said roughly to the tavern-keeper, who had obsequi-
ously come out, hat in hand, to salute him : " In the
name of the National Convention, of which I am the
representative, I order you to strike out that inscription." " Yes, citizen," replied the poor fellow, trembling all over, " but what shall I put in its place ? "

" Put, *à l'épée du peuple*. There should be no other
sword honored in France than the sword of the people."

" Bravo ! " exclaimed Tintin Calandro. " I hope
that history will not forget to relate that one of the
great achievements of the National Convention of
France was to change the name of a tavern."

The tavern-keeper conducted Tintin Calandro and
Lakanal to the chamber destined to the latter, and
retired. That chamber was on the first floor, and its
windows opened on the street. At the moment when
Lakanal was saying to Tintin Calandro, " Now let us
call on the mayor of the town," a newsboy was heard

shouting at the top of his shrill voice: "Who wants a journal with the latest intelligence? News! news! Return from England of the Princess de Lamballe, the friend of the Queen. Her arrest and incarceration at the *Abbaye.*"

"Good God!" exclaimed Tintin Calandro, "she must be saved, cost what may! Lakanal," he said, turning to that individual, who, it must be confessed, showed, in his habitually harsh-looking face, that he sympathized with the intense distress in which he saw the friend of his youth, "help me in setting free the Princess de Lamballe and in removing her to foreign parts. I will engage on her behalf that she will never come back any more. Grant me that, and I will forgive you all that you have done. I will love you as before—nay, I will be your slave, your dog, if you please." Lakanal looked at him with compassion, but shook his head negatively. "I throw myself at your feet," continued Tintin Calandro. "I will kiss them, and kiss the dust of the floor on which you stand, if you grant me the boon for which I implore you. I have never asked you for any favor. It is the first, and shall be the last," and, suiting his action to his words, he embraced the knees of Lakanal.

The stern tribune—the man of stone—was moved. He struggled to raise Tintin from his supplicating posture, saying: "You overrate my power and influence. I can not open the doors of the prison of the Princess de Lamballe."

"Can not Robespierre do it?" asked Tintin Calandro, gasping for breath.

"Yes, *he* could."

"Then, she is saved!" exclaimed Tintin in a transport of joy, "for I once heard Robespierre say, Laknal, that he was so circumstanced toward you, that, should you ever ask him for anything, he was bound to grant it, if he could, and that he had himself given you that assurance. Is it so?"

"It is."

"Save the Princess de Lamballe."

"I dare not. I can not."

"Life for life, Lakanal. I saved yours once. I never would have reminded you of it, but for the extremity to which I am reduced. Grant me the life I sue for, and your debt to me is cancelled."

Lakanal grasped the hands of Tintin Calandro, which he shook convulsively. "Spare me," he said, "the agony of this horrible scene. My heart bleeds, but your prayer can not be granted. Oh! do not look at me thus, but listen. I am bound hand and foot by mysterious bonds which I can not break. I belong to a secret society, and have taken the terrific oath which it imposes. That society has undertaken to revolutionize the world with every element of destruction. Implicit obedience must be paid to its mandates. All that it dooms, be it of flesh and bone, or stone and mortar, must perish. The Princess de Lamballe is one of the doomed—she first, to pave the way and as an experiment—then the King and Queen. According to orders, there will be to-day a tremendous rising of the populace in Paris, and all the inmates of the *Abbaye* and other prisons are to be massacred without an exception. It is, as you see, too late for me to interfere, even if I could."

With a shriek of horror Tintin Calandro darted from the room, and rushed to a stable which was within the court-yard of the tavern, and in which post horses were kept. He flung himself on one of them and galloped frantically on the high-road to Paris, changing at every post station his wearied horse for a fresh one. The distance is about thirty-five miles; he overcame it in two hours and a half. When in sight of the city, his too hard-ridden horse fell from exhaustion. Dismounted, but unconscious of fatigue, Tintin Calandro pushed desperately forward among a crowd of intensely excited people, who, like a hot stream of lava, were pouring into Paris. "The Jacobins were up and doing," they said. "There was a gigantic and bloody insurrection. The prisons had been broken open, and the massacre of their inmates had begun." Each one was striving which should be the foremost to see what was going on. Tintin Calandro's feverish anxiety seemed to endow him with superhuman strength, and he ran, rather than walked, with unabated speed. When he reached the quay on the Seine in front of the Louvre, his further advance was stopped by a dense mass of men and women yelling like demons, and carrying aloft, stuck on a long pike, the gory head of a woman—the head of the Princess de Lamballe. He looked at that ghastly object, uttered a piercing shriek, and fled—a raving maniac.

On the next day, the work of demolition had begun at the *Château de Chantilly*, and when the sun went down, one of the towers had fallen with a crash heard far and wide, and was answered by the long howl of a dog. It was Norlingue, thus named after one of the victories of the great Condé—Norlingue, who had, at first sight, exhibited such antipathy against Lakanal. That howl was repeated incessantly during the whole night, and in the morning, poor Norlingue was found lying dead on the ruins of the tower.

CHAPTER XXVI.

THERESA CABARRUS AND TALLIEN—FALL AND DEATH OF ROBESPIERRE.

EVERY day was demonstrating the appropriateness of the famous comparison of the French revolution with Saturn devouring his children, and there was no Cybele watching over the monstrous appetite of the unnatural parent, to cheat the cannibalism of the near-sighted deity by the substitution of a swaddled stone for flesh and blood. On the contrary, it happened that, more than once, there was some woman who, either voluntarily or involuntarily, directly or indirectly, assisted and encouraged the settled determination of the god to feed on his own family. Charlotte Corday had dispatched Marat. The women of the fish market and of the sewers of Paris had contributed, as much as their male associates, to the fall of the Girondists, by intimidating the Convention and stimulating Robespierre and his party. Danton, the Jupiter of the revolution, had not escaped like his prototype the jaws of Saturn. He, who had flung the head of a king at the feet of all the kings of Europe as the gauntlet of defiance—he who had shouted that "to dare, dare again, and always dare," was the sure way to success, had listened to the appeals of one whom he tenderly loved. She had said: "Let there be no more bloodshed"; she had conquered the heart and the will of the thunderer. He

17   (385)

could not resist that voice; he yielded, and refused a
seat among the sanguinary Committee of Public Safety. It was taken as a censure, and to censure the
Committee of Public Safety, was to engage in a' duel
with death. He had gone farther: he had, in the
presence of Robespierre, let fall some words of blame
against the ultra-revolutionists. It was construed
into a decided act of hostility and reaction. What
was still more fatal to him, his wife had, with pardon-
able imprudence, withdrawn him from the scene of
action, and carried him away from Paris to Arcis sur
Aube, his native place, where the disarmed Titan had
reposed several weeks in the bosom of conjugal love.
When he returned to his seat in the Convention, he
was lost. All had been prepared for his ruin. He
was accused of a conspiracy against the republic,
judged, condemned, and executed without being permitted to defend himself. He had been warned of
the danger, and had replied: "They will not dare."
Strange that he should have forgotten that he was the
apostle of daring, and had formed disciples who had
bettered the instruction! There is a sort of political
infatuation which is striking in the uniformity of its
effects, and yet no ambition has ever been able to
guard itself against its contagious influence. The
hope of being an exception always soars above the
warning given by the undeniable evidence resulting
from historical precedents. What law more invaria-
ble than the one by which it is decreed, that the original mover or abettor of a revolution seldom or never
profits by it? There comes a time when the demon
who has been evoked and enslaved, breaks his bonds
and tears the magician to pieces. There comes the
inevitable hour when the leader discovers that he who

precedes the Juggernaut car of revolution, does it after the fashion of yoked oxen—that he is driven, not driving—and that when he stops, or does not go fast enough, he is trampled upon. In the Cabinet of the many-headed tyrant, whoever accepts the portfolio of the ministry of proscription is sure to wield the sceptre of power. But, whenever he attempts to perform an act of humanity, he falls never to rise again. Revolutions acknowledge no masters ; they are never controlled by the will of man. Onward they move, crushing every obstacle, until they stop of their own accord, or from sheer fatigue, or from the necessity of digesting the food with which they have been gorged. It is only then, at the appointed hour, that, out of the smoke and dust where he had remained concealed from view, appears on the scene the man of destiny, who calls himself Cæsar, Cromwell, Bonaparte. It matters not what name it is.

Robespierre committed the same fault as Danton, whom, in consequence of it, he had sent to the scaffold. He was forty days without appearing in the Committee of Public Safety, or in the Convention, and thus lost more of his influence than he supposed. He thought that the dictatorship which he had desired for himself alone, and not with colleagues, was at last within his grasp. He wished to establish on clean ground the foundations of popular sovereignty, of which he fondly hoped to be the representative, after having swept out of sight the corpses and blood which began to stink in his nostrils, as soon as he had concluded that they were no longer necessary. Therefore, he did not want to appear to participate in the butcheries daily ordered by the Committee of Public Safety. But before beginning to carry his secret in-

tentions into effect, he desired to get rid of some mem‧
bers of the Convention whose opposition he feared,
and he was plotting their ruin. They were not so
blind as not to discover it, and thus a death struggle
ensued between those irreconcilable antagonists. A
woman was destined to have considerable influence in
shaping its final issue. But before she took a part in
it, another woman had attempted to deliver France
from Robespierre. She presented herself at his domicile, armed with two knives. Being arrested, she
avowed her intention, and said "that she wanted to
see of what stuff a tyrant was made." She was twenty years old, and her name was Cécile Renault.
Robespierre had escaped that imitator of Charlotte
Corday ; he had yet to meet a more artful and dangerous enemy in Theresa Cabarrus.

This woman was born in Spain. Her romantic career ended in her dying Princess de Chimay—the wife
of Joseph de Caraman, a descendant‧from a family in
France to which there was no superior save the royal
one ; he was a Spanish Grandee, the first peer of
Hainault, and a chamberlain to the King of the Neth-
erlands. Her father, who was a Frenchman by birth
and distinguished for his abilities, particularly as a
financier, had introduced into Spain the system of
banking, and, for his public services, had been created
by Charles IV. a Count of Castile. He took care
to give his daughter the most brilliant education,
and when she was only sixteen years of age, he presented her, in 1788, to the court of France, whose
expiring glories she witnessed and whose last orna-
ment she became. Her beauty and her graces were
unrivaled, and she possessed that rare endowment
which makes beauty perfect and resistless—that in-

describable charm which can not be analyzed and is
called fascination. She spoke three languages with
equal facility, accuracy, and elegance, and, what was
still more attractive for the frivolous, she sang and
danced divinely. Two nations of antiquity had become the fashion in France; everything was to be
à la Greeque, or *à la Romaine.* Theresa Cabarrus had
to choose a character in harmony with the mania of
the epoch. She did so; but it was not Lucretia,
Porcia, or Cornelia whom she adopted for a model;
it was Lais, Phryne, or rather Aspasia. She would
become the priestess of the doctrine of free love, but
with restricted affinities which would be permitted to
develop themselves only in favor of the privileged
few who dwell on the high Olympus of society. She
would sacrifice chastity and virtue to wealth and
power, without which she could not live, but it would
be with the condescension and refinement of a goddess, and not with the shameless facility of a courte-
san. Thus she, in early youth, sketched for herself
the part she determined to act in the future, and she
performed it with never-failing consistency. She was
an extraordinary compound, and she exhibited,
throughout her long life, the phenomenon of an excellent and energetic heart entirely controlled by the
vicious logic of a splendid intellect. Her first step
on the stage where she was to shine, was taken with
mature deliberation and a frigidity of calculation with
which no impulse or inclination was permitted to interfere. Thus, whilst royalty and nobility were still
in existence and in the enjoyment of their privileges,
although in imminent peril, she selected for her husband, among a crowd of worshipers, a man old
enough to be her father. It is true that he was still

handsome; that he was gay and witty. But probably the main consideration for her was, that he was rich, and Marquis de Fontenay. It followed that the new *marquise* became—what she expected—the rage in all the *salons* of Paris. She breathed like a deity in an atmosphere of adoration, and in her temple incessantly burned the incense offered by all those who by their talents or genius were the pride of France.

After four years of marriage, Theresa Cabarrus discovered that she had not been properly mated. Her coronet of *marquise* had fallen to a very low discount, and the wealth of her husband had vanished. She concluded that the affinities which had led her to his arms were things also of the past, and she contemplated a divorce under a recent law that permitted a separation between husband and wife to take place almost at the will of either party. But the life of Mr. de Fontenay was threatened; he had to fly, and she could not make up her mind, under such circumstances, to abandon her proscribed husband. It was resolved that they should seek an asylum in Spain, and they had reached Bordeaux, when an event happened which changed the destinies of Theresa. Three hundred royalists of that city, ruined by the revolution, were anxious to escape with their lives, if nothing else, and had taken their passage on board of an English ship in the harbor, but, at the last moment, the captain had refused to sail, because the whole of the passage-money had not been paid. When Theresa heard this, she was so fired with indignation as not to listen to the remonstrances of prudent friends. She instantly went on board, and gave the captain the three thousand francs which he claimed. He offered a receipt. "I do not care for it," she said. "Only give me the list of your passengers, that I may know the names of those I have saved." The list was delivered to her, and with it she returned, proud and happy. Unfortunately, this act of generosity became known, and those who had been balked of their prey went to work to ascertain who was the beautiful woman that had dared to save aristocrats. It seems that they were successful; for, the next day, when she went to the theatre, she was hooted by a mob and rudely handled. But her spirit was equal to the occasion. "Look at my cockade," she said. "I am a patriot, as you see. I assure you that you have been misinformed. The persons who sailed yesterday are not enemies of the revolution." "We shall judge for ourselves," shouted one of the crowd. "Give me the list of the passengers, for we know that you have it in your bosom." "Out with it," cried another. "It is useless to deny it. You see that we have good spies." A third one threw himself on her, and tried to force the concealed list out of the place where it was reported to be. She repulsed him with all her strength, and, as he still held in his grasp one of her hands, she took the paper out of her bosom with the other which was free, and tore it with her teeth, exclaiming: "I will not give it; you may kill me first." At that moment, a man stepped through the crowd, and with an imperative sign of the hand ordered them to disperse. It was Tallien, the proconsul, a member of the National Convention, who, with two associates, Isabeau and Lacombe, had been sent to Bordeaux to purge that city of its impure blood. Lacombe had already issued an order for the arrest of *citoyenne* Fontenay, suspected of a want of patriotism. The order was obeyed, and Theresa, instead of the pleasure that she expected at the theatre, had the mortification of being carried to prison.

Under the triumvirate of Tallien, Isabeau, and Lacombe at Bordeaux, to be in prison and accused of a want of patriotism, was to be with the prospect of being decapitated in twenty-four hours. Fortunately for Theresa, she had in Paris, once before, met Tallien, on whom her beauty had exercised the same fascination which it did on everybody else. He had hurried to visit her after her arrest, apparently as an inflexible judge, and came out a devoted lover, determined to sacrifice everything to his passion, if necessary. When he stepped out of the prison, the sagacious jailer hastened to take pen and ink, and wrote to Robespierre: " Everybody betrays the republic. The citizen Tallien pardons aristocrats." The proconsul had not pardoned an aristocrat, but the loveliest woman of her time—an enchantress as powerful as the Armida of Tasso. The penetration of the turnkey had not been at fault. Theresa Cabarrus was free. Tallien, at that time, was young, handsome, full of energy and eloquence. He had acted a conspicuous part in the Convention, had dared to beard Robespierre himself at the tribune, and was backed by reliable and numerous friends. He was one of the most influential leaders of the "*Montagne*"; his star was culminating over the horizon, and there was no telling how high was the zenith which it might reach. For the present, he was a proconsul of the terrible republic. He was armed with immense power, and unlimited wealth was at his disposal, for plunder was the order of the day, and he had nothing to do but to stretch his hands and take largely in the dark out of the well-filled exchequer of confiscation. Clearly

there were irresistible affinities in Theresa which harmonized with those of Tallien. The result of the interview proves it. Mr. de Fontenay was permitted to
cross the Pyrenees in safety, but *alone.* " Remain,"
had Tallien said to Theresa, " and be the Egeria of
the *Montagne*, as Madam Roland was of the *Gironde*.'
" I know nothing of the *Montagne*, or of the *Gironde*,"
was the reply. " I know only of the people. Let me
serve them." So, they were united in some sort of
Jacobin wedlock, and the *ci-devant marquise* became
a plebeian and a patriot. Tallien had gallantly tendered to her for a residence the magnificent hotel
which he occupied on the *Place de L'échafaud*, as it
was called, because it was provided with a guillotine,
which was in such active operation that this *Place de
L'échafaud* might have been considered as decorated
with a never-failing fountain—a fountain of blood.
Theresa, who had no taste for such a sight, refused
the offer. " Then," said Tallien, " I will come to
your own house." " No. It is not you, but the guillotine, that must move "; and the guillotine did move
away. This wonderful woman soon subjugated the
two colleagues of her new husband, Isabeau the tiger,
and Lacombe the wolf, who, spell-bound under the
charm with which she had fascinated them, forgot to
fill up daily, as usual, the death lists, and the guillotine
became an idle and useless instrument.

Theresa was again in possession of what was indispensable to her existence—pomp and power. She
was again a goddess, and one far superior to the other
divinities of the day—such as the Goddess of Liberty
and Reason—for she was proclaimed the Goddess of
Pardon. Since his connection with Theresa, the stern
proconsul had ceased to affect to live with republican

17*

simplicity. The Spartan had become a Persian satrap.
He appeared in public with her, sometimes driving in
an open carriage, in which her exquisite form was set
off to advantage by Grecian draperies. At other
times, in the costume of an Amazon, she dashed
through the streets, and, stopping where she saw a
crowd of people, addressed them in language which
produced the wildest enthusiasm. She literally
reigned over the populace; all delighted to hear her,
with the mellifluous voice of a siren, apotheosize
liberty, and preach a republic of universal peace and
charity. But, when she was within the perfumed precincts of her boudoir, she encouraged Tallien in the
façons de grand seigneur which were natural to him,
and which he had perhaps inherited, for he was reported to be the illegitimate son of a nobleman. It is not
astonishing, therefore, that an observer of what was
going on should have addressed Robespierre in these
words: "There are singular political details about *La
Fontenay*, and Bordeaux seems to be a labyrinth of
intrigue and plunder. We must restore the people
to the sincere love of the real virtues of the republic."

So, Tallien was recalled, and Bordeaux was to be
subjected to the observance of the "real virtues of
the republic"—which meant that heads were again to
be tossed about, thick and fast, like balls in a tennis-
yard. Little did Robespierre dream how fatal to
himself would be that order of recall. Such are the
vain schemes of man! When the hour of adversity,
sent by fate, approaches, it throws forward a shadow
which blinds the eyes of the doomed. Instead of
clipping the wings of Tallien, as he had intended, he
gave them the opportunity of gaining more strength
and amplitude; for, on his return, Tallien was elected

president of the Convention for a fortnight. This
was a bitter pill for Robespierre. He was surprised
at such a success; but what surprised him still more,
was to find that his former pupil was no longer man-
ageable. That pupil had tasted the sweets of authority; he had become bolder and more eloquent; the
cub had grown into a fully-developed beast of prey,
with a genuine roar, a horrific row of teeth, a huge,
angry mane, and paws exhibiting claws which were
not to be despised. In fact, Tallien had become impatient of the curb and *irrepressible.* This was not to
be wondered at, for it was the effect of his natural
temper, and he had an ambitious woman at his elbow.
He and she regretted Bordeaux, and had a secret
grudge against Robespierre. Probably at her instigation, Tallien seemed to have taken pleasure in teasing
and irritating his more experienced adversary, and
more than one lance was broken between them in debate. That was sufficient to make Robespierre resolve to have the head of Tallien. In the meanwhile,
the wheels of the revolution went on grinding faster
than they had ever done before, and the edge of the
guillotine became blunted, so much was it tasked to
fill up with heads the insatiable basket of liberty and
fraternity. This butchery was carried so far, that
Camille Desmoulins, in a daily paper which he published under the title of *Le Vieux Cordelier,* had
said, mockingly: "Yesterday, there was a miracle in
Paris. A man actually died in his bed." This
Camille Desmoulins is an authority which can not be
suspected, for he had styled himself "Attorney-Gen-
eral of the Lamp-post"; and when, a little later, he
was put on his trial and interrogated as to his age, he
answered: "I am of the same age with the *sans-*

culotte Jesus at the time of His death. I am thirty-three years old."

In his efforts to acquire strength and popularity, Tallien was actively supported by her who had assumed to be his wife, and who had taken his name. She danced the *Carmagnole* with the red cap on her head, paraded in public promenades in transparent costumes, and appeared in the *salons du beau monde*, escorted by a host of admirers, with her naked feet reposing on sandals and adorned on each toe with precious stones. She led the fashion, when full-dress meant almost the absence of all drapery, such, for instance, as we might suppose the appearance of the statue of the Medicis statue of Venus, placed under a gossamer veil, merely to increase the voluptuousness of visible and embellished nudity. She even took a bolder step. Appearing before the National Convention, she presented to that body a fluent and lengthy exposition of her republican and evangelizing views and sentiments, beginning in these words: "Citizens and representatives, as morality is more than ever the order of the day," and she went on, entreating that women, now adorned with the noble title of *citoyennes*, might be allowed to find some work to do for the State in training the young and alleviating the sufferings of the poor and the sick. She was warmly applauded. The former *marquise* was evidently playing a farce, but Robespierre thought that it was time to put a stop to such foolish exhibitions. He seemed to have taken a serious view of them ; for he desired the Committee of Public Safety, of which he was a member, to issue an order of arrest against her. Its phraseology was peculiar. She was designated as "one, Cabarrus by name, the daughter

of a Spanish banker, and the wife of one Fontenay
by name, ex-member of the parliament of Paris." It
must be observed that, in this document, she was not
recognized as Madam Tallien. This order was kept
secret for several days. It was executed in a striking
manner.

Theresa, although she had sent over the Pyrenees
the Marquis de Fontenay, had retained possession of
his *château*. It was situated in the environs of Paris,
and was called *Fontenay aux roses*, a very appropriate
name for the residence of its beautiful proprietoress,
or occupant. There she was fond of giving entertainments, where splendor vied with taste. Unconscious of the danger which threatened her, she had
prepared a *fête*, which was to surpass all the preceding
ones. It was to be in honor of Robespierre. She
had a special object in view, certainly deserving of
praise, and which was, to captivate him, and to cajole
him into consenting to the inauguration of a policy
of clemency and moderation. On the day fixed,
Robespierre appeared with his favorite blue coat and
his perpetual bouquet. He was, of course, *the guest*
among the guests, the one on whom her smiles and
powers of fascination were concentrated. She related to him, in tones which would have melted iron,
what triumphs clemency had obtained in Bordeaux,
and she begged that the same experiment be made in
Paris and all over France. Robespierre was moved
to tears. He declared that the god of liberty was
no longer athirst, that the prison doors should be
opened, and that the reign of peace and fraternal
love should begin. She embraced him enthusiastic-
ally and they danced together. When he retired, she,
with a burst of joyful exultation, said to her friends

who gathered round her : " We are saved. He is the most just of men." It is easy to imagine the general congratulations and rejoicings that ensued, but they were suddenly changed into consternation, when *gendarmes* broke in and showed their commission, signed by Robespierre, for the arrest of the hostess. It was dramatic; it produced what the French call a *tableau*, and, years after, was actually put on the stage.

The plan of Robespierre was a crafty one. He wanted a pretext for the arrest of Tallien himself, and he had probably calculated that, by endangering the life of the woman he adored, he might drive him into some imprudent action, or that Tallien would sue for her release, which he would grant on conditions by which his adversary would be tamed down, and which would be guaranties for his future conduct. If, on the contrary, Tallien should remain passive, it was to be presumed that Theresa would resent his not risking everything in her defense. In that case, Robespierre supposed that she might be tempted to say something that would serve his purposes. But Tallien saw the trap, and, although frantic with apprehension, did nothing which the spies of Robespierre could seize upon as a sufficient ground for accusation and death. Defeated in that quarter, the wily monster approached Theresa and offered her life and liberty, provided she signed a declaration of Tallien's treason against the republic at Bordeaux. She nobly replied : " I am only twenty years old, but I would rather die twenty times." So, she remained in her dungeon at *La Force* for a while, and was afterward transferred to *Les Carmes*, where she had at least the consolation of being in distinguished company, for she was incarcerated in the same cell with Josephine

Beauharnais, the future Empress of France, and with the Duchess of Aiguillon. For some reason or other she was taken back to *La Force*. In the meantime, Tallien, unable to effect her release, and trembling lest every hour might prove her last, watched the daily processions of victims. Never had they been so frequent, and never had there been so many women in the death carts. The bodies of countless citizens were thrown into pits full of quick-lime, and it was said that, in the vicinity of Paris, there was a tannery for human skins. It was the "reign of terror."

Theresa was pining away in doubt and anxiety, when, one day, her rough jailer, upon whom some mysterious influence seems to have acted, said to her in gentler tones than usual: "Your health is declining visibly. I will assume the responsibility of allowing you to inhale a little fresh air," and, in the evening, he took her to a small court of the prison, where she was left alone. She was pacing it up and down, when a stone suddenly fell at her feet. She instantly picked it up, and saw that a scrap of paper was attached to it. She was afraid of unfolding the note; invisible eyes might be fixed on her. She retired to her cell, but there darkness prevailed. She had to wait until dawn. How long that night was! At last there was light, and, with a palpitating heart, she deciphered these words from Tallien: "I am watching over you. Every evening you will go into the court at nine, and I shall be near you." For eight days she was permitted to comply with that secret summons, and had the comfort of receiving the assurance, by some token or other, of the presence of a loving heart close to her outside the wall. On the ninth day, the jailer told her that her health was restored, and that she needed no more fresh air. She contrived, however, to send a message to Tallien. Although a silent one, it was eloquent. One morning, when he awoke, he saw glittering on a table by his bed a small Spanish dagger which belonged to Theresa Cabarrus, and which had been deposited there during the night by some unknown and unseen hand. "I understand thy meaning," he exclaimed; and, after pressing it to his lips, he put it within the breast of his coat and went out. The first object he saw was appalling. He stood facing four cartloads of women on their way to the scaffold. He gazed at them with sickening eagerness. Theresa was not among them. Great was the relief, momentary as it was, and he went his way. As chance would have it, he met Robespierre and David, the painter, walking arm in arm. He informed the former that he had a request to address to him. "It is granted, if possible," answered Robespierre with that air of benignity which he sometimes assumed. "Well, then," continued Tallien, "I entreat you to stop this horrid spectacle of women being put to death for political offenses. It is unworthy of the republic to strike such weak and defenseless beings. There is one in particular who is unjustly arrested, and whom I wish to plead for." The piercing gray eyes of Robespierre were instantly fixed on the speaker, and a mocking smile played on his thin lips. Tallien's courage failed, he hesitated, he could not utter the name he had in mind, and he said: "It is the *citoyenne* Josephine Beauharnais."—"I do not know the *citoyenne* Josephine Beauharnais," replied Robespierre dryly. "Besides, no one is arrested illegally." Tallien became more pressing. "That the French republic," he said,

" should fear women is contemptible, almost laugh-able. It would be an eternal disgrace to shed their blood on account of their opinions. Europe is shocked."

" I do not care a straw for Europe," retorted Robes-pierre, with that peculiar hissing intonation which his voice always assumed when he began to be excited. " But, as to women, it is different. You think that they are not dangerous. It shows that you do not know them. They are all our enemies; they love noth-ing but the orgies of royalty. It is by a woman that the republic will perish "; and he turned on his heels.

" Is this your last word?" exclaimed Tallien. " Well, you have said it, cowardly tyrant. It is by a woman that your republic will perish!" and he de-parted. When he was out of sight and hearing, he took Theresa's dagger from his bosom, and swore on it to save her or die.

In the afternoon of that day, Tallien, Barras, Fré-ron, Barrère, Isabeau, Collot D'Herbois, and Carnot, the weather being intensely hot, for it was in July, were dining together outside of a *café*, under the trees in the Elysian Fields. By a curious coincidence, Robespierre and his brother, with David, St. Just, and Lebas, all of them his most devoted adherents, were also dining at the same establishment, but in an upper room, and with closed doors. The evening having stolen on them, and dusk falling, both parties left the Elysian Fields almost at the same time; and, by an-other strange coincidence, found themselves face to face on the *Place de la Revolution*, close by the statue of Liberty. Barras, without consulting his friends, stepped to Robespierre and thus addressed him: " I have the right to speak the truth to you at the foot of this statue. We have established a reign of terror by which we only frighten one another. Let us cease such child's play, and be men."

"Why not," replied Robespierre, coldly. "I make no one afraid, and I am afraid of nobody."

"Then," broke in Tallien, with ill-restrained impetuosity, "if you really wish to make no one afraid, why do you gorge the guillotine as you do? Why are not the prisons thrown open? Why are those who were your friends treated as enemies?"

Barras, interposing, endeavored to pacify him and recommended more moderation in language and manner. "You and Robespierre," he said, "have both done too much for your country to forget it, and to permit yourselves to sacrifice the common cause to private interests and selfish passions."

David chimed in: "I agree to that. Yes, let us unite to save the vessel of State, but let Robespierre remain at the helm."

"I ask nothing else," added St. Just. "I have already declared repeatedly in our Jacobin Clubs that the committees, in whose hands the government now is, must, to insure the safety of the republic, be replaced by one man of genius, patriotism, and energy, as dictator, and that that man is Robespierre, the only one capable of saving us, for you know that the moment for action has come."

"As to myself," said Robespierre, with an air of as much modesty as he could put on, "I am ready to make way for my betters, but it is only true republicans who must be the masters of the situation."

"Are you not absolute master everywhere?" exclaimed Tallien, angrily. "When I say *you*, I mean the *Montagne*."

"No," rejoined Robespierre, "it is just there that I find most traitors."

"Name them," cried Barras. "We have heard that you have a list. Show it to us."

"Here it is," said Robespierre, drawing a paper out of his pocket.

"Let it be torn now without reading it," hastened to say Fréron. "We are all too good republicans to suspect one another. Let us swear to suppress the guillotine!"

"No," replied Robespierre. "Since the paper has been called for, it must be read, and read aloud." And he handed it over to Barras.

The first name on the death-list was Tallien's; then came Barras himself, Fréron, and others. There was in this action of Robespierre an audacity of frankness which was almost sublime, and which struck them dumb with astonishment. A dead silence ensued—the silence of stupor. Tallien was the first to break it. "Since you have shown us our names," he said, with deliberate and marked emphasis, "you mean to efface them, because you believe that union would be strength. You invite us, I suppose, to reconciliation and peace, and not to dissension and mortal combat. Therefore, let us have your programme; and let us see if we can accept it."

Robespierre's answer was a long speech on the critical state of affairs, and a proposition to take Tallien and his friends into confidence, if they would unite with him in effecting the proscription of his enemies. Tallien thought the moment favorable to let out what he had most at heart, and begged the liberty of the *citoyenne* Fontenay, born Theresa Cabarrus.

"Never! Never!" was the reply. "For her you

betrayed the republic at Bordeaux. She leads you like a child."

" Ha! Ha! is it so? Know then that the *citoyenne* Fontenay is my wife, and I will have her set free before the sun goes down twice. If you must have blood, take our heads," shouted Tallien, breaking away from the group. He had become desperate. When he reached his home he was in a state of mind to dare all that man can dare. He certainly needed no stimulant, and yet he found a powerful one in a note which was handed to him, and which ran thus :

AT LA FORCE, 7th thermidor.   }
THE *citoyenne* FONTENAY TO THE *citoyen* TALLIEN. }

The administrator of police has just been here. He came to inform me that to-morrow I am to be tried ; that is, carried to the scaffold. This is very little in harmony with the dream which I had last night. Robespierre existed no longer, and the prisons were open. But thanks to your arrant cowardice, there will soon be left in France nobody capable of realizing it.

Tallien wrote back to her : " Be as prudent as I am courageous. Pray, keep a cool head on your shoulders."

Robespierre had never been known to act from impulse. It is probable, therefore, that when he showed his death list to Tallien and Barras, he had calculated that they would attribute his frankness to the security which he felt in the possession of resistless power, and that they would be intimidated into a reconciliation and submission, which they would believe him capable of accepting with the same frankness he had shown in braving them. But he committed a fatal error, if these were his motives. He had staked too much on one card ; the game was too

high ; the losers would inevitably have to pay in the
end with their heads. He forgot that he was too well
known to be trusted by his adversaries as to any proposed compact. He had shown them that the contest
could not be safely prolonged. Time was precious,
and the most was to be made of it. Hence, his opponents resolved that the next two days should determine which side should be the loser, or the gainer.
There is a secret instinct which tells us that, when
men have to put their fate on the cast of a die, it is the
boldest hand which shakes the box that has the best
chance to win. That night, the next day, and the
following night, every member of the Convention, ·
known or supposed to be hostile to Robespierre, was
seen and tampered with, and when dawn broke on the
9th thermidor, everything was ready for the onslaught.
The plan had been digested, discussed, and adopted.
Every one was to be at his post and knew what he
had to do.

On that great historical day, early in the morning,
there seemed to be something fatidical in the air.
Excited groups had assembled in the streets, and
crowds had gathered in the public places. There was
a general agitation without any known cause. Some
event was expected to happen, but why, and where,
and what was it ? These questions were not answered,
and yet everybody looked and acted as if the answer
would not long be deferred. In the meantime, the
hour for the meeting of the Convention had come.
That body had rarely been so well attended by its
members. An atmosphere of grim solemnity seemed
to have penetrated into the hall of their deliberations
and to have enveloped the whole assembly. It was
observed that many of them looked pale and jaded.

Robespierre was the first to ascend the tribune. He described his own services and zeal for the State, and declared that he had the intention to propose measures which alone could save the country. He said: "I see in many no inclination to be guided by fixed principles, no disposition to follow the path of justice, which the enemies of the republic have tried to obstruct. If I am to conceal these truths, I prefer that the cup of hemlock be brought to me. My reason, if not my heart, is on the eve of having doubts on the possible existence of that virtuous republic of which I had designed the plan myself." "You are the Catiline of the republic," shouted Tallien. "Down with the tyrant!" cried many voices. "It is to men who are pure, and not to brigands, that I address myself," continued Robespierre. He was interrupted by increasing vociferations. Gathering all his strength, and clinging to the tribune, from which his adversaries struggled to pull him notwithstanding the opposition of his partisans, he turned to the president of the Assembly, and said in a loud tone: "For the last time, president of assassins, I demand to be heard." "No! no!" shouted numerous voices, "he shall not be heard; the traitor and tyrant never allowed any one of his adversaries to be heard. Measure for measure." Robespierre continued his efforts to speak, until he was completely exhausted, and until nothing but a gurgling sound or death-rattle issued from his throat. "It is the blood of Danton which chokes you," shouted a member. "Ha! is it Danton you wish to avenge?" gasped Robespierre. "Down with the tyrant, down with the would-be dictator!" was heard on all sides. Tallien rushed toward the tribune, and, brandishing Theresa's small Spanish weapon cried : "I have armed myself with this dagger to pierce the heart of this Cromwell, if the Convention does not decree his arrest." The Assembly tumultuously voted that decree, accompanied with the shouts of, " Long live the republic!" " The republic!" echoed Robespierre, rousing himself, " it is lost, for brigands triumph." He, with his brother, with St. Just and several others who had been comprehended in the same order of arrest, were conducted as prisoners to the city hall. He was rescued, however, by General Henriot, the commander-in-chief of the national guards of Paris, and advised by St. Just and others to march against the Convention and disperse them. He replied: "Such a step would be the proceeding of a tyrant. I will not expose myself to shed the blood of my fellow-citizens to avenge my own cause. My duty, after all, is to conform to the will of the sovereign people. They are free to defend or to abandon me. Should the last be the case, I shall know how to die like Tiberius Gracchus."

In public affairs, the greatest rogues invariably talk the loudest about virtue, and the most abominable tyrants, about liberty and popular sovereignty. On this occasion, the monstrous hypocrisy of Robespierre overleaped the mark and caused his ruin. He waited, and refused to act, no doubt to assume the position of one saved by the people, and not by his own exertions. It would have been better and more convenient for him to have the Convention butchered by others whilst he folded his arms, and to be proclaimed dictator, notwithstanding his protest, and by the force of circumstances. But his partisans, being deserted by their chief, who gave no order, vacillated, hesitated, disagreed, and knew not what to do. In supreme crises, to hesitate is to be lost. It is what happened in this emergency. The golden opportunity presented itself to Robespierre, and he did not clutch it with a firm and resolute hand. It gave breathing-time to his enemies in the Convention. They acted with the vigor which had been lacking in him, and history relates the rest. But let it be remarked that Tallien was a true prophet when he said to Robespierre: "Your republic will perish by a woman." It was Theresa Cabarrus. Robespierre was no less prophetic when he declared that the republic—no matter what republic it was, his, or that of any other man—would also be destroyed by the same instrument; for, by a woman the republic of Tallien and Barras perished in its turn. Its death-warrant was signed when Barras, the president of the French Directory, issued, under the influence of a woman, that commission which gave to her young husband the command of the army of Italy. That woman was Josephine Beauharnais.

But that event was yet in the future. For the present, Tallien and Barras had triumphed, and Theresa Cabarrus became again the idol of the Parisian society. The "reign of terror" was over, and the reign of pleasure began. People were tired of the Spartan black broth in public, when there was no real sobriety in private, and of the ridiculous affectation of Roman virtue, when there was not a particle of virtue of any kind. Life is no longer in danger; let us make the most of it, was the general feeling, and the whole population fell to eating, drinking, and dancing with a sort of rage. "Sullen despair was gone," says a writer, "and now it was: let us seek new ways of killing time and spending money, and accordingly, in this reaction, all Paris danced—danced as if it never could make up for the lost time; danced over graves; danced with crape on the sleeve at the '*ball of the victims,*' as it was called, where the ground for admission was the loss of a relative by the guillotine. From the highest to the lowest, every man, woman, and child seemed seized with a dancing mania—a lucrative time for fiddlers, one would suppose, when there were no fewer than six hundred and forty-four places for dancing in Paris. And what dancing! No longer stately minuets, country-dances, or quadrilles, but the German waltz, in which women, far too scantily clad for former notions of decency, were whirled about in their partners' arms till they almost dropped from exhaustion." License was carried to its extremest limit, and its exigencies beggared the fertility of invention of the most depraved imagination, amidst the saturnalia of this saltatory insanity.

Thus the republic had become a bacchanalian revel, a carnival of bedlamites, and a school for dancing, which was soon to be changed into a military one under the rod of an imperial despotism.

18

CHAPTER XXVII.

THE LEADERS OF MEN AND THEIR WEARINESS OF SPIRIT.

I NOW proceed to relate the impressions which some of the events I have described had produced in America. Washington was on a visit to Mount Vernon, when he received a letter from Gouverneur Morris, dated on the 23d of October, 1792, which awoke his benevolent sympathy in favor of the unfortunate Louis XVI., the ancient friend and ally of America. "You will have seen," wrote Morris, "that the King is accused of high crimes and misdemeanors, but I verily believe that he wished sincerely for his nation the enjoyment of the utmost degree of liberty, which their situation and circumstances will permit. He wished for a good constitution, but, unhappily, he had not the means to obtain it, or if he had, he was thwarted by those about him. What may be his fate God only knows, but history informs us that the passage of dethroned monarchs is short from the prison to the grave."

In the meantime, the arms of revolutionary France were triumphant. "Towns fall before them without a blow," wrote Gouverneur Morris, "and the declaration of rights produces an effect equal at least to the trumpets of Joshua. But I do not draw a favorable augury from this success. We must observe the civil, moral, religious, and political institutions of a coun-

try. These have a steady and lasting effect, and
these only. Since I have been here, I have seen the
worship of many idols, but little of the true God. I
have seen many of those idols broken, and some of
them beaten to the dust. I have seen the late constitution, in one short year, admired as a stupendous
monument of human wisdom, and ridiculed as an
egregious production of folly and vice. I wish much,
very much, the happiness of this inconstant people.
I love them. I feel grateful for their efforts in our
cause, and I consider the establishment of a good
constitution here, as the principal means, under divine
Providence, of extending the blessings of freedom to
the many millions of my fellow-men who groan in
bondage on the continent of Europe. But I do not
greatly indulge the flattering illusions of hope, because I do not yet perceive that reformation of morals
without which liberty is but an empty sound."

Washington shared all the forebodings of Morris,
and had even apprehensions as to the state of affairs
at home. He thought there was too great a disposition to run fast and to innovate. He said to Jefferson: "When men put a machine into motion, it is
impossible for them to stop it exactly where they
would choose, or to say where it will stop. The
constitution we have is an excellent one, if we can
keep it where it is."* How prophetic!

The mills of a revolution work fast. The monarchy, the King, the Queen, the nobility, the clergy
of France, and Heaven knows what else, had been
ground into powder, and the force that kept the
wheels still a-going was not hydrological power, but

---

* Irving's "Life of Washington," p. 170, vol. v.

constant streams of a more precious liquid, which flowed as abundantly as water.

"When will savages be satisfied with blood?" exclaimed John Adams, when he heard of the death of Marie Antoinette.*

Not so with Jefferson, who, from Monticello, wrote to his friend, Tenck Coxe, in Paris: "Your letters give a comfortable view of French affairs, and later events seem to confirm it. Over the Foreign Powers I am confident that they will triumph ultimately, and I can not but hope that that triumph, and the consequent disgrace of the invading tyrants, is destined, in the order of events, to kindle the wrath of Europe against those who have dared to embroil them in such wickedness, and to bring at length, kings, nobles, and priests to the scaffolds which they have been so long deluging with human blood. I am still warm whenever I think of these scoundrels, though I do it as seldom as I can, preferring infinitely to contemplate the tranquil growth of my lucern and potatoes. I have so completely withdrawn myself from these spectacles of misrule and usurpation, that I do not take a single newspaper, nor read one in a month; and I feel myself infinitely the happier for it." †

How painful must have been the sacrifice made by the retired philosopher, when, solely for the good of his fellow-citizens, and not for the gratification of any ambitious aspirations, he allowed himself to be torn away from the "contemplation of the tranquil growth of his lucern and potatoes," to become during eight years President of the United States!

---

* John Adams to his wife.

† Jefferson's Works, vol. iv., p. 104.

But we must return to General Aubert Dubayet. After the terrible events which had brought on the destruction of the Princess de Lamballe, and of the King and Queen, he had missed Tintin Calandro and looked round for him in vain; nobody had been able to tell him anything about the object of his inquiries. At last, when the most diligent search had been fruitless, he accidentally found him in a lunatic asylum. Dubayet, taking charge of the poor maniac, and thinking that a change of scene would benefit him, had dispatched him to Louisiana with a letter for *L'abbé* Viel, his old preceptor, who kept a school in the county of Opelousas, and officiated as the priest to whose spiritual care had been committed that distant settlement, where, in those days, there were almost as many Indians as whites and blacks. In that wilderness Tintin Calandro had ever since remained, after having partly recovered his reason, until, on the departure of *L'abbé* Viel for France, he was, on the recommendation of that ecclesiastic, appointed by the bishop of New Orleans guardian and sexton of the St. Louis Cemetery, in that city, in the discharge of which functions he has been exhibited in a preceding work—"Fernando de Lemos."

General Dubayet had been glad to escape the terrific scenes enacted in Paris in 1793, in consequence of his having been intrusted at that time with the defense of Mayence, on the Rhine. But, after having shown great courage and skill, he had been obliged to surrender. He was arrested, accused of treason, incapacity, or cowardice; for the patriots would not admit that Frenchmen could be beaten fairly. He was, however, honorably acquitted. Not satisfied with that, he presented himself before the Convention, begged to be heard, and exonerated himself and his troops so completely from all blame, that he received a fraternal embrace from the president of that body by virtue of a formal decree. After having been comforted with this theatrical exhibition of good-will and confidence, he was sent to *La Vendée*, at the head of the garrison which had defended Mayence in vain. Fortune did not smile on him at first, for at Clisson he met the terrible Cathelineau, who kept the word he had pledged to the Jacobins when he defied them and Marat in their den, and who, on this occasion, crushed the forces of the republic, capturing eight hundred men with all the artillery and baggage. Cathelineau, on account of his piety, had been surnamed by the peasants "The Saint of Anjou"—a province in which most of his exploits had been performed.

After having repaired his losses, General Dubayet was confronting another army of Vendeans, when he received a dispatch removing him from command on the eve of a battle for which all his preparations had been made. Quietly putting the dispatch in his pocket, to be considered and attended to in due time, he fought and won the battle. After a complete victory he departed for Paris. His laurels did not prevent him from being arrested by order of the Convention. Tried a second time, he was again acquitted, and returned to *La Vendée* where, under General Hoche, he contributed to the pacification of the province and behaved with humanity toward the insurgents, who were called brigands, and had been treated as such by their adversaries in that dreadful civil war. Promoted to the grade of General of division, he was appointed commander-in-chief with his headquarters at Cherbourg. He acted with great energy, re-established communication between Le Mans, Alençon, Angers, and La Flèche, and several times obtained considerable advantages over the enemies of the republic. At one time, he was preparing to march on Paris to put down an insurrection against the National Convention, when he heard of the triumph of that body. Constitutions were fast succeeding constitutions, to gratify the impatient fickleness of the people, who were not long satisfied with what had pleased them at first. A new constitution having been adopted in 1795, Aubert Dubayet was appointed under it minister of war.

One day, when he was complaining to Gouverneur Morris of the vexations which besieged him, the American minister said: "Be comforted, my friend. If our noble and great Washington is constantly attacked by censorious tongues and pens which are ever ready to cavil at every measure of his administration, why should you be fretted by unjust opposition on the part of your countrymen? It is mournfully suggestive of the soreness and weariness of heart with which he sees his conscientious policy misunderstood, or misrepresented, and himself becoming an object of party hostility, when, for the first time perhaps in his life, he is betrayed into expressions of bitter irony; for this is what he writes to me: 'The affairs of this country can not go wrong; there are *so many watchful guardians of them, and such infallible guides*, that no one is at a loss for a director at every turn.'"

Washington's weariness of spirit went on increasing. Not only had he to contend with calumnies and factious opposition, but also with actual insurrections, which struck him with horror at the bare idea of shedding the blood of his countrymen in a civil war. Witnessing the last days of the expiring Roman republic, and determined not to survive the loss of liberty, Brutus, when putting an end to his life, exclaimed : " O virtue, thou art but a name ! " Washington, in the golden age of the American republic which he had founded, was so disgusted with the turbulence of party, with the wickedness of human passions, with the want of truth and patriotism conspicuous around him, and with the difficulties which selfish interests and corruption threw in the way of one who would undeviatingly lead his country to respectability, wealth, and happiness, that he exclaimed : " The post of honor is a private station." Such were the conclusions of Brutus and Washington, although separated by an interval of almost two thousand years! If such is to be the bitter experience of the best men who engage in political struggles, what matters it under what form of government we sweat and groan, draw water and hew wood, during our brief existence !

Marat had died by the dagger of Charlotte Corday, Robespierre on the scaffold, and the " reign of terror " was over. Aubert Dubayet lent himself to the hope that the new republic of France had seen its darkest days and passed its most dangerous ordeal. Whenever he could steal an hour from the time required for the fulfilment of his arduous duties as secretary of war, he would call on his friend, Gouverneur Morris, with whom he loved to talk of the destinies of France and America, which he considered as bound together by the strong ties of past services, of similar institutions, and reciprocal attachment and esteem. One day, he found Morris overwhelmed with mortification and shame. He but too soon ascertained the cause of such feelings, for the American minister showed him a copy of a dispatch which had been found on board of a French privateer captured by a British frigate, and which had been forwarded to the Cabinet of St. James. Lord Grenville had transmitted the original to Mr. Hammond, the British minister at Philadelphia, through whose hands it had reached Washington's. That dispatch was from Fauchet, the French minister to the United States, and addressed to his Government. It strongly implicated the integrity of Randolph, who was then secretary of state. After relating the breaking out of the Western, or whisky insurrection, as it was called, and the proclamation of Washington on that event, Fauchet went on saying:*

"Two or three days before the proclamation was published, and, of course, before the Cabinet had resolved on the measures to be taken, the secretary of state came to my house. All his countenance was grief. He requested of me a private conversation. 'It is all over,' he said to me: 'a civil war is about to ravage our unhappy country. Four men, by their talents, their influence, and their energy, may save it. But, debtors of English merchants, they will be deprived of their liberty if they take the smallest step. Could you lend them instantaneously funds to shelter them from English prosecution?' This inquiry astonished me much. It was impossible for me to give a satisfactory answer. You know my want of power and deficiency in pecuniary means. Thus, with some thousands of dollars, the republic could have decided on civil war, or peace. *Thus the consciences*

---

* Irving's " Life of Washington," p. 222, vol. v.
18*

of the pretended patriots of America have already their price. What will be the old age of this Government, if it is thus already decrepit?"

Aubert Dubayet dropped the paper and shed tears. "Ah!" said Morris, "well may you weep with me over such revelations; and how much more will you grieve, when I tell you that, publicly, before the face of the whole world, in the councils of the nation, in the daily journals of the country for which he has done so much, Washington's military and political character* is attacked with equal violence, and it is proclaimed that he is totally destitute of merit, either as a soldier or a statesman. He is charged with having violated the constitution in negotiating a treaty without the previous advice of the Senate, and with having embraced within that treaty subjects exclusively belonging to the Legislature, *for which an impeachment is publicly suggested.* Nay, more, it is asserted that he has drawn from the treasury, for his private use, more than the salary annexed to his office. Thus, in broad daylight, Washington is accused of being a thief, not by obscure scribblers, slandering him from the dark corners where they are hidden, but by conspicuous leaders who are backed by a powerful and numerous party. O God! is this the beginning of our republic? If it is born in corruption, and if it is possible to publish with impunity in the midst of an ungrateful, or at least indifferent, people, that we have a Dick Turpin at our head, what will be the morals of our successors in one hundred years, and what will our boasted institutions be worth?"

---

* Irving's "Life of Washington," p. 226, vol. v.

Washington himself was amazed at the wide-spread hostility exhibited against him, and wrote as follows to Jefferson:

"Truly,* until the last year or two, I had no conception that parties would, or even could, go the length I have been witness to; nor did I believe until lately, that it was within the bounds of probability, hardly within those of possibility, that, whilst I was using my utmost exertions to establish a national character of our own, independent, as far as our obligations and sense of justice would permit, of every nation of the earth, and wished, by steering a steady course, to preserve this country from the horrors of a desolating war, I should be accused of being the enemy of one nation (the French) and subject to the influence of another (the English); and, to prove it, that every act of my administration would be tortured, and the grossest and most insidious misrepresentations of them made, by giving one side only of a subject, and that, too, in such exaggerated and indecent terms as could scarcely be applied to a Nero, a notorious defaulter, or even to a common pickpocket. But enough of this; I have already gone further in the expression of my feelings than I intended."

This letter must have had the effect of producing a twinge in Jefferson's toe; for he had lately written to Monroe: "Republicanism must lie on its oars, resign the vessel to its pilot,† and themselves to what course he thinks best for them." Thus, according to Jefferson's declaration, the best thing that republicanism could do under Washington's administration was to

---

* Irving's "Life of Washington," p. 241, vol. v.

† General Washington, President of the United States.

"lie on its oars," and wait for better times. If so, Washington was not a republican; and if not, he was not true to the institutions he had founded; and if not true, then he was a perjured hypocrite. Could anything more disgraceful be intimated against him? It is needful, indeed, for the virtuous and the good in this world, particularly those who aim at being the benefactors of their race, to keep their eyes fixed on Calvary. The awful lesson will support their courage and maintain their steadiness of purpose.

CHAPTER XXVIII.

A QUARREL, AND ALMOST A WAR, BETWEEN THE
TWO SISTER REPUBLICS — DEATH OF AUBERT
DUBAYET.

MEANWHILE, Monroe had succeeded Morris, as minister plenipotentiary of the United States in Paris, and the latter had departed from that city for London. This was a painful blow to Dubayet, who was warmly attached to him. He needed such a friend, for whom he had no secret, and in whom he had found the consolations of sincere sympathy and the salutary advice of experience and sound judgment, on more than one occasion. As minister of war his relations had become unpleasant with Carnot, the president of the Committee of Public Safety. He therefore resigned, and was appointed ambassador to the Ottoman Porte at Constantinople. He departed on the 26th of March, 1796, taking with him a numerous suite and a company of light artillery that was to engage in the service of Turkey. Before his leaving Paris, he had read with much satisfaction a letter written by Washington to Monroe, and in which the former said :

" My conduct in public and in private life, as it relates to the important struggle in which France is engaged against England, has been uniform from the beginning of it, and may be summed up in a few words. I have always wished well to the French revolution; I have always given it as my decided opinion, that no nation has a right to intermeddle in the national concerns of another; that every one had a right to form and adopt whatever government they liked best to live under themselves; and that, if this country could, consistently with its engagements, maintain a strict neutrality, and thereby preserve peace, it was bound to do so by motives of policy, interest, and every other consideration that ought to actuate a people situated as we are, already deeply in debt, and in a convalescent state from the struggle we have been engaged in ourselves.

" On these principles I have steadily and uniformly proceeded, bidding defiance to calumnies calculated to sow the seeds of discontent in the French nation, and to excite their belief of an influence possessed by Great Britain in the councils of this country, than which nothing is more unfounded and injurious."[*]

So thoroughly sick was Washington of the atmosphere in which he lived, and so disgusted was he with being at the head of the great republic he had founded for the happiness of others, if not for his own, that he began to count the days and hours that would intervene between his term of office and his retirement, for he had refused to serve more than two constitutional terms in his exalted office. He wrote to his old fellow-soldier and political coadjutor, Henry Knox: " To the wearied traveler who sees a resting-place, and is bending his body to lean thereon, I now compare myself; but to be suffered to do this in peace, is too much to be endured by some. To mis-

---

* Washington's Writings, vol. xi., p. 164.

represent my motives, to reprobate my politics, and to weaken the confidence which has been reposed in my administration, are objects which can not be relinquished by those who will be satisfied with nothing short of a change in our political system."

How mournful is such language from such a man! What a deep sigh of discouragement is here breathed by the wounded spirit within!

Poor Dubayet! He himself had become the victim of a sombre melancholy which he could not overcome, and, on the day before he departed, he overheard a dialogue between two boyish ragamuffins in the streets of Paris, which ought to have excited hir mirth, but which, strange to say, increased the weight of the load oppressing his heart. It seemed to be such a mockery of what had been the idols of his youth, at least in theory, and the objects of his generous hopes!

"Tom," said Nat, "what is that republic of which people talk so much?"

Tom. "Fool! Don't you know? It is wild Lucy, the circus girl, whom Robespierre promenaded through the streets with a red cap on her head, a red flag in her hand, and whom he called the mother of reason. As you see, the republic is no great thing."

Nat. "That was not the name. It was the goddess of reason."

Tom. "What is the goddess of reason?"

Nat. "I don't know."

Tom. "Then don't talk nonsense. I say it was the mother of reason."

Nat. "Very well. I don't care. But what is liberty?"

Tom. "It is, that we can do what we please without being whipped by papa and mamma."

Nat. "Hurrah for liberty! But what signifies equality?"

Tom. "It signifies, that we can break, when we choose, into old Mathew's orchard, and that you have the right to steal as many of his apples as I can, although you are not as big and as smart as I am."

Nat. "Hurrah for equality! But what is general fraternity?"

Tom. "What a goose you are! It is that you and I are brothers."

Nat. "How can that be, when our fathers and mothers are not the same?"

Tom. "That is their fault, and their noses ought to be tweaked for such a mistake. No matter, we are brothers, although they don't know it. The republic says so, and when I have no soup at home, which often happens, I will go and eat half of yours."

Nat. "The old woman won't like that."

Tom. "If she don't, aunt Guillotine will settle it."

Nat. "You are so smart, Tom, that I will ask you one more question. What is communism?"

Tom. "Why!—a thing which belongs to you and me equally. For instance, I have an empty pipe; you have a cent. I say to you, buy tobacco. Good! Give it to me. Excellent! I fill my pipe. That's all."

Nat. (Looking puzzled). "That's all! What is my share in it?"

Tom. "You are very dull, Nat. Whilst I do the smoking, you do the spitting. Is not that fair? That's communism."

This time, little Nat did not shout any hurrah.

"Well," said Dubayet to himself, as he left these boys, the one so inquisitive, and the other so wise, before having cut their eye teeth, " I have seen the birth of two republics, and I have sad doubts about their vitality and their answering the purposes for which they were created. I am curious now to ex-amine the most absolute despotism existing on earth. Let us hasten, then, to the dominion of him to whose decree of death the followers of the prophet of Islam unhesitatingly bend their submissive necks, without one thought of resistance."

Aubert Dubayet was treated with coldness at Con-stantinople. Almost all the representatives of the Foreign Powers were hostile to him. The envoy of rebels who had murdered their sovereign, could not expect sympathy in any country whose ruler claimed to exercise his functions by divine right. He be-haved, however, with such dignity and tact, that he soon conciliated favor and commanded respect. Hav-ing at last obtained an audience from the Sultan, he was received by that Prince with all the marks of the highest consideration.

Meanwhile, John Adams had succeeded Washing-ton as President of the United States. He was sus-pected of being still more in favor of England than Washington was supposed to be, and for that reason was assailed with greater violence. In the treaty which Washington had made with that power, the rights of the people had been represented as not only *neglected*, but absolutely *sold*. It was asserted that it contained no reciprocal advantages; that the benefits were all on the side of Great Britain; and, what seemed to have more weight with the people than all

the rest, and to have been most pressed by the opposition : " that the treaty was made with the design to
oppress the French, in open violation of a treaty already existing between that nation and the United
States, and contrary, too, to every principle of gratitude and sound policy."

Under Adams, the relations between France and
the United States, which had been unpleasant under
his predecessor, became gradually so embittered that
they threatened a rupture. Washington had de-
manded the recall of Genet for improper conduct. It
had been granted ; but the French Government had,
in its turn, insisted on the recall of Gouverneur Morris,
whose political sympathies were considered highly
aristocratic. That request had been complied with.
In these conjunctures, the text of the obnoxious
treaty having been made known, such was the irrita-
ble condition of the public mind that the whole country had been immediately in a blaze.* Not only the
opposition party, but also a portion of the Cabinet,
had been against its ratification. The attack upon it
had been vehement and sustained ; the support of it,
feeble and faltering. The assailants had seemed determined to carry their point by storm. Immense
meetings to oppose the ratification had been held in
Boston, New York, Philadelphia, Baltimore, and
Charleston. The smaller towns throughout the Union
had followed their example. In New York a copy of
the treaty had been burnt before the Governor's
house. In Philadelphia it was suspended on a pole,
carried about the streets, and finally burnt in front of

---

* Irving's " Life of Washington," p. 216, vol. v.

the British minister's house, and amidst the shoutings of the populace.*

Monroe, who had been sent to France as envoy in the place of Gouverneur Morris, had been especially instructed to explain the views and conduct of the United States in forming the treaty with England, and had been amply furnished with documents for the purpose. From his own letters, however, it appears that he had omitted to use them. Whether this arose from undue attachment to France, a feeling common to many, or from mistaken notions of American interests, or from real dislike to the treaty, the result was the very evil which he had been instructed to prevent. The French Government misconceived the views and conduct of the United States; suspected their policy in relation to Great Britain; and, when aware that the House of Representatives would execute the treaty, became bitter and unjust in their resentment. Symptoms of this appeared in the capture of an American merchantman by a French privateer.†
Under these circumstances Monroe had been recalled, and Charles Cotesworth Pinckney, of South Carolina, chosen to succeed him.

Still the resentful policy of the French had continued, because the American Government would not join them in a war against England, and they had issued a decree ordering the seizure of British property found on board of American vessels, and of provisions bound for England, which was a direct violation of their treaty with the United States. A letter which Washington had written to Gouverneur Morris, then in London, had by some accident fallen into the

---

* Irving's "Life of Washington," p. 216, vol. v.   † Ib., p. 242.

hands of the French Government, and had produced much irritation, although it gave very little cause for it, for the part deemed objectionable was as follows:

" I give these details," wrote Washington to Morris, "as evidences of the impolitic conduct of the British Government toward these United States, that it may be seen how difficult it has been for the Executive, under such an accumulation of irritating circumstances, to maintain the ground of neutrality which had been taken; and at a time when the remembrance of the aid we had received from France in the Revolution was fresh in every mind, and while the partisans of that country were continually contrasting the affections of *that people* with the unfriendly disposition of the *British Government;* and that, too, while *their own sufferings* during the war with the latter, had not been forgotten.

" It is well known that peace has been (to borrow a modern phrase) the order of the day with me, since the disturbances in Europe first commenced. My policy has been, and will continue to be, while I have the honor to remain in the administration, to maintain friendly terms with, but independent of, all the nations of the earth; to share in the broils of none; to fulfil our engagements; to supply the wants of, and be carriers for, them all. Nothing short of self-respect, and that justice which is essential to national character, ought to involve us in war."

On Monroe's recall the French Government had gone so far as to declare that it would not receive any new minister plenipotentiary from the United States, until that Power should have redressed the pretended grievances of which the republic had complained. When Monroe had his audience of leave,

Barras, the president of the Directory, addressed him in terms which conveyed a compliment to his own nation, but an insult to the Americans.

"The French republic hopes," he said with arrogance, "that the successors of Columbus, of Raleigh, and of Penn, ever proud of their liberty, will never forget that they owe it to France. In their wisdom they will weigh the magnanimous benevolence of the French people with the artful caresses of perfidious designers, who meditate to draw them back to their ancient slavery. Assure, Mr. Minister, the good American people, that, like them, we adore liberty; that they will always have our esteem, and that they will find in the French people the republican generosity which knows how to accord peace, as it knows how to make its sovereignty respected.

"As to you, Mr. Minister plenipotentiary, you have fought for the principles, you have known the true interests of, your country. Depart with our regrets. We give up in you a representative of America, and we retain the remembrance of the citizen whose personal qualities honor that title."

A few days afterward, Charles Cotesworth Pinckney presented himself as the successor of Monroe. The French Government refused to receive him; and, as if this indignity was not sufficient, he was ordered out of the republic. The next step was to proceed to the capture of American vessels by French cruisers. On being informed of these outrages, President Adams convened Congress. In his opening address he adverted particularly to the language of Barras in Monroe's audience of leave.

"The speech of the president of the Directory," said he, "discloses sentiments more alarming than the refusal of a minister, because more dangerous to our independence and Union ; and, at the same time, studiously marked with indignities toward the Government of the United States. It evinces a disposition to separate the people from their Government, to persuade them that they have different affections, principles, and interests from those of their fellow-citizens, whom they themselves have chosen to manage their common concerns, and thus to produce dissensions fatal to our peace. Such attempts must be repelled with a decision which shall convince France and the world, that we are not a degraded people, humiliated under a colonial spirit of fear and sense of inferiority, fitted to be the miserable instrument of foreign influence, and regardless of national honor, character, and interest,"

The President recommended to Congress to provide for effectual measures of defense, but at the same time announced his intention to institute negotiations in view of an amicable adjustment. Washington, though retired from public life, strongly advocated the course pursued by Adams. In accordance with the policy announced, three envoys extraordinary were appointed to the French republic, viz. : Charles Cotesworth Pinckney, John Marshall, and Ellridge Gerry.

On the arrival of the ministers in Paris, a certain individual, named Bellarni, called on Pinckney, as the secret agent of Talleyrand, minister of foreign affairs, assuring him that citizen Talleyrand had the highest esteem for the citizens of the United States, and was most anxious for their reconciliation with France.

"I am very happy," replied Pinckney, "to receive

such assurances, and so will my colleagues be. We hope, therefore, soon to obtain an audience."

"No doubt," continued Bellarni. "But, to show your good dispositions, it would be proper to offer a present of two hundred and fifty thousand dollars to Mr. de Talleyrand, for the use of the Directory; to agree to expunge certain offensive passages in the speech of President Adams; and to pay a large sum, in the shape of a loan from America to France."

The baseness and the impudence of these propositions were startling; they were indignantly rejected. A few days after, besides the secret agent, an intimate friend of Talleyrand was present at another meeting. They insisted again on the expunging of the passages in the President's message to Congress, but hinted that they might give that up, "provided they had money—a great deal of money."

At a third conference, the same personages fixed at six millions four hundred thousand dollars the amount of the *loan* which they exacted from the United States, with a *douceur* of two hundred and fifty thousand dollars for the private comfort of the members of the Directory.

A fourth meeting was held, and on the plenipotentiaries presenting the object of their mission in what they thought its proper light: "Gentlemen," said the secret agent, "you mistake the point altogether. You say nothing of the money you are to give—you make no offer of money; on that point you are not explicit."

"We are explicit enough," replied the American envoys. "We will not give you one farthing; and, before coming here, we should have thought such an

offer as you now propose, would have been regarded
as a mortal insult."

" You again mistake the point," coolly observed
the agent. " We are above a bribe, and want merely
a fee to advocate your claims, just as you would pay
a lawyer to plead your cause. You had better reflect
on the matter, and let me know the result of your deliberations."

Having continued to reject persistently such disgraceful propositions, the American envoys remained
several months in Paris without being accredited, and
finally returned, without having had the opportunity
to discuss officially the object of their mission.

The Directory, believing the people of the United
States would not support their Government in a war
against France, issued a decree subjecting to capture
and condemnation neutral vessels and their cargoes,
if any portion of the latter was of British fabric or
produce, although the entire property might belong
to neutrals. The United States being at this time
the great neutral carriers of the world, this iniquitous decree struck at a vital point in their maritime
power. *

The Directory had reckoned too much on the par-
tiality of the American people for the French. Such
insults and outrages at once roused their temper,
changed their dispositions, and with an indignant
spirit they prepared for a war which they considered
inevitable. Congress resolved on vigorous measures,
and the President was authorized to enlist ten thousand men as a provisional army, to be called by him
into actual service, in case of hostilities. " If the

---

* Irving's " Life of Washington," p. 271, vol. v.

French come here," wrote Adams, "we will have to march with a quick step and attack, for in that way alone they are said to be vulnerable."

Washington was appointed commander-in-chief, and Hamilton next in command. In recommending him, Pickering, the secretary of state, wrote: " The enemy whom we are now preparing to encounter, veterans in arms, led by able and active officers, and accustomed to victory, must be met by the best blood, talents, energy, and experience that our country can produce."

Gouverneur Morris, who had remained in London, had maintained a regular correspondence with his friend Dubayet, at Constantinople, and had kept him informed of these facts and details. They mortified him so deeply that his health, which had never been strong, gave way entirely. The dreadful shock which he had received in early youth in Louisiana, had never been forgotten, and its lingering effects could be detected in the latent melancholy which he carried with him through life, concealed as much as possible, but doing its withering work in the depths of the heart. As a diversion from his sorrows, he had resolved to keep himself incessantly engaged in the execution of noble and great purposes. He had assisted the successful creation of two republics in two hemispheres, which were the hope of mankind, and which were to spread universal liberty, peace, equality, and fraternity all over the whole earth. What an illusion it had proved to be! The two model republics, on two different continents, although separated by the broad Atlantic, were on the eve of grappling together, not in a sisterly embrace, but in a deadly struggle. One of these republics was already steeped in blood and corruption! What would become of the other, the virgin of the wilderness? Did he not clearly see in her such seeds or germs of demoralization as might, in the course of time, and under circumstances favorable to putrefaction, develop themselves into appalling growth and expansion? In his dejection, he felt as if all incentives to action were gone, since it was impossible to do any permanent good in the world, and to achieve any progress in private or public morals and in the science of government, without a corresponding retrogression, which brought the chariot of civilization back to its starting-point, notwithstanding so many discoveries and improvements in the realm of matter. He considered humanity as typified in the symbolic circle of the snake biting its tail. With a mind in such a condition, and a constitution weakened by a long-indulged sorrow, Dubayet yielded easily to a malignant fever which suddenly attacked him, and died at Constantinople, on the 7th of December, 1797, in the thirty-eighth year of his age, with the knowledge and conviction that, in this world which he left when still so young, " all is vanity of vanities," save the unselfish satisfaction proceeding from the consciousness of the performance of duty under all circumstances, and the internal consolations derived from the divine sources of morality and religion.

THE END.

APPENDIX.

CLOSING REMARKS.

AFTER having described the revolutionary throes accompanying the birth, in the last century, of the two greatest republics of modern times in Europe and in America, the author believes that it will not be inappropriate and foreign to the subject he has treated, to place before his readers, in the shape of an appendix, the following episode showing the last agonies of the ancient Roman republic, when perishing under the deadly effects of lawlessness and corruption, and gradually transforming itself into a social and political condition which, in accordance with eternal and inflexible laws, necessitated the advent of imperial despotism.

A HISTORICAL EPISODE

OF

THE LAST DAYS OF THE ROMAN REPUBLIC.

THE WIFE OF CÆSAR—THE MYSTERIES OF THE GOOD GOD-
DESS — THE TRIAL OF CLODIUS FOR SACRILEGE AND
ADULTERY — THE JUDGES BRIBED — SCENES IN THE
FORUM AND IN THE SENATE OF ROME—GENERAL COR-
RUPTION.*

ON the 5th of December, 692 of the Roman Era,
and 62 years before the birth of Christ, under the
consulate of Julius Silanus and Licinius Murena, early
in the morning, there could be observed in the streets
of Rome a greater agitation than usual. The vast
human hive was evidently in a state of commotion.
In the Forum, and particularly in the *Sacred Street—
Via Sacra*—there were groups of excited men talking
and gesticulating with extreme animation ; a number
of priests were seen moving about in various directions, and when they met, conversed in a low tone
of voice, apparently on a subject which seemed to fill
them with anxiety. Some extraordinary event had no
doubt happened, or was expected. What was it ? Wild
rumors of every sort circulated rapidly. Some said
that another Catiline conspiracy had been discovered ;
others, that Cato, the inflexible adversary of all
agrarian laws, had been murdered by the violent and

---

* The writer of this article has derived the materials with
which he has constructed it, from Cicero, Suetonius, Seneca,
Plutarch, and other authorities, but chiefly from Duniazeau's
" Barreau Romain."

unprincipled advocates of such measures; that Cicero
had quarreled with Pompey and Crassus; that a
Roman army had been entirely destroyed somewhere
—nobody yet knew in what locality and by what
enemy. Suppositions and conjectures increased, as
time flew, in number and in sensational force. Crowds
had gathered densely in front of the residence of each
of the two consuls, in the hope that, from that quarter,
the first reliable news would come out. The excitement was growing in intensity, when the street door
of Consul Silanus opened and let out, to the wonder
of the multitude, the venerated matron, Aurelia, the
aged mother of Julius Cæsar. An expression of deep
grief was in her face; she walked slowly and with
difficulty, supported by the female servants who escorted her. The people crowded around her as much
as respect permitted; her son was already dear to
them. Had he been the victim of some cowardly
and secret attempt against his life, and had she come
to inform the consul? Being eagerly interrogated as
to the truth of this conjecture, she replied: "No,
Cæsar still lives, to serve the Roman people, but asks
redress for the insult offered to his name and to his
household Gods." A few minutes afterward, the
whole population of Rome, of high and low degree,
knew the adventure which, the night previous, had
taken place. On that night, the mysteries of the
Good Goddess were to be celebrated at the house of
Cæsar, the high pontiff, under the direction of Pompeia, his wife, daughter of Quintus Pompey and niece
of Lucius Sylla. What of that Good Goddess?
What of her mysterious worship? In what did it
consist? Nobody ever knew exactly. Her true name,
for she had more than one, was to be communicated

only to women, and they seem to have kept the secret. No man was permitted to be present in the building where those mysteries were celebrated, and even every picture, statue, effigy, or anything whatever, animate or inanimate, in which there was any trace of the male sex, was to be carefully removed, or veiled.

A female slave, named Abra, had been stationed at the door opening into the inner peristyle, to admit the Roman women who, as soon as the sun disappeared beneath the horizon, were seen moving from all parts of the city toward the house of Cæsar. The religious sacrifices were to be accomplished in a large hall prepared for the occasion. A woman presented herself with her face carefully veiled. Her stature was rather uncommon for one of her sex, and a close observer could have detected a slight degree of embarrassment or confusion in her manner. On her being asked her name, she replied: " I am the Milesian Neera, chorist of the Good Goddess in her temple on Mount Aventine." There must have been something preconcerted between them, because, on hearing these words, Abra put her finger on her lips as if recommending silence, prudence, and caution, and taking the pretended Neera by the hand, led her rapidly through a long series of galleries, and left her to herself in a small room of the upper story where complete obscurity prevailed. It was the chamber of Abra.

The person who had thus assumed the character of a chorist was Publius Clodius Pulcher. His illustrious family was traced back to the foundation of Rome itself. He inherited the surname of Pulcher, the handsome, from one of his ancestors, but it seems that he very little deserved the complimentary appellation ; for, Cicero once apostrophizing him in one of his speeches, said : " I believe that, should a mirror be presented to you, you would find yourself to be very far from being *Pulcher*, handsome." Nevertheless, he was a favorite with the women of Rome. He was a haughty, overbearing, impetuous profligate, renowned for his debaucheries, and was even suspected of having an incestuous intercourse with his three sisters—one of them the wife of Lucullus. That personage had changed the orthography of his patronymic name—from Claudius to Clodius. He had become such a demagogue, that perhaps it was to show by this change, that he renounced all connection with his noble ancestors; and in order to be elected a tribune, to which office no patrician could aspire, he at last caused himself to be adopted into a plebeian family, and thus became one of the people. They, in the course of time, rewarded him with the position which he had desired, and from which he expected to derive the authority and influence he needed for the accomplishment of all his nefarious schemes. He was a hideous assemblage of all the vices without one solitary redeeming quality, and his audacity was fully equal to the perverseness of his heart.

This was the man who was in the chamber of Abra, waiting for the object of his guilty passion. But the religious ceremonies had begun, and Pompeia, who performed in them the principal part, could not withdraw without its being remarked. Impatient of delay, and perhaps moved by an irresistible curiosity to peep into the celebrated mysteries of the Good Goddess, Clodius left the room where he was safely concealed and directed his steps to a place where melodious sounds attracted his attention. He lost his way, as he cautiously wandered through the sinuosities of vaulted arches by whose obscurity he thought himself protected. He met a female slave, who proposed to lead him where they could entertain themselves with some amusement or other. He refused; she insisted; he persisted in his silent refusal. Somewhat nettled by his obstinacy, she attempted to drag him to some lighted spot where she could see his face. Clodius then said that he was Neera the singer, and that he was in search of Abra; but his voice, which he could not sufficiently modify to make it support his assumed part, betrayed his sex, and the alarm was given. A shout announced that a man was within the sacred precincts. The frightened women shrieked and gathered together like a flock of sheep; the religious ceremonies were interrupted, and the holy emblematic images used in the celebration of the mysteries were veiled to protect them against a profane eye. Aurelia promptly ordered all the doors to be closed, and with lighted torches a search being made, the audacious person who had sacrilegiously violated the mysteries of the Good Goddess was soon discovered. The indignant crowd of women precipitated themselves upon the guilty one, whom they devoted to the Infernal Gods with the usual imprecations. The tumult was at the highest, when Abra, availing herself of the confusion, got hold of Clodius, hurried him through a gallery which was not lighted, and facilitated his escape by a secret door. But he had been recognized, and at day-break, Aurelia, as already stated, had hastened to give information of this sacrilege to Consul Silanus.

This amorous adventure, complicated with an out-

rage against religion, assumed from other circumstances the character of a political event, which was
destined in its consequences to have a serious influence on the affairs of the State. For some time past
many Romans had reconciled themselves to the idea
that the end of the republic was at hand, and that a
concentration of all powers in one man was bound
to be the necessary result of those fatal intestine dissensions and civil wars which had undermined its
very foundations, by introducing the dissolving element of universal corruption, private and public. The
grand republic, so noble at its birth, had become nothing else than a monstrous, gigantic mass of putrefaction. This had stimulated the unscrupulous ambition
of three men, who dreamed of possessing themselves
of a permanent dictatorship. They were Crassus,
Pompey, and Cæsar. The first based his hopes on
his colossal wealth ; the second on his military glory,
which had made him the idol of the people ; and the
third on the consciousness of his own genius and on
his belief in the fortune which destiny had prepared
for him. Cæsar knew that he was Cæsar. That was
enough to plan the conquest of the world, including
the subjugation of his own country. Those three men
united themselves to remove all the obstacles which
they found in their way, although they subsequently
became divided as soon as they had gathered the
fruits of a common victory. Cato and Cicero struggled against the accomplishment of those schemes of
usurpation that were manifest to all. Cato had all
the energy of a sincere republican and austere stoician.
But Cicero, with all his eloquence, his patriotism, and
his many other virtues, was sometimes weak and
vacillating. His philosophy was not so stern and his

nerves so strong as to impart to his mind that fixed-
ness of purpose which shrinks from no danger, be
they a threatening reality, or existing only in an
alarmed imagination, but no less powerful in their influence. The luxury of certain material and intellectual enjoyments in Rome, or at his famous coun-
try-seat of Tusculum, was too keenly appreciated by
Cicero not to make him alive to the consequences of
risking too much, although it can not be denied that
he fearlessly made great sacrifices in his country's
cause.

The crime of Clodius had been the occasion of a
wide-spread scandal. Notwithstanding the stupendous corruption of the epoch, the religious institutions,
formerly so much respected, still retained a powerful
hold on the mind and heart of a portion of the population, which felt itself profoundly outraged in its
faith ; and the women, particularly, were clamorous
for the punishment of the sacrilegious offense that
had been committed. But the patrician Clodius was
known as desiring to be adopted in a plebeian family,
as already stated, and, therefore, disposed to renounce
his caste. He had assumed to be the warm, or rather
the furious advocate of the interests, wishes, and passions of the people, who were grateful to him for his
efforts on their behalf. They could not forget that
he intended to descend voluntarily into their ranks,
and to abandon all the aristocratic privileges of his
race, which for centuries had been famous for its
haughtiness and its contempt for the lower classes.
He was, therefore, in possession of an immense
popularity, that made him worth being conciliated
by every one of those ambitious men who aimed
at sovereign power, and who hoped to cajole the

people into willing servitude, or into granting the means of destroying their liberties at the opportune moment. Hence, Crassus and Pompey could not but be inclined to serve him, if not by declaring themselves openly in his favor on this occasion, when he had brought himself into peril, at least by secretly helping him with their influence. The interest of Cæsar was the same. It was his policy not to provoke the enmity of that energetic demagogue, but his position was exceedingly delicate. As a pontiff and as a husband he had been outraged in a double capacity. His political interests, however, prevailed over a just resentment, and he joined, as much as decency permitted, his efforts to those of his two associates, Crassus and Pompey, to save the lover of his wife, although he had hastened to repudiate her. In palliation of his conduct, if it can be palliated at all, it must be remembered that in those days of advanced civilization to which Rome had attained, Romans had ceased to care much for the fidelity of their wives.

The consuls, whose term of office was soon to expire, were disposed to follow a policy of prudent inaction, and to refrain from taking the initiative in a criminal prosecution which might subject them to the animadversion of the populace. Less timid, or perhaps actuated by secret feelings of enmity toward Clodius, Quintus Cornificus, who had lately been a candidate for the consulship in opposition to Cicero, denounced the alleged crime to the Senate. This act of virtuous energy on the part of a man who had always shown himself more of an unprincipled demagogue than a rigid conservative, or guardian of public morals, caused universal astonishment. People wondered at the inexplicable motive of his conduct, as his sympathies, considering his character and usual deportment, were supposed to be enlisted in favor of Clodius. Whatever was his spring of action, it is certain that he forcibly related the circumstances of the case, expatiated at length on the gravity of the offense, insisted on having the accused brought before the proper tribunal, and declared that he himself, if no other undertook the task, would appear in the character of public prosecutor. As he was known to be a friend of Clodius, some suspected that his object was to obtain the management and control of the trial, and to conduct it in such a manner as to make it a failure. This was not uncommon at that epoch on the part of those who favored the accused parties, and who had recourse to that stratagem.

There was another anomalous circumstance. Caius Scribonius Curio, the friend of Cicero, and his firm supporter in his former quarrels with Clodius — so much so that he had been beaten, it is said, by the slaves of that ferocious partisan on account of his opposition to their master's schemes—now showed himself favorable to the accused, and, without assuming to justify him, called the attention of the Senate to the fact that, even admitting the truth of what was related, there was a preliminary question to be settled, which was, whether what Clodius had done was a crime or not—alleging that it was the first time that such an occurrence had happened ; that it was not foreseen and provided for by any law ; that inasmuch as it was an affair of a religious nature, the Senate had no jurisdiction over it, and, therefore, that it was indispensable to refer the matter to the consideration of the Sacred College of Pontiffs. The main object of this proposition was to gain time, and to postpone all further action until after the first of January, when the new consuls were to come into office. It was known that one of them, Piso Calpurnius, was completely devoted to Clodius, and it was hoped that, through his influence, the unfavorable feelings and dispositions entertained by his colleague, Valerius Messala Niger, might be paralyzed. After a very animated debate, Curio's motion was adopted, and the affair was referred to the pontiffs. This was one point gained by Clodius. Curio's course, considering his previous antagonism to Clodius, appears enigmatic to posterity, but perhaps was well understood and appreciated by his contemporaries. In a demoralized state of society, made worse by civil discords and intense party excitement, such tackings about, or shiftings of the ship's sails, in which individual interest is the only recognized pilot, or such coat-turnings as may suit the exigencies of the hour, are not unfrequent. The morality of modern times has been more than once shocked by similar circumstances in high places, where the very conspicuousness of the variations might have been supposed to be a check against their occurrence.

The question did not seem doubtful to the Sacred College. It was remembered that, in the year 567 of the foundation of Rome, under the consulship of Postumius Albinus and Marcus Philippus, certain women having been accused of incest during the celebration of the mysteries of Bacchus, the Senate had instructed the consuls to proceed to an investigation, and that several of those women had been tried and punished with death. It was thought by the Sacred College that the introduction of a man into the building where the mysteries of the Good Goddess were celebrated, evidently constituted a sacrilege, and also that the priestly character which Pompeia derived from the sacerdotal dignity of her husband as pontiff, combined with the sacredness of the place where the outrage had been committed, assimilated to incest the adultery of which Clodius was suspected. The Sacred College, therefore, declared that the act attributed to him was a crime *de religione,* or *pollutis sacris,* or *de incestu.*

A report to that effect being made to the Senate, gave rise to immediate discussion. Cornificus delivered a speech in which he again expatiated on the enormity of the offense, and on the necessity of quieting, by an exemplary punishment of the offender, the consciences of the honest and the pious. This was very well thus far; but what was the tribunal, or *quæstio,* which could entertain jurisdiction over the case? It was admitted that there was none. Nobody thought of bringing Clodius before the ordinary and permanent tribunals established to judge assassins, peculators in the provinces subjected to the rule of Rome, plunderers of the public treasury, and perpetrators of the crime of bribery and corrupt canvassing. Consequently, it was indispensable to create, by a special law, a special tribunal, *quæstio extra ordinem.*

Cato spoke after Cornificus, and adopted his conclusions. The sacrilege of Clodius could not remain unpunished, but he feared a scandalous impunity, should the accused be tried by a special tribunal, which, according to precedent and usage, would be composed of judges drawn by lot. "In recent trials," he said, "has it not been demonstrated how weak has become the sentiment of duty and justice in the breasts of the people, from whose ranks the jurors were to be taken according to the accidents of chance, and how easy it was to corrupt those administrators of the law thus improvised at random. What judges, designated by the blind caprice of the drawing by lot, will condemn Clodius, so powerful by his wealth, by his family connections, by the sympathies felt for him by all the enemies of order and peace, and by the secret support of ambitious men, who speculate on the audacity and popularity of this patrician demagogue? Therefore, if this was an occasion for the creation of a special tribunal, it also was a matter of absolute necessity to decree that the judges be selected by the *prætor*, or magistrate, instead of leaving the composition of the tribunal to the uncertain arbitration of chance."

On hearing these sentiments, the partisans of Clodius, who had artfully grouped themselves for effect and mutual support in the Senate, burst into a wild clamor, accompanied by violent gesticulations. "What!" exclaimed Curio, "is Clodius so great a personage in our republic that our existing laws are too feeble to rise up to the height of his importance and power, and that he can be reached only by the extraordinary exercise of an exceptional legislation, applying singly to his person? Or is he the object of such implacable hatred, that men who have hitherto been considered as the most vigilant guardians of the established laws, propose to violate them for the purpose of securing the gratification of their revengeful passions? Exceptional legislation for a special case has always been regarded with disfavor by the Roman people, because one of their most objectionable effects is, to be retroactive—an odious feature, which has been eloquently and energetically denounced by Cicero in the trial of Verres, and explicitly prohibited in the laws cf the Twelve Tables. It is proposed, not only to institute an extraordinary tribunal, but, moreover, to invest it with the power to pass judgment over a sacrilege and an incest. Would not this be a violation of all the sound principles of jurisprudence? Can two crimes entirely distinct be cumulated and subjected to the same jurisdiction? If the Senate should be of opinion that there are good grounds, which I am far from admitting, to order a criminal prosecution against Clodius, there ought at least to be created two tribunals—one for each of the alleged crimes. With regard to the proposition to give to the prætor the choice of the judges, it is a monstrous one, which I resist to the utmost of my ability; and thoroughly convinced I am that, if this body should thus dare to trample underfoot all those usages, precedents, and principles which are matters of common law, the people would know how to render justice in the premises by reprobating and checking such iniquitous proceedings."

Cicero, whose authority had been quoted, rose and said: "True it is that, in the case mentioned, I spoke with the usual energy of my convictions against the abuses of retroactive legislation, but the orator to whom I reply has forgotten that, on the occasion to which he called our attention, it was an edict of the prætor Verres which I assailed. There is no assimilation to be made between an edict emanating from a magistrate concerning private matters, and a law proposed by the Senate and approved by the people. The special laws passed to meet particular cases in analogous circumstances are so numerous, that I do not deem it necessary to re:ite them, because they are well known to all. With regard to the cumulation of accusations, of which Curio complains, I can not explain to myself the position he has taken, except on the hypothesis of his being blinded by the excess of his zeal for the defense of his friend, because nobody can plead ignorance of the fact that the permanent tribunal constituted by the law *Cornelia* took cognizance of the crimes of assassination, of poisoning, and of the bribing of judges, although these were distinct facts, and of a different nature. After all, in the present affair, the necessity of conforming to the same jurisprudence results from the connection of the two crimes attributed to Clodius—a connection which is so close that it merges them into one—because the circumstances of time and place are such that they make of adultery an incest and a sacrilege. I see, therefore, no objection to prosecuting Clodius for the crime *de religione*, according to the conclusions of the Sacred College of Pontiffs. Finally, I am of opinion, in relation to the motion of Cato, that it certainly appertains to the Senate, when it creates a new tribunal, to propose that the people, whose will is sovereign, should ultimately determine, for the best interests of justice, either the number of the judges, or the mode of selecting them, or both, and the forms of the proceedings."

Fierce and long were the debates. Several senators imputed other crimes to Clodius—among others, that of sexual intercourse with his sister, the wife of Lucullus. At last, after the most stormy deliberations, the Senate passed a *Senatus Consultum* decreeing the formation of an extraordinary tribunal to judge Publius Clodius Pulcher, accused of the crime of sacrilege. That tribunal was to be composed of fifty-six jurors, chosen by the prætor presiding at the trial, outside of the ordinary jury list, if he deemed it proper. As to the mode of proceeding, it was to be in conformity to the forms and rules prescribed for the court which took cognizance of peculations. (*De pecuniis repetendis*). The consuls were invited, according to the ordinary formula, to apply to the people for the necessary sanction to convert into law the present Senatus Consultum. (Rogatio).

The decree of the Senate produced a great surprise and commotion in Rome, the general impression having been that the partisans of Clodius would have the upper-hand in that body. He had relied on the influence of Crassus and Pompey, who, probably yielding to a sentiment of shame, had prudently kept aloof. The Consul Piso, who was entirely devoted to Clodius, was indignant at their equivocal conduct, and urged the tribune Fufius Calenus to seize the first opportunity to force Pompey to manifest his dispositions. That opportunity was not long in presenting itself. The tribune, having met Pompey in the circus of Flaminius on a market day, called upon him to declare in the presence of the crowd there assembled, whether he approved the Senatus Consultum which delegated to the prætor the choice of the judges, and what was his opinion about the best mode of composing the tribunal. Pompey was surprised and nettled. He aristocratically answered that it appeared and had always appeared to him that the authority of the Senate should be held superior to any other. The rest of his remarks were prolix, embarrassed, and devoid of any precise meaning. This ambiguity and trimming pleased neither of the contending parties. Shortly after, Consul Messala asked him in full Senate what he thought of the affair of Clodius. His answer did not differ much from what he had already said in the circus of Flaminius. He so enveloped his sentiments in a cloud of words that it was impossible to discover what they were; and after having praised in general terms the profound wisdom of the august assembly, he went and took a seat by the side of Cicero, to whom he said: " Do you not think that I have been sufficiently explicit on that ugly case?" It is fair to suppose that Cicero, who was always cautious to keep on good terms with Pompey, did not give a very positive answer. Crassus rose and spoke in pompous terms of the glories of Cicero's consulship, praised his courage, extolled his services to the sky, but said nothing of the affair of Clodius, whom he was known secretly to favor. This was an artful diversion from the subject on which he suspected Cicero of being disposed to speak energetically and with damaging effect to his friend. He succeeded; the vanity of the great orator was well known, and was prodigiously tickled on that occasion. He wrote to Atticus in an ecstasy of pride and joy: " This day has made me a Crassus man." Then he added, about the speech which he had delivered in reply: "By the Immortal Gods, how handsomely I made my toilet, and in my best dress paraded in the presence of Pompey! If ever sonorous periods, happy inflections of the voice, richness of invention, artifices of language, came to my aid, it was certainly on that day. Hence, what acclamations! It is true that I was treating of the dignity of the Senate, of its perfect accord with the Equestrian Order, of the excellent spirit which prevails throughout Italy, of the expiring remnants of the

Catiline conspiracy, of the low price of grain, and of
the re-established peace. You know how my words
ring when I speak on such a subject. Being convinced that they sounded loud enough to reach your
ears, notwithstanding the distance which separated
us, I will refrain from saying anything further as to
the grand effect which they produced." Evidently
the satisfaction of Cicero was unbounded. But what
of Clodius, whom he had forgotten? Surely Crassus'
must have laughed in his beard and enjoyed hugely
the success of his artifice.

Meanwhile, the day on which the people were to
vote for the approbation or rejection of the Senatus
Consultum had arrived. From early morn the whole
city was in commotion. All the young debauchees
who had joined in the Catiline conspiracy, were seen
actively moving in the most populous thoroughfares
and advocating the rejection of the Senatus Consultum. Piso, who as consul had been officially compelled to submit the measure to the vote of the people, participated in these shameful manœuvres. The
agents of Clodius swarmed at every point and were
distributing ballots for the rejection. On these ballots was inscribed the letter A—meaning : *Antiquo*—
that is, " I vote for what is ancient; no innovation."
The formula of adoption was an U and R — *uti
rogas*—which meant : " Let it be done as desired."
Cato, seeing with what ability the partisans of Clodius
were conducting their intrigues, and fearing a defeat
for the Senate, ascended the rostrum, and called Consul Piso, who happened to be present, to an account
for his conduct. This was done with a vivacity of indignation which produced a profound sensation. Hortensius succeeded Cato whose views he supported

with the animated flow of his usual eloquence. Other orators were heard ; they all agreed in their withering denunciations of the corrupt practices of the friends of Clodius. Their success, however, was doubtful, when fortunately perhaps for the fate of the Senatus Consultum, it was announced that the auspices were unfavorable, and therefore the *comitia* were prorogued. It was a convenient circumstance, which frequently happened whenever it suited the patricians, who alone had the privilege of consulting the entrails of the animals sacrificed to the Gods.

Thus time was gained, and the situation of affairs was considered so important, that the Senate was convened in extraordinary session as in cases of urgency, and a member proposed to invite by a decree the consuls to solicit the sanction of the people to the Senatus Consultum in question ; which was an extreme measure, only resorted to in exceptional circumstances. Clodius, alarmed at this firm perseverance of the senators in their resolution to prosecute him, affected great humility and threw himself as a suppliant at the feet of the most influential. Piso and Curio made great efforts to have the proposition rejected. The decree, however, was adopted by a majority of 400 to 15—the vote being ascertained by sitting and standing. The decree said that the *comitia* should be convened *de novo* to take cognizance of the affair in preference to any other. This was a crushing result, but Clodius was not abashed. He who, when the issue was doubtful, had put on so humble a garb, resumed the attitude of haughtiness which was natural to his character, and addressed Hortensius, his brother-in-law Lucullus, and Consul Messala in the most violent and insulting language, overwhelming them with reproaches and threats. As to Cicero, Clodius ironically complimented him on his marvelous talent to discover conspiracies and all sorts of crimes.

A few days afterward, the *comitia* were assembled. Gifted with that prodigious activity which character-izes the abettors of popular troubles and disturbances, and which Cicero calls *horribilis diligentia*, Clodius had stimulated and raised the courage of his parti-sans, whilst he had by his defamations undermined his adversaries in the public estimation. He had personally attacked Cicero, who from the rostrum re-plied with one of those broadsides which he so well knew how to direct against his enemies, when his fiery zeal for the safety and dignity of the commonwealth had not cooled down into moderation from pruden-tial considerations. He was elated at the manner in which he spoke on that occasion. " Immortal Gods!" he wrote to Atticus. " With what blows I demolished my adversaries! What a carnage I made of them! How I rushed on Piso, Curio, and all those miserable bandits! How I crushed to the earth under the weight of my contempt and indignation those hare-brained old men and those beardless debauchees!" Still there were apprehensions as to the result of the vote. Hortensius, frightened at the turn which the affair took, imagined an expedient which, as he thought, would give satisfaction to the populace, and at the same time save the dignity of the Senate. The main complaint of Clodius against that body was based on that part of the decree which conferred on the prætor the power to compose the tribunal as he pleased. Hortensius suggested to the tribune Fufius, whose opposition he feared, the idea of proposing, as an amendment coming from himself (Fufius) that the Senatus Consultum be adopted in all its provisions, with the exception of what was relative to the composition of the tribunal. Fufius acceded to it with eagerness, and presented the amendment to the people.

This compromise was generally approved, but Cicero opposed it with much earnestness. According to his views, the gist of the law was that very part of it which was proposed to be suppressed, so much so, that, so far as he was personally concerned, he would prefer the absolute rejection to the adoption of the offered compromise, because it was much better to abandon Clodius and leave him to his infamy, than to institute against him a derisive prosecution. Hortensius insisted, being convinced, as he said, that the culprit could not escape, whatever was the composition of the tribunal, and that "a leaden sword would suffice to pierce him." His conclusions were finally adopted by many of those who had been originally opposed to the amendment, and what was called the law *Fufia* passed by the vote of a large majority.

This issue of the first phase of the prosecution profoundly discouraged Cicero. From that moment "he drew in his sails," according to his own expressions, and kept aloof, as if he saw in the future the flames which devoured his house and the decree which sent him into exile.

Four citizens presented themselves before the prætor as the accusers of Clodius. They were the three brothers Lentulus, of the great Cornelian family, and Fannius, one of the Pontiffs. Publius Lentulus, the eldest of the brothers and the highest in dignity, was the principal accuser, and swore that his accusation was not based on any evil motives and was not for the purpose of calumniating the accused. His two brothers and Fannius joined him as secondary accusers (subscriptores). They all signed the *procès verbal* recording the names of the accusers and of the accused, the taking of the oath, the allegation and definition of the crime, together with the date of the day fixed for the opening of the trial, which was, after a delay of ten days. Accordingly, the prætor summoned the accused, the accusers, and the judges or jurors for the 4th of May, 693 of the foundation of Rome, after the Floral games.

II.

Among the great judicial trials recorded in history there are few which present themselves to the imagination with such circumstances of pomp and grandeur. The real accusers were the Roman Senate and people; the accused was the powerful descendant of the great Claudian family, whose origin was coeval with that of the Eternal City. The advocates on both sides were patricians and senators; the witnesses were the mother and sister of Cæsar, Cæsar himself, Cicero, and other illustrious personages. The theatre of the debates was the Forum, and one may be allowed to suppose that among the audience were the invisible Gods, whose temples encircled on all sides the august seats to be occupied by fifty-six judges. In appearance the question was whether a man had been guilty of sacrilege and adultery, but in reality it was, which of the elements of good and evil engaged in a death struggle, would predominate, and influence the destinies of the mistress of the world. The temple of justice had become a political arena, and the verdict of the jury was to be the measure and evidence of that corruption which bred civil wars, destroyed the republic, and made a necessity of the Augustan empire.

On the day of the famous trial, the 4th of May, the Forum was invaded before sunrise by an immense multitude. The porticoes of the temples of Saturn, of Castor and Pollux, of Vesta and of Concord were loaded with spectators, as well as every spot, roof, gallery, or elevated point from which the eye could embrace the Forum. At nine o'clock, a long swell or undulation was noticed in that ocean of human beings, which parted to give passage to Clodius, who was seen advancing with slow steps, and accompanied by his defenders, four in number, by his numerous clients and friends, and by several members of his family, among whom were conspicuous his three sisters, Clodia, Pulchra, and Tertia, who were in mourning apparel. At a short distance behind Clodius came the accusers, followed by many persons of distinction, among whom, the Consul Messala, Cicero, Cato, Catullus, Caius, Piso, Lucullus, and others. The prætor was not long in presenting himself with his two lictors, his clerks, and bailiffs. He took his seat in the centre of the Forum on an elevated estrade. Behind him were exhibited a pike and a sword, as the emblems of command and force. A little lower, at a certain distance on the right, was the bench of the accusers in the shape of a semicircle. In line, on the left, was the bench of the accused and his defenders. The space between the estrade and those benches on both sides was occupied by the seats of the judges, in the shape of a hemicycle. A balustrade about three feet high encircled the whole.

The case being called, the prætor announced that he would proceed to the first drawing by lot (*sortitio*) of the fifty-six judges, or jurors, who were to take cognizance of the accusation against Clodius. He added that the accuser and accused had each the right to recuse twenty-eight ; that is, ten in the order of the senators, nine in the order of the knights, and nine in the order of the tribunes of the treasury. Immediately, the bailiffs brought three urns containing balls, on which were inscribed the names of the jurors who were to serve as such during the year. These urns having been opened, the prætor drew from the first, nineteen names of senators; from the second, nineteen names of knights ; and from the third, eighteen names of tribunes of the treasury—in all, fifty-six judges. The accuser, having risen, declared that he recused twenty one judges, whom he designated. The accused challenged nine. The prætor announced that he would proceed to the second drawing by lot to complete the number of the judges (*subsortitio*). Consequently, he drew again, as he had done before, and exactly in the same manner, fifty-six names. Then addressing the accuser, he informed him that his right being to recuse half of the judges —that is, twenty-eight—and his having already recused twenty-one, there remained only seven to be challenged by him, to wit : six in the order of senators, and one in the order of knights. He also notified the accused that he had the right to nineteen recusations—seven among the tribunes of the treasury, seven among the knights, and five among the senators. He then placed the fifty-six names in a fourth urn, and proceeded to draw again, either party challenging as the drawing went on—the accuser first, and the accused next. The right of recusation being exhausted on both sides, the judges, or jurors, seated themselves and took the prescribed oath. The prætor declared that the tribunal was finally constituted.

These preliminaries had not been gone through without considerable disorder. Each time a recusation was made, shouts of approbation or disapprobation had been heard from the crowd, according to the feelings of the sympathizers with either party. The judges had hardly been sworn, when the public began to conjecture about the issue of the trial, based upon the composition of the tribunal. Clodius had exercised his right of recusation with remarkable tact, and succeeded in setting aside most of the independent and honest citizens whose names had been called. There could be seen among the judges, if Cicero is to be believed, senators of ill-repute, knights in rags, and tribunes of the treasury, "who certainly had no treasury of their own." Three of the judges were of a notoriously bad character, and the presence of a few honest men whom the challenging by the accused had not been able to reach, was not a sufficient guarantee for an impartial judgment.

The prætor informed the accuser that he had the right to open the case.

The law *servilia*, which was enacted thirty-two years before, to put an end to certain abuses, had ordered that, in cases of a specific nature, the pleadings should embrace two days, with an interval of one day. The second hearing, or pleading, was called *comperendinatio*—that is, the pleading of the third day. This proceeding, which, at first, was restricted to special cases, was later extended to several sorts of criminal actions, and it seems that the law *Fufia* had made it applicable to the Clodius case. In the course of time, the advocates, considering that these two pleadings were supererogatory, and were tiresome to the judges and to themselves, because it frequently was a mere repetition of the same arguments, had gradually adopted the habit of reducing the first pleading to a simple exposition of the general features of the affair, reserving for the second hearing the examination of the proofs and the offering of their strongest arguments. They had found it to their advantage to speak only after the testimony had closed, rather than split their discourse into two parts, one before and the other after the proofs. But this course was not very favorable to the accused, because it gave to the accuser the opportunity to reserve his best points, and to comment with more precision and effect on the evidence presented.

Publius Lentulus, therefore, limited himself to exposing the facts of the case as they resulted from the versions which were believed to be the most accurate, and to presenting some remarks based on the gravity of the crime attributed to Clodius, and on the responsibility which rested on the judges. He drew a vivid picture of the situation of the Republic, and showed that it was on the very brink of terrible disasters and final ruin, through the violence of those factions which were the natural results of such causes as the general corruption of the commonwealth, the rivalship of ambitious men, and the ever-growing contempt for the majesty, sanctity, and power of the Gods.

After Lentulus had concluded, the prætor signified to the accused that it was his turn to speak. Then Curio, the principal defender of Clodius, rose and addressed the court. After a pathetic exordium, in which he attempted to enlist the sympathies of the judges in favor of a citizen whose greatest crime—nay, whose sole crime in the eyes of the nobles—was to have always warmly embraced the cause of the people in all conflicts between them and their patrician adversaries, he bitterly complained of the laconism of the argument of the counsel on the opposite side. "Thus far," he said, "on what rests so grave an accusation? Relating merely the gossipings scraped up in the fish-market, the accuser reserves, no doubt, for the second hearing, some great stage effect sedulously concealed from us. Truth ignores these tricks, and does not fear to show herself at once in all her chaste and commendable nudity. Clodius does not require two days' preparation to justify himself. He is ready to establish, without delay, that on the 4th of December, 692, at nine o'clock in the evening, he was in the city of Interamnium, at the house of his friend, Cassinius Schola, and, therefore, that he could not be in Rome when the sacrilege is alleged to have been committed. The alibi will be proved beyond a doubt by a large number of respectable witnesses, and it will be demonstrated to every man of good faith and impartiality that my client is the victim of an atrocious calumny, or a deplorable error." He then reviewed certain circumstances that rendered improbable the facts brought forth by the accusation, and he strove to refute in advance the proofs which the accuser had announced. In concluding, he alluded to the last words of Lentulus: "Yes," he said, "the Republic is in danger; but keep it in mind, Romans, that it is less from the contempt for religion than from the avarice of the patricians." This apostrophe was received with boisterous acclamations from the partisans of Clodius, who had grouped themselves near him as much as possible, and those acclamations were echoed through the crowd to the very extremities of the Forum. When silence was at last re-established, the prætor invited the accuser to produce his witnesses, and the clerks prepared themselves to take down the depositions.

The first witness was Aurelia, the mother of Cæsar. After having sworn by Jupiter to tell the truth, she thus spoke: "You all know it, O judges; the 4th of December was the day fixed for the celebration of the mysteries of the Good Goddess. The sacrifice which was to be offered in the name of the Roman people was to have taken place in the house of the high pontiff, Caius Julius Cæsar, my son. My daughter-in-law, Pompeia, was called upon, on account of the sacerdotal dignity of her husband, to fulfill the ministry of high priestess. At four o'clock in the afternoon, Cæsar departed with all the male persons of his household. All male animals had been sent away. The statues, the paintings, and everything which represented persons or animals of the male sex, had been carefully veiled. When this was done, the Vestals declared that the grounds were consecrated, and pronounced the usual imprecations against any profane intruder who should dare to pollute them by his presence. At 8 o'clock the women invited to the celebration of the mysteries had arrived, the holy things were uncovered, and the ceremonies began. Between eight and a half and nine, a great noise was heard in the *triclinium*, and almost at the same time my slave Ægypta rushed into the *oratorio*, with dishevelled hair and her dress in disorder. 'A man is here,' she cried. Immediately the songs ceased, and the Vestals threw themselves on the sacred objects to prevent them from being seen. I ordered all the doors to be closed. Ægypta informed me that the man she had met was in female attire, and indicated the direction he had gone. We visited the house with lights, even the most secret places, and we found in the chamber of Abra, the slave of Pompeia, a person dressed like a woman, but whom it was easy to discover to be a man. At that moment there rushed in a crowd of women, and availing himself of the tumult which ensued, the stranger disappeared and could not be found again. Early on the next morning, I called on Consul Silanus to complain of this abominable sacrilege. I have said."

Lentulus, having risen, asked her if she had seen and recognized the man of whom she had spoken. She answered: "I saw and recognized him, I believe. I believe* that it was Publius Clodius Pulcher, the son of Appius Claudius." This declaration produced a moment of agitation among the spectators who were the nearest to the tribunal.

"Will you describe the costume of the pretended Clodius?" asked Curio, addressing the witness. "I can not," she replied, "but Ægypta will."

Lentulus expressed the desire to know if Pompeia had left the sacred place of the sacrifice between eight and nine o'clock. The witness affirmed that she was not aware of it, and did not think that she had absented herself.

---

* Witnesses among the Roman people generally gave their testimony with great circumspection. They did not say: "I saw, I heard, but I believe that I saw, that I heard." This formula, expressive of what was the "Socratic doubt," had passed from the Academy to the Forum.

After Aurelia, the sister of Cæsar, Julia, was heard. Her testimony, delivered with clearness and without hesitation, confirmed her mother's declarations. Next came Cæsar. He declared that he had been several hours absent from his house when the incident occurred, and therefore that he knew nothing. Being hard pushed by the accusers, he persisted in the same reserve and even refused to repeat any of the reports which had reached his ears, because it was impossible for him to ascertain if they were correct. "If you know nothing," testily said Lentulus, "how is it that you have repudiated Pompeia?" "Because," he replied, "the wife of Cæsar must not even be suspected."

The fourth witness was the slave Ægypta. She thus spoke: "I had been appointed to guard externally the place where the sacrifice for the Roman people was to be accomplished. About nine o'clock, I discovered at the extremity of a gallery a woman whom I took to be a slave. I went to her and proposed a game of osselets. She did not answer; she turned her head, and walked a few steps from me, as if going away. I followed her, drew her to a lamp suspended from the vaulted ceiling, and asked her who she was, to be so disdainful. She replied that she was one of the singers of the Good Goddess, and that she was looking for Abra. It was not the voice of a woman. I seized the unknown by the arm, but she got rid of me by so abrupt and violent a movement, that I no longer had any doubt as to her sex." The witness then repeated all that had already been said by Aurelia. Curio having asked her if she had recognized Clodius, she answered that she could not have recognized him, because he was unknown to her; but that several of the Roman dames, on seeing the person she had mentioned, exclaimed: "It is Clodius."

Confronted with the accused, she believed that she recognized him as the person in question, who, however, was younger and beardless. Interrogated as to the costume, she declared that the pretended chorist of the Good Goddess wore a saffron-colored robe, a head-dress in the shape of a mitre, purple ribbons, a tucker, and a buskin, such as are used by women, and that she carried a harp.

Abra testified with great unconcern on the facts already known, as if she had not been an accomplice. Keenly interrogated by both sides, she confessed that she had admitted the chorist dressed as Ægypta had described, but averred that she did not know who she was and had lost sight of her immediately after her admittance. She emphatically denied having facilitated her evasion. After Abra, several Roman matrons testified. They all declared that they thought they had recognized Clodius.

Then Marcus Tullius Cicero was called as a witness. On hearing that name, the partisans of Clodius broke out into an immense clamor. Yells after yells of rage resounded far and wide. Alarmed at this threatening demonstration, the judges spontaneously rose from their seats and surrounded Cicero, as if to protect the man who had so well deserved the appellation of "father of his country," and by gestures and words gave the perturbators of the peace to understand that they were determined to defend the illustrious witness at the peril of their lives. This attitude of the tribunal produced a profound impression on the people, and Clodius himself seemed to be struck with dismay. The howls ceased by degrees, and Cicero could give his testimony. He swore that, on the day of the celebration of the mysteries of the Good Goddess, he had seen Clodius at six in the evening in Rome, and had conversed with him on the affairs of the Republic. He added that this fact was so well known in the city, and, if necessary, could be proved by so many witnesses, that it would not have been possible for him not to mention it, even if he had been so disposed.

Curio then rose and said : " There is not one of us who does not know the jealous and shrewish temper of Terentia, the wife of Cicero. She has taken into her head that Clodia, the sister of Clodius, entertains the singular fancy of marrying Cicero after having induced him to repudiate her, Terentia, and that this negotiation is now being conducted by Tullius, a friend of both houses. I ask the witness, whose reverential submission to the will of Terentia is not a secret for anybody, if the declaration which he has just made has not been suggested to him by the necessity of re-establishing peace in his household." This question elicited loud laughter on the benches of the accused and of his friends. When silence was restored, Cicero answered with calm dignity, in a tone not untinged, however, with irony : " That he had never raised his pretentions to the thought of marrying Clodia, although it was well known that she had a tempting dowry of *quadrantes ;** that he was

---

* Clodia was one of the loosest women of Rome. It was related that one of her numerous lovers had once, in derision, sent her a bag of small coins, of very little value, called *quadrantes*, as an adequate price for her favors. Hence the surname of *qaudrantaria* given to her.

far from believing that she had ever thought of him, because he knew her taste for family alliances;* and that, with regard to Terentia, even admitting as true the ridiculous ideas attributed to her, she could not have been so insensate as to desire the removal of a man whose assiduous attentions to Clodia were rather a cause of security for her supposed jealousy than one of inquietude."

The answer produced an explosion of hilarity; all eyes turned toward Clodia, and it was with difficulty that the prætor put an end to this war of sarcasms.

Curio, however, was not put out of countenance. He said that he was not willing to insist on simple conjectures, whatever might be their plausibility. But he thought it not improper to remind the judges that the Vestal Fabia, the sister of Terentia, had been accused of incest by Clodius, and that, although she had been acquitted, yet it was easy to understand that Terentia had cherished against the accused, in the present trial, a resentment which was necessarily shared by the witness.

Cicero, who had withdrawn from the stand, signified by a gesture that he would not condescend to reply.

Other witnesses were heard in support of the accusation. Cato testified as to some facts which were of little importance. Lucullus produced two of his female slaves who swore that Clodius had entertained

---

* It was a matter of public notoriety that Clodius entertained an incestuous commerce with his three sisters, and particularly with Clodia. This infamous creature had married the celebrated Lucullus, and after being repudiated by him, had become the wife of the Consul Metellus Celer ! There can not be a stronger illustration of the moral putrefaction of Rome at that epoch.

a criminal intercourse with his sister, whilst she was the wife of their master, who had repudiated her, not only for that crime, but also for other acts of licentiousness. Several distinguished personages testified as to facts by which it was intended to show that Clodius had been guilty of perjury and peculation, of electoral bribery and rape. Thus it is seen that in Rome a criminal prosecution took a wide range. The accused, when charged with a particular crime, was subjected to a critical review of his whole life, and all his past transgressions were invoked against him as presumptive evidence of his having committed the one for which he was tried. To this day the criminal jurisprudence of France, which is derived to some extent from the Romans, is tainted with the same vicious and unjust mode of proceeding.

At last, at the request of the accuser, some of the slaves of Clodius were interrogated as to the manner in which he had passed his time during the evening of the 4th of December. This was an exceptional proceeding, authorized only in trials *de religione*. But nothing was extracted from them which could criminate the accused.

The evidence being closed on the part of the accuser, the court adjourned to the next day.

On the 5th of May, early in the morning, the crowd again took possession of the Forum—not more numerous than on the preceding day—that would have been impossible—but better disposed for Clodius, because the night had been employed in gaining him partisans. The court being in session, the witnesses for the accused were called.

The first who presented himself declared that his name was Caius Cassinius Schola, a Roman knight, residing in the city of Interamnium. After having sworn to tell the truth, he said that, on the 4th of December, Clodius, at nine o'clock in the evening, had come to his house, where he had passed the rest of the night, and that he had returned to Rome the next day.

Lentulus asked Cassinius Schola what was the distance between Rome and Interamnium. The witness answered that it was about sixty-six miles; that no doubt it was difficult to admit that Clodius could have been seen at both places on the same day, and at the same hour, but that it was not for him, the witness, to do away with this difficulty; and that he considered himself to be called upon to affirm only what was to his personal knowledge. Several of the slaves of Cassinius confirmed this declaration, which gave rise to violent debates, often interrupted by the clamors of the assembled multitude.

After the hearing of several other witnesses who had been picked out from among the vilest creatures attached to the service of Clodius, with a view to corroborate the evidence of the alibi, which was the capital point of the defense, there came the introduction of such witnesses as were needed to establish the good and virtuous antecedents of Clodius and his immaculate morality. It certainly required a wonderful supply of brass for any one to publicly endorse Clodius as a man having even the semblance of virtue—so well known was he to the whole community! Nevertheless, that class of witnesses proved to be numerous, and composed even of many senators on whose devotion Clodius had good reasons to rely. Pompey himself had been cited to render the same service to a man notoriously coated all over with vices and stained with every crime. But Pompey, at least, did not come. Clodius brought also to testify in his favor many notable citizens of neighboring cities, particularly of Lanuvium, which was his birthplace and in which he exercised great influence.

The 5th of May having not sufficed to hear all those whitewashing witnesses, the case was continued to the 6th, and then the list being exhausted, the tribunal adjourned to the 8th, allowing the 7th for the interval, or *comperendinatio*, which was required by the law to elapse before the pleadings could be resumed.

The coming of the 8th of May was not looked to without great apprehensions in Rome. An incident had taken place on the last sitting of the court which was a justifiable cause for those apprehensions. Moved by the pathetic amplifications of the notables of Lanuvium on the generous devotion of Clodius to the interests of the poor of the plebeian class, a portion of the people had manifested much turbulence, and the vociferations had been of an alarming nature. For one moment the populace had broken into the precincts of the tribunal, and threats had been preferred both against the judges and against Cicero, who, notwithstanding the moderation of his testimony, was supposed to be the instigator of the prosecution. Afraid of these demonstrations, which might lead to acts of greater violence, some of the judges had resolved not to take their seats, unless a guard were granted for their protection. All the members of the tribunal deliberated on the subject, and unanimously voted, less one vote, for the furnishing of a guard. The Senate, to which was referred the action of the judges, approved of it, and issued orders in accordance with their desire. This measure gave great satisfaction to all good citizens, and removed, to some extent, their apprehensions. A large crowd went to the house of Cicero to show their sense of his patriotism and eminent services. There was much rejoicing among the sound part of the population when the tribunal, so much distrusted at first, now gave signs of its being determined to do courageously its duty. Moreover, there were such precision and concordance in the proofs adduced, they were so clear and so overwhelming, the falsity of the alibi was so conclusively demonstrated, that nobody doubted that a verdict of guilty would be rendered. The accused himself seemed resigned to his fate. Hortensius, rejoicing at having so accurately judged of the situation when he suggested to the tribune Fufius the amendment which reconciled the people to the Senate's decree, offered to bet that Clodius would not present himself on the next morning, but would prefer a voluntary exile to exposing himself to the blow which was sure to fall upon him.

On the said 8th of May, an immense multitude came from the neighboring cities to see the end of that memorable trial. At dawn, a troop of armed men occupied the porticoes of the old hall of the Forum. To the astonishment of his adversaries, Clodius made his appearance. His face was calm, and his whole countenance was full of assurance.

When the court opened, it was addressed by Publius Lentulus, one of the accusers. After having described in his exordium the situation of the Republic, and dwelt on the necessity of putting an end to the civil discords which threatened it with absolute ruin, the orator reviewed the antecedents of Clodius. " The accused," he said, "after the death of his father, participated with a sort of furious eagerness in all the debaucheries of those suddenly enriched buffoons who disgrace Rome, and sank so low into the mire of infamy as to be guilty of incest with his own sisters. When he reached the age of manhood, he embraced the career of arms, and made himself conspicuous, not by his talents and courage, but by the avidity with which he surrendered himself to the shameful passions of the Cilicians and other barbarians. Having become infected by the new-fangled notions of the day, he communicated the infection to the army, which was commanded by Lucullus, his brother-in-law, and to which he preached insubordination and insurrection. Having failed in that criminal enterprise, he is put on a vessel and sent back to Rome. Attacked by pirates near Nisibis, he is too timid to offer any resistance and is made prisoner. Set free on account of the fear they had of Pompey, his patron, he goes to Antioch, and then sneaks back to Rome. After his return, how does he signalize himself? By charging Catiline with peculation and by taking hush-money for ignominiously dropping the accusation! Having departed for Gaul with Murena, he manufactures in that province all sorts of false statements, puts to death the minors and heirs that are in his way, and associates himself with malefactors to perpetrate a number of crimes of astonishing variety. Back to Rome again after all those exploits, his first step is, to fraudulently appropriate to himself certain sums of money belonging to the people, by cutting the throats, in his own house, of the men who had been charged with the distribution of those funds among the tribes." Lentulus then went into a close

examination of the pending case, and discussed in de
tail the proofs relative to the fact of sacrilege on which
the trial was based. With regard to the alibi, it was
treated by his brother Lucius. The pontiff Fannius
took charge of the general recapitulation and of the
peroration.

The advocates of Clodius also divided among themselves the defense in three parts. Curio spoke first ;
the largest portion of his speech was consecrated to
the justification of his client against the imputations
foreign to the case, by which Clodius had been, he
said, so malignantly assailed. " I beg the judges,"
he added, " to weigh equitably in the scales of The-
mis, on one side the calumnies of which my client is
the object from the nobles, and on the other, the constant devotion of that client to the popular interests.
He shows it by aspiring only to become a tribune of
the people. He has, O Romans, no other ambition !
To obtain that single honor he has relinquished all his
patrician privileges. He has been adopted into a plebeian family—he who reckons among his ancestors
thirty-two consuls, five dictators, seven censors, and
seven triumphers ! His intentions and predilections
are known to all. Hence the hatred of the patricians,
and, in particular, of Cicero—that new man, formerly so proud of his plebeian origin when struggling
against the freedmen of Sylla, and to-day so infatuated with his upstart nobility that he systematically
opposes all reforms ! The sacrilege of which Clodius is
here accused is nothing but a pretext, and it is evident
that what in reality stands on trial now, is, on one
side, the preservation of the worm-eaten privileges of
the Roman aristocracy, and on the other, the development of the progressive theories which are spread-

ing with such force, and which will be carried into practical effect by the new generation. Do you know who are the parties to this trial? It is the usurped wealth of the publicans against the excessive and ever-increasing poverty of the oppressed class. This quarrel does not date from the 4th of December, 692; it is as old as the Republic itself, and the profaner of the mysteries of the Good Goddess is—shall I tell you his true name? It was, in turn and successively, at different epochs, Spurius Cassius, Licinius Stolo, Tiberius and Caius Gracchus, and Servilius Rullus, who all proposed laws, the object of which was to distribute among our poor citizens the lands belonging, or having belonged to the State, that were wrongfully alienated." These last words of Curio were welcomed with immense acclamations, and his friends thronged around him to pour out their compliments.

The remainder of the defense was presented by the other advocates, who attempted to destroy the proofs of the identity of Clodius with the man seen in the house of Cæsar. One of them demonstrated the innocence of the accused by a syllogism, which he maintained that nobody could strive to refute without impiety. "We all know," he said, "that the Good Goddess strikes with immediate blindness the violator of her sacred mysteries. But Clodius has the entire use of his eyes. Hence Clodius can not have violated the sacred mysteries." "Who can know," exclaimed Cicero, "what the Good Goddess would do on such an occasion, since no profanation of the kind ever occurred before the one perpetrated by Clodius?"

The prætor having declared the case closed, the bailiffs delivered to each judge a tablet coated with wax, and a bodkin. The judges wrote their votes immediately and deposited them into three urns, corresponding with the three Orders of which the tribunal was composed. The prætor took out successively the fifty-six tablets, and read aloud the letter inscribed on each one of them. The letter C, meaning *condemno*—I condemn—was on twenty-five tablets, and the letter A—*absolvo*—I acquit—on thirty-one. This result being known, the prætor declared: that Clodius seemed not to have committed the crime of which he was accused—(*non fecisse videtur*), and consequently pronounced his acquittal. The Forum rang with thundering applause, and Clodius was escorted triumphantly to his house by his partisans.

Cicero wrote to Atticus: "You know that baldhead—that Crassus, who lauded me so profusely in the Senate? Well! In two days and through the medium of one single slave, he has brought this whole affair to its shameful conclusion! He invited the judges to his house, he promised, he furnished pledges and guarantees—he gave. Moreover (O Good Gods, what corruption!), he threw into the bargain, as an additional temptation, the prostitution of noble matrons and adolescents." In later times the scandal of this immortal trial was branded by Seneca with singular energy: "The acquittal," he said, "was more criminal than the crime. The adulterer made a distribution of adulteries among the judges, and thought himself safe only when he had rendered them similar to himself."

The deeds of corruption had been so patent and the demoralization of the epoch had reached such a degree of brazen impudence, that the agents of that corruption boasted openly of what they had done. The names of the prevaricating judges were mentioned publicly, and without the slightest reserve, as well as the bribe which each one had received. Catulus said to one of them: "Why did you ask for guards? Were you afraid of being robbed of the money which bribed you?"

On the 15th of May there was an assembly of the Senate. Cicero, who, from the beginning of the trial, had determined to act with the greatest reserve, could not resist the excitement of the occasion and perhaps the perfidious goadings of the secret enemies who surrounded him. Roused into making a speech, he allowed himself to be betrayed into the most bitter vituperations against the judges who had sold themselves, and did not spare even Consul Piso, whom he treated with a harshness that could hardly be surpassed. "Conscript fathers," he said, "you must not shrink from the performance of duty, because you have met with one defeat, and you must not permit yourselves to be discouraged. That defeat, it is true, is of such a nature that it must not be disregarded, but at the same time its gravity must not be exaggerated. It would be insensate to close our eyes to the danger, but there would be cowardice in attaching more importance to it than it deserves. Lentulus and Catiline were acquitted twice. It is but another bandit whom the judges have set free to plot against the Republic. You must not, O Clodius, deceive yourself with any flattering illusion. The judges have given you Rome for a prison. In not condemning you, they wished to deprive you of the liberty of exile. Take courage then, O conscript fathers! Do not forfeit any portion of your dignity. Honest men have still faith in the destinies of the Republic. Their hearts have been filled with grief, but their fortitude remains intact. The evil is not new; but to-day it bears its fruits. A malefactor, loaded with crimes, has found judges as infamous as himself."

Clodius was present, and such language was hard to bear. He was called to his feet by Cicero's violent apostrophe. "How long," he exclaimed, "shall we suffer that this King shall thus dare to speak to us like a master?" "Do you call me King," (*rex*) said Cicero, "because you have a grudge against the memory of your brother-in-law, Marcus Rex, for having forgotten you in his testament?" "You have bought a house," replied Clodius, "with money received from your client, Publius Sylla, in violation of the law *Cencia*, which forbids advocates from accepting any remuneration for their services." "Bought!" exclaimed Cicero. "Are you thinking of your judges?" "My judges! They did not believe your testimony, although given on oath." "Twenty-five believed it," retorted Cicero, "but thirty-one did not put any faith in you, since they compelled you to pay them in advance." This last sarcasm overwhelmed Clodius, who could not conceal his confusion, and who resumed his seat amidst shouts of derision.

The Senate, alarmed at the consequences which might result from the impunity of the crime committed by Clodius, ordered an inquest against the judges who had been corrupted. This was, however, destined to be a *brutum fulmen*, in the condition to which the Republic had been reduced. It would have been wise not to propose a vain measure which could not be executed, and Cicero said in a letter to Atticus that he would have opposed it, had he been present. The Order of the Knights, who, it seems, had many reasons to fear the investigation, considered it a direct attack and separated from the Senate, from which they resolved to withdraw their support in any future conflict with the people. The inquest ordered by the Senate was, of course, a stillborn infant. There was no attempt to give life to it; there was substituted for it a general law against judicial corruption, but the people refused to ratify it. A striking illustration of the moral condition of Rome at that epoch!

Shortly after, Clodius, in violation of all law and precedent, in which he was secretly assisted by Pompey and Cæsar, became, as he had long intended, a tribune of the people on his renouncing his patrician rank and privileges. Armed with the new power to which he had aspired, he burned the house of Cicero on Mount Palatine, another at Tusculum, and a third at Formia, and Cicero voluntarily exiled himself to escape from a worse fate. Clodius enjoyed his revenge, until the gladiators of Milo put an end to his scandalous career.

As soon as public and private virtue ceased to exist in Rome, the Republic virtually perished. It continued to subsist in name and in semblance —not in its former reality and vigorous vitality. This was demonstrated in the trial of Clodius and in the scenes which preceded and followed that event. The day was rapidly coming when Brutus would be compelled to exclaim: "O virtue, thou art but a name!" On that day, when it came, the death warrant of the Republic was signed by Fate—that stern executor of eternal and inflexible laws. An imperial despotism became a necessity, as being a lesser evil than anarchy. Everything in the social body was for sale from head to foot. The conquerors of the world were openly bought like slaves in the market-place. The gold of Crassus elected Cæsar consul, and Cato himself, to defeat that dangerous candidate, admitting in full Senate that bribery had become an indispensable element of influence, recommended its use "for good purposes in opposition to its being employed for evil ones." But Cæsar was the highest bidder, and therefore obtained the majority of the popular vote ; the Republic was dead— and we all know what Cato did to escape what he thought to be the infamy of living under a master. The people shrank into being insignificant factors in the distribution of power; they were succeeded by the Pretorian guards and the legions, who became the electors at the ballot-box of the sword, and who recognized but one authority — one sovereign on earth—one God above—and that was gold! Alas! It is but too easy for one who studies thoroughly the annals of mankind, to be a true prophet—the same causes invariably producing the same effects ; but if there is anything that is entitled to be called "The voice in the wilderness," it is emphatically the voice of History.